INDIA: A GLOBAL POWER

INDIA

A Global Power

Nayyar Shamsi

ANMOL PUBLICATIONS PVT. LTD.
NEW DELHI - 110 002 (INDIA)

ANMOL PUBLICATIONS PVT. LTD.
4374/4B, Ansari Road, Daryaganj
New Delhi - 110 002
Ph.: 23261597, 23278000
Visit us at: www.anmolpublications.com

India: A Global Power

First Published, 2004

ISBN 81-261-1889-X

PRINTED IN INDIA

Published by J.L. Kumar for Anmol Publications Pvt. Ltd., New Delhi - 110 002 and Printed at Mehra Offset Press, Delhi.

Contents

Preface

India is one of the few nations in the world, which have a rich past, prosperous present and bright future. The Indian civilization is one of the most ancient in world history. It has a very rich heritage and esteemed legacy to benefit from. Presently, India as a nation and country is among the fastest developing countries and strongly growing economies on the planet.

Following independence, India has made strides in all fields, be that education, science or economy. In the field of education, India is among the countries, offering best at a lower cost, in comparison to US and Europe. India's tremendous progress in the area of science is acknowledged by the whole world, including some of the most advanced nations like United States, among others. Indian scientists have proved their worth in technology, information and Space Science. Particularly, in the economic field, India has progressed leaps and bounds, during last few decades. In Asia it has a high rank and makes most of nations envious in many areas. Further, in the field of defence, India has acquired a prestigious position. Now, it's a nuclear power also. It can boast of one of the strongest armed forces for defending its honour and borders. Not only that India has a perfect legal system and there is rule of law in the country.

Above all, India has matured as a democratic nation and society, leading the third world in this regard. Over the last 56 years, the democratic system has worked well, against all odds, which in itself is a great achievement.

No body can contradict the fact that India is emerging as a global power in the new world order. This book deals with the same aspect and proves India's worth in all fields and disciplines. It brings India into light, as a strong nation and a civilized society. It virtually covers all aspects and dimensions, in an academic, objective and empirical manner.

This editor is hopeful of being appreciated for this modest effort and acknowledged for the painstaking research and hard work, spanned over a year or so. It is in fact a tribute to the great people of India.

— Editor

1

Introduction

On January 26, 1929, on the banks of the Ravi in Lahore (now in Pakistan), we solemnly resolved that complete independence or Poorna Swaraj shall be the goal of our political struggle.

To realise this goal, we set afoot a total mobilisation of our nation's resources in men, money and material, marshalling our precious heritage, both intellectual and moral, with the uplift of the nation as the one and only objective.

Under the inspiring leadership of Mahatma Gandhi, who had the supreme gift of touching the responsive chord in the hearts of the people in all walks of life, we heroically enacted the saga of satyagraha in 1930, 1932, 1941 and 1942.

These phased programmes culminated in the British agreeing peacefully to quit India.

On September 2, 1946, a national team of talents headed by Pandit Jawaharlal Nehru took office and formed an interim government.

On August 15, 1947, complete power was transferred by Britain to India.

On January 26, 1950, we gave unto ourselves a Constitution, the Preamble of which affirms:

WE, THE PEOPLE OF INDIA, having solemnly resolved to constitute India into a SOVEREIGN DEMOCRATIC REPUBLIC and to secure to all its citizens,

JUSTICE, social, economic and political,

LIBERTY of thought, expression, belief, faith and worship,

EQUALITY of status and of opportunity; and to promote among them all,

FRATERNITY assuring the dignity of the individual and the unity of the Nation"

To what extent have we been able to redeem this "solemn resolve" of the founding-fathers of our Constitution?

What is our record in safeguarding India's sovereignty and territorial integrity?

How far have we succeeded in securing, for our teeming millions, justice social, economic and political?

How much of liberty of thought, expression, belief, faith and worship have we vouchsafed to our people belonging to different faiths?

What is the quantum of equality of status and of opportunity that we have provided for the weaker sections of our society and the linguistic minorities in the states of the union?

What is our record in promoting fraternity among our people, assuring the dignity of the individual and the unity of our nation?

The balance-sheet makes dismal reading.

Why is this colossal failure, after a very promising start ?

After the first few years of independence, the commanding heights of our politics came to be progressively dominated by pugilists and opportunists. This resulted in mental and moral dualism in public life in common parlance, double-think and double-talk in the field of political decisions and governmental activities.

This schizophrenic dualism, this unbridgeable chasm between resolutions and actions, this gnawing gulf between promise and performance, have desecrated our noble temple of freedom.

How shall we reconstruct the disintegrating moral structure and re-enthrone purity in public life?

The basic materials for such reconstruction are right thinking, realistic planning and service-politics.

This cannot come about by mouthing slogans or giving labels to those who hold different opinions. Let us remember that readiness to swallow anything and everything, hook, line and sinker, is an unmistakable symptom of incapacity for independent and imaginative thinking. Whip-driving people to think alike on all matters will result in creating a stagnant pool and, in the words of William Blake, "breed reptiles of the mind".

We must end the slavery to shibboleth; re-create the climate of wisdom, moderation and tolerance; recapture the spirit of selfless, cooperative and constructive politics of the pre-independence era.

"Hatred cannot be conquered by hatred; it can be won only by love." This is the central theme of the teachings of our Vedas and Upanishads, epics and Puranas, saints and sages.

India has a genius for synthesis, harmony. This is the keynote of our ageless culture and the lesson of our history.

The life and work of the broad-minded Al Biruni who, despite his predatory patron Mahmud Ghazni (12th century), dived deep into Indian culture, learnt Sanskrit at the feet of pious pandits and wrote over 20 books on Indian themes, so that his co-religionists might know the Indians "on the basis of their own civilization".

The benevolent and enlightened rule of the bigoted Sikandar's successor, Zain-ul-Abidin (15th century) in Kashmir, and of Husain Shah (15th-16th century) in Bengal; the colourful genius of Babur (16th century) and the significant will and testament lie left to his son and successor, Humayun (16th century) enjoining him, among other things, to "treat the different peculiarities of your subjects as the different seasons of the year, so that the body-politic may remain free from disease"; the idealistic aspirations and endeavours of Akbar the Great (16th century), whom Pandit Jawaharlal Nehru has described as the "Father of Indian Nationalism"; Prince Dara Shukoh (elder brother of Aurangzeb, 17th century), who died a martyr to his eclectic faith; Prince Akbar

(Aurangzeb's son, 17th century), who rebelled against the "suicidal policy" of his bigoted father; the spirit of Kabir (15th-16th century) and other saints who preached that "Ram and Rahim are one"; Guru Nanak (15th-16th century), who, like Kabir, preached the unity of Godhead; and in recent times Sri Ramakrishna Paramahamsa, Mahatma Gandhi and others, who preached and lived the gospel of Sarva Dharma Samanatva, are concrete illustrations of a continual process of harmonisation.

Synthesis and harmony are the other names for love. Unresolved conflict is but a species of hatred. The former is the offspring of sincerity and dedication, while the latter, of egoism and selfishness.

To fulfil the "solemn resolve" enshrined in our Constitution, to ensure a square meal a day, to provide a modicum of clothing and shelter, to eradicate squalor and disease, to improve the standard of living of millions of our less fortunate fellow-citizen, we must make a genuinely concerted and collective effort.

Sloganeering and sensationalism are not the means to achieve prosperity.

Socialism will not descend from the heavens. It is not a negative concept. It cannot be achieved by anti-discipline, anti-production, anti-property and anti-rich stances. Accusations of the better-off sections as callous exploiters and poisonous pests appeals to the poor to envy the rich, and plausible promises to ameliorate their lot without clear-cut, positive, pragmatic and time-oriented programmes will only serve to impede the march to socialism.

Honest, hard, constructive, collective work by all, each according to his aptitude and talents, can alone deliver the goods.

Gandhiji, who was the greatest living socialist of the twentieth century and who alone has given a workable alternative to Western socialism, declared:

"Socialism is a beautiful word and, so far as I am aware, in Socialism all the members of society are equal, none high, none low. In the individual body, the head is not high because it is the top of the body, nor are the soles of the feet low because they touch the earth. Even as members of the individual body are equal, so are the members of the society. This is Socialism. In it, the prince and the peasant, the wealthy and the poor, the employer and the employee, are all on the same level.

"This Socialism is as pure as crystal. It, therefore, requires crystal-like means to achieve it. Impure means result in an impure end. Hence, the prince and the peasant will not be equalised by cutting off the prince's head, nor can the process of cutting off equalise the employer and the employed. One cannot reach Truth by untruthfulness. Truthful conduct alone can reach Truth.

"Therefore, only truthful, non-violent and pure-hearted socialists will be able to establish a socialistic society in India and the world."

When will our warring, self-perpetuating politicians and trade-unionists, princes and peasants, employers, teachers and students, accept and act upon his fundamental truth? When will we realise our responsibility that in the hollows of our hands and upon our honesty or dishonesty, wisdom or stupidity, to a great extent, depend the well-being and prosperity of millions of our brothers and sisters for years to come ?.

The Indian political horizon is pitch dark, full of fierce strifes and sickening personal rivalries masquerading under the garb of ideological conflicts. The disarray of spirit, mind and purpose has assumed alarming proportions.

The heat of unbridled, aggressive politics has resulted in the evaporation, from the waters of national life, of the vitalising vapours of inspiring, infectious idealism bequeathed to us by the galaxy of leaders of modern Indian Renaissance, from Raja Ram Mohun Roy to Paramahamsa, Sri Ramakrishna, Swami Vivekananda, and in recent times Mahayogi Sri Aurobindo, Sri Ramana Maharshi, Mahatma Gandhi and others.

We shall not lose heart. We cannot but be optimists. To the wise, life is a festival.

Clouds are precursors of refreshing, life-giving rains. After thunder and lightning come soothing, fertilising showers. So is, we are convinced, the present political turmoil in India. It is but a passing phase.

Out of evil cometh good. A new era will soon dawn in India. Many discerning observers and students of history hold the view that in the India of today there is going on an unprecedented voluntary, cooperative work more than perhaps at any time in our long history. This tidal wave of harmonious, selfless team work of our good people in every nook and corner of India will soon flood the land and sweep away the filth and froth that are, for the moment, soiling the surface of our national life.

In the midst of World War II, when the Western democracies were locked in mortal combat with the dark forces of Nazism and Fascism, President Roosevelt made an impassioned appeal to the people of all countries ceaselessly to strive for four essential human freedoms:

"First, freedom of speech and expression everywhere in the world.

"Second, freedom of every person to worship God in his own way everywhere in the world.

"Third, freedom from want which, translated into world terms, means economic understandings which will secure to every nation a healthy peacetime life for its inhabitants everywhere in the world.

"Fourth, freedom from fear which, translated into world terms, means a worldwide reduction of armaments to such a point and in such a thorough fashion that no nation will be in a position to commit an act of physical aggression against any neighbour anywhere in the world."

To secure, preserve and protect these four essential human freedoms, we, the people of India, should solemnly pledge ourselves to win one more freedom—freedom from can't and catch words.

2

A New Nation

At midnight of August 14/15, 1947, a jubilant nation celebrated the advent of freedom with great enthusiasm even as each member of the Constituent Assembly took the pledge to dedicate himself in all humility to the service of India and her people to the end that this ancient land attain her rightful place in the world and make her full and willing contribution to the promotion of world peace and the welfare of mankind.

Pandit Jawaharlal Nehru, as the first Prime Minister of Independent India, spoke of the responsibility that freedom and power brought to the people and more so their elected representatives. He prescribed a regimen of hard work to give reality to our dreams (Tryst with Destiny).

Dr. S Radhakrishnan, the philosopher-statesman, however, uttered a note of caution: "Our opportunities are great but let me warn you that when power outstrips ability, we will fall on evil days."

As we celebrate the Golden jubilee of our freedom, do we not miss the exultation that the people felt on August 15, 1947?

Attainment of Independence

In 1946, when the Indian Independence Bill was being piloted by Labour Prime Minister Clement Attlee in the House of Commons, Sir Winston Churchill angrily gave the grim warning that the governance of India would slip into the hands of "men of straw...

rascals, rogues and freebooters of whom no trace will be found in a few years .... Not a bottle of water or a loaf of bread shall escape taxation, only the air will be free; the blood of hungry millions will be on the head of Mr. Clement Attlee. Are we not proving Churchill right and Attlee wrong?

Have we irredeemably fallen on 'evil days'? This thought comes uppermost in our minds as we see strewn around us the debris of our cherished values of *Satya* and *Dharma*, Truth and Righteousness.

When Arnold Toynbee said (in a Foreword to a book on Paramahamsa Sri Ramkrishna) that "the only way of salvation for mankind is the Indian way, we felt flaṭtered." Can India today legitimately claim to provide the moral leadership to the world when, as Prime Minister Inder Kumar Gujral, declared on July 21, 1997, that "the nation is sinking into corruption"?

"On this historic occasion," says Bhavan's President Shri C. Subramaniam, we have to give high priority for the eradication of corruption and nepotism in public life."

Ideals and Values

We must recapture the spirit and ideals which animated us during our unique pilgrimage to freedom and the first few years of Independence of constructive statesmanship, team work, all-pervading sense of participation and binding the will and blending the minds of the people in the creative and thrilling adventure of building up a new and nobler India and a government, fully national in spirit and composition, comprising all the best available talents, pledged to democracy, egalitarianism and the Constitution.

We must go back to the spirit and ideals of those halcyon days when we practised the philosophy of nation first and foremost, when we spoke the language of the heart; when we breathed the air of idealism; when we walked hand-in-hand on the path of selfless service and sacrifice; when all sons and daughters of the motherland prided themselves in being "Indians first, Indians last and Indians always." It is time to find out why we have slipped?

The recharging of the nation with the spirit and ideals of those glorious times alone will enable us:

— to remove the heavy pall of frustration, despair, and despondency;

— to make the people realise that right spring from duties rightly performed;

— to uphold the sanctity of the plighted word, guaranteed by the Constitution which we have given unto ourselves;

— to cleanse our public life of cant and hypocrisy, double-think and double-talk;

— to draw into active political life men and women with wisdom, foresight, humility, ability, spotless character and dauntless courage, so that politics will cease to be a means of promoting personal, parochial and party interests; to save the nation from ethical, spiritual and moral bankruptcy; to restore the majesty of the Moral Law and uphold the supremacy of dharma.

Only if we reactivate the spirit and ideals of that golden era of our national renaissance can we march forward to the "heaven of freedom" of which Gurudev Tagore rapturously sang, for which the best and noblest in the land, during the last two centuries—from Raja Ram Mohun Roy to Mahatma Gandhi and tens of thousands of men and women, known and unknown, from Kamrup to Kanyakumari—tirelessly toiled and laid down their lives.

The nation, like an individual, is an organic whole. Together, and functioning in unison, it is a living, throbbing and creative entity; uncoordinated, isolated, and quarrelling with and hating one another, it generates forces of self-destruction.

Nation First: This should be the prime motivation of every Indian in thought, word and deed.

The first decade of our Independence was not only studded with solid achievements, but was also pregnant with promising possibilities.

Indeed, it was a golden era which witnessed such epic accomplishments as:

a) the successful solving of the problem of rehabilitating some ten million people the biggest migration in world's history who had been uprooted from their hearths and homes in the wake of the partition of India.

b) the framing of Constitution with well-defined fundamental rights enshrined in it; statutory guarantee of equality of opportunity and justice—social, economic and political—to all irrespective of caste, colour, religion or language, a Constitution forged by the amalgamation, of the best features of the progressive and democratic nations of the world and the expurgation of elements which the history of these nations which has successfully stood the storms and stresses of the last more than five decades, while in many of the nations which emerged into freedom along with and subsequent to India, Constitutions have crumbled, leaving the door open to dictatorships of various brands.

c) the miracle of non-violently integrating, within months, "Princely India", covering 48 per cent of India's territory and over 80 million people.

The Noble Goals

These concrete advances towards our "Tryst with Destiny" were possible because, in the early years of freedom, we continued to tread the unique path evolved by our national genius the harmonious blending of Mahatma Gandhi's unswerving allegiance to ethical and spiritual values, Pandit Jawaharlal Nehru's soaring idealism, Sardar Vallabhbhai Patel's down-to-earth pragmatism, Dr. Rajendra Prasad's rock-like moral strength, Maulana Abdul Kalam Azad's unshakeable faith in Indian secularism. Nightingale Sarojini Naidu's grace and Sri. C. Rajgopalachari's far-seeing vision and razor-sharp intellect supported by the best brains and minds of all India.

No less impressive were the achievements of the decades in several fields. Among these were:

1. The Green Revolution which made India more or less self-sufficient in food and put an end to the dependence on imports described decisively as ship-to-mouth living.
2. Expansion of industry output and diversification of industry at all levels, big, small, cottage and handicraft.
3. Expansion of the communication system by rail, road and airways, making the country closely-knit internally and externally.
4. Expansion of the communication system through telephone, radio, paging, electronic mail, cellular mobile service, internet, etc.
5. Improvement in medical health and care and increase in the awareness of population control, leading to a decline in birth rate and death rate per 1,000.
6. Rural rehabilitation through community projects, National Extension Service and Integrated Rural Development Programmes.
7. Infrastructure for promotion of scientific research and technological application.
8. Expansion of the press and the mass media almost on the scale of a revolution.

Through a series of National Development Plans both national and per capita income have substantially risen, and both refflected in a better standard of living in the country as a whole.

Though the problems of poverty, unemployment and illiteracy still remain to be tackled effectively there is much satisfaction to be derived from the gains already made.

At the policy level, socialist control through licences, quotas and permits has been replaced by freedom of enterprise. Liberalisation and globalisation of the economy have become the guiding principle of government action.

Large fiscal deficits, heavy internal and external debt, inflation and near stagnant exports are the economic ills that still afflict the nation despite liberal policies.

The economic gains of development, however, are overshadowed by opportunistic alliances and political instability resulting from hung parliaments and assemblies. The erosion of values, seen the most in the political life of the country, has affected the civil service, the professions and, unbelievably, even sections of the Judiciary.

In such a situation, ' it is we, the people, who have to act. After all, as Mahayogi has said, "the modern politician in any party of the world... does not represent the soul of a people or its aspirations."

In this context, a political voluntary organisations have a decisive role to play. They must inspire the people to action against inequity, injustice, corruption, criminality and communalism. That way lies the path to progress of a great nation rich in its legacy of spiritual wisdom and moral values.

In the chopping and changing sea of time in India, Bhavan's Journal has kept itself afloat for 43-years with its precious cargo. The cargo consists of all things that have a bearing on "life, literature and culture."

Kulapati Munshi set the task for Bhavan's Journal in his note in the first issue of August 15, 1954. He said: "Bharat has a heritage and a mission in history. It should be the privilege of this journal to interpret this heritage and be the instrument of its mission."

In the second year of its publication, Dr. Munshi emphasised the need for the Bhavan's journal to carry the message of the Bhavan to an 'ever-widening circle'. This message he described as follows:

"The Bhavan stands for reintegrated Indian culture anew but Indian way of life, based on the fundamental, moral and spiritual values of Arya Dharma; the inalienable dignity of man, the Moral Order of the universe and faith in God. These values are a challenge to the godless materialism which is at Present fashionable, and the disregard of such values which is often accepted as a badge of modernity."

The eternal values of *Sanatana Dharma* are embodied in the Vedas, the Ithihasas, the Puranas and other sacred literature of India. Bhavan's journal has always tried to carry in each issue something from the literature of the past. The Ramayana is one of these works which has never been out of the pages of the Bhavan's Journal; it has been appearing in some form or other.

Life as lived by the common people is a mixture of the past and the present, and science has a prominent place in it today. While not ignoring faith, the Bhavan's journal has held up reason as no less important. Hence the numerous articles, almost without a break on various aspects of religion and science, and arguments, and counter-arguments on the possibility of a holistic approach theme. History and philosophy have a place side by side with music and dance, indeed all the fine arts. Current topics are discussed in the light of old values and the ephemeral is the eternal.

In great men, it is said virtue governs with the sceptre takes of knowledge and wisdom. The Bhavan's Journal takes pride in celebrating this kind of greatness in its 'Profiles'. Architects and Builders of Modern India. The Divine Integrators and Salutations to Centenarians. The Bhavan's journal has not let go a single opportunity to uphold and extol intrinsic greatness.

Unity in Diversity

India is one and indivisible. Nature and nurture have bequeathed this invaluable inheritance to us.

Nature has marked out India as an indisputable geographical unit, clearly demarcated by distinct natural boundaries and mountains of the north and the seas of the south.

Nature has designed India as a unified, collectively self-sufficient and inter-dependent entity. Nature has distributed India's mineral and other natural resources that for their very survival the different regions of India have to pool their resources and lean on each other.

Balanced all-round economic progress alone can alleviate the poverty of India's teeming millions. Unless we forge unity in the midst of the prevailing divisive tendencies, garibi hatao—banish poverty—will only remain an empty slogan.

Our ageless culture, age-old traditions founded on ethical and spiritual values and priceless literary treasures, epics, Puranas, etc., have from time immemorial, nurtured a sense of oneness of India and emotionally integrated its people.

In 56 years of the advent of freedom, we have chosen to ignore the warning of history. We have forgotten the lessons of history. We have given the go-by to the sense of mission, the all-India outlook and a spirit of selfless service and sacrifice which characterised our unique struggle for freedom under the leadership of Mahatma Gandhi.

We should always remember that if one's loyalty to one's own caste, community, region or religion becomes more paramount, then loyalty of India as a whole will disappear and the springs of our patriotism will dry up. Contradictory and narrow loyalties will fragment and destroy our national unity.

Surveying the national scene objectively, one is overwhelmed with a disturbing feeling: Are we reverting to the pre-Akbar and pre-British period in Indian history when castes warred against castes; regions warred against regions; and when people bent backwards to betray each other at the bidding of foreigners which inevitably forged the chains of slavery?

What has happened to us? What has come over us? What has gone awry? Why this heavy pall of gloom? Why this fanatic fratricidal war? Why are we bent upon a suicidal, disintegrating course?

The Truth is: There is a deepening crisis of character, a crisis of the spirit of India.

To overcome this, our leadership should realise that the mainsprings of India's vitality, creativity and unity are ethical and spiritual values. These values are the life-boats which enable us, through the ages, to successfully survive the recurring, buffeting storms and tempests.

Four decades ago, one of the great architects of our freedom, Pandit Jawaharlal Nehru, prophetically wrote: "We have to face this crisis of the spirit of India. We have neither the old nor the new faith, and we drift, not knowing where we are going. This is a dangerous situation and if not checked and improved is likely to lead to grave consequence ... and failure may well mean disaster."

To keep *India one and indivisible* we must renounce contradictory loyalties, re-enthrone the ethical and spiritual values, restore the Majesty of the Moral Law and revive cultural values in all segments of life, particularly in education.

As Swami Vivekananda asserted: "It is culture that withstands shocks, not a mass of information".

In August 1967, India celebrated the anniversaries of two epoch-making events, significant milestones in our unique pilgrimage to freedom: one, the 25th anniversary of the "Quit India" movement; the other, the 20th anniversary of the attainment of freedom by India.

Our leaders all over India exhorted the people to revive the 1942 spirit. The most eloquent among them was the Chief Minister of Maharashtra, Shri V. P. Naik known for his quiet efficiency and pragmatic approach, and endowed with the great virtue of economy of speech.

An impressive rally was organised on August 8, 1967, at Gowalia Tank Maidan, Bombay, at the very spot and on the very day when, 25 years ago, the soul-stirring "Quit India" resolution was passed; it was moved by Pandit Jawaharlal Nehru, seconded by Sardar Vallabhbhai Patel and sanctified by Gandhiji, by giving the mantra of "Do or Die". The rally was, among others, attended by some of the distinguished heroes of the "Quit India" movement and several other sterling patriots.

Analysing the disarray in our national life, the Chief Minister said: "India needs the 1942 spirit to tide over the present difficulties and to make the nation strong and prosperous." In his pleading, there was a tinge of ardour and fervour, pathos and passion.

Today, the country sorely needs a revival of the spirit and ideals of 1942, of the sense of shared mission, selfless dedication, unadulterated nationalism and all-India outlook.

We must recapture the spirit and ideals which animated us during the freedom struggle and the first few years of independence of constructive statesmanship, team work, all-pervading sense of participation and binding the will and blending the minds of the people in the creative and thrilling adventure of building up a new and nobler India and a government, fully national in spirit and composition, comprising all the best available talents, pledged to democracy and the Constitution.

We must go back to the spirit and ideals of those halcyon days when we spoke the language of the heart; when we breathed the air of idealism; when we walked hand-in-hand on the path of selfless service and sacrifice; when all sons and daughters of the motherland prided themselves in being "Indians first, Indians last and Indians always.

The recharging of the nation with the spirit and ideals of those glorious times only will enable us:

- to remove the heavy pall of frustration, despair, and despondency;
- to make the people realise that rights spring from duties rightly performed;
- to free ourselves from the doctrinaire dogmatism now vitiating our industrial and fiscal policies, which has reduced our economy to a shambles;
- to uphold the sanctity of the plighted word, guaranteed by the Constitution which we have given unto ourselves;
- to cleanse our public life of cant and conceit, double-think and double-talk;
- to draw into active political life men and women with the combination of the qualities of wisdom, foresight, humility, ability, spotless character and dauntless courage, so that politics will cease to be a means of promoting personal, parochial and party interests;

— to ward off the curse of tribalism and, in the pithy words of Sardar Patel, to disarm the "assassins of nationalism" masquerading under the guise of local, linguistic and regional "patriotism" which, if allowed a free rein, will choke off and destroy our freedom and ruin the nation by balkanising it into 17 sovereign independent states, in a matter of a few years;

— to save the nation from ethical, spiritual and moral bankruptcy; to restore the majesty of the Moral Law and uphold the supremacy of *dharma*.

Only if we reactivate the spirit and ideals of that golden era of our national renaissance can we march forward to the "heaven of freedom" of which Gurudev Tagore rapturously sang, for which the best and noblest in the land, during the last two centuries—from Raja Ram Mohun Roy to Mahatma Gandhi and tens of thousands of men and women, known and unknown, from Kamrup to Kanyakumari—tirelessly toiled and laid down their lives.

Integration at all Costs

The nation, like the individual, is an organic whole. Together, and functioning in unison, it is a living, throbbing and creative entity; uncoordinated, isolated and quarrelling with and hating one another, it generates forces of self-destruction.

Nation First: This should be the prime motivation of every Indian in thought, word and deed.

To clamour for linguistic or regional preferences in subordination to national interests is symptomatic of a myopia. This must be extirpated with no compunction.

The country has to be lifted out of the morass into which it finds itself today.

Malignant regionalism cannot be allowed to submerge robust nationalism. The Union of India shall not be broken up.

Unemployment, poverty, pestilence and scarcity are stalking the land. Our prestige abroad is at the lowest ebb; we are scorned and sneered at. Two of our neighbours are lying in wait to prey on us. There are the Mizo troubles in Assam, the Phizo troubles in Nagaland and the threat of a plethora of Naxalbaries all over India. Complacency now towards the other dangers from within will spell disaster.

Shall we allow the lamp of liberty to be blown out? Shall we let India die?

Mere condemnation or persuasion from public platforms, through the press and on the floors of legislatures will not curb the "nation-killers" on the prowl.

Fruits of Freedom Movement

Carl Jung, the world-famous Swiss psychiatrist, who had to treat a large number of Germans in the 1930s, could forecast the coming of the Second World War.

He could read into the minds of those men and see the simmering hatred within which they had to express itself in hatred, violence and war. All wars begin in the hearts of men.

Today we have no Carl Jung with us to make any gloomy prognostication about the future of mankind. But we have evidence enough to realise that men are increasingly fomenting hatred, instead of fostering love.

Almost every field of human endeavour seems to reflect this ugly, killer mood.

In art, which is meant to be an expression of beauty and tenderness, there is much violence. The theatre, the film and even music are not free from sensuousness and violence.

Violence has even made inroads into the field of education, turning temples of learning into training grounds for physical assaults.

We find coarseness in language; writers and the print media give currency to expressions that would have shocked older generations.

In the legal profession, whose aim ought to be the resolution of conflicts, we see perverse influences at work, perpetuating disputes, spreading corruption and undermining people's confidence in the judiciary.

In newspapers, sensationalism finds free-play, and inter-views with smugglers, hate-merchants and terrorists yield good copy.

In trade unionism, we find, instead of settlements through negotiations, agreements made under coercion.

In the world of advertising, there is competition in exciting the baser instincts of people and inducing them to multiply their wants and satisfy them at any cost.

Stock exchanges lure the gullible young into believing that they could get rich quick; the time-tested work ethics is given the go-by.

Where will all these lead to? A mere improvement in the standard of living is not what we want. What we want is an improvement in the standard of life. A lessening of strife. An atmosphere of calmness, conducive to the development of the higher instincts of men instincts of service, sacrifice, common endeavour and harmony, so beautifully outlined in that Upanishadic prayer.

"Let us live together, let us be nourished together, let us get strength from one another, let us become lustrous, let us not hate one another."

The spate of murders and kidnappings in different parts of India following the assassination of Smt. Indira Gandhi, the mass murders in Delhi, the daily killings in Jammu and Kashmir and Punjab, and Rajiv Gandhi's horrendous murder are to be viewed in the wider context of the growing climate of violence. Death by violence has become such a daily occurrence that we seem to be becoming insensitive to mindless killings.

Every life is sacred. Violence is the negation of democracy, and civilised conduct is its essence. Let us return to democracy, not in name but in spirit. Let us return to sanity.

Let us remind ourselves of the great truth proclaimed aloud in our land: "Never in this world can hatred be stilled by hatred; it will be stilled only by non-hatred, this is the Law Eternal."

Let us re-enthrone this great Moral Law in our hearts once again. Let Rajiv Gandhi's be the last of the political assassinations to have befouled the fair name of our Motherland.

Let each one of us who love India decide to unilaterally eschew falsehood and deceit from our daily personal life.

Let our political leaders benefit by Sri Aurobindo's words of wisdom: "The modern politician in any part of the world... does not represent the soul of a people or its aspirations.

"What he does usually represent is all the average pettiness, selfishness, egoism, self-deception that is about him and these he represents well enough as well as a great deal of mental incompetence and moral conventionality, timidity and pretence. Great issues often come to him for decision, but he does not deal with them greatly, high words and noble ideas are on his lips, but they become rapidly the clap-trap of a party.

The deceit and falsehood of modern political life is patent in every country of the world and only the hypnotised acquiescence of all, even of the intellectual classes in the great organised sham, cloaks and prolongs the malady, the acquiescence that men yield to everything that is habitual and makes the present atmosphere of their lives.

"Yet it is by such minds that the good of all has to be decided, to such hands that it has to be entrusted, to such an agency calling itself the state that the individual is being more and more called upon to give up the government of his activities.

"As a matter of fact, it is in no way the largest good of all that is thus secured, but a great deal of organised blundering and evil with a certain amount of good which makes for real progress, because nature moves forward always in the midst of all stumblings and secures her aims in the end more often in spite of man's imperfect mentality than by its means."

An imaginative, massive national movement, cutting across ideological and political interests, pitted against the evil forces of violence and hatred, is our greatest need.

Let words pass. Let deeds speak.

Emergence of an Entity

India is on the threshold of a new twilight, not of an evening but a morning yugasandhya. India of the ages is not dead, nor has she spoken the last creative word: she lives and has something to do for herself and the human race.

Sri Aurobindo

India, our motherland, is a *Punyabhumi*.

To us, the dictum "every saint has a past and every sinner has a future" is not a mere copy book maxim; it is a reality witnessed time and again.

The epoch-making human drama that unfolded with profound intensity in the Chambal Valley on April 14 and 16, 1972, is yet another demonstration of the victory of good over evil; of persuasion over pressure; of nonviolence over violence; of soul force over brute force. The world rubbed its eyes and watched with awe and astonishment the miraculous "farewell to arms" bade by 164 dreaded dacoits, the Ravanas of the ravines, some with prizes of Rs. 1 to 2 lakhs on their heads!

The merciless hands that once delighted in wringing out the necks of people were extended lovingly for being locked in fraternal embrace. The eyes that once emitted the scorching sparks of anger and hatred, shed tears of penitence and purification.

As many as 20,000 terror-stricken villagers of Madhya Pradesh, who used to quail at the very mention of the names of dacoits, saw the great act of conversion and rose as one man to cheer the desperadoes being initiated into a chastened life of peace and respect for low.

Rare and incredible indeed are such noble transformations in the history of men. But to those who know India such miracles are in the very nature of her ancient tradition-unique transformations, soul-elevating episodes and inspiring instances that reinforce man's faith in love, piety, dharma and God.

Significantly enough, every dacoit who surren-dered was given a copy of our national epic, the Ramayana, along with the

Gita. Is not Sri Rama, since time immemorial, worshipped as *Pattita-pavana*-Redeemer of the fallen ?

The very name Ramayana conjures up in the Indian mind the memory of India's Aadi Kavi, Valmiki, a bandit turned-saint.

Chabyan's son, Ratnakar, as Valmiki was known before his spiritual transformation, was a fierce dacoit who indiscriminately waylaid, beat up and robbed unsuspecting wayfarers.

According to Krittivas's recension of the Ramayana, this highway robber once chanced to confront Brahma and Narada when they were passing through the forest.

The thug who knew no mercy cursed his fate for having run into some impecunious mendicants. Little did he suspect that he was to get from them the richest of possessions!

In soft and loving words, Brahma asked of him: "Beloved son, will you tell me why you rob people and indulge in such heinous crimes?"

Came the nonchalant reply: "Of course, to support my family."

Brahma and Narada knew that Ratnakar was honest in his conviction that a householder had to support his family. This was a duty ordained by dharma. Hence he felt no qualm of conscience while robbing or even killing people for discharging his duty. But the all-knowing divines wanted to kindle the spark of divinity in him.

"Noble indeed is your objective. But you must know that to loot, plunder and kill is sinful, even if it were to maintain one's family. Members of your family no doubt share your booty. But who will share your sins? Have you ever pondered over that? Will you please ask those for whose sake you are living the life of a dacoit, whether they would also be sharers in your sin of harming innocent people?"

Ratanakar had no doubt that they would all say 'yes'. Yet, he ran home and put the question to his father, mother, and wife. Each one of them, of course, for some plausible reason, answered 'no' in unambiguous terms.

Ratanakar was stunned. He ran to Brahma and Narada and fell at their feet.

"Mercy, O Holy Ones," he beseeched them with tears. "What I robbed was shared by the four of us and I thought they would undoubtedly share my sins as well. But, alas, one by one I asked all the three and none was willing to share my sins."

"My dear child," flowed forth the soothing words of the Holy Ones, "that is the way of the world. Each one is for himself. Everyone is selfish. As long as you are able to get wealth, so long will your kinsfolk be attached to you. When your body becomes infirm, not one will speak to you, in your own home. When the life breath ebbs away from your body, even your wife will be afraid of it. God alone is unselfish. He alone is unswerving. He alone is full of compassion. You should turn to Him."

"But, how can I, an unlettered brute, so sinful, so fallen, think of Him?"

The Holy Ones consoled Ratanakar and initiated him into the sacred Taraka mantra-Rama Nama Days, months and years rolled by and the bandit Ratnakar was enveloped by an ant-hill. When his heart was purged of all the sins, out emerged from the ant-hill, a new man-Valmiki, the Aadi Kavi, who bequeathed to mankind the immortal Ramayana in words of matchless beauty. It is a superb delineation of the tale of the Lord and His Consort born as mortals, undergoing sorrows and sufferings, and upholding the supremacy of satya and dharma on earth. And Brahma's benediction has come true: "As long as the mountains stand and rivers flow, so long shall the Ramayana be cherished among people and save them from sin."

Legacy of the Rich Past

Buddha, the Enlightened One, proclaimed 2,500 years ago: "Never in this world can hatred be stilled by hatred. It will be stilled only by non-hatred. This is the Law Eternal."

And the story of how he conquered the dacoit of dacoits, Angulimala, is very much relevant to the drama that was enacted in Chambal. Angulimala was so cruel that he delighted in chopping off the fingers of his victims and making a garland of them to adorn his neck. (Anguli-finger; Mala-garland). Just as the peace-loving farmers and cowherds were afraid of the Chambal Valley dacoits, people were afraid of Angulimala, and dared not enter his domain.

The great Buddha heard about the wicked deeds of Angulimala. All alone, the Enlightened One who knew no fear, set out at the forest where Angulimala held his undisputed sway.

The cowherds and farmers warned him: 4'0 Sarmana, please do not go that way. Angulimla will give short shrift to even groups of 30 or 40 people. What then will he not do to you, alone and unarmed!" Thrice they warned, but the Buddha went on undeterred.

From a distance. Angulimala saw a lone man walking into his domain. He was astonished at the temerity of the man and angry that someone had dared to challenge him. With his knife unsheathed, he set behind Buddha to strike him from there. But run as he would, straining every muscle, he found that he was unable to get near the Buddha who was walking calmly.

Impatient and exasperated, Angulimala shouted: "You, there! Stand still."

Buddha turned back and replied in soul-soothing words, "0 Angulimala, don't you see that I am still and it is you who are not still?"

"How do you say that ? It is you who are on the move and not still, and it is I who have stopped and am still."

"No, brother," explained the Buddha, "I am still because I have given up all thoughts of hatred and violence. And you, full of them, are not still."

At once light dawned on Angulimala. He became still in the real sense of the term. Casting away his deadly weapons, he became a follower of the Buddha and attained "Arhathood".

Namdev, (A.D. 1270-1350) one of the great singersaints of Maharashtra, was a sinner-turned-saint. Son of a tailor, Damaseta, of Narsingpur, he was in his youth a marauder and a waylayer. Once he killed 84 horsemen and had forgotten all about it. He found nothing unholy in killing people. Yet he was a *bhakta* in his own way.

One day he happened to go to his favourite temple. There he saw a woman scolding her crying child which was innocently but insistently asking food for its hungry stomach. .

Even the brute Namdeo could not brook the brutality of a hungry child begging for food, being beaten and scolded.

So he chided: "Mother, why are you so heartless`

Sobbing, she replied: "Brother, I am utterly helpless. It is my anguish that makes me angry. I am a penniless young widow. My husband along with 83 other horsemen was mercilessly waylaid and killed by one thug called Namdeo."

The moment of truth had arrived for Namdeo. He was smitten by intense remorse. Realising the enormity of his crimes, he rushed straight into a temple.

"I am a sinner," wailed he. With a contrite heart, he supplicated: "0 God, be merciful to me!"

Overcome by a sense of boundless guilt, he whipped out his murderous scythe and aimed it at his own neck. But lo! The upraised hand stood still!

And God transformed him into a saint, and so great a one that nearly 80 of his songs (*abhangs*) have found their permanent places in the holy Guru *Granth Saheb* of the Sikhs.

All his tremendous energy which was expended on fiendish deeds was now channelled God-ward.

Namdeo is venerated throughout India as one of the pioneers in the sacred art of reciting "kirtans". Historians mark his age as the "Age of Democratic Mysticism". He left his mortal frame in A.D. 1350, and his samadhi at the door of the temple of Vithoba at Pandharpur even today attracts thousands of devotees.

Sri Ramakrishna Paramahamsa used to say that greed and lust are very powerful emotions. If they are calmed and harnessed to worthwhile causes, the energy can be made productive of the highest good and bliss.

The general run of people is immersed in the humdrum of mundane existence. Hence God-realised men coming from their rank are also few. But in the case of daredevils, deadly dacoits and lust-hungry maniacs, once their mind is transformed their devotion would also be intense.

Srimad Bhagawatam speaks of the story of Pingala, the prostitute who, after vainly waiting for someone to turn up one night, suddenly developed intense dispassion and became a beloved of-the Lord.

So sex-obsessed was Tulsidas (A.D. 1511.1637) that one day his young wife Ratnavali,' reproached him thus: "What an infatuation you have for this body of it female constituted of phlegm, bones, blood and arteries! Hast thou but offered half of that love which thou hast towards me, at the feet of Lord Sri Sitapati Rama to the very Vaikuntha thou wouldst have ascended." This touched Tulsidas to the quick and instantly transformed him into the saint who gave to posterity the immortal *Ramacharita Manasa*.

The stories of the admonition of Bilwamangal (A. D. 1300) by his paramour and his transformation into a renowned saint who wrote the soul-stirring Sri Krishna Karnamritam; of Sant Arunagirinathan (latter part of 15th century A. D.) arraigned by his sister for his insatiable lust and his consequent blossoming into a great minstrel of God, whose heart, bursting with devotion to Kumara (Subramanya), broke out into 16,000 devotional songs on

Him which stand enshrined on the walls of 225 temples in Tamil Nadu and Ceylon; and of Mary Magdalene, the fallen woman redeemed by Jesus, are among the several well-known instances.

The Divine Heritage

There is the spark of divinity in every human being. One has to pass through the three stages of inertness, activity and equilibrium which is the balancing of both-Tamas, Rajas-and Satwa.

It is far better to be active than inactive, for in the active man, there is greater manifestation of life and energy. Only an active man can hope to get on to the stage of equilibrium.

Said Swami Vivekananda: "I once met a man whom I had known before as a very stupid, dull person, who knew nothing and had not the desire to know anything. He asked me what he should do to know God, how he was to get free.

"Can you tell a lie? I asked him. 'No' he replied. Then you must learn to do so. It is better to tell a lie than to be a log of wood. You are inactive; you cannot certainly reach the highest state, which is beyond all actions, calm and serene; you are too dull even to do something wicked." The patriot-saint narrated this story to illustrate the point that man must learn to progress from activity to inactivity and thence to perfect calmness.

Newspaper accounts of the Chambal Valley dacoits indicate that, as most Indians, they too are imbued with a religious spirit. Some of them would not even take food before bath. The hunger for real religion is inherent in them. Further, the life of a dacoit is also most miserable-constantly pursued by the police, despised by the people, and every minute unsettled.

All these provided a rich setting for the great conversion of their heart initiated by the venerable Acharya Vinoba Bhave and consummated by (he gentle voiced Loknayak Jayaprakash Narayan.

There is a famous aphorism in the *Patanjali Yoga Sutra*: Ahimsa pratishataayaam Tat sannidhau Vaira Tyagah. When one is truly established in Ahimsa, in his presence even ferocious animals would become peaceful. The tiger and the lamb will play together before that Yogi.

To conduct negotiations with the murderous dacoits needs superhuman courage and the qualities of a *Sthithaprajna*. And the shedding of their violent nature by the dacoits proves that real men established in Ahimsa still tread the sacred soil of Mother India.

The Governments of India and Madhya Pradesh and the handful of dedicated Sarvodaya workers and their leaders, Vinobaji and Jayaprakashji, deserve universal acclaim for this daring experiment in human transformation. May their tribe increase!

Satya and *dharma*, the beacon-lights of Indian culture, are again emerging triumphant.

The altruism which motivated our support to the liberation struggle in Bangladesh, the actual conduct of the willingness to bury the hatchet and negotiate with Pakistan in a spirit of forget and forgive are re-affirmation of the faith in our age-old ideal, the quintessence of our religion and culture-"be good; do good".

Our self-confidence has now been restored. Our words and deeds bear the stamp of maturity. The spirit of service and patriotism has been re-kindled. The Chambal Valley miracle is one of its fruits. This example should prove infectious.

If there is any doubt about the ultimate redemption of these dacoits, we have the categorical statement of Sri Krishna Himself in the Gita. "Even if one of the vilest of evil life, worship me with exclusive devotion, he should be deemed righteous as he is rightly resolved. He quickly becomes righteous and attains everlasting peace. 0 Arjuna! Be assured that my devotee shall not perish."

Mother India has not gone barren and will never go barren. Age after age, India has given birth to great and glorious men and women who consecrated their whole life for the good of the Motherland and for the welfare of humanity-*Sarvabhootahita*.

Dharma *Samsthaapanaarthaaya Sambhowaami yuge* yuge-affirmed the Lord in the Gita.

And true to this Divine-standing Proclamation, this *punyabhoomi* of ours has been blessed, with an unending grand procession of talented, high-souled, dedicated men and women who carried forward our ageless culture, ever re-integrating it to suit the changing needs of time, and at the same time anchored to the fundamentals of dharma: satya (Truth), asteya (non-stealing), and *aparigraha* (non-possession).

Indian civilisation and culture had its origin more than fifteen centuries prior to the Homeric Age. The annals of Bharat run through at least five millennia. There has been an unbroken continuity of Indian culture from the beginning of Time to the present. And from the Vedic Age to the Modern Age, India has been a *Margadarshi–a* Path-setter.

Some recent examples fresh in minds of contemporaries exemplify the truth:

In the 1920-30s, under the leadership of Mahapurusha Mahatma Gandhi, India showed a new path to the world for winning freedom, which heralded the emancipation of millions of suppressed people the world over *Sathyagraha* and Ahimsa

In the 1940s, under the leadership of *Loha-purusha* Sardar Patel, India showed a new path for forging national solidarity by liquidating more than 520 Princely States without liquidating their rulers: Integration without Tears.

In the 1950's under the leadership of Yugapurusha Sri Jawaharlal Nehru, India showed a new path for civilised international relations based on co-existence and mutual respect: The *Panchaseel* Doctrine.

In the 1960s, under the leadership of Yuga-purusha Vinoba Bhave, India showed a new path for agrarian reforms, rural reconstruction and removal of economic disparity, avoiding the unnecessary bloodshed and social conflict that besmirched such revolutions in other countries: *Bhoodan*, *Sampattidan*, and Sarvodaya.

In the 1970s, under the leadership of *Dhairya-prasadini* Indira Priyadarshini, India showed yet another new path of releasing astounding moral strength and of taking up arms for a righteous cause of standing by the persecuted, refusing to be brow-beaten by insolent might and gifting the land liberated by the might of India's arms to its rightful heirs: Dharma Yuddha and Deshdan.

The war into which we were drawn much against our will, in which we sacrificed quite a few valiant flowers of our blooming youth, was verily a Dharma Yuddha. We took up cudgels for upholding human freedom and dignity and that too, in keeping with our heritage, as a last resort after exhausting every conceivable avenue for a peaceful solution.

The wielding of the bow and arrow by Sri Ramachandra, in our national epic Ramayana, against the tyrant elder brother Vali and the crowning of the persecuted younger brother Sugriva as the King of Kishkinda, is one example of Dharma Yuddha.

The dethronement of Yahya Khan, and the release and restoration of Banga Bandhu Mujibur Rehman in his rightful place as the Father of his Nation, remind us of another Dharma Yuddha of close parallel in the Ramayana—the vanquishment of the usurper Ravana and the coronation of the virtuous Vibhishana.

The Mahabharata war which the Pandavas had to wage when their legitimate claim for half the kingdom was denied by the avaricious Duryodhana and his 100 brothers, and when the power-mad Kauravas pooh-poohed even the modest demand of five houses for the Pandavas to live, is a third example of Dharma Yuddha. What Bangladesh demanded was only greater autonomy within the framework of Pakistan. But Yahya Khan and his cronies sent their troops on rampage, to kill, loot, rape, destroy and decimate the whole population of the territory. In the process, like Mahishasura, Bhasmasura Kamsa, Jaraasandha and other tyrants of old, and Hitler and Mussolini of our own times, Yahya Khan also invited destruction on himself.

We won a splendid victory in the war with Pakistan. We helped the 75-million people of Bangladesh to breathe the air of freedom. We staked out all to uphold Dharma.

Dharmop Rakshati Rakshatah: Dharma protects the protector. India of the ages is alive and active. She has a continuing mission to carry forward; a destiny to fulfil.

In his ringing declaration with regard to the future of India during our crusade for freedom. Mahayogi Sri Aurobindo envisaged for Free India a new twilight—not of an *evening yuga sandhya but of a morning yuga sandhya.*

He proclaimed: "India must be reborn, because her Rebirth is demanded by the future of the World. India cannot perish, our race cannot become extinct, because to India is reserved the highest and the most splendid destiny, most essential to the future of the human race. It is She who must send forth from herself the future religion of the entire world, the Eternal Religion which is to harmonise all religions, sciences and philosophies and make mankind One Soul.

"India of the ages is not dead, nor has she spoken her last creative word; she lives and has still something to do for herself and the human race."

3

A Republic Born

Pericles, the great Athenian, defined the essential features of a Democratic State thus :

"The Democratic State must strive to serve the greatest number of citizens, to preserve the quality of all before the law and to work in such a way that the liberty of the citizens derives from the liberty of the State. It must give aid to the weak and call men of merit to the highest posts. The harmonious balance between the interests of the State and the interests of the individuals who compose it, ensures the political, economic, intellectual and artistic advancement of the city, protecting the State against the egotism of individuals and protecting the individuals, thanks to the Constitution, against the arbitrary action of the State."

The Constitution

On January 26, 1950, we gave unto ourselves the Constitution of Free India, "to secure to all its citizens justice, social, economic and political; liberty, of thought, expression, belief, faith and worship; equality of status and of opportunity; and fraternity, assuring the dignity of the individual and the unity of the Nation."

The Preamble, the Fundamental Rights and the Directive Principles of State Policy of the Constitution itself are the quintessence of the knowledge and wisdom and inspiration derived from years of indepth study and discerning appraisal by a galaxy of the best minds and brains of India, of the origin, functioning, rise and fall of nation states the world over during the last 2,500 years.

The Preamble, which is based on the American Declaration of Independence of July 4, 1776, commits the union government to secure to all the citizens of India, justice, liberty, equality and fraternity, the content of which is as much social and economic as it is political.

The Fundamental Rights incorporated in our Constitution are, by and large, based on a study of the Bill of Rights in the American, Australian and Canadian constitutions.

The framers of our Constitution deemed it necessary to define the Fundamental Rights so as to keep them above the vicissitudes of political controversy, to place them beyond the reach of the pendulum of temporary majorities, the whims and caprices of soulless administrators, to firmly establish these rights as legal principles to be applied independent of the human personality, and to guarantee its fullest blossoming without let or hindrance.

The Directive Principles embodied in our Constitution are, in fact, a Charter of Social and Economic Rights guaranteed to the common man. Refuting the criticism that our Constitution did not commit itself to usher in an era of socialism, Dr. B.R. Ambedkar, one of the main architects of our Constitution, declared in the Constituent Assembly: "If these Directive Principles to which I have drawn attention are not socialistic in their direction and in their content, I fail to understand what more socialism can be."

Dr. Sachchidananda Sinha, Provisional Chairman, in his inaugural address to the Constituent Assembly on December 9, 1946, envisaged a truly impregnable framework in our Constitution. But he also warned that strong foundations and impregnable defences are not enough. It is the people, its keepers, who matter. He quoted the internationally renowned jurist Joseph Story: "The structure has been erected by architects of consummate skill and fidelity; its foundations are solid, its compartments are beautiful as well as useful; its arrangements are full of wisdom and order; and its defences are impregnable from without. It has been reared for immortality, if the work of man may justly aspire to such a title. It may, nevertheless, perish in an hour by the folly, or corruption, or negligence of its only keepers—we, the people. Republics are created—these are the words which I commend to you for your consideration by the virtue, public spirit and intelligence of the citizens. They fall when the wise are banished from the public councils because they dare to be honest and the profligate are rewarded because they flatter the people, in order to betray them."

The most significant features of our Constitution are the accent on basic human freedoms, lofty ideals, high moral purpose and various built-in safeguards.

The architects of our Constitution were very keen to uphold the nation's honour and public integrity and the sanctity of pledges and guarantees.

To give an illustration: Replying to a debate in the Constituent Assembly on October 10, 1949, referring to the demur of some of the "Progressives" about the guarantees which had been given to the Covenated Services, Sardar Vallabhbhai Patel said:

"Have you read history? Or, is it that you do not care for recent history after you have begun to make history? If you do that, then I tell you we have a dark future. Learn to stand upon your pledged word . Can you go behind these things? Have morals no place in the new Parliament? Is that how we are going to begin our new freedom?

"Do not take a lathi and say, 'Who is to give you a guarantee? We are a Supreme Parliament'. Have you supremacy for this kind of thing? To go behind your word? If you do that, supremacy will go down in a few days."

The far-seeing framers of our Constitution wisely provided a built-in mechanism for the due discharge of all constitutional obligations and guarantees.

Unfortunately, the spate of amendments to the Constitution over near five decades years have practically nullified and muted it.

Democracy has many facets.

It is a Political Arrangement which treats all people as equals.

It is an Economic Approach which provides equality of opportunity to all citizens, and consciously encourages production of optimum wealth at all levels so as to reduce the gap between the haves and have-nots, ensures equitable distribution of the necessities of life and takes other pragmatic steps to ameliorate the living conditions of the vast mass of people living below the poverty line.

It is an Ethical Way of Life, which, while planning to raise the standard of living, also simultaneously devises measures to raise the standard of life of the people by fostering character-building in all sections of society ministers, legislators and administrators, industrialists, agriculturists and consumers, employers and employees, teachers and students, parents and children, etc.

Of all forms of governments evolved by the genius of man since the beginning of history, democracy is most conducive for the existence of a civilized society. At any rate, despite its shortcomings, democracy is, as Winston Churchill said, the last unsatisfactory of all forms of government.

Democracy being a government by discussion, there is absolutely no place for violence in it. It is rule by consent and not by coercion.

Democracy has been defined as the "abode which man has built for the spirit of liberty". But then a democracy can function as a true democracy only if the spirit of democracy is preserved and those occupying the seats of power and who applaud and swear by democracy are democrats at heart. And if this democratic spirit is wanting, what is designed to be a rule by consent will become a rule by compulsion. Moreover, a democracy in which the spirit of liberty does not reside will ipso facto become a varitable morgue.

"A political institution," Benjamin Disraeli said, "is a machine; the machine power is the national character."

Speaking soon after the adoption of the Constitution in 1950, Dr. Rajendra Prasad, who was the President of the Constituent Assembly, said: "The Constitution we have adopted is like a machine. How good or bad it is, will entirely depend upon the character and capacity of those who work the machine".

What Mahayogi Sri Aurobindo, who was in active politics in his poorvashrama, said about the average politician reads like a prophecy of the shape of things and kind of politicians to come within three decades of gaining of our independence. To quote him:

"...He does not represent the soul of a people or its aspirations. What he does usually represent is all the average pettiness, selfishness, egoism, self-deception that is about him, and these he represents well enough as well as a great deal of mental incompetence and moral conventionality, timidity and pretence. Great issues often come to him for decision, but he does not deal with them greatly; high words and noble ideals are on his lips, but they become rapidly the claptrap of a party. The disease and falsehood of modern political life is patent in every country of the world and only the hypnotised acquiescence of all, even of the intellectual classes, in the great organised sham, cloaks and prolongs the malady ......"

Alas! But with very rare exceptions, our general run of politicians have not got the gift which is at the root of politics, as of all professions that concern the management of men: of distinguishing between what is practicable and impracticable. They are, by and large, selfish to the core. And such elements have a free hand in large segments of national life and administration. False promises are lavishly given, enormous resources, time and energy are expended and all kinds of ruse are adopted for the winning of periodical elections, whereafter unabashed pursuit of power and pelf begins. To cling to power, hotchpotch alliances are forged and defections engineered and encouraged. Without compunction, the saboteurs of cooperative, constructive work-pride and self-will, fear and greed, jealousy and ambition are fanned and allowed to be on the prowl.

The New Era

A generation of boys and girls have been reared and have come of age, solely fed on material values. The truth that only on the rock of moral law and not on the shifting sands of political and economic expediency can stable democratic institutions be built to last is not only ignored but jeered at.

All these are inexorably leading to the desecration of our Temple of Freedom and weakening the very foundations of our democratic system. Our national character has been sullied and moral decay has set in. The nation is verily on the verge of despair on all fronts–moral, social, economic and political.

It is a truism that the only thing we learn from history is that we learn nothing from it. This is a sad commentary not on history but on human indolence, complacency and stupidity. If we continue to be, there is no escape from paying the heavy price for the luxury.

Contemporary history—Russia before the October Revolution, Germany in the grip of economic depression which swept Hitler to supreme power, China in the forties, Egypt in the fifties, Indonesia in the sixties, Greece and Ethiopia in the seventies-teaches us a lesson; that when the ruling elite puts self before party and party before the nation, when scarcity conditions are allowed to prevail for long periods, when inflation is accompanied by shortage of essential commodities and grossly unequal distribution, when administration becomes inefficient, lethargic and corrupt, when dissent is looked upon as treason, when opposition is considered rebellion, when decisions are not taken on the basis of argument, logic and facts, people at large lose faith in the efficacy of parliamentary democracy, national discords arise, economy collapses, subversive forces gather strength and violent revolutions occur. This is the perilous state of the Indian nation today.

What is the way out when democracy tends to go off the rails? Violence? No. Violence is opposed to the very concept of democracy and it is self-defeating and destructive by nature. Hence recourse to violence is certainly not the answer.

Non-violent resistance all the way from appeals, public protests, hungering and thirsting after righteousness, non-cooperation to civil disobedience is the only valid instrument at the disposal of lovers of democracy to safeguard, strengthen and preserve it.

Imagine a mighty chariot crashing down from atop a dizzy precipice into abysmal depths. The reckless and hapless charioteer, the neighing horses, the hurtling chariot, all present an apparent picture of intense drama, intense action.

Let us also view another scene: the same chariot brought to a halt at the edge of the precipice and an expert charioteer in full control of the reins guiding and directing it. An apparent picture of inaction but in reality one of perfect "action within" and "inaction without".

This example of the two aspects of the same chariot demonstrates the Gita dictum of "action in inaction and inaction in action" and the example is equally valid for demonstrating the true traits of violence and non-violence.

Violence is always associated with apparent action, yet in truth it is no action at all, for the simple reason that it is a case of the charioteer giving free reins to the horses.

And violence is always destructive, self-destructive as in the case of the charioteer who plunges to his death with the horse, and also destructive in the case of others just as the crashing chariot destroys anything that comes in the path of its ruinous plunge.

But non-violence outwardly seems to be no action at all because nonviolence springs from inner control, the dexterous control of the reins.

But bereft of selfless, inspired and dedicated leadership, the multitude, which can only associate action with its outward manifestations, is apt to dismiss all nonviolent action as virtual inaction though in reality it is the only real action.

Indisputably, non-violent action has this great advantage over violent inaction: It is not only not destructive but positively creative. Every non-violent movement builds up the inner strength and hastens the redressal of injustice and man's evolution towards the higher goal. All who participate in non-violent action also get a higher pull that uplifts and elevates them personally.

To quote Mulford Q. Sibley, who in The Quiet Battle has made an elaborate and thorough study of the theory and practice of non-violent resistance from the dawn of history to modern times: ,The Spirit of Democracy, surely, is utterly antagonistic to violence; yet it is equally hostile to acts which would stifle free development of personalities and groups. Non-violent resistance offers a means whereby both of these values can be maintained."

India of the Ages is not dead. This is the ancient home where the greatest experiments have been conducted from the beginning of time, in the creative art of life.

Mother India will never go barren of blessed sons and daughters, seers and sages pathfinders. India is great and will remain so.

India has, in the past, given to humanity many outstanding pathfinders like Vedic and Upanishadic Rishis, Vashistha, Vyasa and Valmiki, Buddha and Mahavira, Sankara, Ramanuja, Madhava, Vallabha and a host of others and in this century Paramahamsa Sri Ramakrishna, Maharshi Sri Ramana, Mahayogi Sri Aurobindo, Mahatma Gandhi and others.

In the first half of this century, India discarded the familiar Path of Violent Revolution and showed the world a New Path to break off the shackles of slavery.

It is the duty of every Indian, particularly in the establishment and in the opposition, to maintain a climate of complete non-violence by not harbouring personal malice and ill-will, by not indulging in innuendoes and insinuations, by not provoking violence by word or deed and by earnestly endeavouring to understand and appreciate the good features in each other's approach.

Most of those, in the "fray' are dedicated, tried and tested servants of India. The goal of all is one and the same: only the paths differ. This is nothing uncommon in our national movement.

Like Pandit Nehru, Sardar Patel, Rajaji, Rajendra Prasad and other leaders with widely differing temperaments and ideological differences, the present leaders in both the 'camps' should also learn to discuss their respective points of view in an atmosphere of mutual trust and confidence, compose their differences and chalk out a common programme to take the country to the goal of good government. On the success of this will hinge not merely the immediate future of India but the future of the world.

As during the freedom struggle led by the apostle of ahimsa, Mahatma Gandhi, we are these days living in times of destiny. This is not the time for faint-heartedness, indolence or indifference. Eternal vigilance with intelligent exertion is the price of liberty and good government.

If freedom is to survive, if democracy is to be preserved, if efficient, incorruptible and good government is to be firmly established, we, the people, must bestir ourselves; we must awaken betimes; we must willingly and voluntarily do our duty by the nation as worthy citizens of a Sovereign Democratic Republic.

As Daniel Webster averred: "Nothing will ruin the country if the people themselves undertake its safety; and nothing can save it if they leave that safety in any hands but their own."

In his *Prison Diary*, on July 21, 1975, after about a month of soul-searching introspection and prayerful cogitation in the solitude of solitary confinement, Lokanayak Jayaprakash Narayan, who has given all his life to the country and asked for, nay expected, nothing in return, lamented: "My world lies in shambles all around me."

Like Gandhiji, his master, Jayaprakash had never been pessimistic about the future of this *punyabhumi* of ours. The very next day, on July 22, 1975, he mused: will all the work of a Gandhi, Nehru, Patel, Rajendra Prasad, Maulana Azad, Rajagopalachari be reduced to ashes? It is difficult to believe." And the last sentence of the diary note for the day was a positive affirmation: "Indian democracy will rise from its grave."

Yes, the selfless, dedicated and massive work Bhagiratha Prayatna of the continuous and ever-continuing chain of the galaxy of great architects and builders of modern Indian Renaissance from Ram Mohan Roy to Ramakrishna Paramahamsa, from Mohandas Gandhi to Chakravarti Rajagopalachari and millions of other patriots, did not and will not go in vain.

In less than 20 months (June 1975 to March 1977), did not Indian democracy rise phoenix-like from the ashes and shine effulgent, illuminating and ennobling public life in India once again?

Alas! Its glow was shortlived. In less than 28 months (March 1977 to July 1979), it once again lost its lustre. It was defiled, defaced and decimated. Verily, darkness descended at noon thanks to the congenital incapacity for team work, bloated ego, nauseating self-righteousness, unbridled ambition, unabashed self-seeking, insatiable power lust, contemptible cunning, despicable intrigue and savage stab-in-the back techniques of the coterie of the "selfless servants of India" who were chosen to guard and carry forward the glorious inheritance.

Jayaprakash is the moral conscience of post-Gandhian India. He is the authentic symbol of the collective consciousness of the right-thinking people of our times.

How much more heartrending must be the agony and anguish now of this noble soul who, though seriously ailing, exerted his utmost for the miraculous resurrection, in March 1977, of freedom and democracy in our ancient yet ever young India?

True, Satan races faster than Angels. Evil moves speedily, ferociously like a mad, charging bull, while good creeps slowly but surely like a tortoise. Untruth triumphs in the beginning, whereas truth triumphs only in the end. But it is ultimately *Satya Meva Jayate*.

The hour before dawn is the darkest. Out of evil cometh good. This is the inexorable, immutable Divine Law.

The present crisis in India is not at all the result of the failure of the Constitution, which is the distilled essence of the consecrated, collective sadhana of the cream of the nation's noblest, wisest, most experienced, versatile and unalloyed patriots of the highest calibre who had, for decades, voluntarily and cheerfully undergone the baptism of fire in freedom's battle under Gandhiji's's sublime moral leadership.

The *causus belli* for the current cursed state of the nation is the quarantining of truth, casting away of ethical norms and moral values. It is the outcome, pure and simple of a catastrophic crisis of character at the top level.

People's Power

The vast majority of the Indian people are undoubtedly good and honest men of character. They should not give in to pessimism, indifference and despair. They have a duty to perform for their own and the nation's welfare. They should come out of their self-imposed seclusion and exert themselves to restore the majesty of the Moral Law.

The key to enduring success in churning out nectar from the murky, muddy, befouling filth that is Indian politics today, lies with the large number of good people of India. They must realise that democracy, for its survival and sustenance, needs the intelligent participation of people of high character and unimpeachable probity.

Nature abhors a vacuum. If good shies away, evil will usurp. So all good individuals who remain passive, who shirk responsibility and keep themselves aloof, unconsciously invite and contribute to the weakening and ultimate destruction of the democratic system which alone will ensure them and India's teeming, hungry millions, the bread, freedom, discipline and dignity.

Edmund Burke, that scintillating orator and indefatigable crusader for freedom and human rights, put the whole thing in a nutshell: "All that is necessary for the triumph of evil is that good men do nothing."

Only the indifference of good men gives evil men their power.

Rajaji said: "Individual honesty must be brought into being before we can hope for improvement of our national affairs. It is the drops that make the rain. It is no use saying, I shall be good after I make enough for myself. If each one continues to be dishonest, to better his affairs by wrongful means, the national character will not revive. It will continue to be in disarray character as it is now. It is the totality of the character of each individual that makes what we call national character."

Good men of India! Shirk not. Be up and above for freedom and democracy.

Religious Factors

Upwards of 10 million people had their holy dip at the Triveni Sangam during the Kumbhamela in 1977. The offerings at Tirupati, Guruvayur, Nathdwara and other temples are ever on the increase. In 1933 the offerings at Tirupati amounted to Rs.3 lakh and in 1976 the figure rose to Rs. 12 crore. More and more devotees are visiting the not-easily-accessible Sabarimalai temple atop a hill amidst thick forests in Kerala.

Whether it is the fashionable Paris, the conservative London or the skyscraper city of Manhattan one finds groups of people intensely interested in God and religion.

The audiences that flock to hear celebrated religious preachers like Swami Ranganathananda, Swami Chinmayananda, Swami Akhandananda, Dongre Maharaj, Anjam Madhavan Namboodri and other saintly men are ever on the increase, quantitatively and qualitatively.

Demand for books such as the Ramayana, Mahabharata, Gita, Upanishads, and those dealing with the lives and teachings of saints and sages have gone up hundredfold. There is a spurt in the renovation of old temples and consecration of new ones.

In the last century, may be a Max Mueller or a Paul Deussen showed some interest in Hinduism, that too largely of an academic nature. But today more and more people in the West, belonging to all strata of society, seem to be attracted by the broad tenets of *Sanatana Dharma* to the point of practising it.

The revival in religion, which we observe as a world phenomenon, is a backlash of the lack of faith which plagued the young minds especially, for quite a time.

It was Northcote Parkinson, the celebrated wit and philosopher, justly famous for his Parkinson's laws which constitute the greatest satire on the laws of economics, who said in one of his characteristic epigrams that "industrialisation at its best produces Hippies."

There is more to this statement than cult, the inevitable outcome of the relentless pursuit of material progress, began with the industrial revolution in the 19th century. It is a slap on the face of material affluence and a groping towards God or Light, or call it whatever we may like. In their blind search for freedom from affluence born ennui, many youngsters take to "dope" and alas, are invariably gone forever like poor animals caught in a mire, sinking to their slow death. A few escape because of the hope held out by religion.

It is this redeeming role of religion that is significant today. Certainly it cannot be said that the whole world has overnight become religious or God-minded; such a thing there never was even during the Vedic times. In the Vedas do we not come across the lamentation of a gambler?

India consists of the whole geographical area, bounded by the eternal Himalayas rising tier above tier with their majestic, thunderous sea, skirting the south, east and west.

Himaalayam samaarabhya

yaavad bundu-sarovaram

Hindusthaanam iti khyaatam

aadyantaakshara-yogatah

All those who live within the limits of the Himalayas up to the ocean are Indian in the real sense of the term, whatever may be their race, caste or community.

In fulfilment of the Standing Proclamation of the Lord in the Bhagavad Gita, Mother India, from age to age, has given birth to an unending succession of great sages, seers, philosophers, and institution-builders that ever lived anywhere in this wide world.

These great and good men and women had drunk deep from the eternal fountain of our ethical and spiritual heritage. They carried forward, and handed down to successive generations, our age-old traditions, reintegrating them to suit the needs of the changing times. They assiduously fostered and built up an all-India outlook and unceasingly disseminated the spirit of Bharatiya Vidya, imparting strength and stability to our individual and collective life.

These far-seeing founding-fathers of Indian polity were *nishkama-karmayogi*. They bestowed great thought upon, assigned high priority to, and devoted ample time and resources for the making of men and women of dedication, humility and character. They not merely mouthed the ideals of *samanvaya* (harmony), *sahaveerya* (cooperation) and *samaanatva* (equality) but practised them in their individual, family and institutional life. There was complete accord between their thought, word and deed—*manasyekam, vachasyekam, karmanyekam*. Hence, they and their message came to be invested with such great halo and acquired such an irresistible power that their words found a ready lodgement in the hearts of the people.

This was the *sanjeevini* (ambrosia), the quality of practising what was preached, which enabled our forefathers to survive several foreign invasions, internal convulsions, social and political cataclysms; to preserve our inheritance; to save the Soul of India.

Bharat is the ancient homeland of wisdom and catholicity. In our *punyabhoomi* was born the ideal of universal well-being—*Lokassamastah sukhino bhavantu*. In this *dhartnakshetra* first sprang up the idea of One World, *Vasudhaive kutumabakam*.

Whither today's India and Indians ?

Many of us are now prisoners of dazzling but false and fleeting values, practitioners of double-think and double-talk, linguistic ideologies, of atheism, of jingoism, of class, communal, linguistic and regional viruses.

The thrill, joy, awe, reverence and admiration we instinctively felt, are reflected in the words of Sri Aurobindo, the Prophet of Indian Nationalism: "for the snow-swathed summits of the

Himalayas, the menacing hills of the frontiers, the laughing valleys of Kashmir, the rolling downs of the Deccan, the surge and thunder of the seas, the limpid flow of the great rivers of the country," and these are no more. The love for the spirit and soil of India, one and indivisible, is now fast fading out.

Steeped as many of our "law-givers" and "leaders" in different walks of life are in rank materialism chasing easy fortune, indulging in shameless sense-pursuits at each other, perpetually preoccupied at self-image building and winning ephemeral popularity, feuding to secure concentration of gigantic political and economic power, we are perilously on the brink of an era of decay, degradation and disintegration.

As the Gita has said :

Yad-yad aacharati sresthah tad-tad evetaro janah

Sa yat pramaanam kurute lokas-tat anuvartate

Whatever a great man does,

all that other men also do;

whatever he sets up as the standard,

that the world (mankind) follows.

If we wish to stop this slow but sure descent down the slippery slopes to national extinction, we should urgently set our house in order, get back to our traditional moorings, and steadfastly work for national reconstruction and cultural renaissance.

A peep into the history of great civilizations and cultures such as those of ancient Egypt, Babylonia, China, Greece, Rome, the Western countries as well as India, testifies to the fact that in all these countries each major forward-thrust in national progress and religious, ethical and moral efflorescence took place either during periods of severe stress and strain or soon thereafter.

To give but three significant and relevant examples from our own long and chequered history, it was:

a) at a time when our religion was on the verge of extinction, the great protagonist of Vedic faith, Sri Kumarila Bhatta, the immortal Adi Sankaracharya, Saint

Jnanasambandar and others, came on the scene, rescued it and gave it fresh strength.

b) during the several centuries of Muslim hegemony, the life-sustaining bhakti movement throbbed with redoubled vigour, restoring self-confidence to our crushed and terrorised people;

c) during the two centuries of British rule, when India was in bondage, impoverished and forlorn, the unprecedented, all-round, triumphant modern Indian

Renaissance surged forward, culminating in the establishment of our Sovereign Democratic Republic. We need not, therefore, be pessimistic about the future of this land.

There are already some signs of the declining influence of false prophets, selfish leaders, rabble-rousing techniques, slogan-mongering and empty values.

Our annals run through at least five millennia. There has been no break in the continuity of our culture during these 5,000 years, from the Vedic Age to our own times.

Age-old Traditions

We must have an intellectual understanding of the mighty processes of the history and culture of India, its infinite and enthralling varieties, its unsurpassed vitality and power of endurance, its fundamental values and basic unity. Without cultivating an emotional awareness of our past and the present, without evolving a happy synthesis of the ancient and the modern, India will be reduced to a mere "geographical entity"; and we just cannot generate the will-power and strength to lead our people along the path of constructive endeavours and to navigate the Ship of State in the right direction.

Our first task, therefore, is to look back as far as possible and to draw inspiration, guidance and strength from the heritage bequeathed to us by our forbears. Thence we should adapt ourselves to modern conditions and thereafter plan for meaningful national reconstruction suited to the genius of our people.

Thus alone can we bring about economic prosperity and social equality; thus alone can we hope to usher in cultural renaissance; thus alone can we build tip the India of Gandhi's dreams, an India where satya and ahimsa (truth and non-violence), samanvaya (harmony), sahaveerya (cooperation), samaanatva (equality), maitri (love) and jana kalyan (people's welfare) would prevail. Then only can we lead a purposeful and peaceful life, setting an example to the fear-and-avarice-ridden nations to emulate.

To achieve this ideal we must mobilise all our creative and constructive forces—mental and moral, religious and cultural, social and economic, scientific and technological, literary and educational. This mobilisation should be total and must embrace all segments and strata of national life.

Our democracy, the world's most populous democracy, is now on trial. India is passing through perilous times. Let us not forget that democracy is threatened by the intertia of good people, by the selfishness of most people, and evil designs of a few people. Let us guard our freedom and democracy zealously. Eternal vigilance is the price of freedom and democracy.

In times of grave crisis, we must pause and reflect, turn the searchlight inwards and find out: What has gone wrong? Where? And Why?

The study of history can be the best antidote against political imprudence, which has brought the downfall of many nations, including ancient Greece, where democracy in the West, had its earliest beginning.

Kautilya, in his celebrated book of polity, Arthashastra, counsels that rulers should set apart some time every day for reading the *Itihasa*. The Mahabharata and the Ramayana, which are among the source-books of Dharma, are classified as *Itihasa*-works of history—and Bharat Ratna Mahamaho-padhyaya Dr. P. V. Kane includes them among the source books of Dharma in his magnum opus *History of Dharmasastra*.

The *Ramayana* for its hero Sri Rama who is the embodiment of *Dharma* or virtue-*Ramo Vigrahavan Dharmah*. In the Mahabharata, Sri Krishna, the God Incarnate, is the central character, who expounds the Gita in the most dramatic setting in which a scripture has over been expounded.

The cardinal teaching of the Mahabharata is Dharmo rakshati rakshitah which means Marina safeguards, protects. The Mahabharata brings out the lesson that God Himself is bound by Dharma and that formal obeisance to Him or even kinship with Him is of no avail in saving one from the consequences of transgression of Marina. Sri Krishna's own son, Samba, who violates the rule of good conduct by making fun of a great Rishi, dies in a drunken brawl along with thousands of misdirected youths, power-mad and arrogant.

The distinction between formal religiosity and its observance in spirit is very important.

It is said that when Abraham Lincoln was about to embark on a war someone earnestly reminded him of the need for invoking the blessings of God. Lincoln's reply was that as his opponents too were sure to beseech God to be on their side, the only right course open to him was to take care that he was on the side of God, the side of virtue.

What is the verdict of history with regard to the observance of moral codes?

The illustrious couple, Will and Ariel Durant, in their Lessons of History, the distilled essence of their world famous 10-volume Story of Civilization observe: "A little knowledge of history stresses the variability of moral codes and concludes that they are negligible because they differ in time and place and sometimes contradict each other. A larger knowledge stresses the universality of moral codes and concludes to their necessity."

Indeed, the Mahabharata also points out that subtle are the ways of dharma and they can be grasped only by constant contact with the wise. On his deathbed of arrows, awaiting the onset of the auspicious uttarayana to shuffle of his mortal coil, Bhishma Pitamaha, the elder statesman, imparts to Dharmaputra, the duties of an ideal ruler, Rajadharma, even though in the Great War waged in Kurukshetra, they were ranged on the opposite sides.

In the *Gita*, which is the kernel of the Mahabharata, Sri Krishna says that great indeed is the responsibility of leaders because *Yadyataacharati sreshtha-statat devetaro janahsa yatpramanam kuru te lokastadanuvartate*.

People follow the conduct of the leader; whatever standards he sets, that people follow.

Centuries ago, it was declared that the Mahabharata is the Book of Life. What is not in it is nowhere else. It highlights the dilemmas of those who were caught in the meshes of doubt while reigning mighty empires and how their doubts were resolved by taking recourse to the guidance of the wise. Modern histories may not be explicit in their delineation of the lessons of history but the discerning student can always draw his lessons.

A word of caution here. Those who turn to history for copy book of maxims to be applied straight to all situations of life would do well to remember that history smiles at all attempts to force its flow into theoretical patterns of logical grooves; it plays havoc with our generalisations, breaks all our rules; history is baroque. As affirmed in the Mahabharata, subtle indeed are the ways of Dharma.

A good many are apt to neglect history and at the back of this neglect might be the idea of equating "progress" with the whirligig of time and the feeling that the "moderns" need not bother about the bygone times and the bygone men. They are ignorant of the Law of Life; out of the past is born the present, out of the present is born the future. The present is the past rolled up for action, and the past is the present unrolled for understanding.

Let us remember that while men become instant heirs to the technological advances of their times, they have to learn themselves the moral lessons laboriously, and their character has to be forged on the anvil of personal experience, bitter and sweet. Otherwise, they will grow into rudderless automatons, buffeted hither and thither by each passing wind of change. Experience has to be gained by sweat, toil and tears. It cannot be purchased or inherited.

In the modern scientific age, space and time have all but been conquered and all men are neighbours in geography. But one wonders whether we are neighbours in spirit!

This cannot come about unless mankind wakes up to the realisation of the Vedic ideal-that the World is One Family, Vasudhaiva Kutumbakam. This is as yet an unfulfilled dream of mankind but striving towards this great ideal should never be given up.

The Bhavan's Journal, in its own humble way and in a very small measure, seeks to promote this ancient Indian ideal. It addresses itself, in particular, to the post-freedom generations in India who tend to look down upon the past, and are developing tastes, an outlook and a way of life alien to the priceless heritage bequeathed by our ancients.

Our young boys and girls are not to be blamed for the unfolding national tragedy. They are victims of our shortsightedness, folly. 'The basic causes are:

Free India allowed the distortion of the ideal of secularism as Godlessness, callously neglected the study of Sanskrit, eliminated moral and character-building lessons from school and college textbooks. This has led to Free India rearing up tens of thousands of our talented youth year after year, solely fed on material values, with the sole aim of achieving personal status, success and ever-increasing comforts in life, by any means. They are not taught that right means alone will lead to enduring right ends. Knowledge and skills divorced from character and ethics are dangerous. This is an inexorable Law of Nature.

Raja Bhartrihari (6th century after Christ) in his *Niti Shatakam*, has classified people into four categories.

1. *Satpurushas:* Godly and good people, who are ever mindful and concerned with the welfare of others. Satpurushas, in all countries, are always limited in number, in a minority.
2. *Samanya Purushas:* The general run of people, who are mindful and concerned with the welfare of others, so

long as their self-interest is not adversely affected. Samanya Purushas are generally in a majority.

3. *Manava Rakshasas:* Demons among men, who are not merely solely concerned with their personal welfare, but who also unhesitatingly harm others for advancing their self-interest.

4. *An indefinable category:* Shall we call them Manava Pisachas? Heartless people who gleefully destroy other peoples' welfare, without any benefit to themselves or anyone else.

The students of today are the citizens of tomorrow. Free India has not given them food for the soul. Free India has deprived them of ethical and spiritual nourishment. This has resulted in the steady dwindling of Satpurushas and Samanaya Purushas in our India. More, this has inevitably resulted in the multiplication of Manava Rakshasas.

This is why the nation is in shambles today, despite our successful green revolution, scientific and technological progress and economic achievements.

India will cease to be Bharat if our younger generations are not helped to find their anchorage in India's ageless culture—Sanatana Dharma. The only way to reverse the present suicidal trend is to go in on a massive scale for value-based education imparted by value-based teachers and managed by value-based administrators. Cosmetic, half-hearted measures will not be of any avail. Our curriculum should include lessons in personal family, social and national morals. Our youth should be taught to give allegiance to the Majesty of the Moral Law backed by the elders themselves setting an example.

We should offer our soulful prayers to the Almighty and to our saints and sages:

Give us the strength to raise our mind high above daily trifles;

Give us the strength to make our life fruitful in service. So that India's moral health is restored and India marches forward from Darkness to Light.

4

Evolution of a Democratic Polity

Even if India has been afflicted with numerous ills, she has been continued to be a democracy—the largest democracy of the world - since her journey as an independent state began way back in 1947. In fact, democracy happened to be a core element in the overall programme of our struggle for independence. There have been manifest differences between the programme of the Sepoy Mutiny of 1857 and that of the movement which led to our independence in 1947. In 1857 the only programme was evicting the British rulers from India. Any well-considered alternative system of government for the country was not contemplated except that Bahadur Shah, the last Moghul, would be restored to the throne in Delhi after the British were gone. That is, monarchical rule, pure and simple, would be the order of the post-Mutiny days. By contrast, the goal underlying our struggle for Independence spanning the years, say, between 1885 (the year the Indian National Congress was born) and 1947, was obviously freedom from alien rule. But this goal was, in effect, only a means—a means for the fulfilment of the real goals of the freedom movement. This was because only the fulfilment of the real goals could make national independence meaningful. Freedom for freedom's sake was not, and could not be, tenable any longer. By the advent of the 20th century democracy had become a value to cherish universally. And the attendant attributes of democracy—representative, responsible and responsive government, individual freedom, protection against discrimination and so on—were deemed to be indispensable as the core components of any civilised system of government. There were at least two reasons for this. First, a good many of the frontline leaders of the freedom movement since the birth of the Indian National Congress (INC) had the benefit of an English medium liberal education. As a result, they were familiar with the ideas of democracy as it evolved in Western Europe and North America. Next, and possibly more important, was the reason that Indians in general, and people who participated in the freedom struggle in particular, experienced the high-handedness, racism and wanton repression perpetrated by the Raj. Being the victims of such an oppressive system, India could not but think that when independent India would take to the path of democracy.

Again, the programme of our freedom movement could not remain confined to democracy (as a system of government) only. The reason for this was the singular fact that the man starving in the gutter, without any benefits of health-care, education, and steeped in tradition and superstition, could have little love lost for democracy. Hence, after independence, the Indian state had to be the vehicle for quick economic development and social justice. It would have to face the challenge of the 'revolution of rising expectations'. Else, the edifice of democracy, howsoever carefully crafted, would crumble in no time.

Hence, the task before the Indian state was onerous. It had to help unfold the new vista of freedom in a comprehensive sense. It had to be a vista of what Gandhi called 'Sarvodaya', meaning the rejuvenation of every Indian in all the senses—political, economic, moral, social, cultural and so on. It was a tall order for the new state exploited for centuries, with its historical burden of massive poverty and illiteracy, technological ignorance and little industrialisation coupled with a primitive system of agriculture. Yet, India had to give it a try and tackle these problems and thereby realise the aforesaid goals which were outlined in a sort of blue-print conceived years before independence. India would be a (bourgeois) democracy and adopt a parliamentary systems of government (which would also be federal because of the amazing varieties of regions, religions, languages, cultures and races which, taken together, meant 'India'), as well as a mixed economy guided by a centralised system of planning. There would also be constitutionally guaranteed individual rights and social justice measures (not so guaranteed) under the auspices of the state. With such a programme began our second phase of struggle—the struggle against poverty, exploitation, social ills, illiteracy, etc.

In running a democratic system of government, that is, in ensuring representative and accountable governments, the role of political parties is central. Political parties have varied functions. In this, their roles, inter alia, as the instruments of spreading political consciousness and articulation of interests, and mobilisation of the people are foremost.

In this book we seek to explore the causes of the rise of ethnicity and ethnic parties in India as techniques of political mobilisation. At this stage it may be posited that mainly 'salariat' causes (there are other causes also) have been critical in the rise of ethnicity in India (and in other countries as well) and the 'salariat' class has been at the forefront of ethnic mobilisation and movements which are, by now, scattered virtually all over India.

High Hopes, Low Yields

It is obvious from the above that the policy of 'everything to everybody' stoked the fire of people's expectations. They have been, as if, goaded by the state to look to the government of the day for remedies of all their ills. Hence, under the aegis of development and welfarism the state had to be "everywhere, distributing food, fuel, managing disasters and holding down the prices".' It goes without saying that this stretched the state, given India's historically accumulated drags, to the limits. Hence, a yawning gap between the aspirations of the people and the ground realities was a foregone conclusion. Also foregone were the frustrations of large sections of the people in different parts of India. Such frustrations have been ventilated mainly through the politics of extremism, non-party political formations and ethnic parties. It does not, however, mean that mainstream political parties have not been playing any role in expressing popular discontent. It does not also mean that cases of extremist politics and ethnic politics have not overlapped. Indeed, there are numerous cases of such overlap. And the propensity of various ethnic groups to take to both terrorism' and (ethnic) party politics simultaneously is increasing by the day. We shall, however, deal only with ethnicity in this brief study.

It may not be out of place to indicate here that in a few cases ethnic movements have regional overtones. This is because of the fact that in a number of such cases, those of Jharkhand and Assam for instance, spatial deprivation has been synonymous with deprivation in demographic terms. That is, in cases like Jharkhand, there is, in terms of deprivation, convergence of region, tribe, caste and class. And repetition notwithstanding, in a few such regional-cum-ethnic movements also, the 'salariat' class has acted as the main propellant because it has succeeded in placing 'salariat' interests in the forefront of such movements. This does not, however, mean that such movements, at least the important ones like those in Jharkhand and Assam, are not amenable to other explanations.

At this juncture it is incumbent upon us to engage in a little clarificatory exercise regarding the so-called 'salariat' class. The Isalariat' is not an original class. It is rather an auxiliary one which is a product of British colonial rule and its attendant system of education introduced by the Raj. Hamza Alavi, an eminent Pakistani analyst, defines the 'salariat' as a collectivity which includes "not only those who are in white-collar employment, notably in the state apparatus, but also those who aspire to such jobs and seek to acquire the requisite credentials, if not the actual education itself, that entitle them to such jobs". Incidentally, the expression "the requisite credentials, if not the actual education itself..." in Alavi's definition is crucial to any attempt to understand ethnic politics—mostly 'salariat' led—in India and elsewhere. Plainly this means, among other things, that such aspirants to jobs in the state apparatus usually do not hope to land jobs by virtue of their education and training and on the basis of merit in open competition. Rather, they aspire to such jobs on the basis of certain particular considerations, such as those pertaining to caste, community, tribe and so on. This is, in effect, 'quota politics', the politics of 'reservation'. This readily reminds us of 'Mandal' politics which is a very significant manifestation of political mobilisation on an ethnic basis in India. This stems from the belief (and the fact) that political empowerment is the key to economic empowerment in India. The 'salariat' is not 'middle class', the latter having wider connotations. Nor is it akin to 'petty bourgeoisie'. A large number of the camp followers of the 'salariat' may have a middle-class background. Anyway, the 'salariat' class has, historically speaking, articulated ethnic aspirations and has led ethnic movements in India which have ultimately attracted the urban petty burgeoisie, well-off peasants, well-paid industrial workers, local level leaders including landlords and tribal chiefs. Herein lies the singular relevance of the distinction made by Karl Marx between "class-for-itself' and "class-in-itself ". Ethnicity, as a political phenomenon, is only a "class-for-itself".

Regarding the distribution of the 'salariat' in undivided India, we can gainfully quote Alavi in extenso: "Two factors affect the distribution of the salariat regionally and inter-communally. Regional disparities have much to do with early proximity to nodal points of colonial rule in India such as Calcutta, Madras and Bombay and later Delhi. Differential focus of missionary activities in the field of education have also contributed to regional and communal disparity. Hence, some communities rather than others have traditionally provided cadres for service in the state apparatus...." That is to say, in places like Calcutta, Madras and Bombay which were the hubs of colonial activities in the early years of colonial rule, certain castes, such as Brahmins, Kayasthas and Vaidyas (predominantly in Bengal) volunteered for English medium missionary education and such groups marined the state apparatus and business organisations under the British. Such caste groups had, in terms of missionary educational opportunities and job prospects, stupendous advantage. They were the groups entrenched in power and privilege. And such a situation continued for more than a century after the beginning of British rule in India. The preponderance of this higher-caste-based bureaucracy faced the first challenge from North Indian Muslims through the Aligarh Movement." However, independence and partition, in effect, meant that India inherited this bureaucracy in 1947 both to run the administration and implement development programmes. Meanwhile, discontent started brewing in large parts of India owing to numerous reasons, the most important among them being the frustrations of the newly educated youth aspiring to jobs in the state apparatus, a sense of 'relative deprivation' among individuals and groups across the country and, of course, the staggering regional imbalance. On the one hand, such frustrations and the resultant discontent of individuals, groups and regions overlapped, and on the other, by the same token, such disaffected individuals, groups and regions found a common cause. One singular manifestation of such a phenomenon was burgeoning ethno-politics—ethnic group-based political mobilisation and movements. Economic causes may be the fountainhead of ethnic frustrations, but considerations of primordial identity have acted as an instrument of mobilisation as well as a goal for the same. Even economically advantaged ethnic groups and regions have resorted to ethnic movements. The Sikh separatist movement in India for a separate state of Khalistan is an obvious example. In such cases two explanations may be offered. First, the demand for an enhanced political status (despite the fact that the Sikhs have a considerable say in Delhi) may be a reason. In this, the Basque and Catalonian ethnic movements (both the ethnic groups and their regions being comparatively advantaged) are relevant." Second, the importance of the question of identity in ascriptive mobilisation is highly significant. Dipankar Gupta, while writing on Sikh separatism, argues, "when ascriptive identities, such as those of language, caste, religion or race, become basis of collective mobilisations, then these social identities tend to get 'naturalised', especially in the eyes of the partisans. As one is born into these identities, and as they are not profiles of achievement, the passions they arouse are seemingly prior to one's full range of socialisation, ascriptive mobilisations, therefore, are often of the kind one is willing to die for as they appear to call upon the irreducible essence of one's being".

However, the idea of 'relative deprivation'—basically in an economic sense—of both ethnic groups and comparatively underdeveloped regions where such groups live, has acted as the prime motive for ethnic mobilisation and movements. In regional terms, the explanation generally offered has been christened as 'internal colonialism' which was articulated by Michael Hetcher while explaining England's exploitative and unequal relations with Scotland, Ireland and Wales. Nearby, East Pakistan (now Bangladesh) was a prime example of 'internal colonialism'. In India, Jharkhand and Assam are probably two leading internal colonies. And both these underdeveloped (and deprived) regions have been experiencing prolonged ethnic movements in which the role of the 'salariat' has been critical. Though it may appear to be somewhat queer, both underdevelopment and modernisation (especially in the sense of spread of education and expansion of the middle class) have fuelled such movements. Here, some clarification is called for and in this, we will take up the role of the 'salariat' resulting from the spread of education and the concomitant job aspirations first.

Parliamentary System of Government

India has adopted a parliamentary system of government which pre-supposes a healthy party system. That is a rational approach to politics and the need for political mobilisation on an enlightened basis (not on caste, communal, racial and sectarian basis) was a sine qua non of a healthy party system. But the inevitable frustrations resulting from the failure of the 'everything to everybody' policy, staggering regional imbalances and, of course, from the amazing plurality of the Indian society have led to regionalism and regional parties" and ethnic mobilisation. And these developments have, in many instances, overlapped and coalesced. Indeed, they have been the two inter-twined sides of the same coin which is the frustrations/aspirations syndrome. Marx's idea was that with the spread of political consciousness and the overthrow of the capitalists by the proletariat, ethnicity—

as it was based on a "false consciousness"—would recede into history. Likewise, Durkheim viewed ethnicity as a manifestation of 'mechanical integration' which would pave the way, with increasing division of labour (when every individual would be dependent upon every other individual), for 'organic integration', and ethnicity would then become a thing of the past. But that was not to be. Hence Smith laments: "The dissolution of ethnicity. The transcendence of nationalism. The internationalisation of culture. These have been the dreams, and expectations, of liberals and rationalists in practically every country, and in practically every country they have been confounded and disappointed". The early promise—at least the early expectations of a rational basis of political mobilisation, bereft of racial, communal and caste considerations, gave way to ethinic/caste/religion based on political mobilisation and the emergence of political parties based on such parochial considerations. And paradoxically, such a development is not the result of tradition, illiteracy and poverty that are part and parcel of India. On the contrary, it is the result of modernisation, especially the spread of English education and the expansion of the middle class (the enlargement of the 'salariat', to be specific) that has fuelled ethnic politics in India. In this connection Smith's argument seems relevant. He writes: "The creation of vast factories and plants, massive urbanisation and slum conditions, fierce competition for jobs and housing, the rise of mass literacy and the impact of radio and television, have all tended to bring new insecurities, anxieties and frustrations which unscrupulous demagogues could manipulate by appealing to the comforting warmth of old ethnic bonds."" Two things may be stated here: first, the advancement in communications helped to focus the perception of 'relative deprivation' in sharper contours and hence helped to accentuate the frustrations of the deprived groups, and, concessions to ethnic demands—say, in the form of job reservations—fuelled further ethnic mobilisation, thereby producing a spiralling effect. Thus, what we really experience is the fact that the continually expanding number of intellectuals and the 'salariat', eager to reinforce the legitimacy of the modern bureaucratic state (supposed to be based on scientific rationality) are prepared to man the state bureaucracy. But when such potential bureaucrats flock to the metropolitan centres to find berths in the state bureaucracy, they hardly find any openings. Not only is the short supply of berths a hurdle, but also the new aspirants find themselves pitted against better educated higher caste groups long entrenched in positions of power and privilege. Frustrated and disgruntled, they return to their ethnic groups and are a key factor in ethnic mobilisation and movements. Such mobilisation is reinforced by the masses in underdeveloped, deprived regions where the concerned inhabitants are in an overwhelming majority. As indicated earlier, the petty bourgeoisie, well off farmers, industrial workers, local level leaders and tribal chiefs also join such movements that began primarily as a manifestation of 'salariat' frustrations. As also noted earlier, there is a widespread belief that political power is the key to economic power. Anyway, regarding the impact of modernisation vis-a-vis the question of resistance and endurance of ethnicity as a manifestation of primordial identity, one analyst argues: "In modernisation theory ... ethnic sentiment has been branded as primordial which would disappear in course of development. But as ethnic factors came to pose a challenge to the state, and state development programmes held responsible for the marginalisation of ethnic groups, the gamut of modernisation theory received a jolt." These so-called primordial affiliations, far from being eroded, have set the tenor of politics in many Third World countries" including India. The same analyst writes, "of late the movement in Tripura led by TUJS, and the movements for Udayachal, separate Bodoland in Assam, Jharkhand, Gorkhaland movements have transcended the stage of aspiration limited in culture. The newly emerged elities, educated students youth in these regions prefer to have a share in the power structure".

In order to drive home the arguments presented in the previous section we propose to deal, very briefly, with the instances, primarily, of Assam and Jharkhand. This is because these two instances of ethnic movement may be explained in terms of the concept of the 'salariat' and 'internal colonialism'. In fact, in order to comprehend the dynamics of these two cases, both kinds of explanations may be employed simultaneously.

Assam has witnessed an organised 'salariat' movement for quite some time now. In addition to the 'salariat' factor, there is the other factor - the exploitation of Assam's resources (oil and forest wealth in particular) which have been used for the benefit of areas and people outside Assam. The pattern of exploitation that began during the colonial days has persisted after independence. Only a few years ago an agreement was made whereby Assam was entitled to an enhanced royalty for her oil. Yet Assam can still be deemed as an internal colony. If we consider the questions of non-Assamese control over big business in Assam, continuous resource transfer from Assam, investment (rather, the lack of it) for Assam's development, the per capita income of the Assamese, the pathetic standard of living of the Assamese masses, a resort to the theory of 'internal colonialism' in order to understand Assam's relations with the rest of India, may not be inappropriate.

No less important for Assam is the factor of massive intrusion into Assam of Bengalis, both Hindus and Muslims. This influx has both a demographic and an economic implication with which the Assamese are very legitimately concerned. To quote Myron Weiner, a very keen observer of the Indian scene: "Over the past century, the Assamese speaking people of the state, now numbering approximately ten million, have been concerned with the influx of Bengali-speaking people, both from what is now Bangladesh (which before 1947 was part of a united India) and from the Indian state of West Bengal. At first the Assamese were concerned with the Bengali-speaking Hindus who moved into professions and white-collar service jobs. Subsequently the Assamese became alarmed at the immigration of Bengali-speaking Muslim agriculturists who occupied land. Much of the concern of the Assamese was economic: outsiders were getting the better jobs in the professions, in the government, and on the land. But beyond that was their concern that Assam itself might be overwhelmed by the Bengalis, that the Bengalis would impose their culture upon the Assamese, and that ultimately the Bengalis would take political control over the state." Here it can be stated that the impact of demographic factors on Assamese politics today is considerable. The role of the Bengalis in the Barak Valley and that of the Muslim (say, in the form of the United Minorities' Front), are to be reckoned with. Anyway, on the point of Bengali influx, the Assamese became alarmed and restive since the late 1970s when there was an unusually large increase in the number of people on the electoral rolls. The resultant protests and political turmoil saw the emergence of the All Assam Students Union (AASU) that spearheaded the Assamese ethnic mobilisation. In fact, the AASU has become a sort of a role model for the youth of other areas in India who suffer from a sene of 'relative deprivation'. The movements initiated by the AASU led to the creation of Assam Gana Parishad (AGP) which for sometime now has been the ruling party in Assam. Assam's is a classic case of how an ethnic group suffering from a sense of 'relative deprivation' because of long and continuous economic dominance by non Assamese, has combined with the fact of expansion of the middle class and of the youth with modern education. This has produced, inter alia, 'salariat' discontents and has, ultimately, led to ethnic mobilisation with the 'salariat' at the helm. Assamese ethnic politics is also being carried out through the terrorist mode in which the United Liberation Front of Assam (ULFA) is the kingpin.

As in other areas of society, there are circles within circles in ethnic politics as well. Hence the Bodos, who are less developed than the Assamese, want autonomy (or even separate statehood) and in this, the role of the All Bodo Students Union (ABSU), modelled after the AASU, has been the pioneering factor in articulating Bodo aspirations. In so far as the Bodos seek to get rid of the successors of the plantation labourers imported into their areas from Chhotanagpur by the British, the Bodo movements, having terrorist dimensions, may be branded as, what T.K. Oomnen calls 'insulationist' mobilisation.

Likewise, just across the Assam-West Bengal border, the Rajbansis of the north Bengal districts of West Bengal, feeling deprived vis-a-vis (and because of) the more advanced and privileged Bengalis, now want a separate state of Kamtapur. And in this movement the All Kamtapur Students Union (AKSU) is in the forefront, even though there is also a political outfit for the votaries of Kamtapur—the Kamtapur People's Party (KPP). To be brief, the AKSU is also the very embodiment of 'salariat' aspirations as well as the vanguard of the so-called Kamtapuri movement.

Now a brief look at the Jharkhand movement. Narrowly defined Jharkhand is composed of the Chhotanagpur plateau and Santhal Parganas of Bihar. Amazingly rich in natural resources and home to a very large variety of tribes and a large number of Scheduled Caste people, Jharkhand is a glaring case of the deprivation-discontent protest syndrome. The Jharkhand problem, sui generis by all counts, is not amenable to any single theoretical explanation. Historically speaking, intrusion of outsiders into Chhotanagpur began during the Mughal days and increased considerably during British rule. This has continued unabated even today. Consequently, there has not only been subversion of tribal society and culture but also such intrusion has resulted in wanton exploitation— and concomitant repression—of the tribals. Any contention to the effect that the Jharkhand movement is a compound of ethnic politics and regionalism may not explain all the dimensions of the problem. For instance, in any attempt at comprehending the pattern of exploitation and oppression the consideration of class is significant. Equally significant is the fact that the Scheduled Caste people who live in Jharkhand inconsiderable numbers and have been living there for a long time now, are also victims of exploitation. Hence, the acceptance of 'Sadans' (non-tribals who have been living in Jharkhand for a long time and who have adopted the Jharkhandi ethos) as Jharkhandis in the movement, is significant in that it has an assimilationist dimension. This has helped widen the support base for the movement. At any rate, Jharkhand is the starkest example of internal colonialism in India and it can be contended that Jharkhand is the very embodiment of deprivation in the sense of region, as well as of deprivation of the people who have been living there for centuries.

Jharkhand is a land of numerous tribes, among whom are the Oraons, Mundas, Santhals, Hos, Bhumijs, Kharia and so on. Immensely rich in minerals, forest and water resources, the people of Jharkhand have been exploited in equal measure. This exploitation which was severe during the Raj days has become even worse in independent India, thanks to considerable industrialisation and urbanisation (and resultant deforestation). The tribals of Jharkhand, thus, had to pay a huge price for 'development'. Now they are alienated from their land and forest resources and arc a socially degraded lot.

Again, Jharkhand is an internal colony par excellence. For instance, Chhotanagpur contributes 70 per cent of Bihar's total revenue, while only 20 per cent of the same is spent in Chhotanagpur. It goės without saying that the money (20 per cent of Bihar's revenue) spent in Chhotanagpur benefits the tribals marginally, the bulk of which goes to the exploitative non-tribals in the area.. In fact, the pattern of exploitation in Chhotanagpur may be expressed in concentric circles: exploitation of the tribals by non-tribals (and their tribal cohorts) within Chhotanagpur, and exploitation of Chhotanagpur by North Bihar. Indeed, the development of North Bihar is contingent upon resources transferred from Chhotanagpur. Hence, Lain. Prasad Yadav had threatened that the separate state of Jharkhand / Vananchal would be possible only over his "dead body".

Jharkhand's history of protest is as old as its history of deprivation. During the Raj days there were quite a few uprisings by individual tribes, including the Santhal uprising of 1855.39 At the beginning of the 20th century English educated youth, especially among Mundas and Oraons, emerged in Chhotanagpur as a result of Christian missionary educational activities that started during the preceding century. These English educated Christian youth naturally aspired to government jobs but they found themselves pitted against high caste Hindus inducted into Chhotanagpur first by the Mughuls (a few in number) and later by the British (in large numbers), who were long entrenched in positions of power and privilege. Hence, these educated tribal youth had to fall back upon their tribal identity and engage in ethnic politics. As a result, there emerged, at the turn of the last century, a number of religious, social reform and students' organisations which ultimately provided "the nucleus for subsequent political movements" under the banners of different Jharkhandi outfits. The Chhotanagpur Chhatra Sangharsha Samiti was created in 1978, the All Jharkhand Students Union (AJSU) emerged in 1986, and the Sonot Santhal Samaj was created in 1971 to demand the promotion of the Santhali language and the preservation of Samhali culture and tradition. These are recent manifestations of ethnic politics in Jharkhand which have been mainly, if not wholly, motivated by 'salariat' considerations. In this connection the establishment of the Department of Tribal and Regional Language in Ranchi University in 1980 merits mention. The various Jharkhandi political parties, such as the Jharkhand Mukti Morcha (JMM), the Jharkhand Party (JP) and others, organise their politics on the basis of tribal identity (for identity formation, the tribes and the region are equated) though the tribes in Jharkhand now constitute about 25 per cent of the total population of the area. In fact, the tribes and the Sadans are equally exploited by outsiders. And in deprivation terms, Jharkhand symbolises the congruence of a deprived region (as an internal colony) as well as of deprived human groups (a tribal and scheduled caste people). This has led to the convergence of region, tribe, caste and class in Jharkhand and its inevitable concommitant, regional-cum-ethnic politics.

By all indications, ethnic politics in India will continue to persist. We cannot wish away various political parties and their programmes based on appeal to ethnic identities. The most obvious reason for this is the fact that there will be a continuation of numerous ethnic groups in India as well as their legitimate grievances. We have seen that 'modernisation', especially spread of education, has not eroded ethnicity. On the contrary, it has reinforced the same because of unequal competition in which the 'salariat' belonging to various ethnic groups find themselves marginalised and because political mobilisation based on appeal to primordial identity has proved effective. The experience within

India and outside makes us agree with Dipankar Gupta when he says that "as one is born into these identities" (those of language, caste, religion, race, etc.), and as such identities are not "profiles of achievement, the passions they arouse are seemingly prior to one's full range of socialisation". He continues, "Ascriptive mobilisations, therefore, are often of the kind one is willing to die for .." Further, when the state concedes ethnic demands (which it cannot afford to ignore anymore), it does, in fact, encourage further ethnic mobilisation and articulation of ethnic aspirations.

Again, the decline of the Congress since the mid-1960s has been steady. The results of the 1999 parliamentary elections also confirm this. At the same time, no other party has yet been able to occupy the political space vacated by the Congress. (This is so for the Bharatiya Janata Party as well). Yet, ethnic grievances persist. This has provided ethnic political outfits with larger opportunities to mobilise and bargain with the mainstream parties. In other words, mainstream political parties, the Bharatiya Janata Party or the Congress, for instance, will have to make so on the basis of coalitions—howsoever shifting with ethnic/regional parties. Such coalitions, in effect, have to be the contemporary, and larger, variant of the technique of cooption of ethnic elites practised by the Congress during the first three or so decades since independence. For dealing with the rising ethnic grievances and aspirations, the old Congress technique of cooption is not adequate any more. Further, the Congress mandarins in the earlier years could not ignore local level power structures (as the British rulers could not do so). By the same logic the Bharatiya Janata Party, or any other, will also have to follow suit. Hence, ethnic politics has been and will continue to be an integral part of the Indian political panorama.

Man's journey in the path of civilization, since the dawn of history, has been epoch making though lone, arduous and agonising.

From the Law of the jungle, red in tooth and nail, when the will of the self-willed and the cruel with the dictum "Might is Right" prevailed, man has wearily traversed the Rule of Law, to the free exercise of the will of the people as expressed in peaceful general elections every five years as provided in the Constitution with the popular democratic dictum "Right is Might'.

Millions the world over have laid down their lives to bring about this happy consummation, and millions, in many countries are even today ready to make the supreme sacrifice for preserving this way of life.

But what do we see on the Indian scene?

It is true, we have a Constitution which guarantees for all citizens:

Justice social economic and political;

Liberty of thought, expression, belief, faith and worship:

Equality of status and of opportunity:

Fraternity assuring the dignity of the individual and the unity of the nation.

We have, so to say, a democratic government elected by the people through popular general elections held every five years based on universal adult franchise.

We have proclaimed a Socialistic Pattern of Society as the objective of our economic policy which envisages the raising of living standards, the enlargement of opportunities for all, the promotion of enterprise among all sections of the community.

The record of our government however, betrays a big gulf between promise and performance.

Democracy on Probation

What is worse, an organised, deliberate and masterminded conspiracy to scuttle or subvert the democratic form of government, nay, obliterate the very values we have all along cherished is, consciously or unconsciously, aided and abetted or at any rate, connived or winked at by those many of politically and bureaucratically at the helm.

Strife and violence have become very common in India since the 1967 general elections. Mob frenzy is whipped up by interested parties at regular intervals in the name of religion, language, peasant and labour welfare, students' and teachers' rights and what not. They all take a heavy toll of innocent lives and inflict great damage to public property. This was the first phase of the conspiracy to wreck the democratic governance of India.

The second phase is wanton desecration of the Ramakrishna Ashrams, Gandhi Kutirs, Tagore Niketans and Sarvodaya workers have now been unleashed. This is to systematically wipe out from the lives of our people the innate influence of our ageless culture and civilization, which hundreds of alien rule did not succeed in destroying.

The third phase is the subversion of the Constitution from within and' without; the fourth will be forcible brainwashing; the fifth and final phase will be the ruthless liquidation of values and purity in public life.

What does our Governments do to stem this devilish tide?

Steep all lies in the light of truth?

To explain away crimes, to be complacent in the face of organised, widespread hooliganism and violence, to permit the functioning of paramilitary private armies, is either an unconscious exposure of one's lack of faith in democracy or a tacit admission of incompetency to govern. In both events, it is a gross betrayal of the innocent and law-abiding who repose confidence in the government.

To make India's unhealthy socio-economic conditions a scapegoat for this unabashed orgy of violence is to clothe criminality and banditry with the respectability of great social reforms.

No one denies that there are the landless; no one asserts that there are no dispossessed; no one is happy at the growing unemployment; no one is unconcerned at heartless exploitation of the have-nots by the haves.

Who prevents the government from bringing about far reaching socio-economic changes?

What does government do? After allowing the pernicious crimes to run their disastrous course, the bosses rush to the scene, shed crocodile tears, make high sounding, pious, hypocritical promises and institute Commissions of Inquiry. Where does all this lead to? What value to the stricken humanity are empty jargons and periodical bogus gestures and gimmicks?

Does our government, which professes faith in democracy, realise that the foundation of democratic rule is the possibility of changing the government without resort to violence? Peaceful and orderly change from one government to another can be brought about only as long as violent acts are not allowed to be perpetrated with impunity.

A verse in the Dharmashastras says: "One who sets fire to things, one who poisons, one who attacks an innocent person with lethal weapons, one who snatches away, at the point of the sword, land, money and wife, is an Aatataayin or a great criminal; such a one should be put to death".

It is the paramount duty of any government to maintain law and order. Every other right flows from it, and without it all others are illusory.

The government should deal sternly with all breaches of law and acts of violence. It should categorically and unambiguously declare its resolve to do so and in its own interest, act up to this avowal. Else, the power of the government vanishes, for what gives strength to the statutes of a government is not merely the loftiness of their intentions or the capacity to invent excuses to cover up its failures or manipulation of votes by purchase, piracy or unholy alliances, but the courage of conviction and the strength to back up and enforce the statutes democratically framed.

Popular Sentiments

Centuries ago, during the Dark Ages, Rome was sacked by barbarian hordes. But today, there are not many external barbarians intent on destroying India. But what about the enemies of democracy and freedom within us? They are more deadly and dangerous.

As Plato said, a government is not made either of wood or stone: the character and functioning of a government depends upon the character of the men and women that constitute it. Those who run the government are made or unmade by the people—the voters. The voters, in turn, must get proper lead and guidance from the educated sections of society—the intellectuals and the enlightened.

What should be the intellectuals' task in the face of the grave threat to our great heritage, our very way of life? An analysis of India's own history through the ages provides the answer.

From the Vedic Age to modern times, we have effulgent examples of illustrious men unhesitatingly playing at the call of duty, a dual role: the natural role, that is the discharge of their swadharma: the role of the learned and the pathfinders in society, teaching, spreading knowledge and moulding the character of the people by precept and practice. They have, with equal adeptness, when occasion arose, played another role as *apaddharma*, the role of the crusader, the *dharmagopta*, the defender of dharma.

Srí Ramachandra and Sri Krishna did so for *dharmaraksha*. Chanakya had to adopt the *apaddharma* of a kshatriya to reinstate Chandragupta on the throne; that done, he would have no truck with power; he retired to a hermitage for offering oblations in the fire. Vdiyaranya was ready for battle and willingly shut his Vedantic books. Rana Pratap would have zealously gone on beautifying Mewar with bewitching parks and lakes. Krishnadevaraya would have worshipfully gone on building temples and tanks and visiting punyakshetras and tirthas. Shivaji would have gone on reverentially sitting at the feet of his *guru*, Ramdas, acquiring spiritual knowledge and offering prayers to Goddess Bhavani. Savarkar would have been content to spend his life in an ivory tower, ecstatically composing poems. Tilak would have lovingly taught college lads the intricacies of calculus or discoursed on Vedic astronomy. Gandhi would have devotedly gone on with his phoenix settlement and experiments with truth and non-violence, dietetics and nature cure. Nehru would have delightfully busied himself with scintillating superb word-architecture. Patel would have studiously built up a roaring legal practice and merrily whiled away his leisure, playing bridge and cracking jokes. But, beckoned by duty, they all cheerfully gave up their vocation and stubbornly fought for the independence of India.

The rulers have failed the country. Therefore, the people particularly those who are equipped to show and lead the way in the vital segments of national life should rise to the occasion.

Disappointingly, most of our people, particularly intellectuals, the right-thinking men and women of our land, stupefied as though by the onrush of violence, hatred and militant chauvinism, seem to be incapacitated to think pragmatically and act with courage.

In their desire to lead a life of ease and comfort, or due to disinclination or cowardice, the intellectuals may continue to shirk responsibilities, but their life of case and comfort will be no more than a will -o'-the- wisp once the forces of evil consolidate and emerge victorious. Honest intellectuals will be the first victims. The purges and unspeakable horrors that have followed the assumption of power by the totalitarians and theocrats, wherever they have succeeded, must open the eyes of lovers of freedom to the grim, dreadful prospects.

Smug complacency will not do. Those who stand for freedom and democracy and are wedded to ethical and spiritual values should weld themselves together, courageously voice their protest and go all out to stem the onrush of these demoniacal forces-those who master-mind riots and murders, engineer go-slow tactics and strikes, declare lay-offs and lockouts indulge in adulteration and profiteering and like unhealthy, unethical and anti-social practices.

The continuing attitude of apathy as typified in the selfish motto:

"My food, my bed, domestic bliss

Is all, that worry ?"

is a betrayal of ourselves and the nation. More, it is committing suicide, hara-kiri.

India is burning. Will not our many Neros arise, awake and stop fiddling ?

Andhra the first-ever linguistic state, was brought into existence on October 1, 1953.

This was the 'pioneering experiment' in Bharat's long and chequered history, dating back to 5,000 years and more indeed in world's history, of carving out States based solely on language, ignoring administrative complications, economic considerations, inter-state harmony, the plight of the linguistic minorities and even the paramount requirement of national solidarity.

Nature has designed India as an all-round, cooperative unit, an integrated whole.

Our indisputable geographical unity is marked out by the clear boundaries provided by Nature, the Himalayas in the north, the Hindukush in the north-west, and the great seas in the east, west and the south.

Nature has so distributed in India her bountiful gifts of mountains, rivers, mineral wealth, material resources, flora and fauna, and has endowed the people of all our religions with certain distinctive characteristics and special genius, which are homogeneous in spirit and complimentary in character.

Only if we are united and we pool together Nature's gifts would we be able to lead a dynamic, creative, prosperous and purposeful life.

The spirit of unity is the indispensable prerequisite for the security and progress of this *punyabhumi* of ours.

From the Vedic Age up to the first five years of our post-independence era, our leaders assiduously fostered an all-India outlook.

The history of the last half century testifies to the fact that, with the strength born out of this all-India outlook and resultant unity, we were able to work wonders:

— to wrest freedom from the then mightiest empire of the world;

— to survive the ghastly ravages of partition, migration of some ten million people and their re-settlement, the biggest in recorded history;

— to accomplish the smooth and bloodless merger of "Princely India", comprising 562 states, covering 48 per cent of our territory and over 80 million people, a unique and unparalleled feat of constructive statesmanship; and above all;

— to establish, for the first time since the reign of Samrat Ashoka, but with greater success and covering a strong Central Government whose writ ran in every nook and corner of India, the very description of which, as has come down to us by tradition, is Himavat Setu Paryantam, from the Himalayas to Rameshwaram.

This glorious epoch, studded with solid achievements and pregnant with 'promising prospects, particularly of the post-freedom era, was unfortunately, short-lived.

With the passing away of some of the great captains of our freedom movement and the quarantining of some others, a, quixotic pattern of power-monopoly emerged. This, not infrequently, led to hasty and impulsive decisions, placing personal and party interests above national interests. Naturally, the centre progressively became weak and wobbly. For its survival, it had to resort to a policy of drift, expediency and appeasement. Often, it was obliged to come to terms with the "assassins of nationalism", as Sardar Patel labelled the linguistic and regional "patriots".

The first act of supine surrender to organised violence, coercion and blackmail took place on October 1, 1953, with the creation of a separate Andhra.

Spurred by the success in Andhra, these satanic forces gathered strength and organised riots, arson and loot in other parts of the country. The centre lost courage and appointed, on December 29, 1953, the States Reorganisation Commission.

Since then, the devil dance of the forces of disintegration has gone on and on and on. The demand for separate state of Mithila, Konkan, Sagar Pranth, Vidarbha, Marathwada, Saurashtra, Kutch, Uttara Khand and Old Mysore has already been voiced and reiterated. They will rest content only with the vivisection of our Bharatavarsha into more and more separate states, districts, talukas and perhaps even villages.

We Were Warned.

The turmoil in Telengana is the inevitable outcome of the listless, short-sighted policy we chose to follow.

It is not that we were not warned betimes.

On January 25,1948, barely a week before his martyrdom, Mahatma Gandhi, who led us to freedom, solemnly declared:

— distribution should not militate against the organic unity of India. Autonomy did not and should not mean disruption, or that hereafter provinces could go the way they chose, independent of one another and of the centre. If each province began to look upon itself as a separate, sovereign unit, India's independence would lose its meaning and with it would vanish the freedom of the various units as well.

On June 17, 1948, Dr. Rajendra Prasad, President of the Constituent Assembly of India, appointed a Commission headed by Justice Dhar.

Dr. B.R. Ambedkar, the then Central Law Minister, in his memorable memorandum to the Dhar Commission, stated:

"The linguistic provinces will lead to the break-up of India. Instead of remaining united, India may end up in becoming Europe, faced with the prospects of chaos and disorder."

On December 10, 1948, the Dhar Commission reported its conclusions to the Constituent Assembly as under:

"The formation of provinces on exclusively or even mainly linguistic considerations is not in the larger interests of the Indian nation and should not be taken in hand.... In the formation of new provinces, whenever such a work is taken in hand, the oneness of language may be one of the factors to be taken into consideration along with others, but it should not be the decisive or main factor.

In December 1949, the Dhar Commission's Report was reviewed by the Indian National Congress at its Jaipur Session, which appointed a top-level committee consisting of Pandit Jawaharlal Nehru (Prime Minister) Sardar Vallabhbhai Patel (Dy.

Prime Minister) and Dr. Pattabhi Sitaramaiya (President of the Congress). The super-committee categorically declared:

a) when the Congress had given the seal of its approval to the general principle of linguistic provinces, it was not faced with the practical application of the principle and hence it had not considered all the implications and consequences that arose from this practical application.
b) the primary consideration must be the security, unity and economic prosperity of India and every separatist and disruptive tendency should be rigorously discouraged;
c) language was not only a binding force but also a separating one; and
d) the old Congress policy of having linguistic provinces could only be applied after careful thought had been given to each separate case and without creating serious administrative dislocation or mutual conflicts which would jeopardise the political and economic stability of the country.

In our supreme wisdom or innate cowardice, we ignored the voice of the wise.

During the struggle for Swaraj, there was only one state and two parties. With the advent of freedom, India was divided into two states. With our becoming a Sovereign Democratic Republic, we were further fragmented. We have now 28 states and seven centrally administered territories and within a state, each having four or five parties or even more.

Very few Indians now think as Indians, as Kulapati Munshiji has averred, "the biggest minority in the India of today are Indians".

A Great Fault

The folly of linguistic division has led to the emergence of linguism and regionalism as the most powerful group sentiments, threatening totally to eclipse robust nationalism. One shudders to visualise the prospects ten years hence when the present generation, solely fed on linguistic and regional jingoism, comes of age and assumes the reins of power in different states.

The way the affairs of the nation are run, be it the redemption of the pledge to recover our lost territory; be it the continuing threat to our territorial integrity; be it the containment of Naxalites, terrorists and their ilk; be it the creation of a new district by the ruling coterie in Kerala to keep itself in power; be it the stationing of Central Reserve Police to protect the Union Government's properties in West Bengal; be it the disruption of industrial production and paralysing of economic growth; be it the handling of the present agitation for a separate Telengana reminds one of the historic characterisations by Sir Winston Churchill of the British Government of 1938, which was following a policy of appeasement towards Hitler and Mussolini:

"So they go in strange paradox, decided only to be undecided, resolved to be irresolute, adamant for drift, solid for fluidity, all powerful to be impotent. So we go on preparing more months and years precious, perhaps vital, to the greatness of the nation for the locusts to eat."

The centre should not underrate the dogged determination of the forces of parochialism and their Communist backstage managers, masquerading under different labels: location of steel mills and fertilizer projects, erection of giant dams, enhanced D.A. and job reservations, more powers to the states, decentralisation of the administration, etc.

Their design is to sow the seeds of dissension, to gain a little ground and advance step by step towards the day when the central government would no longer have the will to hold out against them; the day when, through exhaustion, through jealousy and quarrels within the Union Cabinet, the centre would cease to be able to enforce its writ in the various parts of the Republic of India.

There is, however, a silver lining on the horizon. In 1966, Dr. V.V. Giri, the President of India, in a Foreword to Linguistic Vivisection of India—Why not stop it still ? by Sri V.B. Kamath (a Bhavan's publication) wrote:

"The recent border disputes and agitations for the formation of linguistic states and the inter-state rivalries leading to violence, bitterness and disorders have become not only a problem of law and order but even a threat to subvert the unity of India, generating hostility and hatred by people of one state against another. Many of us have come to feel that we should put a stop to this and reverse the trend."

So said the President of the Congress, Sri S. Nijalingappa, in his address at the Faridabad Session of the Indian National Congress in April 1969:

"I have often felt that linguistic states cannot lead to national integration and actually encourage distintegration. We should do away with these linguistic states and reorganise the country on an essentially economic basis."

More and more thinking men and women all over India are veering round to this view.

By nature and nurture, by geographical conditions and historic experience, by religious impulsions and cultural ideals, India is one and indivisible. She must remain so if we wish to retain our freedom.

It is high time that the forces of unity and consolidation in the country got together and organised themselves. Otherwise, it would not be possible for the Union Government to prevent further vivisection, let alone undoing the existing vivisection of India.

Unfortunately, some in the seats of power and authority feel that it is too late to go back upon linguistic states.

Did not Pandit Jawaharlal Nehru, the reluctant architect of linguistic division of India, in his broadcast while releasing the report of the States Reorganisation Commission, emphasise that nothing is permanent in a democracy?

Therefore, let us here and now set about in right earnest to tame and civilize the "tribal instincts" from which linguistic and regional chauvinism springs.

Andhra was the starting point of the linguistic vivisection of our Motherland. Let it also be the starting point of the reversal of that ruinous policy.

Let us work for India the United. That is India's destiny. That is Nature's dispensation. That is Divine Will.

5

Social and Political Fabric

The topic of the seminar has been so structured that it appears to be built on an infinite time-scale. I do not know how much belongs to retrospect, and how much to prospect or the future. I wish to take advantage of this situation, and start from ancient India. This is on account of the fact that though the country today has a political and cultural situation which is totally dehumanising and politically abhorrent, we still have our roots in a continuing cultural and intellectual tradition, which has come down to us from the ancient period of our history. The ancient Indian intellectual and cultural tradition had two main strands in it - one was secular, rational, and this-worldly, and the other was what is sometimes called 'spiritual', and was also based on rituals and dogmatic religious conservatism. The first, broadly materialist and rational tradition, happened to be bigger in size, coverage and volume than the so-called 'spiritual' tradition. Even the Vedas had lot of rational elements in them. They were basically this-worldly, rather than other-worldly texts. They were concerned with material gains. The Ayurveda, Natya Shastra, Arthashastra, and a whole host of other texts and literary works were rational, secular, mundane, concerned with human life, and not with the next world. But a change occurred, to a small extent from the time of the Upanisads, and to a greater extent from the time of Shankaracharya. What was revived in the nineteenth century was not the rational, this-worldly, mundane, scientific and secular tradition. Instead, it was the other tradition—dogmatic, unscientific, superstitious, spiritual, and concerned with other-worldly matters like heaven and hell, which was revived. The supposedly unquestionable authenticity of the scriptures was used to support this tradition. This was a great historical tragedy of the nineteenth century.

Therefore, what is generally called the Renaissance was a perversion of the concept of renaissance. What happened was a sort of religious reformation, which led to a revivalist kind of politics in the first half of the twentieth century. What we have today is the inevitable legacy of this tradition of the nineteenth century, which revived the wrong stream of Indian culture—not the rational, scientific, secular stream, but the superstitious, dogmatic, religious one. Politics today has become totally saturated with this kind of dogmatism, intolerance, superstition, and mythology.

Ancient and Medieval Heritage

Mythology has become an important part of religion. The mythical characters like Rama and Krishna, etc., are neither historical figures, nor based on any rational perception, and cannot be sustained by any sort of scientific thinking. But they have come to occupy a central position in current Indian politics. This is largely because we have discarded our rational and secular tradition and adopted a political culture which is irrational, dogmatic, mythological and without any scientific foundation. This has led back to the middle ages by destroying our secular and rational outlook.

I think it is absolutely necessary to reverse this regressive tradition. I think those who belong to the University have a specific responsibility in this respect. They should not only study subjects like International Relations or Physics but they also have a special responsibility for challenging this religious, dogmatic and other-worldly tradition, and re-establishing the more genuinely rational Indian tradition. The present situation has led to an erosion of India's image as a democratic and secular state. One cannot have a primitive socio-political system, and claim to be a harbinger of change in the international system. This is not a credible position.

The political system is an offshoot of, and is inextricabily intertwined with, this kind of irrational intellectual and cultural context. We are witness to the fact that the Indian democratic system, although nominally liberal and participatory, is in fact entirely dependent on caste and communal prejudices today. Without casteism and communalism, it is not possible to understand the current Indian political system. Indian democracy has sunk to a very low level on account of this perverse intellectual and cultural tradition which we have revived in our politics and national life. A government by the people, is nowhere to be seen. When we speak of 'government of the people, by the people and for the people', it can be 'government of the people' in a very perverse sense, namely, that the government is run in the name of the people. It may be for the people, since the politicians say they are acting and making sacrifices for the welfare of the people. So nominally, our democracy is for the people. But, we will never find democracy by the people on account of the very sharp class divisions in our society. Politics is monopolised by the exploitative upper-classes generally and not by the masses of the people, at least in the greater part of India. Indian politics is known by its specific character of being saturated with the perverse forces of casteism and communalism, and not as a true democracy. So, there has to be an escape from this kind of politics. If this be the retrospect, the prospect cannot be a continuation of the same thing. As in the intellectual and cultural spheres, the prospect in the political sphere has to be in a different direction too—rational, secular, and truly representative. It must be people's democracy, not this perverse form of liberal democracy.

This situation is not surprising, because our economic system is still feudal. There has been no land reform over large parts of India, especially in Bihar, Uttar Pradesh and the entire Northern belt. When this happens, a feudal class dominates politics. It is this feudal class which encourages communalism and casteism, opposes land reform and dominates rural Indian politics, and Indian politics is by and large rural Indian politics.

Elsewhere in India, there exists a perverse kind of capitalism and not true capitalism. It is more or less a trading and financial capitalism. There too, we find the reflection of the kind of politics discussed before, because this perverse form of capitalism is not entrepreneurial. In the rural areas, it is feudalism which controls politics, and the gangsters and rural mafia supply money to the political parties as well as to individual politicians. In the urban areas, the big business houses provide political finance, and the urban mafia dons, criminals and gangsters control politics. Most of us are familiar with the Vohra Committee Report of 1993, which is a government report. It states categorically that there has developed a virtually unbreakable nexus between the criminals and mafia dons on the one hand, and the politicians and bureaucrats on the other. The report also says that it is extremely difficult under the existing penal code and criminal procedure code to bring these people to justice. Criminals get protection from the politicians, who get their money for political funds, particularly election funds, from the former. The policemen and bureaucrats get a share of it too, because they know the modus operandi of the politicians and criminals thoroughly. So, we do not have a true democracy in India. We must create a true, scientific democracy which is not dependent on either feudalism or capitalism. But we cannot do that without abolishing feudalism, and if not wholly abolishing, at least seriously restraining capitalism.

Now I come to matters which are central to today's seminar. When it comes to international relations, it cannot be separated from the domestic issues I have mentioned, because domestic factors are often decisive determinants of foreign policy. One cannot have a primitive cultural or intellectual system, a medieval, feudal, pseudo-Capitalist economic system, and a mafia-based political system, and then expect to play a decisive role in foreign policy. This is not possible, because the structure of a state is a decisive determinant of its external behaviour. Hence, without changing our present historical condition, we cannot have a forward-looking vision of India's role in international relations.

Relations with other Nations

We cannot discuss the entire range of India's foreign policy here, but we will concentrate on what is most topical today, namely, the

Pokhran explosion, nuclear weapons, and Indo-Pak relations and touch on a few other fundamentals of our foreign policy. I would like to emphasize at the beginning that it is wrong to concentrate on the BJP (Bharatiya Janata Party) for the Pokhran explosion, and to relate it exclusively to the communal situation and Indo-Pak relations. It is true that this party has taken advantage of the situation. It is also true that the BJP's kind of politics and its own domestic compulsions have been decisive factors in the timing of the Pokhran explosion, but not in the programme itself. The programme dates back almost to India's independence. It was a nuclear programme, which was officially called a PNE (Peaceful Nuclear Explosion) programme. But actually, it was a nuclear weapons programme from the beginning. The first explosion took place in 1974. At that time and afterwards, the Government of India stated and emphasised the fact that they were keeping the nuclear weapons option open. They did not want to abandon the nuclear weapons programme. If newspaper reports are correct, there were several other occasions (including the last one during the P.V. Narasimha Rao regime), when attempts were made to explode nuclear devices. But apparently, the Americans got wind of the situation in advance. The CIA (Central Intelligence Agency) is always better informed than our politicians and bureaucrats, In the past also, whenever the CIA scented something about to happen in India which they did not like, they always stopped it. Thus, India's invasion of Goa was stopped twice before it was pushed through by Krishna Menon and the defence chiefs, without informing Nehru. This happened again, and the planned nuclear explosions were stopped or stymied on several occasions. What the Indian scientists concerned and the BJP had done was to hoodwink the CIA somehow, and they should be given credit for this. They exploded the weapons. They were not the first who wanted to conduct the explosion; preparations had gone on for decades. Others had tried, but were stopped. Whether this was good or bad is a different question. What I am trying to say is that one should not concentrate on the BJP and Pokhran, and think that as far as nuclear weapons are concerned, this was the beginning of history. Nor is this the end of history so far as the nuclear weapons arsenal is concerned. A lot of infrastructure has been built up, a scientific community of nuclear expert has come into existence, massive investments have been made. No government in the future can roll back this entire process. So, the programme, I am sure, will go on, whatever the colour of the government might be. May be there will be an increase or decrease in the number of declarations made, but subterranean progress of the programme cannot be stopped now.

I would like to state emphatically at the outset that I am totally opposed to the Idea of India and Pakistan manufacturing nuclear weapons which are aimed against each other. I think this is bilaterally ruinous. My vision is different. I consider the prevailing international system to be totally hegemonic. I think the weaker states have a moral duty and political obligation to resist this hegemony and tyranny. I see the nuclear weapons programme of India and Pakistan as one of the ways of resisting this hegemonic system by defying the nuclear monopoly and superiority of the global hegemons.

We have a concert today in the world almost exactly like that Concert of Europe, which came into existence in 1815. What is more, the world has never experienced an imperialism as great as it is witnessing today. Never before in the history of the world, has the entire international system come under the domination of a single state. This is the only occasion in history when this has happened. This is the most important dimension of globalisation, certainly more important than free trade, etc.

In this situation, the common arguments against nuclear weapons are made on wrong grounds. One argument is that we should not spend so much money on nuclear weapons in the midst of so much illiteracy and poverty, and that the nuclear programme has aggravated these problems. Without going into the details of this, I wish to say that the negative correlation, which is thought to be established between military (particularly nuclear) expenditure, and our economic backwardness, poverty and illiteracy, is a spurious correlation. In order to establish a true correlation, we have to eliminate all other intervening variables like the class structure, the performance of the bureaucracy, etc., and establish clearly that our poverty and illiteracy are due only to nuclear weapons. Preferably, it should also be shown that poverty and illiteracy have increased, due exclusively to the nuclear programme. But no critique of India's nuclear weapons programme has done all this. Besides, it is not possible to isolate expenditure on the nuclear weapons programme from the totality of defence expenditures. For all these reasons, the negative correlation sought to be established between poverty and illiteracy on the one hand, and the nuclear weapons programme on the other, may be considered spurious.

Another argument against India's nuclear programme is the astronomical cost of this programme, which is supposed to bring about India's economic ruin. But it is an established fact that the nuclear powers have found nuclear defence to be not only more effective but also cheaper than conventional defence. Had the expenditure involved been truly 'astronomical', neither Pakistan nor North Korea could have adopted a nuclear weapon programme.

Besides, expenditure on the nuclear weapons programme has well known multiplier and acceleration effects on the civilian economy, which should not be ignored altogether.

It has also been said that India and Pakistan have to accept a sub-optional solution comparable to the 'prisoner's dilemma' model of game theory. I presume that there is no need to explain the term here. But this is a completely misplaced analogy. This theoretical model assumes the position of a prison governor for these two countries. India and Pakistan should not consider themselves as prisoners, nor should they accept the dictates of a self-appointed global policeman. This is the first reason why this model cannot operate. Secondly, the 'prisoner's dilemma' model assumes that there is no intercommunication between the two prisoners, and both have to go to their own cells and think of the risk involved before taking a decision. But there is no reason to think that India and Pakistan do not and cannot communicate or negotiate with each other. There is, should be, and probably will be increased communication between them. If that is so, the prisoner's dilemma does not apply to India and Pakistan. If they accept the dictates of global policemen, and communicate with each other only through the latter, only then will this model apply. This suggestion is the result of an inferiority complex, lack of confidence, and a distorted view of contemporary international relations which is based on the assumption of the existence of an authoritarian global policeman.

The New World Order

The international system is a symmetric and anarchical. Thirty-five states with a population of only one million or less, are members of the General Assembly. A small Atlantic island with a population of about 60 million or six crore, is a permanent member of the United Nations Security Council. Bangladesh has double the population of the United Kingdom, not to speak of India which has more than 1000 million or 100 crore, and a huge territory. So, it is an example of the perversity of the contemporary hegemonic and asymmetric international system that a small island is one of the five oligarchs who determine the course of international relations, and not India. This is a situation which no self-respecting nation, individual, or student of international relations should accept. This structure is asymmetric and at the same time anarchical. The central hypothesis of Western international relations theory is that there should be no international regulating authority. The system is supposed to operate on balance of power, which will not work, if there is any regulatory authority. But since balance of power is merely a myth from the empirical point of view, and nothing but a predatory strategy of the global hegemons for their own self-aggrandisement, asymmetry plus anarchy inevitably means an international system characterised by *malsyanyaya* (big fish preying upon the small).

This necessitates the resistance by India and Pakistan against the Non-Proliferation Treaty (NPT) and the Comprehensive Test Ban Treaty (CTBT), which are based entirely on discrimination and the perpetuation of the hegemony of the five nuclear powers. The question is, how is this to be done? My solution is that India and

Pakistan must play a positive and cooperative game with each other, and a negative game against the global hegemons. In other words, they must collaborate to resist the hegemons. Therefore, my solution, which is rational, but may not be immediately practicable, is that India and Pakistan should have nuclear weapons, but these weapons should be jointly aimed by them against the nuclear hegemons. This is the direction in which the foreign policies of India and Pakistan should move.

The problem is that of the new world order which India should strive for. The Western view of the international system is that of complete national sovereignty and informal global oligarchy under cover of formal inter-state anarchy. In fact, the history of Western foreign policy and political thinking with reference to the rest of the world is based on Machiavelli, Hobbes, Nietzsche, and a whole host of other champions of amoral politics, war and imperialism. The concept of a superpower is only an extension of Nietzsche's concept of superman. This is a system of matsyanyaya in the name of state sovereignty and inter-state anarchy which is intolerable for India and other Third World states.

The classical Marxist solution of the international class struggle, the abolition of Capitalism, the disappearance of the state, and the establishment of an international socialist republic has not worked so far. The erstwhile Soviet Union, the rump Russia, and China have all accepted and even legitimised the prevailing inter-state system characterised by state sovereignty, international anarchy, and global oligarchy. Any structural transformation of the prevailing inter-state system can taken place only through a marginal modification of state sovereignty, and not through the abolition of the state. The only feasible solution appears to be the democratisation and empowerment of the United Nations (UN), and its qualitative transformation into a democratic, just, federal and minimal global regulatory authority.

The Third World states, which enjoy an overwhelming majority in the UN, can start a resistance movement in the General Assembly. They can also utilise the Non-Aligned Movement and the Group of 77 for creating a counter-hegemonic movement outside the UN system. They can also enlist the support of the Greens, feminists and other pro-Third World groups in the Western countries. If they carry on a political campaign, eventually the Security Council will be compelled to expand itself. Incidentally, India's permanent membership of the Security Council will not lead to the establishment of global democracy. It will only add one more hegemon to the given global Structure of hegemony.

So what India should really do is not to try for a seat in the Security Council for itself, but spearhead a campaign of the Third World for the democratisation of the UN, and the empowerment of the Third World states. India, as the largest democracy of the world, can play a leading, legitimate, and credible role in an international movement for the democratisation of the LYN and its transformation into a democratic and just global regulatory authority. This, in my opinion, should be the central thrust of Indian foreign policy at the beginning of the twenty-first century.

In conclusion, I come back to where I began. If we do not transform our intellectual and religious culture into something more rational than it is now, and if we do not reform and modernise our political system and destroy feudalism and financial and trading capitalism, then the role that we visualise for our country will be neither credible nor possible in the international relations of the twenty-first century. We shall go on making statements and declaring high international objectives. But Ganga will remain sunken, and the thunder will say nothing. The only boom we will hear will be that of the guns of imperialism.

Political System

If modern politics is democratic politics, the political parties play a key role in it. Political parties organise people's representation, provide effective and responsive government, structure the opposition, transform people's wants into political demands and channelise such demands to the governmental apparatus, make elections meaningful and act as live linkage between the people and their rulers. The health of the parties and the party system reflects the health of the political system. In a word, political parties are the most essential component of modern democratic politics.

In an electoral democracy, political parties are found to be useful for individual politicians as well, for otherwise they would operate as individuals and not join parties, in which case, parties would not come about. A political party is not only a stable coalition of individual politicians with shared preferences. By joining a party an individual politician enhances his pay-off by deciding to act collectively within legislatures. That is to say, because of his party affiliation he achieves much more in terms of bringing about or opposing enactments than he could ever do acting as an individual legislator. Besides, the party as an enduring structure provides a brand name to its members and makes it possible for them to enjoy economies of scale in fighting elections (Aldrich, 1995). Therefore, both from the standpoint of representative politics and from that of individual politicians in an electoral democracy, a system of parties seems indispensable.

Fifty years ago India launched herself as an electoral democratic republic with a string of parties. During the first three elections, numerous parties were represented in the Indian Parliament (Lok Sabha) in a 'single majority district' system of elections under which any candidate receiving a plurality of votes (not necessarily a majority of votes) wins the election. But the presence of numerous parties notwithstanding, the one single party which was overwhelmingly predominant was the Indian National Congress both in terms of votes received and parliamentary seats captured. This had earned the Indian party system the label of 'one dominant party system' or the 'Congress system .

During the first decade and a half, the predominance of the Indian National Congress, founded on about 45 per cent of popular votes and 65 per cent of Lok Sabha seats, enabled the party to provide stable government. This stability was based on, first, the theoretical possibility of a change in the party of governance; second, the pragmatic acceptance by all parties of elections as the instrument of bringing about such change; and third, an acceptance by all parties of the legitimacy of Congress rule.

For the Congress it was possible to perpetuate its dominance because, first, it contained within itself a plurality of political views, and hence, it could effectively work as a centrist party occupying the centre as well as much of the right and the left of the political spectrum. Secondly, it maintained organisational flexibility which made it possible for individual Congress leaders and groups to frequently leave the party and to rejoin it again without in any way bringing governmental stability to the brink. Thirdly, it represented and encouraged a certain amount ambiguity with regard to ideology, programme and policy.

These features made the Congress during this period a truly aggregative political formation in a society characterised by enormous diversity and deep-rooted social cleavages. Some west European states have, over the last few centuries, developed a high degree of social homogeneity. In such states political conflict usually takes place on issues affecting society produced by changes in economy and technology. Political contestations structure around the question of appropriate or desirable policies. The main task of politics in such states becomes negotiating inevitable social changes. Contrarily, Indian society, like many other historical and contemporary societies, is characterised by endemic cleavages built around religion, caste, language, etc. In such societies bringing about social change and harnessing social change to the benefit of the masses are contingent upon the construction of a minimal political consensus with regard to the endemic cleavages constantly threatening to fragment the society. The aggregative stance of the Congress during the first one and a half decades after independence was eminently suited for the task of such political consensus building.

Sometimes, this Congress strategy of building a minimal political consensus has been misunderstood as a consociational strategy. Arend Lijphart, the theorist of consociational politics, has recently so argued (Lijphart, 1997). But if 'grand coalition', 'elite cartel', and 'minority veto' are the benchmark phrases of consociationalism as Lijphart himself would have us believe, then the 'Congress system' certainly did not indicate consociational practice. The Congress during this period had indeed successfully created a broad social coalition as the support base for its political consensus as we will explain below, but this social coalition was certainly not a political 'grand coalition' of parties for manufacturing stable government. Parties of the extreme right, the left as well as parties of confessional persuasion were kept out of governance. Indeed, within the federal framework, when a Leftist government came to power through elections in the southern state of Kerala in the late 1950s, its government was trounced by the Congress.

There is no visible 'elite cartel' either. Neither the confessional parties nor the Communist party was comfortable with the Constitution. The Communist party had openly disagreed with the parliamentary system in principle, though in practice it did accept the institution of elections and participate in it from the very first general elections. The parties to the right like the *Swatantra* had strong reservations with regard to the economic policies adopted by the Congress.

Thirdly, it is indeed true, that the Congress followed accommodative policies with regard to minority rights, both religious and linguistic. But in both cases, and perhaps more so with regard to religious minorities, especially the Muslims, such accommodative policies were the product of its own commitments, its own sense of what was good for India to which electoral compulsions were added somewhat later. To treat such accommodative practices as founded on any claim of minority veto would be utterly wrong. Even the reversal of the Shah Bano judgement through a Parliamentary enactment under Congress initiative much later in the 1980s, which Lijphart refers to as an indicator of 'minority veto', cannot at all be so considered. It was more an instance of wrong priority of the Congress government under Rajiv Gandhi, an example of its thoughtless capitulation to the demands of some bigoted Muslims, which made it vulnerable to all sorts of fundamentalist pressures.

If India's largely prime ministerial system of government within one party dominance during the first twenty years or so of her independence can be labelled as 'consociational' because the government carefully attempted to accommodate representation of linguistic groups and political regions, then perhaps any prudent democratic government, including those of the United States (USA) and the United Kingdom (UK), can be considered consociational; but in which case the label would lose all classificatory significance. No doubt, such labelling betrayed Lijphart's misunderstanding of Indian politics as much as his 'consociational evangelism' (see Lustic, 1997; also, Lijphart, 1982, for an altogether different claim regarding Indian politics and also regarding the relationship between democratic stability and consociationalism).

Therefore, the 'one dominant party system' or the 'Congress system' was not consociational but majoritarian even though its majoritarianism was tempered by political prudence. As a result, the Congress could maintain its dominance without curbing oppositional forces like so many other Third World regimes. Not only was the opposition present, it enjoyed legitimacy by the fact that the Congress allowed 'opposition voices' within itself. Thirdly, the dominant party's ideological ambiguity allowed it to appear as the party of all in general, even though of no one in particular. These features became an indispensable part of the 'one dominant party system' in India.

With these structural characteristics of the 'one dominant party system' in place, the Congress utilised its pre-independence halo built on its past as the party of the freedom movement and the popular deference that Jawaharlal Nehru commanded to achieve a working political consensus. This consensus was as much buttressed by the opposition's realisation that given the disunity amongst themselves, it was absolutely impossible for them to replace the Congress, which commanded nearly half of the total votes, from power as by a social coalition intelligently woven by the Congress. This social coalition, which has also been called 'a composite coalition of interests' (Nayyar, 1998), was based on a combination of support deftly generated by Congress leaderships at different levels of society from quite disparate social groups. It was a combination of support from the urban industrialists as well as from large sections of the working class; from rich farmers as well as from the rural poor; from the Brahmans as well as from the lower castes. But, above all, it was strongly rooted in highly stable support from the scheduled castes, scheduled tribes and the

Muslims, such that these latter groups could be labelled as constituting permanent 'vote banks' for the Congress.

Between 1952 and 1971, the Congress oil an average captured 44 per cent of electoral Support while the largest opposition party could capture around 10 per cent of the votes.

VOTE SHARE IN LOK SABHA ELECTIONS, 1952-99

Year	*Congress*	*Second top party*
1952	45.0	11.0
1957	47.8	10.2
1962	44.7	10.3
1967	40.8	10.2
1971	43.7	10.3
1977	34.5	41.5
1980	42.7	21.3
1984	48.1	06.9
1989	39.5	17.5
1991	36.5	20.5
1996	28.8	20.2
1998	25.8	25.5
1999	28.4	23.7

Sources: Butler, Lahiri and Roy (1997), 158, 16 (for 1952-91); *The Statesman*, 12 October 1999 (for 1991 -99).

But the consensus collapsed in the post-1967 period as the Congress failed to sustain the social coalition. Although after 1967 the Congress could reoccupy its dominant position as the ruling party three times (1971, 1980, 1984), none of these occasions marked a revival of the ,one dominant party system' with all the structural features mentioned above.

It is unnecessary to elaborate how under Indira Gandhi's plebiscitarianism, the Congress not only went through an excessive organisational centralisation and family rule, and tried to transform itself into a cadre-based party but, as the governing party, it also distorted India's federal structure through the politics of centralisation and personalism (for these have been elaborately discussed many times over by numerous commentators on Indian politics). But the net result of it all was that when in consequence of the first fifteen years' democratic politics coupled with some economic development, new inequalities were being created on the ground and the need for managing new conflicts of interests and mass mobilisation at the grass roots level was becoming all the more acute requiring careful handling by a strong party organisation with an effective leadership at the multiple levels of the polity sensitive to the implications of the social changes tinder way, the Congress party organisation after the 1969 split became virtually defunct. It was not possible for such a party to hold the once carefully-nurtured social coalition together. This gave rise to a bimodal party structure instead of a unimodal one of the one dominant party system' days.

Congress vote came down to 34.5 per cent while the opposition Janata party secured 41.5 per cent of the popular votes. That is to say, the distance between the two top parties, which was 34 per cent in favour of the Congress till 1971, came down to only 7 per cent and, that too, against the Congress, Thereafter, excepting in 1984, the distance between the two top parties continued to remain narrow till 1998 when it was wiped out altogether making the system perfectly bimodal. In the 1999 elections, the Congress vote share rose to 28.4 per cent from 25.8 per cent in 1998, while the other major party's, the Bharatiya Janata Party (BJP), votes declined from 25.5 per cent (1999) to 23.7 per cent, making the distance between the two top parties a negligible less than 5 per cent of votes. Nearly the same distance obtained between these two parties but in the reverse direction, when we look at the percentage of votes received by them in the seats they contested in the 1999 elections. Here, we find the BJP's vote, in fact, rose from 33.5 per cent in 1998 to 39.6 per cent in 1999 compared to the Congress 33.9 per cent. That is to say, the apparent decline in BJP's share of the total votes was due to its contesting a lesser number of seats in 1999 than in the year before. Therefore, for the past 23 years from 1977, bimodality has obtained with the only exception of the 1984 elections, which, indeed, were held in very exceptional circumstances following Mrs. Gandhi's assassination.

But even though the distribution of popular votes has become bimodal, this in no way indicates the possible emergence of a stable two-party system. Between 1952 and 1991, the two top parties together used to capture about 5 8 per cent of the votes on an average, although, as we have already pointed out, its distribution was highly skewed in favour of the Congress. This declined to about 52 per cent in the Lok Sabha elections held after 1991. This means that while the distribution of votes between the two major parties has become more evenly balanced and the imbalance has disappeared, yet, together they mop up only half the total votes leaving the other half to be shared by a large number of parties. And if these parties, or at least a substantial number of them could form a bloc, they would have a decisive impact both on the party system and also on the making of the government.

Here, it needs to be remembered that while both the number of national parties and state parties show a declining trend between 1952 and 1991, the number still is very large. Even in the 1999 Lok Sabha elections, there were 30 parties other than the Congress and the BJP (India Today, Oct. 18, 1999: 32). If a few of them are still technically regarded as 'national parties', in fact, all of them are broadly state parties in the sense that none of them has an all-India strength on the basis of which it can hope to act as a prime mover in the formation of the Central government. Perhaps, the CPI-M (Communist Party of India-Marxist) was marginally in such a position during 1996-98, but it is no longer so. To think of any possibility of synthesising these state parties into a single bloc, given the changing scenarios in the states and the divergent interests of these parties, goes against both common sense and recent experience.

After the collapse of the social coalition built by the Congress as the foundation of its predominance, the other major national parties, the Janata and the BJP, during the 1980s and the early 1990s tried in turn to build similar social coalitions around caste and religion through Mandalisation and Hindutva respectively, in order to ensure their predominance at the hustings. While both attempts have deeply affected Indian politics, they proved abortive in creating any alternative social coalition or stable vote bank behind either of these parties. If the Janata has gone quite out of the reckoning as a national party in the process, for the BJP it seems unlikely that its electoral base can any further be expanded significantly, at least in the near future, on grounds of Hindutva. It is somewhat naive to argue, as some within the BJP are doing, that the BJP's disastrous performance in terms of Lok Sabha seats in 1984 was due to Atal Behari Vajpayee's liberalism and its later success was the product of Lal Krishna Advani's ratha yatra and the vulgarity of the Babri demolition. The 1984 elections were very special in that the Congress had at that time most blatantly put on the communal hat inducing even the RSS (Rashtriya Sevak Sangh) to see greater hopes in that party than in the newly formed BJP. But despite that, the BJP could secure about seven per cent of the popular votes which was no less than what its earlier incamation, the Jan Sangh, could muster. On the other hand, all talks and deeds and (mostly) misdeeds in the name of Hindutva did nothing to help the BJP avoid a downslide in the Uttar Pradesh assembly elections in 1993 which, the BJP leaders had claimed before the elections but denied after the elections, was to be a referendum on the Babri demolition; nor did it help it to improve its vote share at all between the 1991 and 1996 Lok Sabha elections. That is to say, the limits of Hindutva either as an ideology or as a campaign strategy are blatantly manifest for anyone who cares to see.

To sum up our arguments so far, the 'one dominant party system' of the first decade and a half after Independence functioned through a political consensus based on a firmly-grounded social coalition forged by the Congress rather than on any consociational engineering. Secondly, between 1969 and 1979, this social coalition collapsed bringing down the political consensus behind one party dominance. Thirdly, between 1977 and 1999, gradually a bimodal party structure has evolved, but the bimodality being weak, it is unable to give rise to an effective two-party system. Fourthly, half the electoral space remains occupied by thirty odd basically state parties (I think regional party is an inappropriate and vague term to describe such parties as the Dravida Munnetra Kazhagam (DMK), the All India DMK (AIDMK), the Telugu Desam Party (TDP), the Asom Gana Parishad (AGP), the National Conference (NC), etc.), which are strong in their respective states but are no longer able to construct a 'third front'.

Given this party scenario, what is its possible political outcome in the short run? First, it is quite unlikely that single party dominance would at all recur at least in the foreseeable future. The complexity and diversity of mobilisation and counter-mobilisation of various social segments based on caste, ethnicity, language, religion and gender, make the construction of any social coalition by a single party completely unfeasible. In the absence of a broad-based coalition of interests behind a single political party, even a single party rule, not to speak of dominance, becomes highly improbable. Contrarily, the longer coalitions of the sort of the National Democratic Alliance (NDA) remain in power, the more coalition government per se becomes legitimised and the more the possibility of minority governments of the Narasimha Rao type recedes into the background. Under such conditions, either of the major parties would act as a pole of attraction for smaller parties to coalesce. Which of the two major parties would be more successful in binding a coalition together would depend on its flexibility of approach, the level of its confidence in running a government in a difficult environment as perceived by its coalition partners, and its leadership quality.

Secondly, both the national parties, the BJP and the Congress, would find it extremely difficult to expand not only for the lack of appeal of their ideology even if they had one, but the more so because the divergent compulsions of politics within each state would make it very difficult for the national parties to control their state units. Local considerations will weigh heavily on them compelling the state units often to refuse to toe the national party line in toto within the framework of state politics. This will happen because the strategy appropriate for the national parties to gain or to hold on to power in Delhi comes into conflict with the strategy considered appropriate by their state units for securing power in the state capitals. This explains why Mamata Bannerjee had to split from the state Congress in West Bengal and form a parallel outfit like Trinamool Congress. The more recent experiences of both the BJP and the Congress with their state units in Uttar Pradesh, Bihar, West Bengal and Karnataka are cases in point. The near complete hijacking of the state Congress by the Trinamool in West Bengal during the Rajya Sabha elections in March 2000 in that state is, however, a limiting case.

Thirdly, the federalising process within the polity will continue to strengthen. As the theory of federalism would suggest, there is an inherent tension between a federal political system and a 'national' (i.e., centralised or all-India) party system. For several reasons, into which we need not presently go, during the first decade and a half after independence this tension did not emerge in India. Studies on Indian federalism during this time were focused on an appropriate description of the federalism established under the Constitution. But from the late 1960s, as the Congress party had to give way to various other parties and fronts for ruling a number of states, and with Indira Gandhi's decided tilt towards centralisation indicating a persistent refusal to accept ground realities, this tension came to the fore. From the late 1980s through the 1990s it has become quite explicit that the ,national' parties are under pressure from the federalisation process.

This is happening in two ways. First, most states in India now either have strong state parties or stable ruling fronts hinged on to a strong state party. This not only has given more governmental stability to states than has been available of late at the Centre, but also, as many of these state parties are essential partners of the central coalition government [UF (United Front) or NDA], they come to possess a sort of veto power on the Centre's handling of the states. Unlike in the 'Congress system', when state Congress parties utilised or depended in various degrees on the popularity of the Congress prime ministers for retaining power in the states, these state parties are autonomous of control by and free of dependence on the dominant party in the central coalition. They know that their life and death depend on their popularity within the relevant states. Contrarily, the dominant party in the central coalition finds support from these state parties indispensable for running the government and implementing its agenda. These together empower the state parties to assert their own autonomy, and along with it the autonomy of the states vis-a-vis the Centre.

The federalisation process is strengthened in a second way also. As we have just now mentioned, the divergent contexts and contents of state politics, and in many states the presence of firmly-rooted state parties, compel the state units of 'national' parties either to follow a course most appropriate for the state concerned or to follow the central unit's diktat and remain largely irrelevant in state politics. This either/ or situation is the product of an increasing individuality of the political processes in the states. Thus, there is hardly much similarity between the political processes in Assam and West Bengal, or those in Bihar and Orissa, or Tamil Nadu and Karnataka, for instance. This allows little scope for a generalised 'all-India' approach by a 'national' party while it creates excellent conditions for autonomous state parties to thrive. This would increasingly compel the 'national' parties to grant a large degree of autonomy to their state units which would, in turn, strengthen the autonomy of the states within the Indian Union.

Earlier we have referred to Arendt Lijphart and we agreed to accuse him of 'consociational evangelism' when he claimed that Indian democracy has always been consociational: 'strong' during the Nehru era, and 'weak' thereafter. We attempted to show that it had never been consociational. On the contrary, we would like to argue that, in view of the increasing indispensability of coalitional governments at the Centre produced by a weak bimodality in the party system and the probability of an increasingly large degree of autonomous party configurations in the states, a dose of consociationalism now becomes urgent for maintaining political integration and democratic development in India. Without an element of consociational agreement among parties across the political divide, thin coalitions would become hamstrung, Lok Sabha proceedings will come to a standstill, the non-elective judiciary will be compelled to show 'activism', the bureaucracy will increase its fiat, the Centre's influence over the states will fall below the threshold required for national unity, economic development will be jeopardised and the country's political integrity and security will be at stake. But then, hidden agendas, phoney leaderships, and political parties' subservience to extra-party forces will act as big hindrances to bringing about a working consociational arrangement.

In her first address to the nation, after re-election as Prime Minister, Smt. Indira Gandhi spoke of her wish to enlarge the areas of participation, consultation and discussion to seek partnership in progress, as she put it, and to keep open, and enlarge, outlets for the creative talents of our people which provide aesthetic and inspirational force to uplift and sustain the Indian revolution. Those are noble ideas, nobly expressed.

When she was first chosen Prime Minister in February 1966, then also she had given expression to similar sentiments. Did she not then give a clarion call of "Nation first and party next?" This is eloquent testimony of her lofty ideals and patriotic motivation.

But what of performance? Unfortunately, it has been a sad story of disappointment. In her one-year stewardship, the nation was submerged in a slough of despondency and despair and was verily brought to the brink of disaster. What is more, the party that she led sank to the bottom. The one-time high and mighty Congress was for the first time on the run. Nay, it had missed the bus.

Sweet are the uses of adversity, it is said. But is the Congress leadership of the day made of that rare species which can buoyantly fight back disaster? Can it make the grade? Has it got the statesmanship to snatch opportunity out of adversity and covert it into an advantage?

The post-election spectacle does not promise any such development. The petty preoccupations of the Congress leadership betray a singular disarray of spirit, thought and purpose. At this crucial hour, when its very existence is in jeopardy, the fierce controversy raging inside the organisation is about the trees, not the wood!

Though mauled and battered throughout the length and breadth of the country, though stripped of power in many states, though its vote has been reduced to a paltry 37.87 per cent, though its majority in the Lok Sabha has shrunk from 114 seats to a verily wafer thin, it has not given up its gyrations of intra-mural politics, manipulations and machinations, and the employing of political sleight of hand to establish itself in power.

When calamity overtakes a party, the path of wisdom is ruthlessly to stamp out chronic in-fighting, to give short shrift to the politics of personalities and power, to gracefully accept the inevitable, and manfully set about concerted action to retrieve the position.

Let the leadership look back and draw lessons from the past. The first five years of our independence were studded with solid achievements. It was the "golden age" of India, as it were. For the first time in our long and chequered history, emerged an India, pragmatic and purposeful, strong and united as never before, not even during the days of Ashoka, Vikramaditya, Akbar or Aurangzeb. What was the alchemy which overnight heralded this wondrous transformation?

When freedom dawned in 1947, the Father of the Nation was there to lead us on to unselfish action, to inspire us to adhere to ethical and spiritual values. He unequivocally declared that the fruits of freedom were not the monopoly of the Congress. He insisted that it should share power with those who stood aloof from the freedom movement, nay, even opposed it. After all, decreed the Mahatma, freedom was a common inheritance, won by the collective suffering and sacrifice of several generations of Indians of differing political persuasions, social philosophy and economic theories, for the common good of all. Which was why non-Congress stalwarts like Dr. Shyama Prasad Mookerjee, Dr. B.R. Ambedkar, Sir N. Gopalaswami Aiyangar, Dr. John Matthai, Sir R.K. Shanmukham Chetty, Dr. C.D. Deshmukh and others happened to be inducted into the first two Central Cabinets. History will record the achievements of that period in letters of gold.

No doubt, slogans like "Nation first and party next"' "Partnership in progress" are inspired by noble impulses. But it is no use merely giving expression to pious platitudes. People cannot be roused to constructive action by empty rhetoric. Deeds, and deeds alone, shall bear testimony to the earnestness of intent and purpose.

Let us look around. Let us take a lesson from post-election events in the Federal Republic of Germany. Since the founding of the Federal Republic in 1949, like India, in West Germany too, there was no opposition worth the name till then.

In the wake of the General Election in the autumn of 1965, Professor Ludwig Erherd formed his second Cabinet representing a "small coalition" of CDU/CSU and FDP (CDU 196, CSU 49, FDP 49 = 294 in a House of 496). The coalescing parties had some things in common. But in less than a year, there was disagreement over budgetary and taxation policies, which resulted in the break-up of the government.

In the interest of the nation, therefore, the leading parties there put ideological issues into cold storage and resolved upon a "grand coalition" of CDU/CSU/SDP CDU/CSU 245. SDP 202 = 447 in a House of 496. West Germany was none the worse for this act of wisdom and far-sighted statesmanship and willing sharing of power among the major parties with differing political ideologies, in consonance with the will of the people as expressed through the General Election.

Prolonged one-party oligarchic rule of unshared power has reduced our country to shambles. Will our union government at least now free itself from the enchantment for power-monopoly and display humility, sense and statesmanship by seeking the cooperation of democratic parties and talented individuals to lead the nation forward to progress and prosperity? In the ultimate analysis, the worth of a government is the worth of the individuals composing it.

After all, many of the stalwarts who are in opposition today have given the best part of their lives in the service of the nation through the Congress. It was only when the Congress drifted away from Gandhian moorings, when it underwent a metamorphosis and remained national only in name, that these sterling patriots, impelled by the sense of compelling patriotic duty, abandoned it. Many among them are leaders of the highest integrity and ability.

The present union government, with its slender majority, is no better than an "ambulance government". For every important vote in the Lok Sabha, the government would have to transport in ambulance, if necessary, each and every indisposed member of its party from sick-bed to the portals of Parliament House. Nothing can be more uncomfortable for a government. How long can this endure?

That the mandate of the people is clearly for a national policy, in the best and most progressive sense of the word, is an indubitable fact. That the immediacy and magnitude of the tasks on hand call for a concerted, cooperative crusade for at least ten years, is recognised by most thinking and patriotic Indians. That this can be accomplished only by providing inspirational leadership, that an "ambulance government", holding the reins of power on account of the caprice of an electoral system and not by majority suffrage, cannot provide such an inspirational leadership is a self-evident reality.

Revolutionary Change

It is one thing to have a de jure majority; it is a different thing to have a firm control over the commanding heights of power. But the crux of the matter is that no government, unless it is backed up and sustained with unwearied and unflinching constancy, by a comfortable majority agile, enlightened, well-informed and dedicated can successfully put through any effective programme of national regeneration. This is particularly so in India, with its vastness and diversity, more especially in the India of today, hamstrung by unimaginable difficulties, conflicting pulls and confusion and in the throes of cataclysmic political polarisation.

To decide major issues of national importance on the strength of a technical majority is an open invitation to violence and disorder. The anatomy of all bloody revolutions reveals that the casus belli is the imposition of de facto minority decisions on the majority.

Mahatma's Legacy

Gandhi, the master, led us to liberty. It was he who chiselled into shape the Congress as the chosen instrument to win freedom. Soon after the advent of independence, Gandhiji in the manner of Vyasa, the master, in the Dwaparayuga, in disdain and despair, cried out:

"But yesterday the Congress was unwittingly the servant of the nation, it was Khudai Khidmatgar-God's servant. Let it now proclaim to itself and the world that it is only God's servant, nothing more, nothing less. If it engages in the ungainly skirmish for power, it will find one fine morning that it is no more."

This warning was as blunt as it could be and was given at the very beginning of the era of moral erosion. Now that it has come full circle, one hopes that the Congress will go back to Gandhiji. That alone is the magic wand which would resuscitate the party from the political quagmire into which it has fallen.

This done, as Congress happens to be catapulted at the helm of affairs at the Centre, people can reasonably look forward to some change for the better, otherwise, they will have to suffer a further, though certainly briefer, spell of trials and tribulations. In such an event, the galloping discontentment and mounting despair of the people will sweep away the Congress bell, book and candle on to the dung-heaps of history. If monopolistic tendencies are given up, if a policy of give-and-take is pursued, if a climate of humility and sanity prevails, the Congress can save itself from such an ignoble fate and also spare India's teeming millions avoidable privations. As things are, it is still in its hands to make or mar itself and the nation.

A pooling and harnessing of all the best available talent and wisdom of the nation is the need of the hour. This will result in tremendous accretion of strength to the government. More, this will make the people in all walks of life, everywhere in India, feel the glow of freedom, and generate in them an urge spontaneously to participate in national reconstruction. This will release the mystic power to touch chords in men's heart that transcends politics. This will set millions of hearts all over the land to beat in unison. The gathering national crisis is of such dimension that nothing less will do.

Means and ends are inseparable. Right means alone will lead to right ends. This is an age-old, eternal, natural law.

Good means marked our freedom struggle and bore rich fruit. Their abandonment has yielded a wild crop of poisonous weeds.

The inexorable law of means and ends has come down alike on the ruling party and on those who seek to dethrone it.

For securing deliverance from foreign yoke, the best and noblest in the land built up, as a cooperative endeavour, a truly national movement, over a period of half a century.

But, within a few years of the dawn of freedom, the movement progressively lost its national character. By slick manipulation, it was reduced to a party caucus.

The name of the party was, however, preserved. This enabled it to retain a readymade, famed fortress, a very useful equipment in electoral battles. To this were added several other sophisticated weapons to win the battle of the ballot box, the exploitation of the halo that naturally shone around a national movement for liberation; the advantage of being inheritors of power from the erstwhile British government; and the utilisation of the limitless opportunities for practising political sleight of hand.

This resulted in two decades of uninterrupted power monopoly, leading to a sense of invincibility, indispensability and irreplaceability. In turn, it brought about all sorts of aberrations, which bred authoritarian and despotic tendencies on the part of the ruling party.

All the other democratic parties which came up in the post-freedom era had to start from scratch.

After three attempts at the hustings, it appeared to be an exercise in futility to penetrate the old fortress. Frustration and despair inevitably came, over the democratic opposition.

Thence they were driven into hotchpotch alliances, with all and sundry in the attempt to end the octopus grip of the monolithic party.

Compulsions of political developments and the then prevalent circumstances forced the democratic opposition somehow to make a dent in the ruling group.

In this desperate effort, they seem to have ignored the paramount need to give the people a clean, good and efficient government, upholding the sanctity of the Constitution and enforcing the Rule of Law. Thus, in the strength process of building up a democratic alternative, India's democratic structure is getting petrified.

The United Fronts that we have now in India are akin to the Popular Fronts which emerged in pre-war Europe. Their experience was none too happy.

In the post-war era, the experiment of the great Dr. Eduord Benes of Czechoslovakia in inducting a Communist in his cabinet resulted in the extinction of himself and democracy from his beloved country.

The experience of the popular Front formed by the Congress Socialist Party and the Communist Party in the 'thirties', was true to pattern. In, the 'forties', the Hyderabad State Congress joined hands with the Communists. That resulted in the State Congress being weakened and the Communist giving armed battle to the government of the Republic.

There is hardly anything to choose between the Left Communists and the Right Communists. The friends, guides and philosophers of both are outside our country. The basic aim of both is to destroy the strength of the free world and augment the strength of the Communist world.

They coalesce with others not to give but to take

They have no scruples to snipe at the unanimously chosen captain of a team from the quarter deck, as the Chief Minister of West Bengal, a Gandhian and good Samaritan, is now learning after bitter experiences.

The Left Factor

The Communists and their henchmen are adept at utilising the democratic machinery to destroy democracy itself.

Let there be no mistake about it. The object of the Communists in sponsoring or joining the United Fronts is to pursue their own goal of strangulating and ultimately destroying their partners; undermining democracy; total domination and ruthless dictatorship.

The *raison d'etre* of United Fronts, according to the Communists, is best summed up in the advice of Lenin himself, when a similar proposal was mooted in the twenties in Great Britain:

"I want to support Henderson with my vote in the same way as a rope supports one who is hanged" (Lenin in Left- Wing Communism).

And of a leading British Communist:

"I would take them by the hand as a preliminary to taking them by the throat" (T.A. Jackson in the British journal Communist).

Communists, both the brands, have a vested interest in scarcity and starvation, unrest and anarchy, wherever the democratic way of life prevails.

"The road from Moscow to London passes through Shanghai and Calcutta," declared Lenin, 50 years ago.

Let the democrats, in all parties, ever remember the lesson of Communist design and perfidy the world over. In their anxiety to retain power-monopoly or dislodge the monopolists of power, as the case may be, let the democratic forces not walk into the parlour of the sworn enemies of democracy.

Indian politics is characterised by a very high degree of diversity. This political diversity is as wide and peculiar as its social and regional diversity. India is the country where almost all categories of political ideologies—from extreme right to extreme left—co-exist. Such political diversity has its origin in the long history of colonial rule. During the period of the freedom struggle, the Indian National Congress was the first and only political party which worked as an umbrella organisation representing all varieties of political beliefs and opinions. The country got the characteristics of a bi-party system as soon as the Muslim League came into being. After independence and the introduction of the Constitution, a number of political parties representing various ideologies came to the forefront. India thus got the characteristics of a multi-party system with a variety of ideas and ideological beliefs.

In a country characterised by a wide variety of social, economic and regional diversity, politics is bound to be something more than the usual phenomenon. In such a situation politics is always a dynamic affair. It is pretty well known that the country has experienced a very high degree of growth in terms of political development in spite of its failure to gain such pace on the economic front. This is significant specially in the context of India being the largest democracy in the world.

Thus, as of now it is a very interesting exercise to account for the experience of the last half of the twentieth century and to predict the future on the basis of past experience. The purpose of the present paper is, therefore, to reveal and highlight those major changes and shifts which have happened over the past fifty years or so. Among the major developments, it is imperative to focus on the growth of regional parties, caste and class based politics, women's reservation and political corruption.

As already mentioned, the multi-party system became an inherent part of parliamentary politics ever since the introduction of the Constitution. In a country so diverse socially and regionally, a multiparty system is the best possible way through which the interests of various segments of society can be reflected. The party system of a country reflects not only what is happening in practical politics but also the basic requirements of the society combining economic, social, cultural and political necessities.

One important characteristic of fifty years of parliamentary politics is the emergence of a number of regional political parties.

Such an event may be termed as the 'regionalisation of politics' The Congress, as a national party, represents almost all social classes across regional, provincial and linguistic boundaries. Besides, the Congress leadership had a type of socially cosmopolitan character so far as the Nehru Gandhi family was concerned. The Congress was the largest national political party, but until recently, there was no competing second largest national party which had influence across regional and provincial boundaries. Thus, there was a long unfulfilled need for a national level opposition party. Such a need culminated in the emergence of a number of regional parties.

Regionalism on Rise

The emergence of regional parties and their dominance over regional and even national politics was rooted in the diversity of social interests. It is no secret that in every society some social classes take up a dominant position in politics while other classes remain recessive. These dominant classes may also constitute the majority in the concerned society. Sometimes, however, the ruling social classes do not constitute the majority, but they give the impression that they represent the majority.

This trend is very much present in India where the emergence of most political parties has occurred as a result of the specific interests of the various social classes in the different regions and provinces. This trend is present in most states and can be traditionally explained by the term 'caste and politics'. In the Hindi-speaking states of the north, all contemporary leading political parties have their bases rooted in some social class or the other. Also, most of these parties have their origin in the interests of some caste. Even when a party emerges as a result of a split in a national party, it immediately appears to get some sort of social class character. This is also true of all southern states, whether it is Tamil Nadu or Karnataka. In the northeast, too, all regional political parties are based on ethnic identity.

Caste-based politics exist in almost all states, though the intensity of the phenomenon may not be the same everywhere. In an underdeveloped and socially diverse country caste is a very important factor in social grouping. According to Surendra Mohan, a senior Janata Dal Leader, "when all social relations take place within the caste group and therefore all blood relations are confined therein, caste naturally becomes the most vital social unit".' West Bengal is the only state in which political parties claim to be free from any sort of ethnic or communal identity. But as far as the idea of social dominance is concerned, such a claim cannot stand when tested in the light of actual social circumstances and situations.

In West Bengal, politics has never taken on a violent form as it has done in some other states. But the situation in West Bengal is very much different. So any effort to draw a parallel comparison with respect to 'caste and politics' between West Bengal and any other state, is doomed to fail. Comparison may be a useful method of analysis when the background under which political events occur is almost similar. That is why when some politicians, academics and others try to prove the immunity of politics in West Bengal from casteism or communalism, it does not present a true picture.

The background of West Bengal politics lies in the mass exodus of refugees from East Pakistan in 1971 during the period of the freedom struggle in Bangladesh. However, the process of migration actually started as early as 1947 just after partition. During the period 1970 to 1980, there was a massive change in the social balance of the state. Traditional power relations were destroyed and a new variety of social power relations developed. Here, an important point which should be noted is that the people who have migrated do not constitute any integrated social class or community. These people are characterised by a lot of heterogeneity, and therefore, do not have any direct inclination towards any particular political party.

In view of this historical and social background and also the present spectrum of politics in the state, it will not be wrong to conclude that no analysis of West Bengal politics can be undertaken without taking the concept of social class into account. Politics in any country or part of it always tries to follow the interests of the dominant class, whether it is a pure social class or a combination of various elements which may seem to be a reflection of the social class. This is the reality which has also determined the politics of West Bengal since the 1970s.

The current trend in Indian politics is towards both regionalisation and nationalisation. The trend towards nationalisation became visible as soon as the Bharatiya Janata Party (BJP) came to the forefront of national politics very recently. However, this trend is very limited in scope and its viability is yet to be tested. But as far as the trend towards regionalisation is concerned it is very clear and conspicuous all over the country. The politics of West Bengal is also no exception to such a trend. The Communist Party of India (Marxist) (CPI-M) is supposed to be a national party. But its major policy decisions have more or less been dominated by regional interests. A few instances, in this regard, may be given to justify the above proposition.

West Bengal has a very long common border with Bangladesh as some other northeastern states also have. Illegal migration is rampant all over the territories along the Bangladesh border. While the northeastern states are very concerned over the incidence of migration, West Bengal has remained largely silent. One explanation for this is that the incidence of illegal migration appears to be in no way against the interests of the dominant social class of the state.

The recent issue of reservation for women in the Union and State Legislatures has also drawn a lot of attention. The issue is so important that it has almost become a part of our societal values. The women wings of various political parties are almost unanimous on the issue. However, the difficulty lies with the modalities as to how such a measure can be arranged. The Constitution had already adopted a reservation policy for a segment of the society. It becomes difficult to accommodate a new set of reservations for women within the present Constitutional framework. According to Sri Rajindar Sachar, formerly the Chief Justice of the Delhi High Court, "The framers of the Constitution did not intend further fragmentation of the legislatures".

Corruption under Democracy

Another trend which has very recently become an important part of our political culture is corruption. The extent of corruption in both politics and administration is so large and its incidence so frequent that India is among the most corrupt countries of the world. Once, the extent of corruption in politics was confined to parliamentary politics with regard to defections, splits and the formation of new parties. Now, it is rampant in almost every area of political decision making. Sometimes corruption is the result of the nexus between politicians and administrators. This nexus can be found in all the cases that have surfaced in the past few years. The most well known was the Jain hawala case in which the list of accused contained the names of leaders from the entire political spectrum barring the Left parties and a few regional outfits. Even the present Union Home Minister, L.K. Advani, while inaugurating a conference of police officers, highlighted the gravity of the situation.

There is another aspect of political corruption which has its exposure in the events of political murder, kidnapping and sabotage. Political analysts have conceptualised these happenings under the heading 'criminalisation of politics'. The increasing involvement of criminals in politics and the nexus between the criminals and some corrupt politicians have destroyed the morale of democratic politics in the country.' In some states such elements are so strong in both politics and the society at large, that it has, in fact, resulted in a 'terrorisation of politics'.

However, amidst such a corrupt social and political environment, some institutions have taken an active role in trying to curb the ongoing corrupt practices prevalent in both politics and administration. Some of these institutions are recognised and have been established by the Constitution of India. While some have only legal or administrative status but no Constitutional recognition. The Supreme Court has always tried to act according to the values of the society. This is conspicuous in the various rulings and orders of the Court. On 17 November 1998, the Court ordered the framing of charges against the accused in the Rs. 133

crore urea scam. In some cases, the Court has even issued orders to the government, fixing a deadline forsetting by a Special Court for executing the orders issued by it. The role played by the Supreme Court, the Election Commission, the Central Bureau of Investigation, has always been active and positive with regard to coping with all the ills that the country has witnessed in the past fifty years of parliamentary politics, India is the world's largest democracy and it has maintained its democratic' institutions despite diverse threats and pressures. In the coming century as literacy spreads, it is to be hoped that India's democratic roots will strengthen further.

6

Society, the New Facets

India at the end of the twentieth century presents a very different picture from India at the end of the nineteenth century, politically, socially as well as from the economic point of view. But is it all that radically different? There are pockets in rural India where time appears to have stood still, while middle class ways of thinking in urban areas, despite the modern gadgetries which abound in middle class homes, often reflect nineteenth century social attitudes and values. Politically, however, India has been an independent and democratic country for the past 56 years with Indians exercising their electoral rights every five years or less, which is a revolutionary change from British dominance and autocratic rule at the beginning of the twentieth century. Economically, too, India has moved from British controls and a policy of imperial preference to one which adopted ideas from both the socialist and capitalist worlds, and more recently, parallel with the end of the Cold War and the collapse of the Soviet Union, to a more liberalised economy embracing a new economic policy involving deregulation of industry, easing of controls on trade and foreign exchange and removal of restrictions on investment. There have been major social changes as well, prodded especially by Constitutional provisions and the rule of law to promote the interests of the previously underprivileged castes, tribes and other backward classes. The position of women has undergone a dramatic transformation through the course of the past fifty years, although the impetus for bringing women out of their homes came from the national movement itself.

In the New Millennium

Today's India, at least its large cities and small towns, is a very different place from what it was a hundred years back. If we compare the past century and its developments with the century before that and go back in history using 100-year units and compare these to the immediate preceding centuries, the multifaceted changes in twentieth century India probably outdo all other 100 year periods. This, however, is true of most other countries as well, whether it is the United States of America or Russia (which became the Soviet Union and then reverted to Russia again in this period) or Argentina, Iran or Thailand or many of the regions which are now states, but which did not have any independent status prior to the twentieth century. Today's world, in fact, is a very different and a much smaller place than what it was a hundred years back. It is a world where one sees the formation of larger and larger trading blocs at the regional level, mega-mergers at the corporate level and an explosive growth of global production, financial and capital flows and technological virtuosity. Small states have been subjected to a kind of "one cap fits all" policy by major international trade and financial institutions and this has resulted in system failure in certain economies. In this world of hegemonic power and economic globalisation, where does India stand?

So far as politics is concerned, there has been a globalisation of democracy with more and more countries accepting political and economic freedom and basic civil liberties as the norm. Samuel Huntington, in his book The Third Wave: Democratisation in the Late Twentieth Century, calls this trend "the third wave" (which had its inception in 1974), the second wave having occurred after the Second World War. But then, there had been the second reverse wave with more than twenty developing countries falling to military dictators or civilian autocrats. Currently, too, there have been blatant reversals as in Pakistan and Sudan and break-down of government as in the Republic of Congo, Sierra Leone, the

Gambia, Somalia and many other African countries. In India, democracy appears to have become consolidated, but is this democracy really stable? Foreign analysts writing on India at the end of the last millennium, perceive a pervasive lack of accountability and weak rule of law that permits corruption, violence, personalisation of power and abuse of human rights, in addition to economic problems like continuing poverty and stagnation. There have been dire predictions about the sustainability of Indian democracy in general and the unity of the state as it is currently, in particular.

It is with many such questions and thoughts in mind that the Department of International Relations, Jadavpur University, Kolkata, organised a seminar in March 1999, on the theme, "India at the End of the Twentieth Century: Retrospect and Prospects". It has taken some time to collect and update the papers which were presented, as well as invite a few selected specialists, in addition to contribute their viewpoints. But we have finally succeeded in bringing it all together in the form of this book. The seminar was divided into sections dealing with Indian politics, Indian foreign policy, economic policies and trends, and social and cultural patterns and trends. The book, too, largely follows these divisions.

The Indian democracy was not born through any large-scale war of independence against colonial rule, which may have increased the depth of national feeling among all sections of the people (though the histories of some countries which underwent such wars do not always corroborate this view), but through the blood of sectarian violence. Though the length and nature of the Indian national movement ensured a fairly stable national political party and politicians experienced in self-rule, and there could be a smoother transition of power than in many similarly colonised countries with little or no national movement, where the succeeding elite had hardly any understanding of governance and hence were unable to prevent coups or civil wars, etc., India's long struggle for freedom also left some adverse legacies. Communal, caste, regional and other differences had enough time to grow, consolidate and proliferate and later haunt independent India.

It is, indeed an amazing feat that the new State was able to survive all the differences that make up the country and still remain a democracy. It was largely under the British that what is today called India came under one rule (though the princely states had a different status) after about five thousand years of civilisation. But it is also true that the British, in their interest, fomented the innate divisions which existed in the country. So, the country that we won from colonialism was fractured socially, politically and economically. Yet, it was enthused with a new sense of freedom, a keen sense of national identity (at least among the educated), perhaps for the first time in its long history. Its differences, both actual and potential, were addressed in its new Constitution, which not only declared India to be a sovereign, socialist, democratic republic guaranteeing the fundamental rights of its citizens, but emphasised secularism, judicial independence, federalism and through the Directive Principles of State policy, ensured that all citizens would have the right to an adequate means of livelihood with equal pay for equal work and that the operation of the economic system would not result in the "concentration of wealth and means of production", among other things. Not content with a mere non-discrimination clause on the grounds of religion, race, caste, sex or place of birth (Article 15), Article 17 abolished "untouchability", making its practice punishable under law. On the whole, the Constitution found solutions to some of the most baffling problems of divisiveness in the country, be it language, caste, region or religion.

Yet, at the end of the old century and the beginning of the new one, it is these very problems which plague the country. There is growing ethnic and sectarian violence with movements verging on secessionism. The Constitution has been amended over 75 times and recently, the National Commission to Review the Working of the Constitution recommended major changes including 10 new fundamental rights, for instance, the strengthening of the Right to Equality which should also say that people should not be discriminated against because of "ethnic or social origin, colour, age, language, political or other opinion, property and birth", in addition to the grounds already mentioned.

The problem is that despite its many achievements, India has not been able to find credible institutional formulas to manage regional and ethnic divisions peacefully. And this is partly because of the vested interests of political parties. India, as envisaged by the framers of the Constitution, was to be a secular, casteless, equal society. Yet, by creating a system of reservations (however noble the motives), and making special provisions for certain minorities as well as states, it created vested interests which could be exploited by politicians. The introduction of adult franchise at one stroke among a predominantly illiterate people had its own dangers and an absence of a viable opposition in the beginning to the Indian National Congress, followed by the emergence of splinter groups, regional parties and coalitions of these at the Centre and even at the state level, also had its dangers. In many newly independent Third World countries, the issue of power and empowerment has led to the politicisation of ethnicity and religion. India, too, has not escaped this and, in fact, there has been more of such politicisation in this country—politicisation of language, politicisation of regional issues, politicisation of caste, etc., leading to the formation of small local/regional parties with limited local/regional outlooks which sometimes coalesce to form the national government. Moreover, organisational weakness is a pathology which is shared by virtually all political parties including the Bharatiya Janata Party (BJP), although it still shows more cohesion than some of the others. In the intrigue and infighting which plague these parties, ideological consistency is lost and individual ambitions and self interest which fuel these parties can, in the long run, corrode democracy. From a more or less one party ascendancy in the early years after independence, we appear to have moved towards a two coalition system, but the composition of both these alliances at the Centre is not constant because of coalition-hopping by parties and party-hopping by individual leaders. Under the circumstances, political instability, which can fuel further fissiparous and centrifugal tendencies, appears to be becoming endemic.

Political Corruption

Also endemic is the level of corruption in politics as well as in the officialdom. It was the Indian bureaucracy which had earlier provided a stable backbone to the fledgling democracy. But today, even the ranks of the bureaucracy, of which there is a great abundance (getting a government job having become an end in itself), have been penetrated by corrupt practices. Further, despite this massive number of officials from the smallest 'block' level to the top-most ministry level, decision-making, remains highly centralised, rendering the services of many of these officials to be essentially clerkish, dressed in a better garb. In other words, there is a marked administrative ineffectiveness and incapacity in addition to corruption, which does not auger well for the country. Reform in the institutional structure of the bureaucracy is something that the government should seriously consider in the near future to ensure impartial and effective governance.

Fissiparous tendencies have found renewed vigour in politicised religion and the promotion of the idea of the state as a Hindu nation. While it is true that in millennia past it was the religious identity which acted as a token of identification for the diverse region that was India, there has never been any such thing as Hindu fundamentalism and therefore, a Hindu fundamentalist state. Hinduism has no church, no compulsory beliefs or rites and no single religious book enjoining the worship of any particular godhead. One can be an atheist or an agnostic and still be a Hindu and its various rites and rituals are marked by regional variations. Hinduism is eclectic and embraces a wide range of doctrines (if one can call them that) from monism to monotheism and pantheism to polytheism. But independent India was born through the surgical division of the country based on the 'Two Nation' theory which had religio-cultural overtones. While Pakistan embraced Islam, its raison d'etre, India proclaimed itself to be secular. However, Pakistan's very existence as an Islamic state and its tortured relations with India has added fodder to the fires of Hindu communalism which had its origins during the national movement as a kind of reverse mirror image of Muslim communalism. With the Hindu masses providing an ample electoral base, Hinduism has been manipulated for political purposes in a very perverse way, where not only Muslims but Christians and other religious minorities are being demonised. It should be remembered that the concept of Ram Rajya' does not imply a Hindu State, but is based on the idea of tolerance and peaceful co-existence, of tigers and deer drinking from the same waters.

Today, cultural pluralism, an ideal sought by many of our earlier nationalist leaders, is threatened by the issue of multiple identities. In practice, one can be an Indian, a Bengali as well as a Hindu or Muslim, at the same time with great case. The problem arises when the regional, ethnic or religious identity clashes with the national identity or becomes more important than the others for whatever social, political, cultural or economic reasons. In many Western countries, nation Consciousness appeared either before the formation of the state or it was in almost simultaneous process. In the Third World, most states were formed before national integration could take place. It is tragic that even after more than 55 years of existence as an independent and United country, the Indian government still has to promote programmes to raise the national consciousness with billboards and bus advertisements proclaiming 'Hamara Bharat Mahan' (Our India is Great).

There are several essays in this book on some of the issues mentioned above. Rakhahari Chatterjee, Sekhar Ghosh and Kanak Sarkar discuss recent trends in Indian politics with particular reference to political parties. While Chatterjee analyses the structural transformation from more or less single party dominance to a bimodal pattern of voting and underscores the importance of a stable party system in democratic politics, Ghosh brings in an analogy of 'salariat' causes and the 'salariat' class which he gauges to be at the root of ethnic mobilisation and party formation. Sarkar, on the other hand, discusses various issues like corruption, ethnicisation of politics and the growth of regional parties with special reference to West Bengal politics. Shibashis Chatterjee's essay is a survey of some of the reigning ideas of the new millennium, both at the domestic and international levels. In the area of domestic politics, he examines the ideas of secularism and economic reforms in the hands of an "outfit" ideologically committed to a "brand" of economic nationalism. Joyobroto Sanyal, Siddharta Dasgupta and Kakoli Sengupta have a joint essay on a state where the legacies of Partition are most evident and where minority sub-nationalism in collaboration with external terrorist forces poses a constant danger to the state. They discuss the local, regional and international dimensions of the Kashmir conflict with a view to explaining the inherent problems of bringing about a sustainable peace in the state and they come to the conclusion that the absence of the necessary preconditions for sustainable peace is largely the result of New Delhi's "inappropriate" Kashmir policy.

Amalendu De, Samir Das, Indrani Chatterjee and Jahar Sen analyse the socio-cultural problems of India at this juncture of its history. While De traces the Islamic theological scenario from pre-colonial times to explain the current situation, Das concentrates on the problems ethnic communities face and are likely to face in the future. His focus is mainly on India's northeastern states, although his conclusions are more or less general to all minority-ethnic communities. Chatterjee, in her essay on 'The Politics of the Unhomely', discusses the Indian women's movement in the light of how "one's specific interests or group identity (as women) might relate to one's political activity as citizen". Sen traces the Indian government's cultural policy since independence, because "culture" is an important part of civilisation and the government has played a significant role in "rebuilding India's cultural structure", assuring support for arts "previously patronised by the princes".

State of Economy

In the field of economic development, the major challenge at the beginning was the transformation from a colonial economy to an independent one, and here, there was a discourse between foreign models, including the Marxist, and alternative strategies generally called 'Gandhian'. The early leaders adopted a kind of mixed model, essentially foreign, setting up both a private and a public sector, but the motive for adopting from foreign models was genuinely nationalistic. The Nehruvian vision initially encompassed a heavy industrialisation strategy to modernise the economy, and an economic development planning programme was initiated, which aimed at public sector-led fast-paced, capital intensive industrialisation, leaving the private sector to play a complementary role, largely restricted by bureaucratically imposed import control designed to ensure priority to the public sector. However, this meant drawing on vast foreign-aid resources since there were little internal resources as well as problems with internal resource mobilisation, specially because of the emphasis on the public sector. A decline in foreign aid, neglect of the agricultural sector and a regional imbalance in economic development later led to a change of emphasis and a New Agricultural Strategy based on high yielding seed varieties was adopted in the late 1960s, together with agrarian or land reform to alleviate rural poverty. However, agriculture being a state subject, the Central leadership could only set guidelines and persuade the state leadership to implement land redistribution. Since landed interests were represented disproportionately in the government in virtually every state, land ceiling legislation became somewhat farcical. It was only in West Bengal and Kerala that moderately effective land reform was undertaken.

While the growth performance of the Indian economy was generally poor when compared specially with some of the dynamic economies in the developing world, yet, when it is measured in terms of its early development goals which emphasised self-reliance and import substitution rather than export promotion, its relatively low growth status can be understood. India's nationalistic policies based on its urge to manoeuvre independently in all areas, were also reflected in its economy. What is significant is that India managed to avoid the heavy debt burdens which countries like Mexico and Brazil incurred on their path to development. Though its outstanding external debt as a percentage of the Gross National Product (GNP) increased from 13.7 per cent to 18.7 per cent between 1970 and 1988, this was the lowest among all developing countries except China.

However, major obstacles persisted in its progress towards self-reliance, including poverty, unemployment, literacy and issues concerning public health and this affected its economic status in the world. Market changes in the world economy since the mid-1980s also made it imperative to shift emphasis in economic planning in order to prevent marginalisation. It was in Rajiv Gandhi's time that there was a marked movement towards technological modernisation in the Indian economy and the capital goods sector and this trend has continued through the United Front period to the BJP government under the policy rubric of 'liberalisation'. While the first-generation reforms steered clear of critical areas like agriculture, labour market reforms and institutional reforms like privatisation, the BJP-led National Democratic Alliance (NDA) has shown a determination to deepen reforms by its decisions to open up the insurance sector to private enterprise, increase plan allocation for agriculture, bring down the government's equity in non-strategic public sector enterprises and delicence coal, lignite and petroleum. The second generation of reforms was initiated in April 1998 by the government's decision to move more swiftly on phasing out quantitative restrictions on imports, including consumer goods, and hastening the process of bringing India's economy in line with the global economy. The reformist intentions of the BJP-led government were also clear in its quick approval of many foreign investment proposals, the introduction of a bill in Parliament in June 1998 to convert state electricity boards into independent state electricity commissions to rescue them from bankruptcy and the repeal of the Urban Land (Ceiling and Regulation) Act to promote investment in the area of housing. The BJP, in its earlier 1998 election manifesto, had emphasised 'internal liberalisation' over 'external liberalisation" that is swadeshi, which meant that local firms, throttled by state controls for decades, should first learn to compete among themselves before confronting total foreign competition. Thus, the BJP wanted Foreign Direct Investment (FDI) in only priority areas but not in areas where the domestic industry was functioning well, which amounted to a kind of 'computer chips yes; potato chips no policy'. However, after its election victories, it moved towards a further opening up of the economy. According to the Home Minister, L.K. Advani, "No economic philosophy should become a dogma" and "[swadeshi] does not mean xenophobia or belief that everything foreign is bad". This stance was further elaborated by the Finance Minister, Yashwant Sinha, who noted in an interview that "I understand swadeshi basically as a concept which will make India great. And India can be great only when we become an economic superpower... We can be great by being able to compete".

But have these reforms paid off in terms of economic growth and alleviation of poverty? While there has been a 'robust' growth in the services and industrial sectors and net foreign institutional investment has crossed the $10 billion mark, there has been a further deepening of regional inequalities as states which have been more progressive and pro-reform have attracted more investment. The states which have been failing behind, mainly situated in the North (excepting Delhi, Haryana and Punjab) and in the East, are also among the largest and poorest and this may have troubling political consequences in years to come. Also, the reforms so far have largely bypassed the rural sector which contains two-thirds of India's vast population. Interestingly, while the reforms-led growth has not translated into a decline in the general poverty level, neither does there appear to be (statistically) a particular increase in inequality, although urban-rural disparity has grown.

There are three essays in this book on economic policies and trends. Abhirup Sarkar discusses the issue of state intervention in economic activities in India in the background of recent suggestions for structural reforms. He expresses the view that there are some areas in the economy where free market has to be introduced with more caution, specially the agricultural goods sector, and concludes that the "government should not go for an all-out policy of free trade". Basabi Bhattacharya discusses human development issues in the Indian context using indexes like the human poverty index, and notes that India is grouped among the low human development countries by world standards. She, however, examines the regional disparities within India and points out that it is the low human development indexes (HDI) of some states which pull down the general HDI and thus, this index gives only an approximate picture of development in India. She emphasises that attention should be paid to formulating human development strategies and providing basic facilities. Biju Paul Abraham's essay is an analysis of India's search for self-reliance in the fields of science and technology and he points out that despite its successes, India still remains dependent on technology imports. He mentions that with globalisation, it is imperative that India should keep up with the rapid advances in technology worldwide. He suggests that Indian research and development (R & D) institutions should move closer to Indian industry and that there should be a "consortium" approach to technology development, since technologies are becoming more and more complex.

One area which is not covered here but should be examined is that today, globalisation is under attack in the West as well. Moreover, the creation of large market blocs put individual countries at a disadvantage. Despite world trade agreements, economic giants tend to 'bully' other countries through national legislations. Future trends in the world economy will have a deep impact on India now that it has decided to open up its economy. It is imperative that this area should be analysed by scholars and policy-makers with a view to formulating policies which would put emphasis not only on India but on the South Asian region in the context of global trends.

Regional Factors

The South Asian region has always been significant to Western powers for its geo-strategic position! Earlier, apart from its importance as a producer of primary goods much needed to fuel European industrialisation, it was also a gateway to other primary producing areas in Southeast Asia and the Far East. Its importance in the present day, however, is more related to its positioning vis-a-vis oil rich West Asia, on the one hand, and China, on the other. In this region, India emerged as the major power after the 1971 war and now has ambition of playing a much greater role in world politics.

This vision of India's (and also Asia's role was projected by Nehru even before Independence. In the post-Independence period, it culminated in the Non-Aligned Movement (NAM), which, in a word, can sum up India's foreign policy in the Cold War period. It served India well till the late 1980s, helping it to maintain its independent status during the alliance politics of this time. However, there were many other foreign policy issues of perhaps greater long-term significance, which continue to focus attention. The nuclear issue which had remained an option till 1998, is central to India's current policy-makers in the country's emergence as a great power. This brings in a host of other matters like acceding to international treaties and regimes, for instance the Comprehensive Test Ban Treaty (CTBT), the Missile Technology Control Regime (MTCR) and the Fissile Material Cut-off Treaty (FMCT), quite apart from the Nuclear Non-Proliferation Treaty (NPT) which India has long refused to sign in its present form. Such matters could complicate its relations with the current hyper-power, as well as affect its standing with international organisations. The decision to go nuclear will have a bearing on its future relations with Pakistan, which has also gone nuclear, thus introducing the perennial threat of nuclear blackmail in bilateral relations with that country. The viability of the South Asian Association for Regional Cooperation (SAARC) under the circumstances of strained relations between two of its largest members, both of which are now declared nuclear powers, is also a vital issue. Moreover, the rise of ethno-nationalism in neighbouring states is also a challenge to India and the SAARC. India has new nuclear security requirements and this will definitely be a major factor in shaping its foreign policy, which has moved a long way from the idealism of the Nehruvian era to modern day realism and pragmatism. However, there are severe limitations in India's security apparatus and these were exposed during the recent war in Kargil and the hijack of an Indian Airlines aircraft to Kandahar. While the army appeared to be ill-equipped and even vacillating in Kargil, the crisis-management and decision-making institutions were found to be faulty during the Kandahar crisis, as the division of responsibility seemed to become a victim of the red-tapeism of the National Security Council, the Prime Minister's Office (PMO) and the Crisis Management Group headed by the Cabinet Secretary. Additionally, a bit of the corruption which has tainted civilian life appears to have permeated the defense bureaucracy also, as promotions and transfers have been abused by the civilian government as an instrument of favouritism and political control.

The new century holds multiple challenges and if India is to really become a great power, it must improve and restructure its key institutions, make the running of these institutions more transparent, divide responsibility effectively and tone up the various new bodies which are being created to meet any crisis situation with promptness and effect.

Prof Jayantanuja Bandopadhyaya, in his keynote address, emphasised the foreign policy aspects; of Indian politics. His suggestion that India and Pakistan, now that they are both nuclear powers, should "collaborate to resist the hegemon", is worthy of note. Prasanta Kumar Ghosh discusses "the dilemma of non-alignment" at the end of the twentieth century and questions whether the internal divisions within NAM will lead to its marginalisation in the future. Anindyo Jyoti Majumdar analyses the role of the people, leaders and "messiahs" on the road to India's nuclear explosions. Purushottam Bhattacharya's essay is on the concept of regional cooperation in relation to the South Asian region and he examines India's role in the context of a "road block" or a "facilitator". Surarijan Das' article emphasises the importance of dialogue and economic cooperation between India and Pakistan in the quest for South Asian peace and stability.

India won freedom in a unique way, unparalleled in the annals of the world, through a civilized war without violence. Inspired and led by a leader, who practised what he preached. A luminous symbol of sincerity and selflessness that was Mohandas Karamchand Gandhi. He led the people and did not follow them cowardly for fear of losing illusory, ephemeral popularity.

During India's freedom struggle, Gandhi, the master, transformed hundreds of thousands into "Indians first, Indians last and Indians always". The simple secret of his phenomenal success was that he lived the ideal. That was the elixir which rejuvenated India and hastened the advent of freedom from the then mightiest empire of the world.

Today, where is India? Where are Indians? Of Gandhiji's dreams? Of the dreams of the numerous great architects and builders of Free India from Kashmir to Kanyakumari? Ram Mohun Roy, Rabindranath Tagore, Rajaji and Rajendra Prasad; Aurobindo, Annie Besant, Khan Abdul Ghaffar Khan; Ansari and Ajmal Khan; Jawaharlal Nehru and Jayaprakash Narayan; Bal Gangadhar Tilak, Bipinchandra Pal, Bhimrao Ambedkar and Bhagat Singh; Feroz Shah Mehta and Prakasam Garu; Gopalkrishna Gokhale, Gangadhar Rao Deshpande and Gobind Ballabh Pant; Veer Savarkar, Sardar Patel, Subhas Chandra Bose and Sarojini Naidu; Dadabhai Naoroji and Deshbandhu Das; Madan Mohan Malaviya, Motilal Nehru and Maulana Azad; Zakir Husain and a host of others, too numerous to be listed here.

India is on the verge of ceasing to be the age-old, legendary Bharata Varsha, encompassing Setu (Rameshwaram) in the southern-most and Himalayas in the northern most tips of India-Aasetu Himachala Paryantam.

In today's India regional patriotism and linguistic fanaticism have practically submerged national patriotism and even human values. Our politics have become "pollutics". Corruption—political, intellectual and monetary—has become a way of life with most people. Indians have become rare biological specimens.

Alas! Our simple, innocent people are sought to be de-Indianised by arousing parochial feelings and by fanning religious, linguistic and regional hatreds. All this for petty transient, political mileage.

"Freedom is in peril. Defend it with all your might!" was the clarion call given by Nehru years ago.

Our mind goes back to the National Integration Conference convened in September 1961, in the wake of the savage Assam-

Bengal language riots. The Conference met in all seriousness; eminent statesmen and thinkers participated in the deliberations and the Conference set up the National Integration Council to review all important matters pertaining to national integration and to make recommendations thereon.

The country hailed the move as the first major step to foster national unity since independence. Much optimism was aroused; great expectations were raised.

The first and only meeting of the Council was held in June 1962. Thereafter, as Shri Jayaprakash Narayan stated in his letter declining to attend the Srinagar meeting, "a wholly whimsical decision was taken on the morrow of the Chinese invasion to put the original Council in cold storage on the plea that the invasion had already brought about National Integration."

What is the balance-sheet today? Has there been progress or retrogression? Has the objective of unity and solidarity been brought any nearer?

Alas! We have been steadily drifting towards disintegration. The governments, at the centre and in states, have looked askance at:

1) the plethora of regional and factional senas, all of which, under some specious plea, are allowed to carry on their divisive activities, without let or hindrance;
2) the spate of violent agitations on inter-state disputes relating to border, river water-sharing, location of dams, steel plants, etc.
3) the series of subtle discriminatory orders, rules and procedures via domicile regulations and the like, in the matter of employment, education, grants, loans, etc.
4) the continued selection of candidates for general elections, mid-term elections in some states, several by-elections to parliament and legislatures, municipal and panchayat elections, primarily on considerations of caste, religion and language.

Perhaps many leaders and ministers at the centre and in states feel that, if they soft-pedal in matters communal and more particularly regional and linguistic, their vote catching potential will be ruined; that in the prevailing atmosphere, it is not real politik to denounce or deal firmly with or completely shed "regional and linguistic patriotism".

In the harum-scarum brawl of power-politics, let it not be forgotten that what is at stake is the survival of India as a nation.

Violence, whether linguistic, communal, student or labour, is violence and should be ruthlessly dealt with as such.

The growing tendency to be complacent or explain away violence indulged in on certain issues and by certain bodies should cease.

Those in power, and those who want to wrest it, should look upon any breach of the peace, first and foremost as a law and order problem, irrespective of the purpose for which it is perpetrated or the persons who are behind it, however powerful or politically useful.

If our governments adopt a dual standard in matters of law and order, a stage will soon come when their police forces will develop a crass partisan attitude, ignoring even unambiguous ministerial orders to the contrary, in dealing with violent demonstrations and acts of vandalism by "we, the sons of the soil" against "they, the outsiders".

Such a development would be wholly repugnant to the equality before law guaranteed to all the citizens by our Constitution; nay, it would be the negation of a civilized government.

There are no states, not even districts, in India without "outsiders", i.e., without a dozen or more linguistic groups.

If such groups are treated as "minorities" and discrimination goes on without effective check in several states, and a weak centre does not take action against the offending states, it would be an invitation to anarchy and enslavement, for the virus may spread to the defence services—the sheet anchor of our stability and security.

The soul of India is still sound. Barring a microscopic, aggressive and fanatic minority, all our people, in all the states of the Indian Union, are patriotic, peace-loving and decent citizens. Given inspired, dedicated and selfless leadership, they will rise as one man and cheerfully give their 'blood, sweat, toil and tears' to defend the unity and integrity of their motherland. They did so during the Pakistan and Chinese aggressions and the Bangladesh war. They will certainly do so again.

The stakes now are much higher. The very existence of Mother India and the values she has stood for through the ages are in jeopardy.

The union government and leadership of all political parties, social, literary, educational, sports and other organisations should tarry no more.

Indeed, India today is in a more perilous position than what Britain was in the darkest days of World War II, after the fall of France and when America had not joined the Allies. Britain's political leadership surmounted the calamity by forging a grand National Alliance, putting party politics in cold storage till the threat to its very existence was decisively removed.

Positive action alone will spur the nation to constructive endeavour for unity and solidarity and galvanise the forces of national integration all over the country.

Let words pass. Let, deeds speak.

Jaya hey Bharata Bhagya Vidhata.

Issues at Stake

The present state of the nation is anything but healthy. Instability of administration and insecurity to person and property are on the ascent. The demoniac forces are on the prowl with impunity.

"When the Ganga is in flood, the water is turbid. The filth comes to the surface. When the flood subsides, you see the cool, clear, pure, blue water of the Ganga which soothes die eye," said Gandhiji years ago.

With the martyrdom of Mahatma Gandhi in 1948, and with the demise of Sardar Patel two years later, there has been a flood in the affairs of India. And when, in 1964, Pandit Jawaharalal Nehru passed away, there was a veritable deluge.

Gloomy as the present state of the Indian Republic undoubtedly is we should not feel downcast and despondent.

A peep into the long and chequered history of India testifies to the fact that each major forward-thrust in our national progress and religious, ethical and moral efflorescence took place during the periods of severe stress and strain.

To give but three significant examples from our history, it was:

a) at a time when our religion was on the verge of extinction that the great protagonist of the Vedic faith, Sri Kumarila Bhatta, the immortal Adi Sankaracharya, Saint Jnanasambandar and others came on the scene, rescued it and gave it fresh vigour and strength;

b) during the several centuries of Muslim hegemony, the life-sustaining bhakti movement gushed forth from all parts of the country, restoring the self-confidence of our crushed and terrorised people;

c) during the two centuries of British rule, when India was in bondage, impoverished and forlorn, the unprecedented, all-round, triumphant modern Indian Renaissance surged Democratic Republic. What India is passing through at present is yet another Great Churning-Amrutha Manthan.

This is the first phase of the fierce contest between the forces pledged to build up the nation step by step and ensure social, economic and political justice according to our national genius, and those who wish to do so at one stroke, not realising that shortcuts are invariably slippery and disastrous.

After the first phase will commence the crucial and decisive encounter for supremacy between the large majority of our people who have faith in God, and stand for truth, religion and culture, democracy and freedom, and the militant group who ridicule ethical and spiritual values, and who stand for coterie rule, dictatorship and totalitarianism.

True, the present churning has so far brought forth only poison. And alas! There is no Mahadev in the shape of it Mahatma Gandhi to contain this poison in his throat.

Yet, as has been the case all through our history, the nectar, amrit', will soon issue forth.

Rejuvenated by such nectar, all the patriotic and democratic forces will rise to the top of their consciousness; and saturated by selflessness, they will assign supremacy to national interest, above party and self-interests.

This will be a harbinger of harmony among themselves. And then all the creative and constructive forces, mental and moral, religious and cultural, social and economic, literary and educational, scientific and technological will come together and embark upon and successfully implement a massive cooperative programme of national reconstruction and bring about the long overdue amelioration of our teeming, downtrodden millions, with malice to none and goodwill towards all.

Thus alone can be held at bay the enemies of democracy and freedom, the forces of exploitation and disruption.

India has a genius for synthesis and harmony and a peculiar capacity to evolve unique solutions to baffling problems. This is the keynote of our culture and the lesson which history teaches us.

The vicissitudes and trials of 50 centuries of our history bear witness that we have taken the challenges of Time in our stride as the tests of our Truth of Vision.

It is a common experience that after thunder and lightning come the fertilising showers. However, oppressive, dark and frightening the clouds on the horizon, that are really precursors of the refreshing rains.

The hour before dawn is the darkest. The whirligig of Time has come full circle. A new and glorious dawn is round the corner.

India's Vision is sempiternal. It is rooted in her soul.

India of the Ages is not dead. She has still a destiny and mission to fulfil. She has yet something more to do for herself and the human race.

Soon will emerge an India, strong, united, democratic and truly secular, anchored to ethical and spiritual values.

Its vital manifestations are already evident at various levels in all segments of national life.

As Veda Vyasa, our Eternal Master, proclaimed centuries ago, *Yatho dharmasthatho jayah: Dharma,* Truth and Righteousness will ultimately triumph.

7

Peaceful Existence

On August 15, we celebrate the birthday of Independent India. But the spontaneous and natural gaiety, joy and enthusiasm which marked the early years of the advent of freedom have been registering a progressive decline year after year.

How did this come about? By pursuing a confused, halting, wooden approach to national problems.

How shall we get out of the rut? By evolving a harmonious, comprehensive, all-embracing, cooperative policy of harnessing the best from all to build up the nation.

"Hatred does not cease by hatred, it ceases by love is the central theme of our Vedas and the Upanishads, the Epics and the Puranas, and the teaching of the numerous saints and sages, Hindu, Muslim, Christian and Parsi and Sikhs, who have sanctified this ancient land through the ages.

Synthesis is another name for love; and conflict, whether of class or caste, or communal is but a sort of hatred. The latter is born of ignorance and intolerance, the offspring of dogmatism, inferiority complex, and assertive arrogance. The former is the offspring of self-confidence, humility, an open mind, understanding of and consideration for others, which are the quintessence of the Indian heritage.

Those who have taken upon themselves the onerous duty of administering the country and shaping its destiny, would do well to follow the guidelines glistening through our great cultural heritage. 'They should remember that:

a) Indian heritage is as old as the civilizations of Harappa and Mohenjodaro; as rich and exalted as the Himalayas, and as veriegated as the vernaculars of the sartorial styles of India.

   It has the integral unity and cohesiveness of the Indus Valley Civilization, the persistence and stability of the King of Mountains, the basic kinship and coherence of speech and dress patterns of the subcontinent;

b) Indian heritage is neither wholly Aryan nor wholly Dravidian; neither wholly Brahminical nor wholly non-Brahminical; neither wholly religious nor wholly secular; neither wholly Hindu nor wholly Muslim;

c) Indian culture is a sober synthesis, harmonious blend of so many elements, and its attitude is one of selective, assimilative acceptance of the best and noblest from everywhere, and not of indiscriminate, outright rejection of anything from anywhere;

d) Indian culture is neither so exclusively idealistic as to be utopian, nor so sordidly "matter of fact" and sensate as to make it unethical and unspiritual.

Unfortunately, the deliberate distortions and twists given from time to time by selfish, ignorant leaders to one facet or other of our ageless, complex heritage, torn out of its proper perspective and context, have led some leaders and their unthinking followers to look upon it in the manner of "the seven blind men reporting on the elephant". The reality is that Indian inheritance is neither akin to a rope, a pillar nor a fan! It is a dynamic, growing, whole living ensemble, all along absorbing the vitalising new elements and forces that sprout from time to time in any and every part of this wide world in the course of humanity's continuing pilgrimage to the cherished millennium and at the same time shedding the worn out, obsolete and outmoded ones.

Crusade against Evils

Our leaders have rightly declared a war on the "twin enemies" of communalism and poverty. Generations of Indians sacrificed their all to win the struggle for freedom precisely for this purpose.

But without following the basic tenets of our heritage, viz., fostering synthesis and harmony, creating a climate for pooling talents, resources and cooperative working, and profiting by the remarkable examples replete in our long and chequered history, this war on communalism and poverty just cannot be won.

Babar, the Mughal conqueror, who had come in personal contact with Guru Nanak, left to his son and successor Humayun, the following Will and Testament, discovered in Bhopal, reflecting the enlightened and comprehensive outlook of the Age of Ramananda, Kabir and Nanak:

"O, my son! People of diverse religions inhabit India, and it is a matter of thanksgiving to God that the King of kings has entrusted the government of this country to you.

It, therefore, behoves you that:

1. You should not allow religious prejudices to influence your mind, but administer impartial justice, having due regard to the religious susceptibilities and religious customs of all sections of the people.
2. In particular, refrain from the slaughter of cows, which will help you to obtain a hold on the hearts of the people of India; thus you will bind the people of the land to yourself by ties of gratitude.
3. You should never destroy places of worship of any community, but always be justice-loving, so that relations between the king and his subject may remain cordial and thereby secure peace and contentment in the land.
4. The propagation will be better carried on with the sword of love and obligation than with the sword of oppression.

5. Always ignore the mutual dissensions of Shias and Sunnis, otherwise they will lead to the weakening of Islam.
6. Treat the different peculiarities of your subjects as the different seasons of the year so that the body politic may remain free from disease.

Akbar, whom Jawaharlal Nehru hailed as the "Father of Indian Nationalism", was a faithful Muslim. He, however, made searching enquiries about the truth of each religion and he spared no pains to understand their fundamentals. His policy declaration as recorded by the Jesuit writer, Bartoli, will rank as one of the noblest of all times:

"For an empire ruled by one head, it was a bad thing (declared Akbar) to have the members divided among themselves, and at variance one with another..."

We ought, therefore, to bring them all into one, but in such a fashion that they should be one and all with the great advantage of not losing what is good in any one religion, while gaining whatever is better in another. In that way, honour would be rendered to God, peace would be given to the people, and security to the empire.

Shivaji whom Nehru described as representing India's religious-nationalist revival, was a staunch Hindu. He gave relentless battle to Aurangazeb but was not opposed to Islam as a religion. The attitude of this peerless and brave patriot, devotee of Amba Bhavani, disciple of Samartha Ramdas, is well expressed in his famous epistle to Aurangazeb protesting against the latter's barbarous bigotry and the folly of his fanaticism. The Muslim chronicler, Khafi Khan, has recorded:

"He (Shivaji) made it a rule that, wherever his followers went foraging, they should do no harm to the mosques, the Book of God (Quran), or the women of any one....

"The infamy of persecution (declared Shivaji) will be recorded in the Books of History that the Emperor of Hindustan collects the jiziya from paupers, mendicants, ruined wretches, and the famine-stricken, and (thereby) dashes down to the ground the name and honour of the Timurids! May it please Your Majesty! If you do believe in the true Divine Book and the Word of God, you will find therein that Allah is styled Rabbi-ul-alamin (Lord of all men) and not merely Rabbi-ul Mussalmin (Lord of Mussalmans only).

"Verily, Islam and Hinduism appear as contrasted terms; but they are diverse pigments used by the Divine Painter to fill in his picture of the whole human race. If it be a mosque, the call is chanted in remembrance of Him. If it be a temple, the bell is rung remembering Him alone to show bigotry towards any man's creed and practices is tantamount to altering the words of the Holy Book. To draw new lines on a picture is to find fault with the painter .....

"If you imagine that piety consists in oppressing the people and terrorising the Hindus, you ought first to levy the *jiziya* from Rana Raj Singh who is the head of the Hindus. Then it will not be difficult to collect it also from me, as I am your humble servant. But to oppress ants and flies is far from displaying valour and spirit. I wonder at the strange fidelity of your officers who neglect to tell you of the true state of things, but cover a blazing fire with straw. May the sun of your royalty continue to shine above the horizon of greatness!"

Like the legendary Vikramaditya, the noble Akbar and the valorous Shivaji, our present-day rulers of the centre and the states should so conduct themselves and formulate such policies, let us repeat, as would attract the best talent in the nation from all walks of life. For this, our leaders should;

a) develop a syncretic genius to harmonise the diverse elements constituting the nation;

b) acquire the foresight and statesmanship to bring about constructive and workable adjustments between all the classes, castes and communities;

c) cultivate the capacity and wisdom to stimulate the idealistic aspirations and patriotic impulses embedded in all sections of the people without distinction.

They must discourage go-slow tactics and strikes, curb corruption and profiteering. They must ensure more and more production in our farms, factories and offices.

There is no magic wand to usher in harmony excepting through synthesis and co-operation. There is no shortcut to equality excepting through increased prosperity.

Prosperity will not descend from heaven. We cannot get it from any country as a loan or dole. Nor can it be grabbed. The Indian nation as a whole must cheerfully sweat and toil for it.

To quench the communal fire, the talisman is to alchemise old hate into the gold of love and make it current.

To kill poverty, the panacea is to inspire the people by words backed by deeds, to search for synthesis, to live in harmony and to learn to work, work and work, with a sense of devotion and dedication.

All the political parties should look upon India as One and Indivisible. They should propagate that Mother India is the mother of us all; that the good of India is the good of all its regions; that the glory of India is the glory of all its constituent states. Which state will live in freedom, peace, prosperity and dignity if the Union of India disintegrates?

Whence did the USA starting from scratch and without foreign aid generate and build up her unprecedented economic prosperity, unsurpassed scientific strides and unparalleled military strength within a short span of 200 years, outstripping all the old and advanced European countries? The secret is the composition of its population, the happy mingling of people of varied racial and linguistic stocks-from Europe, Asia and Africa with their God-given special aptitudes and talents, harnessed to their own and at the same time to the common good.

Leadership is at once a cross and a prize; and it needs the highest qualities of impeccable character, unalloyed patriotism, and above all, supreme moral courage to steadfastly stand for and, if need be, forsake everything in the cause of the whole of India rather than mere parts of it.

The mantle of such constructive and dynamic leadership can be donned only by men and women of wisdom, imagination, far-sightedness fortitude, courage, selfless and total dedication.

The people of all the states, particularly the leaders, should look upon themselves as Indians first, Indians last and Indians always.

What ails the progressive nations of the world, Capitalist and Communist?

Political floor-crossings? No.

Economic stagnation? No.

Slow progress in science and technology? No.

Inadequacy of educational facilities and medical care? No.

Negation of the necessities of life? No.

Widening gap between the haves and have-nots? No.

What, then, is the basic cause for the rising tide of chaos, criminality and anarchy in affluent societies ?

What is the *casus belli* of the creeping cankerous and contaminous sickness physical, mental, moral and social plaguing the "advanced" nations, whom India and other "backward" countries are sheepishly striving to ape, enticed by and enamoured of their vaunted prosperity?

Are not the root causes of the malaise:

a) rearing up of generations of young men and women solely soaked in material values?

b) dangling before the people the ideal of the undefinable and limitless higher standard of living, which in fine, is interpreted as indefinite multiplicity of wants and non-stop fostering of insatiable craving creature for comforts, a philosophy of acquisition of wealth, conspicuous consumption and self-aggrandisement as the goal of human existence?

c) building up of affluent society, bereft of the moderating influences of the home and traditions and customs?

d) contemporary acceptance of the theory that ends justify the means?

Have not, in the process, all moral values been progressively relativised and atomised?

Has this not, inevitably, led to the erosion, if not the end, of the all-pervading authority of ethical and spiritual values in the governance of the affairs of men and nations?

Mammon worship and relentless, exclusive pursuit of material success in life will submerge the noble instincts in man and transform him into a brute.

As an individual, so a nation: when ethical and spiritual values are devalued and sensuous values are glorified, the very foundation of the nation, its inner peace, ballast and stability get into dangerous and might even end up in its historical and cultural death.

We, in India, who, with borrowed crutches, are feverishly engaged in the race to "catch up" with America and Europe, must draw the right lessons from the deepening crisis of Western civilization and diligently diagnose its whys and whats.

Let there be no doubt about it. The stakes are very high. Neglect of man-making, in the ceaseless preoccupation with technological progress and the intense hunt for money and more money, for pleasures and power, will spell the death of civilized existence.

Mahatma Gandhiji, who led us to freedom, cautioned years ago :

If we provide food for the body which is perishable, then, surely it is our primary duty to provide food for problems and solution, which is imperishable.

What we witness the world over today is the result of starving the soul, the moral atrophy against which Gandhiji had repeatedly warned.

From time immemorial, India has been the homeland of ethical and spiritual values. Every one of us, and the nation as a whole, should hearken to the gospel of Gandhiji, the master. We should all so conduct ourselves in our individual and collective lives as to restore the majesty of the Moral law dharma and carry forward India's ageless message non-violence, truth, faith, self-discipline and dedication ahimsa, satya, shraddha, samyama and samarpana.

This is the only straight and safe pathway to steady and sure progress, well-being and happiness, for individuals and for the nation.

Adi Sri Sankaracharya in his Gita Bhashya points out that the Eternal Dharma which the Lord propounds at the beginning of each Cycle of Creation appears, at certain periods of Time, to be under a cloud, lustreless, dim and overawed by Adharma.

This is because the powers of True Perception and Right Discrimination—Viveka of the people in general and the elitist class, or what Arnold Toynbee calls the "creative or dominant minority" in particular, gets progressively contaminated and corroded by *kama* (lust), *krodha* (anger) and *lobha* (greed).

The present state of our nation makes it crystal-clear that the hydra-headed monster of utter unrighteousness and decadence, unbridled selfishness and greed Adharma has menacingly reared its ugly head. We also witness the revolting and sickening spectacle of those who are devoted to the Dharmic way of life, being branded, isolated, reviled at, stifled and thwarted at every step by the demonaical forces.

The sufferings of the hapless, dumb millions have touched the breaking point. The Godly and the good are desperate and desolate.

The present disconcerting state of affairs signifies that the time for deliverance is near at hand. Deliverance always comes when it seems impossible.

According to the Divine Standing Proclamation in the Gita, it is at such critical junctures that the Lord arises again to overthrow the powers of darkness, to re-lit the lamp of discrimination, righteousness and wisdom, to re-enthrone the majesty of the Dharmic way of life.

It is not that the venomous three musketeers—*kama, krodha* and *lobha*—have all of a sudden surfaced and gone on a rampaging spree.

Kama has marshalled for its justification an impressive array of sophisticated arguments, nay built up a whole philosophy that not only ridicules restraint but rationalises promiscuity, advocates unlimited indulgence and glorifies conspicuous voluptuousness.

Krodha has manifested in every sphere of life. In his selfish pursuit, man is confronted with fellowman and what, with the law of diminishing returns operating in the realm of Nature, the springs of compassion and understanding are drying up. There are more hands to grab whatever is available, and naturally anger has a free field.

Lobha has assumed monstrous proportions and the whole earth, without thought of the future, is being plundered and bled white in order to amass all at once, all that Mother Earth can give.

In his arrogance and avarice, man has forgotten the age old warning: "Nature will bless if she is treated as mother, but Nature will kick if she is treated as a mistress."

As Ruskin has said, mostly matters of any consequence, good or bad, are three-sided. *Kama, krodha* and *lobha* are the three gates to hell according to the Gita. They take us to *naraka*.

Tradition of Love

A legend concerning Deepavali tells us that the great demonaical king, Narakasura, kept imprisoned 16,100 princesses, and Sri Krishna, the Lord, in answer to their prayers proceeded to Pragjyotishpura with Satyabhama who killed Narakasura and liberated them. It is also said that these princesses sought the hand of Sri Krishna in marriage.

That is the mythology, the old-world made of abstract thinking translated into delectable stories.

What does this legend signify? What lesson does it hold out for us?

Within limits, like all qualities, *kama, krodha* and *lobha* have certain utility. But owing to lack of the sobering, civilizing influence of culture and fear of God, which is the beginning of wisdom, the set limits are transgressed with impunity and then sought to be rationalised by all sorts of fabricated justifications.

Narakasura is the personification of the three great demonaical forces-uncontrolled and deified *kama, krodha* and *lobha*—that lead man unto hell. Whosoever develops a philosophy of life on the wrong foundations, extolling those forces that do not make for the real happiness of mankind and builds on bases which are insecure and destructive is a *Narakasura*. But, for the time being, they seem alluring, magnificent, formidable and secure. Society, by and by, gets itself dissipated, allows decadence to set in, and is cast into a state of all-round gloom. That is the darkness which needs light.

The Lord or His Power, *Shakti*, in various forms appears on the scene on the darkest night, the *Amavasya*, the thirtieth day of the month in the lunar calendar. He lights a lamp and the terrifying darkness vanishes.

But the Lord appears not anywhere and everywhere. Time and again, God arises again in mortal form and glory only where his *bhaktas* prayerfully seek Him.

What does this signify ? The lesson is that the only way in which we can rid the world of its darkness is by lighting a lamp of virtue in our own individual lives, unmindful of what others do or do not do. This lamp will shine and throw out beams and inspire others to light their own lamps too.

Our great books are full of such stories and mythical accounts.

In the *Vedas* it might be the *ushas*, the dawn that rises, that will rise for ever, dispelling the darkness. But the lesson is the same, the lesson of the imperative need for virtuous living and the abandonment of the three roads to destruction, that the Gita has warned us of-

Trividham narakasyedam dvaram nashanamat-manah

Kamah krodastatha lobhas tasmadetattrayam tyajet.

Three-sided indeed is the way to hell and to the destruction of one's self. It is through *kama* or lust, *krodha* or anger and *lobha* or greed. Hence, man must control these three.

Let us start dispelling the fiendish darkness that has descended on Mother India.

India is facing hard times.

Centrifugal forces, group sentiments and linguistic fanaticism threaten to submerge our nationalism, impair our age-old cultural unity and desecrate our very way of life.

Our economy is in great strain.

Strikes and lockouts, intimidation and violence are menacingly on the prowl.

Population explosion continues unabated.

Love of ease, less work and more pay have become the credo of most working people in all fields of national endeavour.

Love of wealth with utter disregard for quality and honesty has become the creed of most businessmen and industrialists.

Love of power and position has become the craze of most public men. Power and position meant for public service are being misused for self-aggrandisement. Consequently, the institutional structure of our society is disintegrating. The family bond is becoming weak among large sections of our men and women. Marriage is losing its sanctity. The moral authority exercised from time immemorial by parents, elders, teachers, public men and religious and social institutions is crumbling.

How shall we stem the rot, reverse the ugly trend? How shall we preserve and nurture our national character, our precious inheritance.

This can be done only by a determined and sincere effort at reconstruction of our individual and national life: through an appropriate system of education.

Hand and training in the practice of ethical and spiritual values through the institution of inviolable marriages and reactivated family bonds, the two nurseries of self-discipline; through reordering of the economic systems and readjusting capital-managerial-labour relations on the basis of *asteya*, i.e., self-imposed trusteeship of all wealth-material, managerial, intellectual and physical.

Confucius, one of the sentinels of Eastern wisdom, has said:

"The ancients, who wished to preserve the clear and good character of the world, first set about to regulate their national life. In order to regulate their national life, they cultivated their family life. In order to cultivate their family life, they rectified their personal life. In order to rectify their personal life, they elevated their heart. In order to elevate their heart, they made their will sincere. In order to make their will sincere, they enlightened their mind."

To enlighten our mind, we must once again expose ourselves to the energising light of our ageless culture. We must hearken to the call of the Vedas, listen to the message of the upanishads, learn the morals of our epics and puranas, and make our sages and saints, ancient and modern, continuously speak to and guide us from the cradle to the grave.

In sum, we must ceaselessly foster moral and spiritual values, the foundation of enduring achievement.

As Arnold Bennet has said: The manner in which one single ray of light... will clarify and energise the whole mental life of him who receives it, is among the most wonderful and heavenly of intellectual phenomena."

Let us light the three Lamps of Discrimination, Righteousness and Wisdom.

Godhead is Light. Nescience is darkness. Where there is Godhead, there is no nescience, no darkness.

Tradition of Morality

When we look around, what do we find? The immortal Veda Vyasa cried out: "With upraised hands do I cry *Artha* and *Kama* flow from Dharma and so why not follow Dharma?" But it has fallen on deaf ears.

Likewise, judging from the stinking depravity all around, and the endemic devaluation of values, years of ceaseless effort by the Bhavan's journal to disseminate the message of *Dharma Satyam* (Truth) *Shivam* (Love) *Sundaram* (Beauty); *Shraddha* (Faith); *Samyama* (self-discipline) and *Samarpana* (dedication) does not appear to have made any noticeable impact. This is a sad situation.

The ethos of Indian life—religious, social, political, educational, cultural and commercial-is today characterised by an all-pervading moral bankruptcy, double-think and double-talk.

Successful public work has come to mean fox-like evasions, putting the expedient before the equitable, bandwagon jumping, twisted tongues and cold hearts.

Slandering others has come to be reckoned as a form of public service and a substitute for one's own good behaviour!

There is a rapidly enlarging vacuum in the sphere of ethical and spiritual values, disarray of spirit, mind and purpose.

Pride and self-will, fear and greed, jealousy and ambition—these common saboteurs of team work are on the prowl.

Alas! Our temple of freedom and culture has been turned into a prison-house for puerile and wily impulses of unabashed self-seekers.

How shall we recapture the spirit of selfless service and silent sacrifice which characterised all our individual and collective activities in the pre-independence era?

As our seers and sages were never tired of repeating, in all our plans and programmes, we must give paramount importance to the aspect of reconstruction of man by simultaneously fostering ethical and spiritual values, which alone go to build up character.

Character is a by-product of a great, ceaseless and supreme unilateral offering called duty. It is the humus on which everything worthwhile and stable grows.

Character rests on the foundation of Truth.

Truth is identity between thought, word and deed.

These days, as Churchil remarked during World War II, referring to Russian deceptions, "truth has become so precious that it has always to be attended by a bodyguard of lies!"

"The essence of lying", said Ruskin, "is deception, not in words. A lie may be told by silence, by equivocation, by a glance of the eye attaching a peculiar significance to a sentence. These kinds of lies are worse and based by many degrees than a lie plainly told."

Deceit and cunning as a policy, mendacity as a tenet, perfidy as a permanent institution can never succeed because of their unethical foundation; for, in the history of nations, as in the lives of individuals and institutions, there is a Moral Law which cannot be broken with impunity.

We must turn to the prophets, seers, saints and mystics who, by their vision and experience, have given a firm basis to the all-pervasive Moral Order by living up to it. We must learn from their experience.

The universal experience of men and women of all ages, who adhered to the Moral Law is that happy relations are the end-product only of sincerity; abiding achievement is the end-product only of honesty; that profound sincerity and honesty are the twin basis of all talents as of character.

The Moral Law is unchanging; unchangeable. It operates universally regardless of status, class, place, time and unity.

The need of the hour is continuous recommunion between us and the great saints and sages of all ages who symbolise the Moral Law; to make them, so to say, regularly "speak" in a form and language easily understandable to the captains and crew of all segments of national life.

The prayer, which Gurudev Rabinranath Tagore poured forth in the darkest days of our slavery, is very relevant today to achieve our aim:

Where the mind is without fear and the head is held high;

Where knowledge is free;

Where the world is not being broken up by narrow domestic walls;

Where the words come out from the depth of truth;

Where tireless striving stretches its arms towards perfection;

Where the clear stream of reason has not lost itself in the dreary desert of dead habit;

Where the mind is led forward by Thee into everwidening thought and actions;

Into that haven of freedom, my Father, let my country awake.

We in India again stretched our hands of friendship to Pakistan through our Prime Minister Shri Atal Behari Vajpayee undertaking a Pilgrimage of Peace and Harmony-Shanti Maitri Yatra in the form of the Bus journey from New Delhi to Lahore on Sunday, February 21, 1999. This was much in the manner of the immortal Pilgrim of Peace, Harmony and justice, Poorna Purushottama Sri Krishna. He was not unaware of the mind-set of the Kauravas. Yet He undertook the journey to the conceited, unscrupulous Kauravas seeking elementary justice for the Pandavas. This is the legacy bequeathed by Sri Krishna who blessed mankind with the immortal Song Celestial, Bhagavad Gita, the ever-relevant comprehensive Philosophy of Life, the core of which is to stand up and squarely fight for justice and fairplay, after exhausting all peaceful avenues.

The Gita was the inspiration of Mahatma Gandhi, Father of the Indian Nation, who led the Indian Subcontinent to Freedom, a part of which is today's residual Pakistan less than half of what it originally was in 1947 (Post-1971 Pakistan: Population 69 million, Bangladesh 71 million).

Kashmir Issue

The leopard never changes its spots. Born in hatred, peddling fanaticism, pulverised by pusillanimity, peeved by frustration, prodded by petulance and propelled by evil intentions and its arrogant and short-sighted military cohorts, unmindful of their earlier suicidal Himalayan blunders of 1962, 1965 and 1971 which ended up in their disgraceful rout and left permanently truncated since 1971, seem to be heading for another collossal misadventure which may ultimately be its Hoo-doo and nemesis.

Who could imagine that behind the outwardly smiling welcome of the Pakistan's Prime Minister, a devilish conspiracy was being hatched by the diabolic military to perfect deception to a fine art and to clandestinely send hordes of Pakistani army personnel and trained mercenaries to Kargil and other sectors of Kashmir crossing the Line of Control which has been settled, acknowledged, sanctified and accepted as inviolable by India and Pakistan decades ago and also upheld by the international community.

Born in beastly banality, bred in jealousy, the belching brigands of Pakistan have spurned the hand of friendship proffered by India. Once again, India has been forced to stand up and throw out the intruders, who are undoubtedly aided and abetted by Pakistan.

The world at large has been provided incontrovertible evidence by the release of transcripts of taped conversation between the Pak Army Chief, General Pervez Musharraf and the Chief of the General Staff, Lt. General Mohammed Aziz, that the real power in that country is still wielded by the military brass that democracy in Pakistan is a sham. The tapes also blast lies mouthed by various Pak authorities that the intrusion in Kargil was an autonomous Mujahideen affair.

Let Pakistan be under no illusion. India will not rest content till the last of the intruders are thrown out of their hide-outs in the crevices and crannies of the Kargil, Drass and other mountain ranges. If our territorial integrity is violated, the whole of India from Thagla Ridge to Thiruvananthapuram, from Burdwan to Mumbai will again rise as one man and ruthlessly repel the intruder, lock, stock and barrel.

At this crucial juncture, whatever our, vocations, religious denominations and political persuasions, there are no Congressites, Janata Party, Janata Dal, Communists (Right or left) or, Regional Parties—all will join hands as a united nation to fight aggression.

This betrayal, this aggression on trust, has spontaneously resurrected and reinforced the Patriotic Fervour Collective Will and Determination of all our citizens.

There are now no Hindus, Muslims, Parsis, Christians, Buddhists, Jains and Sikhs. Only Indians, Indians, Indians.

There are now no Andhras and Assamese, no Bengalis and Biharis, no Kashmiris and Keralites, no Maharashtrians and Mysoreans, no Madhya Pradeshis and Uttar Pradeshis.

There are now no teachers and students, no capitalists and workers, no rich and poor.

If any of India's political parties fails to resist the temptation of fishing in troubled waters and put personal and party interests above national interest in this grave hour of national crisis, the people of India will contemptuously and for ever disown them and consign them into the dustbins of history.

Therefore, political differences, economic disparities, regionalism, communalism and sectarianism and short-sighted transient party interest will be buried in our, common crusade for safeguarding the nation's territorial integrity and preserving and protecting peace, harmony and justice.

In the words of Dharmaputra, the Eldest of the Pandavas of Mahabharata fame, whom all Indians through the ages have hailed as Ajatashatru; "We may be five (Pandavas) against hundred (Kauravas), but against a common enemy, we are hundred and five.... Beware of the anger of a sober and patient leadership and peace and harmony-loving people. It will be disaster to you. Forget not that the Law of Karma is inexorable and irreversible. "

Should the foolhardy political adventurists and the mad Pakistani military marauders think of escalating the situation in the Kargil region and thrust a war-like situation upon peace-loving and freedom-cherishing India. Pakistan will have once again to face the might and fury of 980 million Indians united and firm as a rock.

Our inherent bond is stronger than that of blood. Fortified as we are by our ageless cultural heritage of undying vitality and blessed with a truly Democratic Secular Constitution and the Rule of Law, we, all the citizens of India, owe common allegiance and reverence to our, Motherland—*Matrubhoomi*, on whose breast we are born and where we all will one day die.

Come what may! We will not flinch from our inalienable duty. We will not forsake dharma. As the Gitacharya Sri Krishna has decreed *Samsaya-Atma Vinashyati*. We will not be *samsaya-atmas*—doubting Thomases. We will not shirk a fight for dharma, if it becomes inescapable.

Yato dhartnastato Jayah: 'Where there is dharma, there is sure victory'.

Pakistan continues to nurse the illusion that they are the only champions of Islam and sole protectors of Muslims. They forget that the Democratic Secular Republic of India has more Muslims than Pakistan. They are all full-fledged citizens. India has the third biggest Muslim population in the world, the first being Indonesia and the next Bangladesh. India legitimately prides itself over the fact that our Muslim brethren, like all Indian nationals, have guaranteed enforceable Constitutional rights far more than their counterparts in Pakistan where there is perpetual confrontation between Shias and Sunnies, between Sindh, Punjab and NWFP, to which the history of Pakistan bears irrefutable testimony.

As in Pakistan, there are no second class citizens in the Indian Republic. It is heartening that Muslims, young and old, intellectuals and professionals and venerable Imams—Spiritual Leaders, all over India have volunteered to go to Kargil to fight shoulder-to-shoulder with our brave Jawans in defence of motherland.

India believes, now as ever, in *Sarva Dharma Samabhava*—equality of all religions. India's secularism is not a propaganda stuff. It is the nation pith and essence. The highest offices are open to all. Those who have eyes to see can also note that the many veterans who fought and won all the previous wars against Pakistan belong to different faiths, including Muslims.

We know that as Napoleon Bonarparte averred : "There is no place in the heads of fanatics where reason can enter."

Yet, let us sound an earnest note of warning to the petty and power-mad politicians and the Military die-hards of Pakistan: Make no mistake : For the sake of Peace, for the true well-being of our Muslim brethren in Pakistan, and in the true spirit of Islam, desist from the ill-advised misadventure embarked upon the Kargil and other sectors, call back the intruders and restore status-quo-ante scruplously respecting the Line-of-Control in Kashmir. This is a fervent call to Reason, to follow the path of Sanity, Discrimination and Wisdom.

Let not hate belching Pakistani leadership, military and political, and like-minded despots forget the inexorable Law of Karma. True dictators and their cohorts will for a time succeed in entrenching themselves in power by hook or by crook—by rabble-rousing, by peddling poisonous canards, by whipping up religious frenzy, by rousing aggressive nationalism, by terror and persecution, by molestation and murder. But they cannot for long escape Divine Retribution: their own compatriots and people will disown them, force them to commit suicide or, put them to death and ridicule and revile them even after they are no more. Such ignominious end of the for-a-time-all-powerful Hitler of Germany, Mussolini of Italy, Stalin of Russia and General Tojo of pre-World War II Japan is recent history. Alas! The power hungry maniacs in all countries never heed the warnings of history, and learn the lessons of history.

Tension in Subcontinent

We both—India and Pakistan—have a Greater War to win the War on Poverty and Pestilence. This non-destructive war will be a non-stop war. This Great War can be won only if selfish politicians of both Pakistan and India resist the temptation of mutual recrimination and mudslinging, power-hunt and pleasure-lust.

The task ahead is stupendous. Let us jointly win this Great War. With a common plan and strategy. With all the resources Pakistan and India can garner.

Salutations and adorations to our valiant jawans and officers of the Indian Armed Forces. We pledge our full moral and material support and pray for their safety, the welfare of their families, and the success of their mission.

Let us repeat: we solemnly pledge to uphold the integrity of our, Motherland, come what may. We will sacrifice everything to defeat the evil designs of the aggressors. We will Do or Die. Who lives if India dies?

Communal Harmony

When theocratic Pakistan was wrung out of an unwilling and heart-broken Gandhiji in 1947, the Mahatma uttered these prophetic words.

"Hindu-Muslim unity has been my passion from early youth .... Partition means a patent untruth. My whole soul rebels against the idea .... God fulfils Himself in strange ways. He may, in a manner least known to us, fulfil Himself and open the way to an honourable understanding ...."

Prof. Aurobindo Ghose, fiery patriot, and visionary, who later blossomed into Mahayogi Sri Aurobindo, declared on the midnight of August 14, 1947-the eve of India's independence and birth of Pakistan:

"But the old communal division into Hindus and Muslims seems now to have hardened into a permanent political division of the country. It is to be hoped that this settled fact will not be accepted as settled forever or as anything more than a temporary expedient. For if it lasts, India may be seriously weakened, even crippled : civil strife may remain always possible, possible even a new invasion and foreign conquest. India's internal development and prosperity may be impeded, her position among the nations weakened, her destiny impaired or even frustrated. This must not be; the partition must go.

"Let us hope that, that may come about naturall by an increasing recognition of the necessity not only of peace and concord but of common action, by the practice of common action and the creation of means for that purpose. In this way, unity may finally come about under whatever form—the exact form may have a pragmatic bit not a fundamental importance but by whatever means, in whatever way, the division must go; unity must and will be achieved; for, it is necessary for the greatness of India's future.

"India of the ages is not dead, will never, die...... She has much more to do for herself and the human race."

Mahayogis are endowed with the divine gift of envisioning the future. Their words are potent, prophetic.

The last century of the concluding millennium has seen the disintegration of Soviet Union and Yugoslavia into several nation states. Emerging unity-oriented Europe which embraces States which were constantly at war with one another for several centuries, has now worked out pragmatic working relationship that has resulted into the European Union and a unified European Community.

Mahayogi Sri Aurobindo prophesied this wholesome welcome transformation in Europe when he was a student in England in the early years of the 20th Century.

Legendary statesman Prime Minister Sir Winston Churchill advocated this process in 1946, at the end of World War II, half a century later.

Saints and Sages are endowed with the Divine gift of peering into the future. That was why in ancient India, these Moral Monarchs (Raja Rishis) were accorded by all sections of the people precedence over Political Monarchs—Maharajas, Presidents and Prime Ministers.

There will be strength, growth and prosperity only in unity. Constructive and co-operative working together of India, Pakistan and also Bangladesh, would ensure the rapid and all-round development of the underprivileged millions of the whole subcontinent.

'Pak means pure. Let Pakistan not become 'Na Pak'–impure, unethical. Let Pakistan not become a Rogue State as it appears to be fast degenerating.

Inscrutable are the ways of the Almighty.

We invoke Divine blessings for India that is Bharat, which is *bhagya vidhata*. Also for the people of Pakistan.

8

Academic and Cultural Development

Mulk Raj Anand has defined culture as "the integral process of creative life for the self-realisation of the individual within a social group, community or milieu. It is not a decoration of human life to appease the vanity of a person or society, but the need of the soul for sustenance as is the daily bread for the body. It is an unconscious process when it is habitual culture, but a conscious effort at renewal when it is a living culture".

The conjunction of "daily bread for the body" and "the need of the soul for sustenance" affirms that culture is a total concept. The *Sanskrit* word for culture is *Sanskriti,* which is derived from *Samskara.* It means some refinement and modification of original nature. *Prakrti* is nature and *Saṁskrti* is culture. Among the languages in India, *Prakrit* is the crude form of language, while its polished form is called *Sanskrit.* Culture involves betterment of the conditions prevalent in nature. Culture is refinement in human life, thought and activity. The process and the sum-total of such refinement are also called culture. "If the forest symbolises nature", R.R. Diwakar illustrates, "a garden connotes culture. If a mountain stream is the work of nature, a dam and a canal may be said to be the work of civilisation".' What we call culture is full of amorphous, elusive and all-important elements.

Cultural exchange in modern times is a well-known jargon in international relations. Many countries maintain their cultural foreign service which deals with cultural diplomacy. People debate the reciprocity of cultural exports and imports. Daniel G. Boorstin argues, "In my opinion these are exercises in futility, efforts to compare the incomparable, to measure incommensurable". Boorstin explains:

> The boundaries and divisions of nations and states and cities are needed for social services, for water and sewage, for protection of property and the administration of justice. But the cultural world—the world of books and ideas—is indivisible. The barriers needed to direct traffic, to prevent crime, to control drugs or to promote domestic economy—these too have no place in the librarian's world.... The world's cultures and the culture of books may be defined by languages, by traditions, by historical movements. But they are not confined by national boundaries. Ideas need no passports from their place of origin, nor the visas for the countries they enter. All boundaries in the world of culture and ideas are artificial and all are doomed to be dissolved.

Various Institutions

Since India's independence in 1947, the formulators of New Delhi's cultural policy have endeavoured to disseminate India's great and little traditions. Their activities have remained confined to distribution, regulation and allocation of resources, opportunities and honour. They have tried to preserve what is old and dying and promote what is new and valued as essential paths to national unity. The Government of India defined its cultural policy as rebuilding of India's cultural structure. It assured continuation of Support for arts previously patronised by the princes.

The Sangeet Natak Akademi was established in 1953 to promote dance, drama, music and film. The principal tasks of this organisation were to encourage research, establish theatre centres and training institutions, publish books and journals and sanction grants to other cultural institutions. In 1954, the Sahitya Akademi and Lalit Kala Akademi were established. The members of the first board of the Sangeet Natak Akademi included H.H. Maharaja Shri Jaya Chamaruja Wadiyar Bahadur, the governor of Mysore,

T.L. Venkatarama Aiyar, the chairman of the Law Commission, S.N. Majumdar, industrial consultant, N.R. Ray, M.P. Dharma Vira, A.K. Ghosh, J.C. Mathur and A.V. Venkateswaran, the four secretaries to the Government of India. The chairman of these Akademis is appointed by the President of India and the financial adviser by the Government. The General Council forms the Executive Board. Some members of the General Council are nominated by the Government. There are ex-officio members who join the General Council as representatives of ministries or other akademis. The co-option of additional members attaches due importance to the knowledge of music, dance or drama or other achievements in these fields. The Kathak Kendra in Delhi and the Jawaharlal Nehru Manipur Dance Akademi have been sponsored by the Sangeet Natak Akademi. The funds of the akademis are provided by the Ministry of Education (now Ministry of Human Resource Development).

The Indian Council of Cultural Relations (ICCR) was inaugurated in 1950. The main purpose was to establish, revive and strengthen cultural relations between India and other countries. It has its regional offices in Mumbai, Kolkata, Chennai and other cities. Its activities include dissemination of Indian studies abroad, translation of Indian works into various languages, publication of books and journals, services for foreign students in India, organisation of talks and lecture demonstrations, holding exhibitions of arts from foreign countries, performance by foreign artists, sending Indian artists abroad for performances, and extending invitations to distinguished foreign guests. The ICCR is funded by the Ministry of External Affairs. The administration includes a president appointed by the General Assembly of the ICCR, a financial adviser from the External Affairs Ministry, an executive secretary appointed by the Government of India and nine members elected from and by the General Assembly of the Council. The General Assembly includes a number of people eminent in various fields of Indian culture as well as representatives from the three national akademis, and scientific, educational and cultural organisations and universities in India.

The three national akademis and the ICCR, though supported by annual government grants, are described as autonomous.

In 1964, a committee under the chairmanship of Homi G. Bhablia, a leading scientist of the country, was formed to review the activities of the national akademis and the ICCR. Eminent persons like Kamaladevi Chattopadhyay (chairman, All India Handicrafts Board), M.A. Chidambaram, A.K. Ghosh (secretary, Ministry of Education and B.N. Bhardwaj (deputy-secretary, Ministry of Education). Bhardwaj was the secretary of the committee. The Bhabha Committee Report recommended that eminent practitioners and critics in the relevant field of art should be appointed as fellows of the akademis. As fellows they should be treated as ex-officio members of the governing bodies of the appointing institutions. There should also be a gradual decrease in the influence of nominated members and bureaucrats and a corresponding increase in the influence of the fellows. The organisation of the akademis of the arts "on the European pattern" should be gradual. The measures that the committee recommended are as follows:

First, the General Council of the Sangeet Natak Akademi should meet at least three times a year.

Secondly, the terms of appointment of its members should be reduced from five years to three.

Thirdly, grants to institutions should be disbursed directly by the Ministry of Education on the advice of the Akademi.

Fourthly, the chairman and secretary of the Akademi should have direct access to the secretary of the Ministry of Education.

There were recommendations on specific items such as library, theatres, scholarships and publications. The authorities of the akademis disagreed with the recommendation is of the Bhaba Committee.

In 1970 another review committee under the chairmanship of Justice G.D. Khosla was appointed to review the workings of the akademis and the ICCR with reference to their objectives and the recommendations of the Bhabha Committee. The members of the committee were: Amrit Nahata, Professor Hirendra Nath Mukherjee, D.M. Tewari, Loknath Misra and Professor Saiyid Nurul Hasan, all members of parliament; Dr. Narayana Menon, Sham Lal, Professor A.K. Narain, Dr. Umashankar Joshi, Professor Rasheeduddin Khan, Girija Devi (vocalist), Rukmini Debi Arundale (dancer and founder of the Madras Kalakshetra) and M.F. Hussain. Hasan subsequently became a minister and resigned from the Khosla Committee. A.K. Narain resigned to join an assignment abroad. The committee addressed itself to an evaluation of the impact of the akademis and the ICCR on "the cultural life of the people" and a study of "the involvement of the creative artists in the national pattern of culture and art". The Khosla Committee framed the following questions for the purpose of investigation:

1. Were the akademis and the ICCR delivering services promised and expected?
2. Had the powerful akademis and officially-sponsored institutions taken on roles which should have been played by arts' professionals?
3. How could accountability for public funds be reconciled with the workings of the akademis as autonomous bodies?

The committee visited different regions and states of the country excluding Assam and Meghalaya. A comprehensive questionnaire was sent to 1500 persons. It elicited approximately 700 replies.

In 1972 the Khosla Committee Report was submitted to the Ministry of Education and Social Welfare. Respondents complained that younger artists were ignored and older artists were preferred in the selection of award recipients. On the basis of these responses, the committee expressed its view that:

> On the whole all occupational groups, and specially Academicians and Artists think that the Akademis have been unsuccessful in raising the standard of arts, bring [sic] art nearer to the common man, strengthening the cultural unity of the country and evoking art consciousness among the

public. The Sangeet Natak Akademi has succeeded to a greater extent than the other two Akademis in this regard.

The committee echoed the grievance of many respondents that the representation of artists and art critics on akademi governing bodies was inadequate.

> The root cause of present dissatisfaction is a feeling among general body of artists, especially the younger artists, that their views and needs are not heard, and a cultural policy in which they have no voice is imposed upon them.

The Khosla Committee's recommendations were as follows:

First, a number of sub-committees should be appointed to deal with specific projects and programmes sponsored by the Sangeet Natak Akademi.

Secondly, a comprehensive inventory of the various cultural institutions in the country should be compiled to facilitate selection of institutions deserving support.

Thirdly, each akademi was asked to prepare panels and to recommend artists for foreign tours and the government was to honour their advice.

Fourthly, a national school of dance and a national school of music should be established. Such institutions should be financed either by the Sangeet Natak Akademi or directly by the government. But Kathak Kendra, which was then under the financial and administrative control of the Sangeet Natak Akademi was to be restored to an autonomous status.

In March 1977 the Emergency rule collapsed. The Janata Party assumed power in New Delhi. Encouraged by the changed political situation, the classical dance stars of New Delhi arranged a press conference at India International Centre on 26 April 1977. The protesters were led by Sonal Mansingh, Yamini Krishnamurthy, Rani Karna, Swapna Sundari, Leela Samson and Madhavi Mudgal. The memorandum issued at the end of the press conference called for a new "dynamic and genuinely motivated apex body which used the resources at its command for larger purpose than the Sangeet Natak Akademi's". They suggested the establishment of a national school of dance so that "a large reservoir of trained talent would be available for projecting a dynamic and contemporary image of Indian culture both within the country and abroad". They demanded an enquiry into the use of public funds allocated to the Sangeet Natak Akademi, the Song and Drama Division of the Ministry of Information and Broadcasting, the ICCR, the Kathak Kendra and other bodies. The memorandum suggested that a panel of experts, drawn from all major forms of dance and music should be formed to ensure an impartial selection of performing artists.

The protest of these Delhi dancers brought to focus a number of long-standing problems and immediate demands. These are as follows: effective autonomy of the akademis; the role of experts in selecting and honouring artists; the need for improved facilities for artists; proper allocation of available resources and their distribution; the balance among bureaucratic, political and artistic concerns in policy formulation and the demand for a new national cultural policy.

Since 1977 some reform measures have been introduced. Some of the recommendations of the Khosla Committee Report have been implemented. In 1982 the Executive Board of the Sangeet Natak Akademi was reconstituted. Still, some questions, pertinent as they are, remain unanswered. Joan L. Erdman who has deeply studied the case of the Delhi dancers, has clearly articulated some of these questions.

> If autonomy allows the akademis to refuse the recommendations of an expert committee report, then are autonomous akademis desirable? Moreover, to what extent are akademis and councils autonomous when they are financially dependent upon government allocations, and their executive and council officials are in (or retired from) government service? Can the arts be treated instrumentally, as are defence, development, and science? Or are the arts special because they require interpretative efforts and opportunities for creative growth and experimentation?

It is true that the activities of the Sangeet Natak Akademi have not been totally fruitless. In urban areas the audiences for classical performing arts have grown considerably. Indian classical music and dance have earned appreciation around the world. But the cultural policy of the Government of India has projected only India's traditions and past accomplishments. It has not encouraged experimentation. Joan L. Erdman has drawn our attention to a glaring limitation of New Delhi's cultural policy.

> The national integration policy of post-independence India promoted the concept that the classical arts helped unite India culturally. Fears of an unruly and fissiparous regionalism were met by giving particular regional forms of classical arts national recognition. The reviving, preserving and reshaping of indigenous arts (including visual, literary, and performing arts) characterised the pre-independence period. After 1947, Sanskritisation, i.e., textual legitimisation for performing arts—and enlargement of regional styles to all India importance became the dual motifs of cultural policy. While Western (European) cultural progress has been premised on change - i.e. the acceptance of new directions in the fine and classical arts - India's state-supported cultural development featured dissemination of extant cultural forms to an urban and sophisticated audience which segregated religious and secular performances previously conjoined. Even the folk performing arts, presented annually in New Delhi as part of Indian Republic festivities, are designed and choreographed to promote the goals of secular national integration.

A bunch of documents entitled Samarthan published in 1998 by the Department of Culture, Ministry of Human Resource Development, Government of India, has examined the meaning of culture in contemporary Indian society. It states:

> The role of culture lies not only in the context of the promotion of economic growth but also in relation to other objectives of creating an environment that nurtures self-expression and exploration on the part of the individual and communities besides support to arts and artists, correcting some of the distorting effects of free market mechanism and involving the people at large in a sense of cultural commonality and finally, developing creativity as a social force."

The Department of Culture nurtures various institutions and schemes. The preservation of cultural heritage is maintained through the Archeological Survey of India, Museums and Archives. The three National Akademis of Performing, Literary and Visual Arts encourage creativity through incentives, awards and fellowships. The Department of Culture has set up institutions that prepare audio-visual and printed materials, aiming at inculcating aesthetic and cultural values. Seven Zonal Cultural Centres have been set up to stress cultural kinship and foster a spirit of national integration.

A special scheme has been launched to provide building grants to private, non-governmental organisations to enable them to establish permanent centres of cultural interaction. Financial assistance to individuals and groups has over the years been provided to encourage experimental and innovative original works in the literary and performing fields. Spe'cial one time grants are also offered for celebration of centenaries of important personalities in different fields, who have contributed to social reforms, culture, education and other nation-building causes. There is, moreover, the Scheme for Preservation and Development of the Cultural Heritage of the Himalayas which encourages the study, research and documentation of the cultural heritage of this region.

Similarly, a scheme aimed at giving financial assistance to voluntary Buddhist/Tibetan organisations including monasteries engaged in the propagation and scientific development of Buddhist/Tibetan culture and tradition and research in related fields, has also been launched. The criteria for grants are as follows:

- i) The voluntary institution/organisation and society should be registered as a society under the Societies Registration Act (XXI of 1860) or similar State Acts;
- ii) Only those organisations which are mainly devoted to Buddhist/Tibetan studies and have been functioning at least for the last three years will qualify for applying for a grant;
- iii) The organisation should be of a regional or an all-India character;

iv) The grants will be ad hoc and of a non-recurring nature;

v) Grants from this scheme will be given only to those organisations which are not in receipt of grants from any other source for similar purposes; and

vi) Organisations which are doing good work in the field and have resources for meeting the matching funds will be given preference.

Financial assistance may be given for all or any items listed below upto a maximum of Rs. 2.00 lakh per year for any single organisation. The ceiling for any single organisation for each item is listed below:

i)	Maintenance/Research Project	Rs. 40,000/- p.a.
ii)	Repairs, restoration, renovation of ancient monasteries, etc., of historical and cultural importance	Rs. 60,000/- p.a.
iii)	Award of fellowships/scholarships/ holding of special courses	Rs. 50,000/- p.a.
iv)	Purchase of books, documentation, cataloguing	Rs. 50,000/- p.a.
v)	Financial assistance may also be given for construction of hostel building	Rs. 2,00,000/- p.a.

The grant on any of these items will be shared between the Union Territory/Central Government and the State Government/Union Territory or the concerned organisation in the ratio of 3 : 1. Each project will be considered on merit.

The Department of Culture operates fourteen schemes of financial assistance to help individuals, groups and voluntary organisations to sustain and encourage cultural activities in the country. The Government of India proclaims in no uncertain terms:

> We have been deeply conscious of the fact that it is not for the state to guide culture as culture is around us, behind us and ahead of us. We have only to create necessary infrastructure

facilities so that cultural values could inform our development policies and programmes besides manifesting themselves in a manner what Indian sages called *'Satyam, Sivam, Sundaram'*.

Tribal/folk culture attracted the notice of the Government of India immediately after independence. The scholars who are engaged in the study of folk culture have noticed significant differences between folk culture and elite culture. These are as follows :

	Folk culture	*Elite culture*
1.	Natural and unsophisticated culture	Artificial and purely sophisticated culture
2.	Collective culture	Individual craftsmanship
3.	Open air culture	Club-based Culture
4.	Hereditary, spontaneous forest and agrarian in nature	Acquired, mechanical and urban in nature
5.	Simple	Complex
6.	Traditional	Modern
7.	Heartfelt and mass based	Brain-oriented and sectional
8.	Unwritten, oral, shruti	Written and bookish
9.	Animistic in faith	Organised religion
10.	Optimistic	Pessimistic
11.	Propogates national integration	Partly integrative
12.	Production-oriented	Non-productive
13.	Egalitarian (manual labour)	Stratified, reluctant to do manual labour

"From the above comparison", argues Prafulla Kumar Mahato, "it can be deduced that general Folk Culture is the culture of general mass (mother Culture of the nation of Bharat Varsha) whereas elitist culture is the product of the folk culture nourished in urban centres and hence elitist Culture does not cover the sense of a total culture of people".

The Fifth Schedule of the Constitution of India made provisions as to the administration and control of the scheduled areas and scheduled tribes. This provision did not apply to Assam, Meghalaya, Tripura and Mizoram. The Sixth Schedule of the Constitution made provision as to the administration of tribal areas in the states of Assam, Meghalaya, Tripura and Mizoram. Article 46 of the Constitution says: "The state shall promote with special care the educational and economic interests of the weaker section of the people, and in particular, of the Scheduled Castes and Scheduled Tribes, and shall protect them from social injustice and all forms of exploitation". Article 164 has specifically laid down that "in the states of Bihar, Madhya Pradesh and Orissa there shall be a minister in charge of tribal welfare who may, in addition, be in charge of the welfare of the Scheduled castes and backward classes or any other work". The Constitution of India has also introduced universal suffrage. This has qualitatively transformed tribal society.

Since 2nd October 1952, the Planning Commission of the Government of India introduced Community Development Programmes in the tribal areas of eleven states, namely, Andhra Pradesh, Assam, Bihar, Bombay, Madhya Pradesh, Orissa. Madhya Bharat, Manipur, Tripura and NEEA. The community project administration started work in 60 community development blocks and 188 National Extension Service Blocks covering approximately a total population of 28,984,249 of which about 15,576,370 belonged to the scheduled tribes and 13,407,879 to the scheduled castes. Improved methods of agriculture and new arts and crafts were introduced. New schools were opened and generous stipends were granted to encourage education of tribal students at all levels. A large number of tribal welfare centres and multipurpose cooperative societies were also established. All these measures have tremendously transformed and modernised tribal life. In this connection, N. Dutta Majumdar, then Director, Department of Anthropology, Indian Museum, uttered a note of caution:

> The aim of the Five year Plans and of the Community Projects Administration is to raise the standard of living of all sections of the populations of India. But in order to achieve this aim it

should be constantly come in mind that the standard of living is but an aspect of the life and culture of a social group, and that proper account ought to be taken of the role of culture as a whole. This caution is all the more necessary in dealing with the cases of tribal peoples, whose cultures have been used to functioning for a long time on a plane far removed from what is known as the modern way of life. There should be no attempt to frame a programme of action in the ivory tower of a central office and then to impose it on a tribal people. Such a plan unrelated to the socio-cultural context of the tribes is not only bound to be a failure, but also to cause irreparable damage to large human groups.

Two years ago a scheme for the "Promotion and Dissemination of Tribal/Folk Art and Culture" was announced by the Department of Culture, Government of India. The details of the scheme are as follows:

1. The scheme will be known as the Scheme for Promotion and Dissemination of Tribal Folk Art and Culture. Under this scheme financial assistance will be provided to the voluntary organisations and institutions engaged in the preservation and promotion of tribal/folk art and culture on a recurring or non-recurring basis.
2. The scheme will address itself mainly to the well identified and urgent need for the preservation, promotion and dissemination of tribal and rural art and culture. Its objectives will be:
    a) to provide the tribals with opportunities to conduct their cultural activities including the 'Utsavas' (festivals and festivities) in their environment and to collect and preserve their art and craft in their milieu so as to ensure the continuity to the traditions of tribal art and crafts;
    b) to promote and support documentation, research and survey, particularly the preparation of photographic record of such artistic and craft heritage and manifestations of tribal and rural

India, as face the threat of extinction as a consequence of rapid development;

c) to assist the educational authorities of the State Governments concerned in identifying projects which will help to integrate the educational system particularly the curriculum (in both formal and non-formal systems of education) in tribal areas with the cultural traditions of the tribal and rural communities;

d) to disseminate the awareness of the richness of tribal/rural culture, particularly among the urban educated people so as to inculcate in them respect and admiration for the contribution of tribal/rural communities to various facets of Indian culture; and

e) to promote the preservation and development of tribal art and crafts and other facets of tribal culture by all other means.

3. To achieve the above objectives, it is proposed to give grants or subsidies to the registered voluntary organisations, institutions and individuals both tribal and non-tribal who have either been associated or will associate themselves with some institution having the necessary infrastructure facilities for their projects and who are engaged in the area of preservation of tribal art and crafts for undertaking projects for:

a) documentation, research, survey and photographic record

of artistic manifestations;

b) identifying projects in the system of formal and non-formal education to disseminate awareness of the richnesses of tribal culture and life; and

c) preservation and propagation of tribal art, crafts, oral

traditions and other facets of tribal and rural culture.

4. Grants or subsidies will be provided on the basis of approved programmes and projects including construction of cultural huts attached to school buildings or community centres in tribal areas. The grants will be recurring/non-recurring in character, subject to the limits laid down for different components of the project by the Advisory Committee which will consist, among others, of the representatives of governments dealing with tribal welfare and culture (such as ASI, RMS), experts in the field of tribal art and crafts and tribal people themselves. The projects approved by the Advisory Committee will normally be of the duration not exceeding one year at a time. The Advisory Committee may recommend extension of the project for a suitable period thereafter. The amount of grant may be upto Rs. 2 lakh which will cover all items of expenditure included in the approved project/ programme selected for assistance in a particular year.
5. In selecting individual projects for assistance, care will be taken to ensure that different tribal groups in all parts of the country are covered as far as possible.
6. The Department of Culture will invite from time to time applications for assistance under this scheme. In the normal course these applications from voluntary organisations may be sent through the respective State Governments, which may recommend them with their observations as to the standing and contribution of these organisations towards the preservation of tribal art and culture.
7. The Advisory Committee will recommend the manner of the utilisation and disbursement of the grant.
8. At the end of each year an Evaluation Committee will be set up by the Department of Culture to make an

> overall assessment of the project, in terms of its impact on the cultural life of the tribal area. The Committee will submit its report within six months from the close of the financial year in which the project is completed. The reports of the committee will be taken into consideration by the advisory committee at the time of selecting fresh projects for assistance or for further assistance to continuing projects.

On the occasion of the inauguration of the Indian Council of Cultural Relations in 1950, Jawaharlal Nehru explained in his inaugural address the meaning of culture and the relevance of culture in international relations. His speech highlighted the essence of cultural policy in India since 1947 in marmoreal expressions. I quote below excerpts from this speech:

> Does culture mean some inner growth in the man? Of course it must. Does it mean the way he behaves to others? Certainly it must. Does it mean the capacity to understand the other persons? I suppose so. Does it mean the capacity to make yourself understand by the other persons? I suppose so. It means all that.

If that is culture, how far is it represented in the modern world and among the nations of today? Obviously, if it was represented more than it is, many of our problems, national and international, would be far easier of solution.

Almost every country in the world thinks that it has some special dispensation from Providence, that it is of the chosen people or race, and others may be good or bad or secondary, somewhat inferior human beings. It is extraordinary how these human feelings persist in all nations without exception, whether of the East or of the West.

Culture that is essentially good, looked at from a wrong point of view, becomes essentially not only static but aggressive and something breeding conflict and hatred. How are you to find a balance, I do not know.

And perhaps that is the problem of today apart from the political and economic problems of the age, because behind it there seems to be a tremendous conflict in the spirit of man today, some search for something which it cannot find.

One thing that troubles me is this, that often enough people who understand each other more and more, begin to quarrel more and more. Nevertheless, you cannot say from that we should not try to understand each other because that will be completely limiting oneself and that is something which really cannot be done in the modern context of the world. Therefore, it becomes essential that we must try to understand each other in the right way. The right way is important. The right approach, the friendly approach is important, because a friendly approach brings a friendly response. I have not a shadow of doubt that it is a fundamental rule of human life that if the approach is good, the response is good. If the approach is bad, the response is likely to be bad too.

So, if we approach our fellow human beings or other countries in the right way, not in any sense of surrending anything that we consider of essential value to truth or to our genius but nevertheless in a friendly way, with our minds and hearts open and prepared to accept whatever good comes to them, then that will lead not only to understanding but the right type of understanding.

"I have obtained knowledge that has earned the praises of mighty kings and I have obtained many a thing coveted here on earth," sings Sri Sankara Bhagavatpada and queries "but what next?" The interaction on the last question, in Sanskrit, tatah kim? tatah kim, leads one to a state of exasperation.

Scientific Culture

Science has made such spectacular strides that the common man, looking at its achievements, is awestricken and baffled.

The great and magnificient achievements of science, accomplished with the collaboration and cooperation of millions of people belonging to different climes and continents, leading to the recent epoch-making feat of moon-landing, are indeed remarkable and laudable.

But at the same time, surveying the bloodbath that goes on unabated in the world, the tribal in-feuding, hatred, jealousy, cruelty and violence that dominate it; and the freezing looks of people when they see others cast in a different mould, one comes across humanity at its basest level and sinks into disillusionment and despair.

Pitirim Sorokin, one of the greatest sociologists of our times was a senior colleague of Lenin in the making of the October Revolution. Later, when he resisted the crusade launched by the new rulers of Russia against individual liberty and freedom of thought 'stifling the divine essence in man, he was arrested and condemned to death. However, in view of his intellectual eminence, Lenin himself granted him reprieve. He fled Russia and spent years in a detailed and scientific study of the problems of society. His scientific studies and experiences led him to affirm his faith: The expressions of a cold intellect and plaintive murmurs of a saddened heart in the redeeming Power of Love.

"Whatever may happen in the future, I know that I have learned three things which will remain forever convictions of my heart as well as my mind.

"Life, even the hardest life, is the most beautiful, wonderful and miraculous treasure in the world.

"Fulfilment of duty is another marvellous thing making life happy. This is my second conviction.

"And my third is that cruelty, hatred, violence, and injustice never can and never will be able to create a mental, moral or material millennium. The only way towards it is the royal road of all-giving creative love, not only preached but consistently practised."

Sorokin's conclusions on the Law of Love, given below, are the result of 40 years of sustained and penetrating study and many significant first-hand experiences:

"Hate begets hate, violence engenders violence, hypocrisy is answered by hypocrisy, war generates war, and love creates love.

"Unselfish love has enormous creative and therapeutic potentialities, far greater than most people think. Love is a life-giving force, necessary for physical, mental and moral health.

"Altruistic persons live longer than egoistic individuals.

"Children deprived of love tend to become vitally, morally and socially defective.

"Love is the most powerful antidote against criminal, morbid and suicidal tendencies; against hate, fear and psychoneuroses.

"Love is an indispensable condition for deep and lasting happiness.

"Love is the finest and most powerful educational force for the ennoblement of humanity."

The peer of Arnold Toynbee, Sorokin, is compared by some to Comte and Spengler. It is significant that Sorokin, who "reverentially dedicated" one of his best works Reconstruction of Humanity (Bhavan's Book University publication) to the 'deathless Mahatma Gandhi' arrived at the same conclusions through the rational process of scientific analysis, which our ancient seers and saints did through their intuitive wisdom and experience. All religions, in their inmost essence, declare the high potency-redeeming Power of Love.

In this and every other essential respect, religions remain one and the same. If we dive deep into the depths of all religions and look for the Truth in them, we will grasp their essential unity, we will realise that the core and kernel of all religions is one.

Paramahamsa Sri Ramakrishna, true to the disciplines of a sanyasi, undertook the experiment of living each religion and realising divinity. Gurudev Rabindranath Tagore proclaimed and strove for the same ideal. Mahayogi Sri Aurobindo stood for the Religion of Humanity. Sri Ramana Maharshi stressed the need to erase the ego and lived Universal religion. Mahatma Gandhi made Satya, Ahimsa and Sarva Dharma Samanatva the cornerstones of his mission.

St. Augustine in his retractions tells us that what is known as Christianity was also being practised by people before Christ, only that it was not known by that name. In the Gita we have the Lord telling us that the same Yoga was taught to Vivaswan or the Sun-god ; and in spite of passage of several centuries, the same is being preached. Aldous Huxley in his admirable work, the Perennial Philosophy, has also demonstrated the essential unity of all religions.

The Upanishads pose two contradistinct concepts: the *alpa* (finite) and the *bhooman* (Infinite). Where the mind of man sees differences, it has only the consciousness of *alpa;* where it sees unity and harmony, the Oneness of all things, it is gifted with the *bhooman*. It is towards this ideal of *bhoomanubhave* (realisation of the Infinite), which generates the unifying power of love, that we should ever aspire.

Badshah Khan, a true servant of God, by his life and work, has proved that the truly religious man can have no cause for quarrel and differences; that a man of religion is saturated with compassion and love; that religious fanaticism and human egoism can be transformed and channellised into creative and constructive endeavours by unilateral, unselfish love and affection.

Peace, prosperity and happiness are the by-products of love.

Hatred disturbs equilibrium, breeds fanaticism and saps vitality. As our ancients have said "Whatever we love, we are its masters; whatever we hate, we are its slaves."

In sum, this is the message of Badshah Khan, the living embodiment of the Mahavratas enunciated by all religions : Ahimsa, Satya, Astheya, Brahmacharya and Aparigraha. He sees humanity as one having the divine spark in every individual to whichever faith one may belong and by whatever name one may call the All-Pervading. In Badshah Khan there is always complete accord between thought, word and deed—manasyekam, vachasyekam, karmanyekam—the hallmark of a real Mahatma.

May the Lord give us the strength to give up cant and hypocrisy, to realise and follow the power and ways of Love and to tread steadfastly the path of Sarva Dharma *Samanatva*.

Role of Music

A unique feature of *Bharatiya Samskriti*—Indian culture—is its ingeniously built in, unifying, integrating ingredients.

Our art—be it dance, music, painting or architecture is permeated by bhakti and conceived as a consecration to the lotus feet of the Lord.

Music has been one such unifying force that has transcended all delimiting and obstructing barriers.

Indeed, the galaxy of India's saint-singers has been rightly hailed as Divine Integrators. Whatever integration still remains with us is solely because of the indelible contribution to bhakti and dharma made by them through *bhajans* and *kirtans*.

Even our own contemporary national life provides ample evidence of this integrating nature of music. This fine art has wrought the magic, where exhortations and exhibitions have only accentuated differences of caste, colour, religion, region and language.

The great singer of modern India, Bade Ghulam Ali Khan, who passed away in Hyderabad was acclaimed to be at his best when he sang his exquisite khayal in Darbari Kanada beginning with the words Maheswara Mahadev. The soul-captivating manner in which he used to render the Komal Gandhara notes in this raga, the religious fervour that he put into the song, made listeners wonder whether the singer was not a devout Hindu Saint.

The same was the feelings one got when Sri Yesudas, a Christian, recently gave a full-length Carnatic music concert in Mumbai and rendered with piety and devotion, among others, Kritis of Rama-bhakta, Tyagaraja and *slokas* from Narayaneeyam by Krishnabhakta Meppatur Nampoodiripad. Considerations of caste and creed did not come in the way of this Christian musician being conferred the title of "Sangeeta Raja" by the Bheeshmapitamaha of Carnatic Music, the septuagenarian, Chembai Sri Vaidyanatha Bhagavatar.

No one ever lets his mind be vitiated by narrow or sectional thoughts or national boundaries when listening to Yehudi Menuhin's superb performances in India and other, countries in the East, or when Padma Bhushan Smt. M.S. Subbulakshmi, Pandit Ravi Shankar, Smt. Indrani Rehman, Kumari Yamini Krishnamurti and other artists give performances in Britain, Russia, America and other countries.

Music in particular obliterates all differences; nay, it promotes fellowship and camaraderie.

Bhakti and music are inter-related, and each gives strength to the other. 'The essence of Music is *Bhakti*. *Bhakti* helps erase the ego! *Bhakti* instills compassions, selflessness and promotes harmony and brotherhood. The key-note of all great music compositions is bhakti and dharma.'

The spell cast by good music makes the listener oblivious of everything else.

Music enables man to regain his essential nature music *Anandamayattya* the nature of bliss which he loses as he gets enmeshed in morbid, mortal ventures.

It is no wonder that this is so. Lives there a man who is not moved by sincere *bhakti*-laden music? As the great Bhartrihar has said

He that knows not music
Nor letters, nor art
Is but a beast incarnate,
Of what use is he indeed,
Sans tail, sans horns,
He lives, but eats no grass,
'That is the only good
He confers on men.

Have not we christened as Song Celestial, Lord Krishna's gospel of life imported to his disciple, Arjuna, on the battlefield of Kurukshetra some three-thousand years ago ?

Music has something compelling about it by its measure and melody, by its rhythm and harmony.

Music is a manifestation of a divinity, the Cosmic Order or Rita that the Vedic sages divined in their moments of institutional inspiration.

Music is the perfection of human expression, symbolising the sublimity to which man can rise, expressive of the unity, the sweetness and life-giving elements of life.

All great musicians, like all great scientists, are endowed with child-like innocence, utter humility and unshakable faith in God.

Day in and day out, bickerings, tolerance and mutual accusations stifle our, voice now-a-days. Public life everywhere is full of this foul discord. One is sick of malice and malevolence, vengeance and violence. The atmosphere is filled with loud, hypocritical shouts and unabashed self-aggrandisement.

Music, soul-stirring and leavened with *bhakṭi*, has the power to help man over-power his baser instincts and sublimate the love which every mother feeds him with in his infancy. There is a responsive card in every human breast. All human beings, even the meanest and most vicious, have coursing in their veins some unselfish love and the milk of human kindness which their mothers have implanted in them in their childhood. Even ferocious animals and poisonous snakes respond to the captivating call of enchanting music.

Music exudes relaxation. It provides nourishment to the senses and the soul. Speeches build up tensions, distort and soil the soul. Music unites people. Speeches divide them.

All great musicians, like all great scientists, are endowed with child-like innocence, utter humility and unshaken faith in God.

Day in and day out, hatred, intolerance and mutual accusations stifle our world nowadays. Public life in our country is full of this foul discord. One is sick of malice and malevolence, vengeance and violence. The atmosphere is filled with loud hypocritical shouts and unabashed self-aggrandisement.

Music, soul-stirring and leavened with faith, has the power to help man overpower his baser instincts and sublimate the love which every mother floods him with in his infancy. There is a responsive chord in every human breast. All human beings, even the meanest and most vicious, have coursing in their veins some unselfish love and the milk of human kindness which their mothers have implanted in them in their childhood. Even ferocious animals and poisonous snakes respond to the captivating call of enchanting music.

Music provides relaxation. It provides nourishment to the senses and the soul. Speeches build up tensions, distort and soil the soul. Music unites people. Speeches divide them.

9

Rise of Ethnic Groups

This chapter seeks to anticipate some of the prospects of ethnic Communities in twenty-first century India from the retrospect of the present one. Viewed in this light, it has at least four major limitations which need to be mentioned at the very outset: one, whatever one has to argue, it draws overwhelmingly and at times exclusively, from some of the current researches on ethnic politics in north-eastern India. This, however, should not lead us to think that the experience of the region offers an excellent prototype of ethnic politics—whether in India or in the world as a whole. Our familiarity with the region is admittedly a little better than it is with other parts of India, let alone the world. Plainly speaking, our illustrations from the north-east are cited more for reasons of convenience than anything else. Two, author proposes to concentrate on the problems ethnic communities face or are likely to face only after they become ascendent, rather on those that they face or more accurately, are required to fact in course of their becoming ascendent. The distinction is necessary, though of course, there is no denying the face that some of the problems may be common to both the pre- and post-ascendent states.

Three, we assume that the advent of modernity has among other things, contributed to the ascendence (variously termed as 'revival', resurgence', 'recrudescence', 'explosion', etc., in social science circles) of particular ethnic communities in two very substantive ways: first, we all know that the advent of modernity has made it obligatory on the part of an ethnic community to define its collective self in opposition to what it considers to be its other with the implication that one's membership to it becomes so exclusive that one no longer enjoys the option of belonging to another at the same time.' Indeed, the self-other distinction is so strong in the north-east that almost every community invests the other with what in social anthropology is known as 'a negative evaluative meaning'. Not all distinctions in social life connote a hierarchy of the superior to the inferior. But, the other, under conditions of modernity, is necessarily defined as both distinct from and inferior to the collective self imagined by a particular ethnic community. Thus, the distinctions between the Khasis and the Dkhars, between the Maitheis and the Mayangs, between the Angami Nagas and the Disphrames are also illustratives of the presence of deeply-rooted hierarchies of evaluation in which the other is always held as a dirty word. Secondly, modernity has also transformed communal identities into powerful instruments that their members can promote, mobilise and manipulate at their will in order to attain their economic and political interests. The Rajbangs' demand for certification of their community as a 'Scheduled Tribe' is intended to serve the dual purpose of acquiring certain social and economic opportunities that they have otherwise been denied and also the political mileage of aligning themselves with other Mongoloid groups scheduled as tribes and forging in the process, a pan-Mongoloid unity across the entire region. In sum, ethnic ascendence is taken to mean ascendence of individual ethnic communities rather than that of a particular type of social relations that, for Weber, shows a distinct tendency of influencing other 'non-ethnic types' of social relations hinder modern conditions. The distinction between ethnicity defined as a type of community and that defined as a type of social relations is too significant to be brushed aside. While it is true that ethnicity defined in the first sense cannot but imply a particular type of social relations, their coincidence is neither given nor unalterable. This is because the communities may not be interested in bringing the type of social relations characteristic of them, to bear on each and every sphere of their social life as much as the type of social relations that we are talking about. This may not necessarily by confined to the ethnic communities alone. The Assamese community, for instance, appears to be much less 'ethnic' today than what it was at the time when the Assam movement (1979-85) was in full swing. I have shown elsewhere how ethnicity in the Bhadralok society of nineteenth century Calcutta existed more as a type of social relations—implicit and unacknowledged, yet powerful enough to influence other sectors of social life including the public sphere. I have designated this phenomenon as the 'communitarianisation' (or 'ethnicisation') of the public sphere. In other words, ethnicity at that time in Calcutta seldom existed as a constellation of determinate ethnic communities at loggerheads with each other. We, however, assume here that ethnicity is necessarily embodied in and expressed through the living ethnic communities.

Four, the theoretical part of this chapter is obviously very sketchy, primarily for reasons of space and only secondarily due to the fear that it may sometimes appear to be not pertinent enough; though, of course, it has quite a lot to do with the problem of discovering an appropriate methodology that will enable us to anticipate the prospects by way of reading, the retrospect—provided if at all by the century that has just been completed.

As we have already pointed out, the task of anticipating the prospects of ethnic communities in the twenty-first century opens up a series of thorny methodological questions which unless properly dealt with at the very beginning, might simply deter us from developing our arguments at the end. Some of these questions for instance are: how does one read, and make sense of the retrospect provided by a century? Do all the variegated forces operative with in the span of one hundred years submit themselves to one single and over-arching retrospect? How then, does one read a plurality of retrospects? Does that reading enable us to anticipate the prospects? Quite understandably, many of these questions do not form directly a part of our present inquiry.

One way of reading the retrospect that history supposedly presents to us, is to conceive of it as a veritable maze of sufficiently exclusive and identifiable forces—ideologies, institutions, classes of whatever, in the sense that each of them can unite with another only on condition of what Hegel describes as its 'self-destruction' Insofar as a force visualises its objective of being united with another in these terms, it realises its 'Spirit' located by definition outside its own boundaries. For, the 'Spirit' being Universal cannot be particular to any of the forces under review. Hegel envisaged a dichotomy between matter and Spirit in this connection and argued:

> The nature of the Spirit may be understood by a glance ... at its direct opposite—Matter. . . . Matter possesses gravity in virtue of' its tendency toward a central point. It is essentially composite, consisting of parts that exclude each other. It seeks its unity; and therefore exhibits itself as self-destruction, verging toward its opposite [an indivisible part]. If it could attain this, it would be matter no longer, it would have perished. It strives after the realisation of its Idea; for its unity exists ideally. Spirit, on the contrary, may be defined as that which has its centre in itself.'

History according to Hegel comes to an end as soon as it realises the Spirit. It is no wonder that most of the prophecies of 'endism' which by now have become a integral part of the popular lore of social sciences, have their origins in Hegel's Philosophy of History.

Hegel influenced Francis Fukuyama via Alexandre' Kojeve. The "triumph of economic and political liberalism of the West" as Fukuyama contends, has been precipitated by "a total exhaustion of viable systematic alternatives to Western liberalism". Western liberalism has now become the 'Spirit of the Age' because it is the only ideology that has the unique potential of resolving the 'issues' that have hitherto remained irresolute within the ideological framework of either of its two alternatives—fascism and communism.

Such a reading of history excises ethnic communities from the retrospect of 'World History' on the ground that they do not posit any systematic alternative" to the triumphant liberalism. In a passage significantly overlooked by his otherwise vociferous critics, Fukuyama observes:

> Only systematic nationalisms ... can qualify as a formal ideology on the level of liberalism or communism. The vast majority of World's nationalist movements do not have a political programme beyond the negative desire of independence join other groups of people, and do not offer anything like a comprehensive agenda for socio-economic organisation. As such they are compatible with doctrines and ideologies that do offer such agendas. While they may constitute a source of conflict for liberal societies, this conflict does not arise from liberalism itself so much from the fact that the liberalism in question is incomplete. Certainly a great deal of the world's ethnic and nationalist tension can be explained in terms of peoples who are forced to live in unrepresentative political systems that they have not chosen.

We may say that Fukuyama does not count "nationalism and other forms of ethnic consciousness" as either "systematic" or "an alternative". Hence, they do not constitute a part of the retrospect in which only sufficiently exclusive and identifiable forces 'destroy' themselves in order to bring about a transcendental Spirit and form a System. Those forms of consciousness in other words, have no place whatsoever, in the larger scheme of 'World History'.

Conversely, another reading that has of late become very significant, places them at the foreground of the history of the present century. For purposes of convenience, it my be encapsulated into three very closely inter-linked statements: first, while acknowledging that Western liberalism may have the potential of representing and transcending "nationalism and other forms of racial and ethnic consciousness", it at the same time draws our attention to numerous instances in which ethnic communities are seen to stand up against their absorption in the ideological fold of Western liberalism or, for that matter, in the fold of any "systematic" ideology with a claim to universality. In other words, resistance according to these communities, is a prerequisite for their survival as distinct ethnic communities. Many a time they feel it necessary to resist and, if possible, to continue to do so even when odds are heavily against them and they know fully well that their resistance in the ultimate analysis, may end in a whimper. They do not seem to harbour any illusions about their potential strength. The Nagas for instance, are certainly not foolhardy when they take on the 'colossal invading might of India' for they know that their 'enemy' is disproportionately superior to them. Yet they believe that their survival will be at stake as soon as they bid farewell to arms. After all, the necessity of a fight lies in fighting rather than winning it:

> We are safe as we fight to save ourselves.... [The] issue is not a contest of struggle but of upholding our historic fight against oppressive forces.'

Even as late as in June 1990 when army operations had looked very imminent in Assam, Siddhartha Phukan, Publicity Secretary of the United Liberation Front of Assam (ULFA), admitted in no uncertain terms that "our members are not prepared for taking oil the army (and) we prefer the direct fight with the state apparatus (rashtra-yantra) sometime later". The subsequent experience, however, shows that the insurgent organisation had willy-nilly to engage itself in what in the process turned out to be one of the protracted confrontations of post-colonial India.

Besides, these instances also point to the fact that the ascendence of ethnic communities taking place roughly at the same time all over the world almost without any exception, is bound to cut into liberalism's potential for resolving their problems. The trouble with Fukuyama's analysis is that he considers these problems as potentially resolvable within the ideological framework of Western liberalism: "The point is to ask how the impervious, seemingly all-embracing code might be deployed, or thought so that at least a glimpse of its finitude, a vision of what might constitute as 'outside' to it". Viewed thus, ethnic problems may contain the potential of turning Universalism of whatever variety by its head and of constantly preventing it from ascending into what Hegel described as the 'Spirit of the Age'. In our obsessive concern for Universalism, we often lose sight of these fragments which are never organisable into an integral whole and the multifarious critiques developed by them from time to time.

ULFA's critique of Western liberalism per se rather than the variety exemplified by the Indian state may serve as a case in point. For purposes of convenience, we propose to concentrate on only one aspect of this otherwise valuable critique. The organisation accuses Western liberalism of what I have elsewhere called, an inherent mainlandism. 'Metropolitan India' exercises its hegemony over 'the Indo-Burma region' in much the same manner as Western Capitalist countries do it over India. There are two sides of the critique which should not escape our notice in any way: one, ULFA believes that Western liberalism by virtue of what it is, cannot but perpetrate this bias and thereby creates systematically an 'outside' beyond its so-called Universal gamut. To put it in a slightly different way, Western liberalism, according to ULFA, is constitutive of this 'outside'. It turns into the opposite of what it is 'outside' the so-called mainland and presents itself as illiberal hegemonism in north-eastern India. If 'Delhi-ism' (Dilli-had) is a poor mimicry of Eastern liberalism of the Westminster type, the region represents its true cenotaph. It is precisely liberalism's vast dumping ground where rules scrupulously observed in the mainland can be inflected, bent and broken at the sweet will of the rulers without having to clutch on to an alibi. That is why there is no question of 'completing' the unfinished task of the liberal project. Two, inasmuch as ULFA accuses 'metropolitan India' of having inserted Assam into its fold, denying thereby what it reckons as a community's inalienable right to self-determination, reducing her to one of its most wretched 'colonies' and making a mockery of the liberal-representative system—widely considered to be indispensable to the functioning of Western liberalism, it does not harp on any agenda of overhauling the existing system of political institutions. One of the major limitations of this critique that the organisation appears to be perfectly aware of, is that it does not possess a 'complete blueprint' of the future and hence, is groping in the dark on the question of whether the critique ought to be pushed to its consummate end by way of making a decisive break with whatever is associated with Western liberalism—let alone its representative political institutions, in any future scheme of post-revolutionary 'socialist' reconstruction."

Secondly, ethnic communities remaining "outside" the compass of the 'Spirit of the Age', however, are neither irreducible nor immutable. For one thing, there are communities within communities and there seems to be no end to this process of infinite fragmentation. Thus, what once was known as the great Assamese community (Asomiya Barghar) during the movement of 1979-85 is now fiercely divided into the Bodos, Santhals, Karbis, Mishings, so no and so forth, apart from the Assamese-speaking Varna-Hindus. Likewise, what earlier looked like a homogeneous and unbreakable community on the eve of the birth of Mizoram as a separate state within the Indian Union in 1987, can hardly be said to include today a significant portion of the Hmars who have been demanding a separate Hmar Ram (state) of their own, outside the state. The growing polarisation between the Hindus and the Muslims in Srinagar valley has already reached a point where one rarely speaks of a generic Kashmiri identity (Kashmiriyat) Cutting across their respective communal boundaries. Parallel to this, there is also the process of alignments and realignments. Autochthonous communities of the Chotanagpur plateau have often felt the necessity of coining together and forging a common Jharkhandi identity while politically combating their common adversary. Both these processes taken together, play a significant role in bringing about visible transformations in the composition and functioning of communities.

Thirdly, history according to the second mode of reading, is devoid of any master-key like Spirit and gives unto itself what Jacques Derrida calls, "many ages" presumably governed by "many spirits" (with both ,a' and 's' in small letters)"—each of which is distinct and hence, cannot be subsumed under another. History "at the edge of the twenty-first century" is condemned to be a maze of particularities - of "racial, ethnic and religious groups demanding their right to be - and to remain different"." Difference, in other words, is the keyword of contemporary history. This has two implications: on the one hand, any attempt at incorporating history into the grid of so-called Universality is bound to obliterate differences. As soon as the varieties and differences are reduced to one Universal Spirit, stories of history are substantially simplified and are forced to illuminate what is called 'the grand narrative, irrespective of the time and place of their occurrence. It enjoins upon a historian the responsibility of telling his/her story within the framework of a grand narrative, may be with some modifications here and there that are too benign to challenge its fundamental pre-suppositions. While much has been said about the 'death of the Universal' ("God is dead"), whether by mourning or by celebrating it, the present chapter proposes to concentrate on the second implication.

Two, the 'death' of the Universal does not automatically connote the ascendence of ethnic particularities. We have already seen how the penetration of the forces of modernity has resulted in a certain ascendence of ethnic communities all over the world. In the wake of their ascendence, they are likely to be plagued by a number of anomalies which unless appropriately tackled, might thwart the tempo of their ascendence. We define anomalies as special kinds of problems that the members of a particular community take notice of only after they realise that the world has changed irreversibly and the rules they had hitherto adhered to which thereby formed the basis of their solidarity, are no longer adequate in coping with and successfully resolving them. I think, several features of this definition stand out as important: first, we must recognise that there is a difference between problems that a particular community faces and the ones that it takes notice of and feels necessary to resolve. Viewed in this light, there may be problems among the members of a community do not, or maybe, fail to take notice of, but nevertheless, face. As we will argue later, various ethnic communities do very much face ecological problems but, are extremely slow in realising their exact nature and intensity. Secondly, there is a set of canons and rules that the members of a community agree more—more often than not, tacitly to abide by, and it is on the basis of their common agreement that a community comes into being and sustains itself. To the extent that they continue to subscribe to them, to that extent the community can survive as a collective entity. The ascendence of ethnic communities in the contemporary world has brought into the limelight a quartet of such rules and canons that they may find increasingly difficult, if not impossible, to abide by in the twenty-first century. Unless they recognise the importance of changing them, the tempo of their ascendence is going to be severely disturbed. The quartet comprises the following:

1. that an ethnic community is necessarily rooted in a given sub-territorial space.
2. that an ethnic community seeks to establish and wherever established, tighten its control over the life-bearing resources of the sub-territory;
3. that the female members of an ethnic community under conditions of patriarchy, are vested with the special responsibility of embodying their community's honour—literally, in their bodies;
4. that an ethnic community arrogates to itself the prerogative of setting forth the agenda of rights and thereby, to situate itself at its centre.

As we see, the communities of the twenty-first century are likely to discover that the world has changed in a manner that it becomes impossible on their part, to abide by the same rules and at the same time, ensure their collective survival in the future. Thirdly, the discovery of this problem might encourage them to undergo what Thomas S. Kuhn has termed, 'a paradigm shift' where by the rules of the game are sought to be changed. The symptoms of this shift are slowly yet unmistakably cast in the distant horizon.

Ethnic Feelings on Rise

I define ethnic sub-territoriality as a site where the territoriality of the nation-state is constantly replicated and as a result, contested. In more negative terms, it does not refer to the subsumption, whether real or potential, of ethnic sub-territoriality under the abiding framework of state territoriality. The 'sub-' of the word sub-territoriality is used in our case as a sub-text that underlies the so-called territoriality of any modern state. How do the ethnic communities replicate the principle of state territoriality? For obvious reasons of space, we will restrict ourselves to an analysis of only two examples in this respect. Most of the insurgent outfits operating in the region under review—very like the modern Indian state, are reported to have enunciated their own land revenue acts which they try to enforce within their respective sub-territorial spaces with much rigour and enthusiasm. The 'Tripura Land Revenue Act' of the Tribal National Volunteers (TNV), the 'Nagaland Land and Trading Regulation' enunciated by the National Socialist Council of Nagaland (I-M), are only illustrative of this point. Moreover, these outfits—more often than not claiming to act on behalf of particular ethnic communities—assign to themselves the crucial political task of defining and maintaining 'law-and-order' within the sub-territorial spaces that the modern states are otherwise supposed to perform. ULFA, for instance, has banned all closed-door performances of Bihu dances—taken widely as an inseparable part of Assam's public life. This was expected to protect female bodies from public exposure and its commodification inside closeted parlours and auditoria meant mainly for commercial use. In course of carving out their respective sub-territorial spaces, they often come into direct conflict with the Indian state. This point is borne out by one of Subir Bhaumik's insightful comments that in the north-east, we come across "a situation where possibly two administrations exist—that of the Indian state by day, and that of rebels by night". The notion of nocturnal sub-territoriality robs the Indian state of not only its monopoly authority of enunciating and enforcing the laws within its territorial ambit but what is usually considered to be its essence—the stability of its political borders. The replication of state territoriality cannot but amount to its violation. Ethnic sub-territoriality, in other words, points to the rootedness of an ethnic community to a particular geographical space.

The advent of modernity or more particularly, its new avatar, globalism, has resulted in what Arjun Appadurai calls, 'de-territorialisation' of ethnic communities all over the world. On the one hand, members of an ethnic community no longer remain confined to any particular geographical area as they have hitherto been. They are now scattered literally all around the globe. On the other hand, members of other and hither to unknown communities are also seen to migrate to what once was held by the members of a particular community as their homeland. Appadurai in this connection introduces the notion of 'ethnoscape' in order to bring home the point that the technology of more intimate and instant communication has made it possible on the part of various segments of the same population strewn all across the world, to communicate amongst themselves without any fetters and most importantly, without wasting any time and to re-establish and rejuvenate their ties cutting across their distinct geographical spaces." What he designates as 'ethnoscape' replaces in its wake, the sub-territorially anchored ethnic communities of the yesteryears.

Appadurai's contention, we think has to be taken with utmost caution especially with respect to a country like India and a region like the north-east. For one thing, while some communities (like the Sikhs) are known for their higher geographical mobility, some others are believed to be far less mobile than what the contention would have us believe. The Assamese for instance, are according to one estimate, the least mobile of all communities in India. In case of the less mobile communities, actual sub-territory seems to be the only place that their members can look forward to and woo as the land of their ultimate refuge. Sub-territorial attachments are inevitably very high in such cases. An editorial published in Dainik Asom, one of Assam's premier vernacular dailies, mostly known for its sympathies with the Assam movement, for instance, observed: "If the Assamese are reduced to a minority in their own state, then where do they hope to retain their language and Culture". In some cases, this lament has given way to acute acrimony and genocide. When the Bodoland Autonomous Council was denied jurisdiction of over 500-odd villages which the Bodos claimed to be their own, on the ground that they did not constitute a numerical majority in them, the leaders got the clue, went inside the villages and cleaned them of the non-Bodos—whether by massacring them in thousands or by threatening them to leave their homes bag and baggage, in a bid to restore the demographic balance in their favour.

For another, the highly mobile communities seem to have converted their sub-territories into objects of collective imagination.

'Khalistan' may be looked upon as one of such powerful objects that instantly caught the imagination of various Sikh diasporic groups settled in the United States, Canada and Great Britain and drove them to extend active support, both moral and material, to the movement. John Rex's study of the diasporic Sikhs of Great Britain points out that the leading Sikh families which have actually been benefited from "communal solidarity protected across the world" and "who could apparently become mutual enemies", have been able to understand "the use and advantages of the solidarity and network that have made them what they are and play an instrumental role in sustaining them"." Robbin Burlings' study of the 15,000-odd Garos of Modhupur in the district of Mymensingh, now in Bangladesh, points out how "the Garos of Bangladesh" are "distinct" from "their cousins north of the border" in the Indian state of Meghalaya. Whereas the former have uncritically assimilated themselves into the Bengali-speaking mainstream with the effect that "only rarely can they read or write their language", their counterparts in India are never known to have expressed support for Assamese or Bengali in their classrooms. But still, the former look upon the Garo Hills as the ultimate land of refuge, so much so, that when they were threatened by the Pakistani army way back in 1971, "virtually the entire Garo population fled across the border of India". Notwithstanding their Cultural distinctions, the Garos of Bangladesh perceive the Garo Hills on the other side of the border as the land of their collective imagination.

While such intimate and instant means of communication facilitated by the forces of globalism, have led to a sustained increase in communications and networking amongst diverse, geographically scattered diasporic groups, communities are expected to face two mutually inter-related challenges in the next century: first, it is only natural that a diasporic group would imagine the sub-territorial space in the light of the experiences specific to itself and there is no reason to believe why one's vision of a 'homeland' would coincide with that of another, The problem assumes all the more serious proportions in view of the fact that both of them consider themselves as parts of the same community. Glenn Bowman's classic study., for instance, shows how the construction of 'different Palestines' correspond to the different experiences of Palestinians in the places of their exile. The second or third generation Nagas settled in Great Britain have very little to share with their brethren fighting against the Indian state from the deep jungles of Myanmar till the other day. It may be that the divide on occasions becomes insurmountable and the diasporic; groups tend to project themselves as separate communities. Thus, even if the Kukis of the Manipur hills and their cousins living in present-day Mizoram share the same ethnic lineage, several Kuki organisations harbour deep anguish in their hearts that the latter have not been extending their hands in the way they should. Secondly, given that divergent images of the ethnic homeland are likely to inspire equally divergent political practices, ethnic communities may not be equally successful in clinging to a World-wide agenda and implementing it on a world scale. Samuel P. Huntington's grim prediction that the world is going to be shattered by what could well turn out to be world history's fiercest 'clash' between the Islamic and Judeo Christian civilisations in the coming century, to my mind, downplays many of the rifts and strifes internal to either of them, more than exaggerating their consolidated character. In fact, one is inversely proportional to the other. When the hiatus between the Assamese Muslims and the immigrant ones settled in Assam is too yawning to be brushed aside, the Islamic dream of organising the Muslims on a civilisational scale appears to be blown out of proportion. The Muslims of Assam are so heterogeneous that they have not been able to evolve a generic Muslim identity till date. Much will depend on how the communities organise themselves and coordinate their activities in the foreseeable future. The more the communities are broken into diasporic and footloose groups, the more difficult the task of internal consolidation and coordination becomes. Ironic yet true, ethnic communities in the era of globalism have still to grapple with the twin problems of internal consolidation and coordination and unless they are effectively able to overcome these, the forces of globalism are destined to blow them away.

Ethnic movements in twentieth century India have by and large aimed at establishing and tightening their control over subterritiorial resources. The point bears out a two-fold significance for us: first of all, the crystallisation of their principal aim is invariably preceded by a deep-seated grievance that their 'homelands' are being indiscriminately impoverished of their precious resources by aliens and outsiders. A sense of injustice backed by an intense feeling of being grievously wronged, lies at the heart of ethnic movements in India. Sometimes, the feeling is so pronounced that it also makes them realise that since they are denied access to the corridors of political power, they can easily be duped and deprived of their resources that they feel legitimately belong to them. Political power in this sense, is regarded as the means through which a community establishes and tightens its grip over the sub-territorial resources. When Atul Bora and Samujjwal Bhattacharyya, President and General Secretary of the All-Assam Students' Union (AASU) ask for "the right of the people over the natural wealth of Assam" in one of their jointly signed statements, what they imply is the re-structuring of political power in such a manner that the Assamese people become entitled to enjoy the freedom of politically asserting themselves through peaceful means within the given federal system of India, so that they will no longer feel compelled to submit to forces over which they do not have any control. Only the politically empowered can establish their control over the natural resources of the region.

Conversely, a number of insurgent organisations including ULFA discover a persistent nexus between 'the semi-capitalist, semi-feudal forces' and 'the state apparatus', so much so that the latter is supposed to be an instrument in the hands of the former. The ULFA also makes an advocacy for destroying the nexus through violent means. Destruction is a pre-condition for gaining control over the natural wealth and resources of the region. An ULFA statement for instance, argues that 'the state apparatus' in India acts so much at the behest of the vested interests that "whenever the people of a nation [in an obvious reference to the community/nationality, SKD] wishes to assert its right over the national [jateeya] resources, it is sought to be silenced through guns and bayonets"." In other words, resources of the region are taken to be 'national' in the sense that they belong to the nation/ community inhabiting it and the ULFA demands an absolute right to ownership and control over them.

Revelations by Scholars

Most of the research studies on the subject under review tend to conclude that a community's attempts at establishing control over sub-territorial resources coincide in time with the emergence of a middle class from within its ranks. It is nevertheless true that the potential strength of the middle class varies from one society to another. G.S. Arora's research -perhaps the only of its kind ever conducted in the region in question, amply demonstrates that the emergence of a "commercial and bureucratic middle class" basically thriving on the non-productive, tertiary sector has not disrupted "the traditional system of (natural) inter-dependence", but created class differentiations within the community and has led to "a large-scale decimation of natural forests in the eastern Himalayas". As a result, hundreds of tribal people who are now hardly left with any other means of wherewithal except dependence on natural forests, are simply thrown on to the road to permanent penury and total devastation.

Negatively speaking, the question that the ascendent ethnic communities have brought to the forefront is not so much that since the resources are both life-bearing and non-replenishable, their mindless destruction by outsiders is destined to spark off a crisis of survival for the native communities—sooner rather than later. The question as we have said, is rather one of simply getting hold of the resources on the ground that they are indigenous to the region. If the communities are handsomely compensated - albeit in crude monetary terms, for what they have been divested off, they see no reason why they should grumble against indiscriminate and mindless extraction of their resources. Besides, there is no guarantee that if ownership and control pass over to the autochthonous hands from those of the aliens and outsiders, the ecological problems will automatically take care of themselves. The indifference of the autochthonous communities can be as much, maybe, more acute and dangerous than that of their adversaries. Such a caveat has recently been sounded by a group of socially responsible political economists. Pranab Bardhan, for example, maintains:

> ... one cannot wish away some of the externalities of the development process which the decentralised authority of local communities are unable and sometimes unwilling to cope with ... one such example of externality and inadequacy of local control mechanism is in the case of upstream deforestation causing floating and soil erosion in the downstream countries. Another case is when the local community is not only insensitive to larger environmentalist concerns, or when issue of local livelihood competes with preservationist issue."

Hence, more than simple ownership and control, much will depend definitely on how the communities propose to use the resources and most importantly, whether and to what extent their preferred modalities of use are compatible with the larger and longer-term concern of their sustainability and that of the mankind as a whole.

In this connection, it may not be out of place to note that some of the insurgent outfits operating in north-eastern India have already earned a notoriety for having pushed the issue deliberately under the carpet. A significant part of their funding is believed to have flown from their involvement in (illegal) trading in natural resources—forests, minerals, coal, etc., which they allegedly sell at throwaway prices to non-ethnic businessmen in order to meet their already massive and ever-shooting expenditures. The Bodo Militant Force (Bd. M.F.), for instance, was singularly blamed for rapid deforestation in the predominantly Bodo-inhabited areas along the northern banks of the Brahmaputra as early as in the late 1980s. Prem Singh Brahma, the Chairman of the organisation, has, however, categorically denied the a] legation: "...We have engaged ourselves in the movement keeping the interests of the Bodo people in mind; if we wipe out the forests, we are going to be the ultimate losers, If you go to the interior (villages), you will notice how our people are guarding our [sic] forests". Besides, the deep and dense jungles of these areas often provide safe hideouts for the militants who are on the run, beyond the prying eyes of the security forces. Their presence not only disturbs the flora and fauna of the region but goes a long way in impairing the ecological balance as a whole. While a proper ecological audit of their performance is still a far cry, they can only afford to neglect the crisis at their own peril.

It seems that a glimmer of ecological consciousness is slowly catching the imagination of the ethnic groups and more particularly, the organisations claiming to act at their behest. They are showing signs of gradually coining to terms with the quandary that has so far beset their political practice. In May 1994, ULFA issued what it had dubbed as 'the last warning' in which it fervently pleaded for "the preservation of the resources for future generations". To my mind, none of the ethnic organisations in the region has brought in the issue of 'preservation' for the benefit of the future generations' ever before. ULFA's concern for the 'future generation' has placed the issue of ethnicity in the larger perspective of its sustenance and reproduction. The plea is, however, based on the assumption that once ownership and control pass on to the hands of the Autochthonous communities and are effectively freed from the clutches of the vested interests, the issue of long-term sustainability will automatically take care of itself. For ULFA, the ecological conundrum is very much an epiphenomenon of the existing relations of production. Will the ethnic organisations of the north-east be prepared to undergo what Thomas S. Kuhn has called, a 'paradigm shift' in the next century?

Ethnic communities in the next Century have also to grapple with what in contemporary social science is designated as the women's question. It has been seen that ethnic assertion all over the world including India has made women particularly vulnerable to patriarchal pressures. In this connection, attention to only three factors which, in combination, have contributed to the vulnerability of women: first, the female members of a community are everywhere burdened with the special responsibility of embodying, that is, incorporating in their bodies, the honour of their community with the effect that the community is. Honour is represented by the inviolability of the female body. The community and its women thus share the same symbolic field in which one is taken to be the synonym for another. A report prepared by a Militant organisation of Kashmir way back in July 1990, warns "the women that severe action will be taken if they do not maintain purdah" and on 13 May 1993, members of Dukhtaran-e-Millat (Daughters of the Nation) asks its women "not to come outside without wearing burqa" as prescribed by the Islamic law." Even an organisation like the ULFA, that by its own admission, Subscribes to 'Socialism' as one of its ideological creeds asks 'the mothers and sisters' of Assam to wear mekhela-chador (a skirt considered to be typical of the Assamese women) and discard such dresses and apparels that are supposedly alien to the land. Similarly, the ULFA's call for observing Bihu (a festival marking the harvesting season—once again considered to be typical of the state's culture) in the open (mukoli bihu) was construed by one and all as an important step necessary for protecting female bodies form public exposure and commodification inside closeted parlours and auditoria meant for commercial uses. All this points out how the community's symbols are etched oil to the female body, and in the same vein are wrenched away from their biological subjects. Male members, oil the other hand, do not have to share any such responsibility. Their bodies are looked upon as essentially virile whether as resolute defenders of their community/women or as instruments invested with the biological potential of undermining the honour of other communities/women.

Secondly and as a corollary to the first, since female bodies are burdened with the special responsibility of bearing in them the honour of their community, the only way to undermine the honour of their community is to violate them. It is no wonder then, that their bodies become obvious sites of violation—rape, molestation, torture and intimidation and such other forms of gender-specific abuse. An Amnesty International report, for instance, argues that the incidence of rape in the north-east increases whenever counter- insurgency operations of the armed forces are in full swing.

Finally, the 'victimhood' of women is usually regarded as absolute not simply because their bodies are vulnerable to violation but because the violence they are met with, also deprives them of a language necessary for articulating their pathos and pains and voicing their minds. The fear of reprisal from their own community—should they refuse to bear the special responsibility assigned to them, is sometimes so acute that they do not find it expedient to come out in the open and speak their minds. The report of the Human Rights Watch cited above, notes that "the code of silence combined with fear prevents the people of Kashmir valley from openly condemning such abuses by the militant organisations". This has two major implications: on the one hand, anybody who minds the 'pain' violence has inflicted on her and complains about it, is publicly stigmatised as a black sheep unfaithful to her community. It is simply a taboo on their part to sixth sense pain and talk about it. In the absence of a language, she is unable to share her experience with the fellow victims for any such gesture is immediately regarded as an acknowledgement and therefore, 'sensation' of pain. She is singled out, individualised and showcased as one who has transgressed the norms of her community. 'Sensing' the pain is as good as being thrown out of the community. Two, any refusal to 'sense' pain also deprives the aggressor of the pleasure of violation and inflicting it on the victim. It thus shows the interstices of any act of aggression, howsoever brutal and savage that could be. Refusal viewed in this light, is not the supine acceptance of aggression unleashed against her as well as her community. Ironically, refusal may serve as a vehicle of protest.

Crises Faced by Women

In a world where hedonistic quest for individual happiness and concern with one's body have become nearly obsessive, it is very unlikely that pain will continue to remain 'unsensed' for far too long and voices of protest are already being heard in the far corners of the country. Apart from drawing public attention to the insurgency-related problems that the Naga mothers or women in general have to face, the Naga Mothers' Association has undertaken a series of pro-active measures that it hopes, would presage a new era of dialogue and understanding between the government and the underground rebels and pave the way to an early end to hostilities. The realisation that women everywhere have to bear the brunt of ethnic assertions is expected to bring about new and hitherto unknown gender cleavages within the community. Ethnic communities of the twenty-first century have to reckon with many of these cleavages, if they are to survive as solid and homogeneous communities. Moreover, since women everywhere are facing the same kind of crisis, it is not unlikely that their solidarity might cut across their respective communal boundaries. Such formations of trans-ethnic solidarity would be a stumbling bloc to the crystallisation and exacerbation of inter-ethnic divisions. Communities of the next century may not find it easy to 'discipline' their women in the way they have been doing at present and make the women perform what they have assigned to them without raising any hue and cry.

Human Right Issues

The question of rights is going to be one of the most hotly-debated questions in the next century. We all know that the community—ethnic, tribal or otherwise—has arrogated to itself the prerogative of defining the agenda of rights with the implication that all other types of right are now showing signs of being subsumed under community rights. Their subsumption means at least two things: on the one hand, feelings of alienation, deprivation and violation nowadays take on a communal character. Thus, it is alleged that the Assamese people are allowed to be swamped by the almost incessant influx of foreigners from across the borders because they are Assemese people whose language and culture are regarded as dispensable in the state's scheme of things. A similar plight according to them could not have happened to any other single ethnic community. From this it is just a small step to characterise the state in ethnic and communal terms. According to the National Socialist Council of Nagaland (now, Nagalim) (I-M), the Indian state champions and represents the cultural ethos of 'Aryavarta'. Its Manifesto accuses the Indian state of having introduced an absolutely unfamiliar and alien cultural ethos to the people of Nagaland.

Insofar as the community becomes ascendent in matters pertaining to the agenda of rights, it is likely to be plagued by a couple of anomalies which unless appropriately tackled, are bound to deal a debilitating blow to it: first, the position of an individual vis-a-vis her community may be one of the most knotty questions in the years to come. At one extreme, we may refer to the communitarians who seem to argue that since the individual is constituted by the community he/ she belongs to or may have chosen to belong to, 'he/she is what he/ she is by virtue of his/ her community that makes him/her what he/she is'. In such a situation, any plea for an individual's right (to dissent) against his/her community not only lacks substance but turns out to be overtly self-destructive. As the 'community thinks in him/her', he/ she cannot think of any right beyond the purview of his/her community. The survival of his/her community is a pre-condition of his/her enjoyment of rights. At another, we may conceive of those who in a truly Kantian fashion argue that rights essentially pertain to individuals and one can enjoy them to the extent that one is capable of 'emancipating' oneself from the tentacles of one's community. 'Dissolution of the community' according to them, is a pre-condition of the enjoyment of individual rights. Most of the discourses on rights in India fall somewhere between these two extremes.

We do not feel it necessary to delve into a discussion of the finer points of this otherwise fascinating controversy within the brief span of this paper. Suffice it to say here, what today looks like an apparently innocent theoretical controversy contains the potential of converting itself into one of the most crippling anomalies of the twenty-first century. Even if we assume that the individual is constituted by the community, it does not mean that the individual is necessarily bound by his/her community in every segment of his/her personal and social life. Nor does it imply, that the enjoyment of individual rights is always predicated on one's ability to successfully withstand its pressures or to dissociate from it. For an appreciation of this argument, we need to place it in the larger theoretical perspective. Communitarian Political Theory tells us that community, whatever it is—is based at the minimum, on a notion of what its proponents call 'public good', over and above the multifarious and conflicting interests of its individual members. Indeed, the notion is so strong that an individual member is often prepared to sacrifice his/her self-interest at the alter of the community, should a conflict arise between them. While any community at any given point of time is permeated by such a commonly-shared notion, the latter is neither given nor immutable. In other words, whatever freedom the individual may be said to enjoy in a society like that of India, it is very much in consonance with the broader parameters set forth by the individual's community.

In more positive terms, the individual is free to define the 'public good' of the community in the way he chooses and thereby enter into a debate on the notion with his fellow members. He is as Seyla Benhabib says, free to 'situate' himself within the community. Viewed in this light, individual freedom lies in his right to read his meanings into the notion. While a concern for the community and its 'good' is commonly shared, the question of what constitutes it, is subject to a plurality of representations. Rhoda Howard's distinction between 'traditional' and 'modern' communities may be instructive in this respect:

> There can be community in modern society, although it is weaker and thinner than community in traditional society.... I define community as a group of individuals who have a sense of obligation toward one another. The obligation can be thicker or thinner as one moves from smaller local communities such as the city or the nation.

It is a freedom that does not permit the individual to do away with the community. But it is surely one that enables him to renegotiate the terms of his relationship with the larger whole. The Assamese identity at no point of time was immune from such a plurality of representations." While 'modern' communities cannot be insensitive to the issues of individual rights and freedom, they may find it increasingly difficult to evolve requisite mechanisms through which a plurality of representations can be coordinated, orchestrated and effectively managed. Thus, it is not without reason that the Assamese society presently happens to be on its scams and the apparently no-holes barred consensus of the early-'80s has given way to the dangerous fragmentations of the '90s.

Secondly, as communities all over the world have started asserting their right to be different, the necessity of resolving (as distinguished from 'dissolving') their differences is bound to be more deeply felt: first of all, inasmuch as the differences give rise to inter-ethnic warfares and warfares appear to be increasingly unwinnable in any decisive manner by either of the parties involved in them, a Hobbesian 'war of all against all' proves to be mutually disastrous to both of them. It is in the fitness of things that the communities will try their best to get out of this impasse'. The conflict between the Nagas and the Kukis in the hills of Manipur and that between the Bodos and the Santhals in the northern plains of the Brahmaputra valley have been harmful to all who have joined them. Secondly, our experience of the recent past history has shown that the region is so composite in character that no amount of administrative re-organisation would be able to make the units ethnically homogeneous. It is a region where not only the minorities feel unsafe but the majorities are constantly under the threat of being reduced to minorities—thanks to the incessant flow of 'foreigners' from across the borders. The Assamese fear of being overwhelmed—both demographically and culturally by the immigrants, serves as a classic case in point. Last but not the least, the survival of a community as a distinct cultural entity today depends so much on the survival of mankind as a whole that it has made it obligatory on our part to respond to the pervasive crisis, including the ecological one, in a concerted and harmonious manner. The communities of tomorrow cannot simply afford to keep them aloof and isolated because they face a common crisis of survival and the very nature of the crisis demands that they come together and respond to it collectively.

These factors among other things, have already forced them to look forward and experiment with alternative modalities of resolving their differences. In this connection, it may not be irrelevant to refer to two rather distinct modalities that the communities of the next century may find highly effective in pursuing this objective: first, they may think it proper to agree with a set of rules and institutions which they believe would go a long way in bridging their mutual differences and ensuring their common survival. Neera Chandhoke, for instance, stipulates beforehand a number of such rules (based on such values as freedom, equality and democracy) which according to her, would be absolutely indispensable to the functioning of a macrocosm consisting of a multiplicity of them. While rules and values may be instrumental in bringing into existence the greater macrocosm or what she calls, civil society, both Paul Hirst and John Keane underline the inherent incapacity of the ethnic communities of the Third World countries to transcend their mutual differences and submit themselves to an over-arching civil society independently of the mediation of the state. Both of them—very unlike Chandhoke, recognise the importance of the state in organising and maintaining a civil society in these countries. There is no denying the fact that many communities of the north-east still look upon the Indian state as the agency par excellence for resolving inter-ethnic conflicts. I have argued elsewhere that the Assam movement (1979-85), despite its rabid intransigence on many other counts, was also marked by an unwavering faith in the Indian state for one of its principal objectives was to make the state do what it had not otherwise done—to build the nation and incorporate the Assamese community into its ambit." According to the perceptions crystallised in the course of the movement, the Indian state has 'abdicated' its responsibility of building the nation insofar as Assam is concerned.

The second modality seeks to articulate diverse ethnic communities into what Chantal Mouffie calls, "a radical political community". Quite analogous to the civil society, the political community is also governed by a set of commonly agreed-upon values. But whereas in a civil society, rules are of an 'overriding' nature always trying to prevent the communities from doing certain things that they, left to themselves, might do, the rules of apolitical community offer to the diverse ethnic communities a variety of 'subject positions' with which they can identify themselves and allow for a plurality of specific allegiances'. In other words, the establishment of a political community does not entail an obliteration of ethnic communities. On the contrary, it means that the 'plurality' that these communities represent, can be enacted and played out within its realm, Much, however, will depend on how respective communities can negotiate the terms of their relationship within it. The United Reservationist Minority Council of Assam's (URMCA) objective of transforming India into 'a voluntary Union of States' my be interpreted in this light. Since the Union is voluntary, each of the federal units retains the right to secede from it. The right gives each unit an opportunity to assert its subjectivity even beyond the federal framework. The right to secession, according to the Council, is an inseparable part of 'national self-determination'. Furthermore, states within the Indian Union 'may' and equally may not 'delegate some power' to the Centre. In other words, it is a political community without a Centre. With this de-centring in mind, URMCA seeks to unify and mobilise all the forces that are opposed to the centralisation of power in the hands of New Delhi. At the same time, the formation of such a political community presupposes what Chantal Mouffe calls, "deconstruction of certain identities". The collapse of 'Delhi-ism' for instance, is a prerequisite for the coming into being of a radical re-organisation of India's federal structure. It is a community that does not represent the antithesis of the 'sovereignty of federal units'

The world has changed unrecognisably and unless the communities change themselves to keep pace with these, the whirlwind of change is likely to sweep them away in the next century.

10

Economic Power

One of the fundamental questions over which economists have debated over centuries is concerned with the possible role of the state in stimulating economic activities. On the one hand, there are strong believers in the market mechanism who are against any state intervention. On the other hand, there are those who believe that the market mechanism is basically faulty and to correct market imperfections and failures, state intervention is essential. Extremists in the latter group talk about central planning and government control in every sphere of economic activity; those with less extreme views would like to use redistributive taxes and transfers as well as monetary and fiscal policy instruments. Not very long ago, governments all over the world believed in substantial doses of state intervention. It all started with the great depression of the 1930s. The great depression made economists believe that a free market economy, left on its own, might face periodic downswings. State intervention, in one form or another, was, therefore, thought to be necessary. The theoretical works of John Maynard Keynes provided the dominant economic doctrine in those days. Keynesians pointed out that the free market economy suffers from occasional crisis because of a lack of effective demand. To solve the problem, the state has to create demand artificially either by printing money or by taking up directly income and employment generating investment projects or both. Accordingly, from the mid-thirties governments tried out these Keynesian remedies to pull their countries out of the depths of the great depression.

The dominance of Keynesianism continued after the war right up to the beginning of the 1970s. Gradually, through imprudent and excessive use, Keynesian policies lost their credibility. Now, Keynesian policies can work only if there exists excess capacity all over the economy. If some sectors are supply constrained, demand generating Keynesiam policies are bound to give rise to inflation. This is exactly what happened in some of the countries of Latin America. Governments used Keynesianism as a shield to defend their budget deficits. The excessive volume of money printed every year was used to distribute favour to selected groups. This led to alarming hyperinflation and stagnation. At the same time, government run enterprises lacked economic incentives and exhibited marked inefficiencies. Theoretical developments, challenging Keynesianism, also gained force. By the 1980s the belief became widespread that the lack of government control was the key to economic prosperity. This belief was further strengthened by the downfall of the former Soviet bloc countries. By the early 1990s most developing countries as well as the former socialist nations were seriously talking about structural reforms.

It is in this background that we shall analyse and evaluate the recent policy changes in India. In particular, we shall look at the changing role of the Indian state in the process of economic development of the country. There are, in fact, three different but not mutually exclusive aspects of government intervention that we shall look at. First, we shall look at some micro-economic aspects of government intervention. Thus, for example, we shall discuss how in the past the government has intervened with the free market mechanism and how far the recent deviations from the earlier policy are desirable. Here, the focus of our discussion would be reforms related to international trade. Second, we shall look at the change in the attitude of the government towards macro economic stabilisation. Here, we shall look not only at the recent attempts of the government to reduce the budget deficit, but also at issues like devaluation and capital account convertibility. Finally, we shall look at the role of the state in human capital formation. In other words, we shall analyse the performance of government investment in certain key sectors like health and education. Investments in these sectors are essential for long-term growth and we shall see how the Indian state has fared in this regard.

In what follows, we shall discuss certain aspects of trade reforms in section 2. Section 3 talks about macro-economic stabilisation. In section 4, we look at the role of the state in human capital formation and as an investor in infrastructure. Section 5 concludes the paper.

Reform Measures

The Indian economy has gone through a long period of government control. Right from independence up to the mid-eighties, economic activity, to a large extent, was moulded by the state through successive five year plans. Taxes and quantitative restrictions on the volume of transactions distorted prices. These distortions were especially present in the sphere of international trade. During the heydays of planning, special emphasis was put on attaining self-reliance. As a consequence, deliberate restrictions were put on international movements of goods and services. An important part of structural reforms, therefore, consists of removing the restrictions on international trade. In this section, we shall talk about the possible consequences of removing such restrictions. We shall, in particular, talk about three specific trade-related reforms. First we shall talk about the economic consequences of removal of tariffs and quantitative restrictions on imports. Second, we shall discuss the advantages and disadvantages of direct foreign investment in the Indian context. Third, we shall talk about the effects of trade liberalisation in the agricultural sector.

Starting with David Ricardo, there is a long tradition among scholars of international economics to uphold free trade. Free trade, it is argued, maximises welfare through efficient allocation of resources. Trade, it is further argued, acts as an engine of growth as well as a vehicle of progress and development. Then, why have less-developed countries like India resorted to protectionism in the past?

One of the arguments put forward in favour of protectionism is the so-called infant industry argument. The argument is put forward in the context of less-developed countries in particular. In a less developed country, the level of technology is in general backward as compared to that of developed nations. This implies, among other things, that costs of production are higher in the less-developed countries. As long as the costs are higher, these countries are unable to compete with their developed counterparts. Thus, it is argued that in the initial stages of development, industries in less-developed countries need to be protected from outside competition. It is pointed out that over time, through learning effects and increasing returns to scale, these infant industries would become more efficient and would be able to compete in the world market. When such efficiency is reached, protection may be withdrawn.

In the case of India, as in the cases of many other less-developed countries, the infant-industry-protection argument has not worked very well. Indian industries received tariff and quota protections for a long time, yet they failed to mature. Prolonged tariff protection led Indian firms to believe that protectionist policies would continue indefinitely in the future. This created a serious disincentive to improve technological levels and reduce costs. Because of the lack of competition, R&D (research and development) expenditure was kept to a minimum. In short, Indian industries failed to reap the long-term benefits of protectionism. There were, on the other hand, inefficiencies associated with protectionist policies. The most serious of them was that protectionism gave rise to domestic monopolies. Under tariff protection, domestic monopoly houses restricted output to charge higher prices. Lower output meant lower employment and lower national income. By the middle of the 1980s it was realised that the policy of excessive protectionism could not work any longer. Then, at the beginning of the last decade of the twentieth century, India was plunged into a serious balance of payments crisis. The crisis forced the country to borrow from the International Monetary Fund (IMF) and the latter in its turn imposed conditionalities on the loan. The conditional required that India would open herself more to the international market. Over the next few years, tariffs and import quotas were significantly reduced. How far were these reductions justified?

The most important reason behind the reduction of tariff and quantitative barriers was that protectionism gave rise to monopolies. On the other hand, a case for partial protection could be established if under some tariff protection, domestic output and employment could be expected to increase. The two, taken together, would imply that if tariffs could be reduced to the point where domestic monopolies are forced to charge competitive prices and produce competitive outputs, then the optimal would be achieved. Let us see how this may be done.

If full tariff protection is granted, that is, if imports become virtually restricted, the monopolist will charge a monopoly price and produce a restricted monopoly output. When tariffs are reduced, the consumers have the option of buying from the international market and therefore the monopolist, in order to remain in the market, must charge a lower price. But as the price goes down, market demand will go up and the monopolist will expand output. It is to be noted that as tariffs are reduced, the domestic monopolist virtually becomes a price taker. How far should tariffs be reduced? Theoretically, tariffs should be reduced up to the point where the tariff-ridden international price (which is also the price the monopolist is forced to charge) is equal to the marginal cost of production, that is, the cost of producing air additional unit of output. This is precisely the point where the competitive output and price gets determined. Accordingly, at this point, the optimal tariff is also implicitly determined.

The net offshoot of the discussion is that for a less-developed country the optimal tariff is positive. At this optimal tariff, employment and output is maximised in the country. Thus, optimal structural change does not require the country to go for complete free trade; the government must intervene and set tariffs at the optimal level.

Advocates of liberalisation and structural reforms argue that one of the main advantages of lifting government imposed barriers to international transactions is that it will make the inflow of foreign capital more easy. It is pointed out that inflow of foreign capital or foreign direct investment is a desirable thing because it creates employment in the domestic country. In other words, if an additional unit of a product is imported from abroad, it creates additional jobs in a foreign country. If, on the other hand, foreign capital comes into the country and produces this unit with the help of domestic labour, it would evidently increase domestic employment. This is, in short, the argument for encouraging foreign direct investment. We shall show that this argument cannot be accepted without qualifications.

Casual empiricism suggests that in the past while some countries have benefited quite a bit from the inflow of foreign capital, some others have not been able to make any notable progress in spite of significant foreign direct investment. Roughly speaking, countries with small domestic markets, that is, countries like Taiwan, Singapore, Hong Kong or even Thailand and Malaysia have had a good experience with foreign direct investment. On the other hand, countries with large domestic markets, like Brazil or Mexico, have not been able to reap the full benefits of foreign capital inflow. One wonders, is there any negative connection between foreign direct investment and the size of the domestic market?' In fact, we shall argue that is indeed the case.

There are, in fact, two main reasons for foreign firms to invest in a less-developed country like India. First, a foreign firm may wish to set up a plant or a factory in a less-developed country simply because the domestic market is large. By setting up a plant in that country, the firm can serve the domestic market without any worries about tariffs or transportation costs. This is clearly an advantage. Secondly, the firm may set up a factory in a less-developed country because labour and other raw materials are cheaper there. In the latter case, the main objective of the foreign firm is to produce at a lower cost in the less-developed country but sell the product in the international market. In a recent survey, several foreign firms were interviewed and specifically asked why they wanted to invest in India. Most of them considered the largeness of the Indian market as the prime cause for investing in the country. Proximity to cheaper sources of inputs including cheap labour along with an objective to export were apparently less important reasons.

We would now argue that foreign investment, which comes to a less-developed country primarily to serve the domestic market and not to export, might create a number of problems and may actually decrease the level of employment in the domestic country. On the other hand, if the commodities produced with foreign capital are mainly exported, then the domestic country will experience an unambiguous increase in its level of employment.

Our argument is as follows. Suppose the country concerned is small. This means that the amount of goods the domestic market can absorb is limited. When there is a fresh inflow of foreign capital into this country, new goods and services are produced. Since the domestic market is limited, these goods cannot be absorbed domestically. Hence they are exported. This directly leads to an increase in the level of employment in the country. The profit generated in the production of these additional exports accrues to the foreign firms. This profit is repatriated abroad in foreign exchange. The additional foreign exchange requirement is, of course, met by additional exports. There is no balance of payments crisis.

If, on the other hand, the domestic market is large, the additional goods produced by foreign capital will be absorbed domestically. Additional profit will be generated which will be repatriated abroad in foreign exchange. Where will this additional foreign exchange come from? In this case, there has been no increase in exports. Thus, to pay for profit repatriation in foreign exchange, the country will face a balance of payments deficit. It can handle the balance of payments deficit in different ways. First, to reduce the deficit, the exchange rate may be devalued. This may solve the balance of payments crisis but will invariably increase the rate of inflation. Second, if the country does not want to devalue its exchange rate, it will have to increase its exports, to solve the balance of payments problem, by reducing domestic absorption.

Reduction in domestic absorption will be possible only if the level of income and employment goes down in the country. A possible channel through which domestic absorption may fall and exports increase is a process of general deflation. In this case, exports will increase because of lower prices and increased competitiveness in the world market. At the same time, with lower prices and relatively rigid money wages, the real wage will go up which will lead to a reduction in output and employment. Thus, in short, a country with a large domestic market will have to handle the balance of payments problem associated with a fresh inflow of foreign capital, either by allowing devaluation and inflation or by bringing about a general deflation and a corresponding fall in the level of employment and output.

The above argument apparently does not fit into the recent Chinese experience. The People's Republic of China has, in recent years, been able to achieve a spectacular rate of growth. Undoubtedly, this high rate of growth has been partly made possible by a high inflow of foreign capital into the Country. It is also true that the domestic market in China is quite large. Does it contradict the theory we are proposing?

Actually, the economic success of China, in our opinion, lies in the perfect synchronisation of government intervention with an inflow of foreign capital. In China, the government, by imposing suitable restrictions, has been able to direct foreign capital exclusively to the export sector. This has resulted in a booming export sector and a consequent growth in output and employment. The Indian government can pretty well learn a lesson from the Chinese experience about how one should go about handling the inflow of foreign investment in a country with a large domestic market.

Structural reformists, both in India and abroad, have repeatedly pointed out that no liberalisation programme can be completed without introducing free trade in the agricultural sector. The Indian agricultural sector, so far, has been insulated from the world market. Before the green revolution, India, had to import food grains to meet occasional deficits. But afterwards, when production increased significantly, and a surplus situation was created, exports were not encouraged. Advocates of liberalisation argue that this policy of export restriction has had a discriminatory effect against the producers in the agricultural sector. It is pointed out that if the farmers had been allowed to sell their products in the world market, they could have got a much higher price than they got domestically. In this sense, the government, by disallowing exports, had forced the terms of trade to go against the agricultural sector.

Throughout the 1960s and 1970s the arguments of the Leftist economists in India were just the opposite. Their argument was that the big farmers and traders lobbied with the government to keep agricultural prices artificially high. Thus, on account of high agricultural prices, higher wages had to be paid in the industrial sector, which, in turn, thwarted industrial growth. Moreover, in some cases, industrial wages did not catch up with the rising food prices. This led to a reduction in the real wages and the purchasing power of the industrial workers. The reduction in the purchasing power of the industrial workers reduced effective demand for industrial goods leading to on industrial recession. In short, the leftists argued that throughout the 1960s and 1970s, the industry-agriculture terms of trade went in favour of the agricultural sector and this was a major cause of industrial recession.

The reformists, favouring free trade in agricultural goods, have made some calculations to support their argument. They have calculated that even if all subsidies on agriculture are removed, but the farmers are just allowed to sell their product at the free world market price, they will be significantly better off. It is well known that in India agricultural subsidies cause a significant drain on the government exchequer. Thus, free trade will not only make the farmers better off, but will also make it easier for the government to balance its budget.

The argument of the reformists regarding free trade in agricultural goods has to be examined carefully. It is clear that the opening up of international trade in the agricultural sector will increase agricultural prices. The rise in agricultural prices, especially the price of food grains, will have a direct impact on poverty. The poor in the urban sector will be adversely affected because they spend most of their income on food. In fact, if food prices go up, most of them would have to manage with a lesser amount of food and hence the level of poverty and starvation will go up. Since food is a necessity, the middle class and the rich in the urban sector will now have to devote a higher fraction of their income on food thus reducing their expenditure on industrial goods. This will reduce industrial demand.

Scene in Rural Areas

In the rural sector, too, the poor will be adversely affected. It is well known that the rural poor in our country consist of landless labourers and small farmers. These people have hardly any marketable surplus to offer. Thus, they will not benefit from the price rise. On the other hand, most of them have to buy a part of their consumption requirements from the market. As the prices rise, they will lose out as consumers. The effect, once more, will be an increase in rural poverty. In fact, it is the large farmers and big agricultural traders who will gain most from the price rise. The middle farmers will also gain. These people will increase their demand for industrial goods. This increase has to be weighed against the fall in demand coining from the industrial sector. The net effect on industrial demand, therefore, is ambiguous. Finally, as trade opens up, the farmers' income will become more volatile due to fluctuations in world prices. In a country like India, where there is little insurance available in the agricultural sector and where income is always fluctuating due to the vagaries of nature, further fluctuations are clearly undesirable. To summarise, opening up of trade in food grains will increase poverty, at best it will have all ambiguous effect on industrial demand, and add to the uncertainty in the agricultural sector. One should take all these things into consideration before one thinks of opening up agriculture to international trade.

Much has been written on the need for macro-stabilisation, especially the need for the government to balance its budget in a less developed country like India. In fact, when the IMF gave a loan to the Indian government, it required the government to reduce its budget deficit to the maximum extent possible. The main logic behind the reduction of a budget deficit is that by reducing wasteful government expenditure, it checks inflation. If inflation is lower, domestic goods become more competitive in the world market and therefore, exports go up. This would enable the debtor country to pay back its loans more easily. India, in fact, has been able to impose quite a bit of fiscal discipline on herself in recent years. Budget deficits have not been alarmingly high, like they had been in some Latin American countries, and consequently, the rate of inflation has also remained manageable.

The other requirement of the IMF is that the government should make the Indian rupee fully floating and convertible. There was a sharp devaluation of the rupee at the beginning of the '90s decade when the IMF loan was taken. That devaluation was aimed at raising export earnings and reducing import bills, thereby easing the balance of payments situation. After that massive devaluation, the value of the Indian rupee, although showing a downward trend, had not exhibited any wide fluctuation. The relative stability of the rupee becomes particularly pronounced if we compare it with other all Asian currencies. Clearly, the monetary and Fiscal authorities in India have done a good job.

The other recommendation of the IMF regarding full convertibility of the rupee is to be looked at with caution. Recent experiences of some of the south east Asian countries like South Korea suggest that full convertibility of the domestic currency may lead to wide fluctuations in the exchange rate, balance of payments and the national income. In particular, with the domestic currency fully convertible, a sudden change in the expectations of foreign investors may lead to serious capital outflows. These outflows are often magnified by speculative attacks. In other words, the experiences of some of the south-east Asian countries suggest that for a country like India, where investments are still risky from the point of view of foreigners, it is not prudent to make the domestic currency fully convertible in the near future.

Even strong believers in the market mechanism would agree that the government has to undertake certain investments which the private sector will not find worthwhile to take up. These investments create positive externalities for the economy as a whole. The most important examples of such investments are investments in health, education and infrastructure. These investments are especially important for developing economies. It has been repeatedly emphasised by Sen and others that in India, the state should increase the volume of such investments so as to attain a reasonable rate of long-term growth. There can be little doubt about the importance of their assertion. However, the manner in which these investments need to be undertaken is never clearly specified. Let us take the example of investment in education.

Education and Literacy

It is no doubt true that education levels in India, as measured by literacy rates, are quite poor. It is, therefore, suggested that the government should spend more money for providing education to the people, especially to the poor. It is, thus, implicitly assumed that the educational level will improve if the supply of educational services goes up. We shall argue that the problem lies not only with the supply but also with the demand. It is to be noted that in villages where the government has provided free schools, the dropout rates are pretty high. Why are the dropout rates high? They are high simply because the prospective students do not find it worthwhile to go for primary or even secondary education.

The fact of the matter is that on the one hand, there is a tremendous disparity in the earning levels of the educated and the uneducated workers and, on the other hand, there is a very large gap between the educational levels of the educated and the uneducated. The affluent person wants his children to reach a high educational level and earn a high income. To guarantee this, the typical affluent family over-invests in education. There is over-investment because the number of vacancies in good colleges and universities are limited.

The poor, on the other hand, know that it has to invest a lot in order to go to the high income group. It is impossible for the poor to invest that amount of money. But investing a little, which is the amount the poor can afford, does not make any significant difference in his level of earning. Thus, he has no incentive to invest at all. In other words, because of over-investment by the affluent group, it becomes prohibitively expensive for the poor to invest in education. We wish to point out that unless this anomaly in investment across classes is removed, the government policy of simply increasing the number of free schools is not going to work.

As for the health sector, in our opinion, the problem is more related to the proper implementation of government-run health programmes rather than to under-investment in health by the government. It is often forgotten that government expenditure (as a percentage of the GNP) in the health sector in India is among the highest in Asia. Yet, most Indians, who can afford it, prefer to go to the private sector for health services. Even the less affluent, who can ill afford private health services, go beyond their means and go to the private sector for health care. This simply points to the massive inefficiency with which health services are run by the government.

Finally, the importance of investment in infrastructure can be hardly overstated. Investment, growth and infrastructural facilities have a very high co-relation. It is, therefore, necessary for the government to provide infrastructure before it could expect investment to grow in the country. But once more, implementation is a problem. Take, for example, the case of telecommunications. Development of tele-communications is a pre-condition for industrialisation and growth. But in India, the telecommunications industry is dominated by the government and, as expected, is run very inefficiently. It could do a lot of good to the country if some competition from the private sector could be brought in. The same comment applies as far as construction and maintenance of roads and highways are concerned. The inefficiency of the government makes one wonder if some private capital could be brought in here as well.

In this chapter, we considered the question of state intervention in various economic activities in India. We looked at this old question in the background of the recent suggestions of structural reforms. While we certainly agree that there is a pressing need for government de-control in many key areas of economic activity in the country we pointed out that there were certain other areas where the free market has to be introduced with more caution. In particular, we looked at a few trade-related reforms and came to the conclusion that there are certain negative aspects to these reforms. In other words, the government should not go for an all-out policy of free trade as is often suggested. A similar caution is to be applied to the international movement of capital in and out of the country. Finally, we tried to evaluate very briefly the role of the government in long-term developmental expenditure. We came up with the conclusion that in many instances, especially in the case of health and infrastructure, efficient utilisation of funds seems to be more of a problem than the lack of expenditure.

Menace of Population

India constitutes only 2.4 per cent of the world's land area. But we comprise 14 per cent of the world's population.

In the beginning of the century, we were 238 millions. In 1971, we swelled up to 548 millions. We more than doubled ourselves.

During 1971-75, our birth rate recorded an annual growth of 2.6 per cent.

Experts estimate that (a) at present 55,000 babies are born every day in India; (b) each year there are 21 million births and 8 million deaths, i.e., a net annual addition of 13 million. Thus, we have already been crossed the 1,000 million mark.

In concrete terms, this means that every year we will need 1.265 lakh more schools, four lakh more teachers, 25 lakh more houses, 1,887 lakh more metres of cloth, 125 million quintals more of foodgrains and 40 lakh more jobs not to speak of corresponding additional medical and recreational facilities.

Despite vigorous efforts, Free India has yet miles and miles to go to ensure a reasonable standard of living to most of our brothers and sisters who now number about 600 million. Will we be at all able to generate in 24 years, the barest minimum resources to cater for another 400 million?

In the circumstances, can any patriot question the imperative need for arresting our galloping population growth, which sets at naught the most ambitious and vigorously-pursued programmes of our well-meaning planners?

All these years, our family planning message has been purely negative. It is high time that it is made positive.

Family planning guidance should not merely be confined to stressing the need for performing the sex act without causing pregnancy. It should extend to physical culture, yogic exercises, steps to gradually develop self-restraint and the all-round blessing of sober life.

We should educate our people about the evils of over-indulgence, the debilitating effects-physical and mental-of unrestrained conjugal life. The sanctity of family life, its purpose, and the joys and rewards of a regulated, disciplined life should also be emphasised.

The main plank of the programme should be to liberate people from the oppressive atmosphere with its over-emphasis on sex to the point of making them feel that obsession with sex is the most natural thing in life.

There is such a proliferation of pornographic literature today that even many respectable publications are turning lewd and can no more be read together by all members of a family. "Sales dropping? Add a liberal dose of sex." That seems to be the easy solution. At whose cost? Surely, this is a region where the government can easily step in. It can discourage in a thousand ways those publications which are clearly bent on making money by peddling sex. They should be sternly dealt with and those others which are tending to be so should be suitably warned.

As for advertising, sex appeal has become a "must". A casual glance at any newspaper or periodical any day is enough to convince that everything from a cake of soap to a plane ticket is being advertised with the aid of sex. Are we so bankrupt of ideas? Cannot the government devise measures to discourage advertisements which are blatantly sex-oriented?

True, of late, there are some advertisements—their number is yet so small-which belong to the morally-elevating category. Cannot the government provide incentives to encourage this trend?

Another major corrupting influence, of course, is the modern cinema with its money-spinning formula of sex and crime. While the government should help those films that measure up to aesthetic standards, it should not hesitate to put down the pernicious ones.

While there is the need for popularising by all the available means, the message of a smaller family, let there not be the open invitation to people to enjoy without paying the 'price'.

On the positive side, let people be exposed to the minimum of temptations and be educated in the benefits that flow from living a moral and religious life.

The need for ensuring the quality of children should also be stressed. And indeed healthy and good children will only be born out of prayerful longing of the parents.

Let me quote a moving passage from Swami Vivekananda: "Why should mother be worshipped? Because she made herself pure. She underwent harsh penances sometimes to keep herself as pure as purity can be. For, mind you, no woman in India thinks of giving up her body to any man; it is her own. When a man comes in physical contact with his wife the circumstances she controls through what prayers and through what vows! It is the greatest prayer between man and wife, the prayer that is going to bring into the world another soul fraught with a tremendous power for good or for evil. Is it a joke ' Is it a simple nervous satisfaction? Is it a brute enjoyment of the body? The child must be prayed for.

"Those children that come with curses, that slip into the world, just in a moment of inadvertance, because that could not be prevented what can we expect of such progeny?" The patriot-prophet of India spoke these words from the innermost depths of his being, and today modern science itself is recognising the value of pre-natal influence about which extensive studies are being conducted.

For example, Dr. Alexis Carrel, a Nobel Prize winning biologist, warns: "The drunkenness of wife or husband at the moment of fecundation is a positive crime, for children conceived in such conditions often suffer from incurable nervous or mental taints. Generally speaking, parents who are rash enough to ignore the obligations of eugenism are automatically punished by their own children."

What Dr. Ashley Montague, an authority on genetics, says about pre-natal influence is also worth remembering: "During the pre-natal period, that is, the nine months between conception and birth, a human being is more receptible to his environment than he will ever be again in his life. What happens to him then can help him in his development, or it can hinder him; it can promote his growth or it can interrupt it.... The events that take place before his birth, and his reactions, to them will influence him for the rest of his life. When he is 20 or 40 or 60 there will still be aspects of his body or his mind or his emotions that will be traceable directly to the influence that acted on him before he was born."

In other words, bringing up good and healthy children does not merely depend upon the number begotten, or feeding them with the choicest baby food or giving them the costliest education. The self-restraint and discipline and the moral standards of the parents have the greatest bearing on the birth of good children.

How many couples who are constantly being bombarded with incitements for unbridled sexual indulgence are aware of this ancient, eternal truth which has been attested by the findings of modern science?

We must not be hasty in adopting wholesale Western concepts though certainly we should not fight shy of accepting anything that is positively beneficial from any part of the world once we are convinced of their suitability to our conditions.

Take the case of sex education itself. There are many amidst us who vigorously plead for it without even waiting to understand its impact on the nations which have gone in for it. Dr. Bickshoff, writing in the famous British medical magazine, Lancet, avers: "In all countries where sex-instruction has been widely adopted, there has been a phenomenal increase in illegitimate births (almost doubling in eleven years in Britain). There has also been a lowering of the age of the illegitimately pregnant and of those who commit aggressive, sexually symbolic offences (formerly committed by adults only); and the increasing immaturity of parents has resulted in more psychiatric disturbance in their offspring. A senior girls' remand home, known since 1952, has recently turned turtle in character. Originally the girl with sexual experience was unusual and pregnancy was rare, but now all girls interviewed have had sexual experience and the most common offence is some form of flight, coupled with sexual misdemeanour; pregnancy is fairly commonplace and abortion not unknown.

"All these girls, in contrast to those of 1952, have had full sex and V.D. instruction, and most have received instruction, illustrated by dramatic pictures, films, and even pathological specimens, about contraception and abortion".

In modern India there is a tendency among the so-called "progressives" to dub as "Puritans" anyone who talks of self-restraint, ethics, religion or morality. But when it comes to fundamental matters of national interest, every voice deserves to be heard.

Prof. Wigfield, another eminent medical authority, says: "Education should be towards civilization and citizenship. To adulthood rather than adultery. To personal pride, self-esteem, responsibility and altruism .... At least our self-appointed educators should learn not to make sex synonymous with orgasm."

In India, the ideal of *brahmacharya* even in *grihasthashrama*, is time-honoured. Let us hold up before the people the ideal of *brahmacharya*. It has its positive effects on physical and mental health, in addition to the much-needed advantage of restricting the number of children. The union of husband and wife for the sake of children is not considered a violation of *brahmacharya* by our shastras.

In this age of science, it is absolutely essential to stress the physiological processes involved in the process of celibacy, to quote Dr. M. Sivaram: "The spermatozoa are produced in the germinal layer of the testes. A hormone from the pituitary gland stimulates the production of the sperms. This hormone is called the follicular stimulating hormone. The sperms produced by the several groups of germinal cells, flow out through various seminferous tubules into a main spermatic duct. The spermatic duct passes through two glands, the prostate and the seminal vesicles. These glands pour their secretions on to the sperms and thus the semen is fully conditioned. When the semen that has accumulated is discharged as in a sex-act or wet dream, then the germinal cells of the testes start producing another batch of sperms.

"The supply is conditioned by the demand. If for some reason or the other the semen is not discharged, then the germinal layers of the testes lie dormant. The follicular-stimulating hormone is not utilised and the body can make use of it for other purposes; mainly for mental and meditative purpose."

Every religion has emphasised the virtue of self-control and every moral giant, through the ages, has been a standing demonstration of the benefits of a self-regulated life.

It is true that self-control cannot be practised by all at all times. But that does not mean that the ideal should be lost sight of and not propagated. If a man with an ideal commits a hundred mistakes, a man without one would commit a thousand mistakes. So it is always good and necessary to place the highest of ideals before our people and educate them to make an earnest and honest effort.

Better Living Standards

The quality of life is more important than life itself. Is sex the be-all and end-all of life? Certainly not.

At the same time let us not view sex from the puritan angle as something vulgar and debasing.

It has its place in life. It is sacred. It is divine. It has its role in married life to be instrumental in giving birth to quality children who will flower into responsible, disciplined citizens of tomorrow to ensure the unbroken continuity of the family of man.

Family planning, devoid of a positive approach, will surely lead to sex anarchy, with catastrophic consequences to the individual, to the family and to the nation. It is already changing the lives of men and women more radically than any other revolution of our time. And it is giving birth to an ugly child-Drug Culture, which is fast establishing itself as a significant symbol of youth culture. Therefore, it is imperative that effective steps should be taken expeditiously to transform family planning into planning for citizenship.

11

Security for Peace

Protagonists of realism in international relations have recently challenged the thesis of increased interaction and interdependence as guarantors of 'strategic stability'. In an effort to rehabilitate the legitimacy of balance of power politics, they have undermined the role of international or regional cooperative institutions in promoting the cause of global peace. Institutions have been essentially seen in this literature as reflections of distribution of power in world politics where institutions of cooperation do not exert any 'independent effect on behaviour'. This unfortunately represents a pessimistic and skeptical attitude to international politics. On the other hand, a number of scholars stress the importance of interdependence and cooperative bilateralism—especially at regional levels—in changing traditional state behaviours and preferences. This argument is in consonance with the institutional approach to international politics which considers institutions as capable of discouraging states 'from calculating self-interest', thereby reducing possibilities of war. Studies have demonstrated how states can mutually benefit through free flow of information, reduced transaction costs, credible commitments and reciprocal actions.' In this perspective inter-state cooperative engagements can create conditions for a peaceful world. Mention may be made of confidence-building measures through cooperative monitoring, sharable technologies and treaty verification system.' The broad objective here is to enhance regional security by containing the urge to acquire mass destructive weapons, developing arrangements for cooperative security and applying existing technology for new cooperative applications. Such cooperative monitorings are designed to compliment and not replace national capabilities. Placing itself within this analytical framework, this article identifies the potential for Indo-Pak constructive bilateralism that should create conditions for regional stability in south Asia.

South Asia is a site of multiple contradictions. It represents only 3 per cent of the world's area, but houses 21 per cent of the earth's population. The region is a repository of rich and mostly untapped natural resources, but remains one of the world's poverty-stricken areas. The sub continent has the potential of being the largest market for industrial products, although it continues to be an underdeveloped economic region—plagued by unemployment, inadequate economic growth and insufficient social progress. Again, south Asia constitutes an environmental region with a conjoint ecological cycle and a common river, ocean and mountain system. It shares a rich cultural legacy too. Yet, the region remains a fragmented entity, characterised by 'desegregated' levels of power potential, strategic dissonance and political complexities.

India and Pakistan—the two major constituents of South Asia naturally share the region's economic, social and political distortions. In terms of human development indicators their positions are almost similar—India, occupying the 132nd and Pakistan the 134th rank among the 174 nation states. The following indicators are illustrative. Between 1980 and 1992 the GDP per capita average annual growth rate for India and Pakistan was only 3.1 per cent. While the percentage increase in human development index in India declined from 43.7 per cent in the 1960s to 29.1 per cent in 1993, the fall for Pakistan in the same period was from 56.8 per cent to 36.9 per cent. The under-five mortality rate for India in 1993 was 122 per thousand live births as against 137 in Pakistan. Physician availability per 100 people in 1990 in India and Pakistan were respectively 2.5 and 2.9. Adult literacy rate in 1992 was 49.9

per cent for India and 35.7 per cent for Pakistan. Indian and Pakistani governments spend respectively 17 per cent and 28 per cent of its budget for defense, although the share for health and education in the national budget of either country does not exceed 4 per cent. Both in India and Pakistan there is an acute concentration of wealth. In 1993 the per capita income for the lowest 20 per cent of the Indian population was 537. US dollars compared to 3,306 US dollars for the highest 10 per cent of the population. For the same year the per capita income for Pakistan's lowest 20 per cent of the population was 911. US dollars as against 5,468. US dollars for the highest 10 per cent of the population.' The fruits of development thus tend to be monopolised by a microscopic minority in both south Asian states. According to a World Bank study, India is today "home to the majority of the world's poor". While the rate of poverty reduction, particularly in the rural sector. slowed down dramatically in the nineties, the gap between the rich and poor in India widened considerably. A 1999 study has revealed yet another striking dichotomy for India: increasing food production coincides with one-third of its population, an estimated 320 million in 1997, remaining malnourished.

Resolution of such developmental dichotomies in India and Pakistan certainly requires a structural change in their political economies. Yet, the two countries can adopt some short-term measures for ensuring a balanced developmental process in the two countries. This, however, requires curtailment of their defense expenditure and increased resource allocation for social and economic overheads. According to one estimate a mere 5 per cent reduction in the annual military budget of the two countries would release about 2 billion US dollars which could go a long way in fulfilling basic social needs of the people in the region. The diversion of a major chunk of Pakistan's defense expenditure to developmental spheres in one single year can guarantee primary education for its children and tubewells for its villagers. Still larger benefits should accrue to the Indian people in the event of a curtailment of its defense budget since the sum involved in monetary terms is much higher. In his work, the distinguished Pakistani political economist Mahbub-ul-Haq reckons that south Asia requires 129 billion US dollars for a 15-year period of 1995-2010 or 8.6 billion US dollars per year to provide the people of the region with universal primary education, basic health services, child nutrition and family planning. With a projected per cent annual growth of GDP in South Asia, the sum involved would be only 1.6 per cent of the region's GDP. Haq persuasively argues that bilateral and regional cooperation can easily mobilise these resources.

Such regional cooperation cannot, however, be envisioned without substantial contraction of tensions between India and Pakistan and replacement of traditional perceptions of hostility and suspicion by mutual understanding and trust. A series of military CBMs, at one time did improve the relations between the two neighbors, but they still fell far short of the desired results. The present submission argues that people-to-people contact, free flow of information, economic cooperation, and use of appropriate technology to develop mutual confidence and verify cooperative agreements should be able to accomplish important breakthroughs in the normalisation of Indo-Pak relations. This work thus goes beyond the strategic or security studies paradigm and argues that an expansion of cultural, economic and technological cooperation could erode much of the mistrust and misgivings between India and Pakistan, creating a favourable climate for resolving pending military, political and strategic dichotomies in the region.

Changing dynamics of international political economy in the post Cold War period have imposed on India and Pakistan new compulsions for economic and technical collaboration to sustain their pace of growth. Firstly, official Western financial assistance is now diverted mostly to successor states of the former Soviet bloc, the per capita international aid for south Asia being presently only US $ 5. Secondly, the rate of economic growth in major industrialised states is likely to be relatively slower in coming years. This implies that India and Pakistan cannot count upon traditional Western markets for their exports. Thirdly, formation of regional economic groupings like the North American Free Trade Area (NAFTA), European Economic Community (EEC), ASEAN Free Trade Area (AFTA), Caribbean Free Trade Area (CARIFTA), Central American Common Market (CACM), Latin American Free Trade Area (LAFTA), Andean Subregional Group, Central African Customs and Economic Union, East African Community, Arab Common Market (ACM), New Zealand-Australia Free Trade Area and Common Market of the Southern Cone (MERCOSUR) will impede expansion of Indian and Pakistani commerce in those regions. Fourthly, the decline of the Soviet Union led to a shrinkage of South Asia's external markets. India's export trade to Eastern Europe alone having decreased by 10 per cent. Fifthly, the eclipse of the USSR and the American disengagement from Afghanistan released both India and Pakistan from their traditional international alignments, enabling them to look more to south Asia itself. Finally, Pakistan's old allies—the US and China—are pushing Islamabad to replace its conflictual attitude by a cooperative posture towards New Delhi.

Commentators have also pinned hope for Indo-Pak economic cooperation following the adoption of structural adjustment programmes by both countries. Since 1992-93 the growth rate in India has tended to rise almost consistently, the increase for 1997-98 having been 7 per cent. After years of sluggish GDP figures, Pakistan too, recorded an almost 6.4 per cent rise in the same period. The 1990s even witnessed a shift in the 'sectoral composition' of the two economies. Share of agriculture in the GDP of India and Pakistan declined to one-third and one-fourth respectively, and the contribution from commercial, transport and trade sub-sector correspondingly increased substantially. The saving-investment ratio in South Asian countries has improved too. Besides, unlike the developing world in general, India and Pakistan have been relatively spared of the vice of hyperinflation. A World Bank report on south Asia's Integration into the Global Economy (1997) predicts the region is likely to experience the world's fastest growth in exports in the period leading to 2028". Unfortunately, much of these apparent signs of economic growth tend to be offset by a phenomenal rise in India's and Pakistan's external debt, thanks to their large-scale borrowings from the IMF and World Bank in the 1990s.

Relations with Pakistan

India and Pakistan are today thus faced with a contradictory situation: prospects for economic growth juxtaposed by increasing external indebtedness. In a world widely perceived to be characterised by American unipolarism, and a north-dominated global economic order, both India and Pakistan need to fall back on regional cooperation to preserve their economic interests and restore, what one. Pakistani commentator calls, 'their economic sovereignty' from the clutches of the International Monetary Fund and World Bank.' In this perspective, it is possible to identify areas of commercial and technical cooperation between the two south Asian neighbours which could contribute to a subsumation of bilateral political tensions. Realisation of these potentials of constructive bilateralism should also enhance prospects for south Asian stability.

Up until August 15, 1947, India and Pakistan were parts of the same economic unit. Unfortunately for Pakistan, she did not inherit those areas of British India which were industrial conclaves. In 1947 only 7 per cent of the industrial work force was located in Pakistan. To minimize adverse economic implications of the partition, a standstill agreement was concluded in August 1947 for maintaining status quo in matters of Indo-Pak trade until February 20,1948. But the agreement was violated more than it was observed. Yet, in 1948-49 more than 70 per cent of Pakistan's trading transactions were with India, 63 per cent of Indian exports to Pakistan comprising manufactured items and 92 per cent of Pakistani imports to India consisting of food and raw materials. The end of 1949, however, witnessed a rapid downturn in Indo-Pak trade relations. Although between May 1948 and-March 1960 as many as Indo-Pak Trade and Payments Agreements were concluded, the bilateral official trade declined from 184.06 crore of Indian rupees in 1948-49 to 13.63 crore in 1958, and to an all-time low of 10.53 crore in 1965-66, which incidentally coincided with the second Indo-Pak war. The Pakistani economy remained particularly insulated from India by high tariffs and quantitative restrictions on imports from across the border.

Informed sections of public opinion on both sides of the border gradually realised how the severance of bilateral commercial relations in the post-1949 period forced both Pakistan and India to adopt economic adjustment programmes that impeded their efforts to attain self-sufficiency. Pakistan's plan of rapid industrialisation became dependent upon Western technology and capital. She imported coal, steel and iron from the West, China and south Korea when she could have purchased them from India at half the price. Similarly, Pakistan could have imported viscose filament yarn and viscose staple fibre from India instead of looking to suppliers from outside the region. India has an exportable surplus of aluminium from which Pakistan might have also drawn upon at an economical rate. Even for an agricultural item like wheat, Islamabad turned to Australia, although she could have imported it from India and saved hard currency. Pakistan was compelled to accept another dose of adjustment in its foreign trade in 1971 when its eastern part seceded to emerge as Bangladesh. At the same time India incurred considerable 'opportunity cost' in rearranging her economy in the aftermath of Independence. For instance, areas more suitable for paddy cultivation were converted to jute cropping in order to counteract the crisis caused by Pakistan's decision to prohibit export of raw jute to the other side of the border. India had to import pig iron and iron scrap from outside the region, while she could have purchased them from Pakistan for a much lower transportation cost, especially for furnaces located in the Western part of the country. India also suffered a great deal from the scarcity of natural gas for which she could have relied upon Pakistan if normal bilateral relations had prevailed.

The new structure of international political economy in the post-Soviet era and the triumph of democracy in Pakistan during the post-Zia period, however, opened new possibilities for Indo-Pakistan commercial relations. Following the 1972 Shimla Treaty, formal bilateral trade had resumed from November 1974, the value of which reached 108. 18 crore of Indian rupees in 1988-89. In November-December 1981 Pakistan joined the Delhi International Trade Fair. Thereafter, exchange of trade delegations between the two neighbours occurred in quick succession. In 1986 India and Pakistan became signatories to the final document of South Asian Regional Cooperation (SAARC) which committed itself to "promote the welfare of the people of South Asia, to improve their quality of life, to accelerate economic growth, social programmes and cultural development... (and) to devise common policies and approaches for finding solutions to the shared problems". By July 1989 Pakistan agreed to import 322 Indian items. The installation of the Nawaz Sharif government in 1991 coincided with a new boost in Indo-Pak trade, its size rising from 168.09 crore of Indian rupees in 1990-91 to 522.59 crore in 1992-93. Besides, both New Delhi and Islamabad acknowledged how a thriving informal underground smuggling trade across the border was denying them substantial revenue. This undercover trade is estimated to be to the tune of 16 billion Indian rupees a year, four times more than the official trade between the two countries. The size of this informal trade touches 20 billion Indian rupees per annum if we consider the supplies received by India and Pakistan through third countries. Indian textile machinery, tannery equipment, chemical goods, viscose fibre, stainless steel utensils, cosmetics, cashew nut, cotton fabric, ayurvedic medicines and confectioneries reach Pakistan through suppliers based in Dubai, Hong Kong and Singapore. Pakistani goods entering India along unofficial routes include plastic goods, fibre fabrics, second hand clothing, plastic ware, melamine dinner sets, woollens and vegetable oil.

In 1996, Pakistan enthusiastically participated in the first SAARC industrial exhibition in Delhi. The Punjab-Harayana-Delhi Chambers of Commerce and the Federation of Pakistan Chambers of Commerce and Industries cooperated to prepare a potential inventory for normal bilateral trading relations between India and Pakistan. While Indian businessmen selected 207 exportable and 34 importable items, their Pakistani counterparts identified respectively 153 and 152 goods. Items earmarked for Indian export to Pakistan included agricultural machinery, tractors, motorcycles and automobile parts; diesel engines and electric motors; dyes and textile machinery, cement, food processing, telecommunication and engineering items; railway track and generators; industrial and pharmaceutical chemicals; biri and betel leaves; wheat, sugar, onion and potato; tea; coal and iron ore. The list of possible Pakistani exports to India included leather, sports and surgical goods; industrial alcohol, textiles; stainless steel, pesticides and insecticides; fertilisers; precious and semi-precious stones; raw cotton and wool and blended fabrics; medicinal herbs; mineral substances; vegetable oil and nuts. It was also felt that removal of hindrances to open trade might create opportunities for the use of idle or Surplus capacities in Indian and Pakistani industries to meet the demands of a larger regional market.

The above roster reflects the maximum convergence of interest' since the economic cost for India and Pakistan in this proposed trading structure would be substantially lower compared to export-import trade in these items with any other part of the world. The two countries have also discussed the possibility of the right to transit through each other's territories. While this would provide India with an easy access to central Asian markets, transit facilities through India could help Pakistan's trade with Bangladesh, Bhutan and Nepal. Besides, India and Pakistan can pursue joint export-import strategies, which could enable them to gain maximum economic advantage. For instance, the two countries compete with each other in the world market in rice and marine products. But a coordinated marketing strategy can help both to win a higher price for those items. Similarly, India and Pakistan might receive a better deal for their imports if they work through a consortium of state trading organisations.

Initiation of a structural change in the intra-regional trading relations under the auspices of the South Asian Regional Cooperation has helped the acceleration of the pace of Indo-Pak trading relations. The extent of intra-regional trade within south Asia is still significantly low. Only 3.1 per cent of import and 3.8

per cent of export trade of south Asian countries are tied to the region at a time when 63.4 per cent of West Europe's commerce represents intra-European Economic Community trade. While about 0.8 per cent and 3 per cent of Indian exports and imports respectively are concerned with south Asia, Pakistan conducts only 1.5 per cent of her import and 4.9 per cent of her export trade with her neighbours. But the South Asian Preferential Trading Arrangement (SAPTA)—concluded in December 1995—introduced an integrative trading arrangement in the region. The first round of SAPTA negotiations, popularly known as (SAPTA-I), resulted in tariff concessions for 226 products by the participating countries. In the second round of SAPTA negotiations (SAPTA-II), the total number of products identified for preferential treatment rose to 2,013—India offering concessions to Pakistan for 375 items and Pakistan reciprocating it for 230 products. The SAARC Chambers of Commerce and Industry is even envisaging a South Asian Economic Union to cope with the challenge of globalisation and overcome socio-political differences in the region. The US-based Centre for Trade Development has estimated that removal of trade restrictions and lowering of tariff between the states of south Asia would lead to a fives fold increase of intra-SAARC trade from the present $ 3 billion to over $ 15 billion by 2000 AD. Since India and Pakistan are major partners in intra South Asian trade such a development would be advantageous to both.

Regrettably, the full potential for increased trade within the SAPTA-II framework remain unrealised. For instance, in 1995-96 India imported from Pakistan only 17 out of the 375 products and exported only 37 of the 230 products that were granted preferential concessions. Multinationals and their collaborating business houses in Pakistan which sell over-priced consumer goods have tried to sabotage normalisation of Indo-Pak trade. 16 Islamabad also suspects that India gained relatively more advantages from SAPTA-II. If 14 products for which India received tariff concessions were already among the top 50 items she exported to Pakistan, Islamabad could receive similar concessions in respect of only five of the items that were within her top fifty products imported by

India." This discrepancy should be rectified in future SAPTA deliberations. Compared to Pakistan the Indian trade policy is alleged to be even less transparent, highly complex and restrictive. SAPTA was originally viewed as an element in a total package of instruments aimed at trade expansion of the individual countries of the region. The scheme was intended to be essentially a liberalisation scheme on a products by-product basis. But commentators now suggest that SAPTA, to be effective, should be converted to 'an across-the-board trade liberalisation scheme'.

Nevertheless, the writing on the wall seems to be for a better Indo-Pak bilateral trading relations in the coming days. Business groups in both countries have realised that India and Pakistan produce goods that can fulfil mutual requirements of a combined GDP of about $ 300 billion, and a regional market only second in size to China. Common tastes and Culture Should facilitate the establishment of a regional market for goods produced in any part of the region. Pakistani analysts have themselves demonstrated how their country could particularly benefit by importing items like medicines from India where they are sold at less than 30 per cent of the Pakistani prices. J N Dixit, India's High Commissioner to Pakistan from 1989 to 1991 and then Foreign Secretary of India from 1991 to 1994, testifies to the refusal of leading businessmen in Lahore, Karachi, Peshawar and Quetta to accept the traditional contention of their government that the Pakistani public would not accept normalisation of economic relations with India Without a resolution of politico-military dichotomies. A member of the Lahore Chamber of Commerce thus told an Indian journalist: "Let the politicians do what they like, trade charges, make statements against each other and other populist stuff. Leave businessmen of the two countries out of this and let them get on with their work".

Similarly, Indian business leaders like Abhaya Kumar Kasliwal, the President of FICCI, asserted at a SAARC function, "We have found that a climate exists (in the region) wherein businessmen have realised not to take pressures between themselves but act as one for improving bilateral trade". [The News, April 29, 1997].

The fact that economic bilateralism is feasible, irrespective of political differences, was demonstrated in the autumn of 1990 when India helped Pakistan to tide over a sudden potato and onion crisis after she had failed to secure imports from Turkey, China and Spain. The then Indian High Commissioner to Pakistan, J N Dixit, recollects that although the Pak government preferred not to inform the public about the Indian imports, "everybody in the market knew the truth"." Again, at the beginning of 1997, Pakistan imported 50,000 tonnes of sugar from India to face a sudden shortfall. By March of that year the National Shipping Corporation of Pakistan also urged Islamabad to scrap the 1975 Protocol Agreement which prohibited Pakistani vessels to load cargo from Indian ports to a third country. Indian businessmen too are increasingly persuading New Delhi to unilaterally initiate all open ful-fledged trade with Pakistan. H S Tandon of the Punjab Haryana-Delhi Chambers of Commerce and Industry is convinced: "The voluminous unofficial trade between our two countries is an indication to the mutually-profitable opportunities in the bilateral business and the intense suppressed desire of the two business communities to trade with each other. The opening up of trade and the free movement of the businessmen will only help in strengthening the trade ties between India and Pakistan for mutual benefit".

New Delhi has already accorded Pakistan the Most Favored Nation Status. Reciprocation from Islamabad should be forthcoming, particularly in view of pressures from within Pakistan itself. In 1978 a Pakistani dealer of the Italian Vespa scooters had used his influence in Islamabad to prohibit private sector trading from across the border, apprehending threats to his interests from the less-expensive Indian Bajaj scooters. But in a 1993 seminar the president of the Lahore Chamber of Commerce emphasised the necessity to strengthen Pakistan's trading connection with India, of course, without jeopardising her industrial interests. The former Pakistan commerce minister Ahmed Mukhtar. who led his country's delegation to the January 1996 Delhi meeting of the SAARC Trade Ministers, himself admitted that conceding the MNF status to India would only be a matter of time. At a November, 1996 seminar organised by the Management Association of Pakistan, the participants agreed that an open Indo-Pak trade would be particularly beneficial to Pakistan, although the country's commerce minister Chaudhuri Ahmed Mukhtar suggested a step-by-step approach'. The president of the association, Tariq Ikram, reminded the participants of the seminar that when both India and Pakistan were signatories of the World Trade Organisation, the question was no longer if the two states should trade with each other, but how Pakistan could gain most from open trading with India. Participating in the discussions, Tariq Sayeed Saigol, a leading manufacturer and exporter of textiles, alleviated fears of adverse impact of open trade with India, provided his colleagues optimised the cost of production and ensured quality production. It was also noted how Pakistan's agriculture could benefit from low-cost Indian machinery. Addressing a meeting of SAARC officials in New Delhi in April 1997, Pakistan's commerce secretary, Faiz Ahmed, remarked: 11 am optimistic of greater movement of goods from Pakistan to India and other SAARC nations as a result of lowering of our tariff levels..." (Pakistan and Gulf Economist, November 2-8, 1996). On another occasion, the former Pakistan foreign minister, Mubashir Hasan, went to the extent of remarking that not politicians—who held temporary offices—but commercial groups on both sides of the border could constructively contribute to a better bilateral commercial relations.

A new climate for Indo-Pak trading relations was reflected in the signing of MOUs between the Federation of Indian Chambers of Commerce and Industry (FICCI) and the Federation of Pakistan Chambers of Commerce and Industry (FPCCI) on December 23, 1996. In March 1997, an agreement of cooperation was concluded between Federation of Indian Micro Small and Medium Enterprises (FISME) and Federation of Pakistan Chambers of Traders and Cottage Industries (FPCTC). In April 1997, India and Pakistan decided to expand the number of items in official bilateral trade. Observers have also suggested the formation of an India-Pakistan Commission on Free Trade—possibly headed jointly by the two

Prime Ministers—to use the new congenial business spirit for promoting bilateral free trading.

India, however, has to alleviate Pakistan's fear that the opening of her economy carries the risk of the establishment of Indian hegemony over her domestic market. At the same time, India has to assure Pakistan that she would not undermine the SAARC by joining the Rim Association for Regional Cooperation. One way of gaining Pakistani confidence is to adopt 'a phased manner approach' in the elimination of trade barriers. Significantly enough, business lobbies in India and Pakistan have already suggested categorisation of tradable commodities into non-competing, competing and exempted products and adoption of different timeframes for the extension of preferential tariff treatment to them. Non-competing goods comprise those raw materials, intermediate and manufactured products which Pakistan imports from India but are not produced in Pakistan. Tariffs on these items could be eliminated in the first phase of normalisation of trading relations. Competing goods are those which are produced both in India and Pakistan and in which open trade entails risk for domestic import competing industries. These items are required to be gradually and carefully brought within the preferential tariff system. Exempted products are those that the two countries consider 'sensitive' and tariff barriers for them need not be immediately eliminated. The introduction of preferential trading in such a phased manner could provide a level-playing field to the Pakistani business community. This is particularly important since we are now negotiating the transition from the South Asian Preferential Trading Arrangement to a South Asian Free Trade Area (SAFTA) in 2005 which would allow a grouping of two or more regional states for trade without fiscal and institutional hindrances. To quote a perceptible commentator:

> Only by achieving balanced trade—and much will depend on the attitude of India and Pakistan as the larger economies—can the region enhance its self-sufficiency and lessen its dependence on Western sources which offer no comparative advantage other than the ability of the supplier to also provide credit.

Summarising the economic benefits of free trade between India and Pakistan, Khan aptly remarks:

> A free trade area can considerably improve cost efficiency in the Indian Pakistani manufacturing sectors, enabling industrialists to benefit from cheap production imports (industrial raw materials, intermediate products, finished capital goods) and the lower freight costs stemming from both states' geographical contiguity."

Complementary technological relations are necessary to sustain improved commercial connections. Recognising that technology "would dominate the developmental challenges of development in the 21 st century", a SAARC study group on economic cooperation prescribed regional technological cooperation to meet the requirements of global competitiveness. The group correctly recognised three dimensions of this regional technological challenge: (a) Identification of sectors where collaborative efforts would aim at technological upgradation to maintain global competition; (b) Improvement of technical capabilities in areas where 'global technological horizons' are changing fast; (c) Substitution of old technologies to meet ecological demands. In all these realms there are strong potentials for Indo-Pak collaboration.

India—contributing 78 per cent of the total manufacturing value in the region—has an unmistakable technological superiority in both capital and intermediate technology. Compared to Western technology, this expertise is more economical and suitable for south Asian needs. A technical partnership between Islamabad and New Delhi would be, accordingly, particularly beneficial to the former since about 60 per cent of its development budget relies on foreign credit to import capital and intermediate goods. Bilateral cooperation for technological upgradation in textiles, leather goods, jute manufactures, tea, rubber products, micro-electronics, biotechnology, and photo voltaic should be economically fruitful in the face of global competition. During the 1980s in the Hazara region of Pakistan, large deposits of rock phosphate were discovered which could have been processed economically with

Indian technology. Similarly, such Indian enterprises as the Tata Iron and Steel Company can help in the establishment of coal washeries to free the high ash content of Pakistani coal. In paper production. India and Pakistan may collaborate to replace the wood-based technology with the relatively environment-friendly biogas-based technique. The Council of Scientific and Industrial Research(CSIR) in India is credited for having developed over 2,000 patents in industrial technology and this knowledge has to be transmitted to Pakistan. Likewise, India can profit considerably, from the projects of the Pakistan Council of Scientific and Industrial Research in the realms of food and fermentation technology, ore processing, metallurgy, glass and ceramics, paints and plastics, fine chemicals, polymers, industrial chemicals and leather. Joint efforts of the Pakistan Agricultural Research Council and the Indian Council of Agricultural Research cannot only enhance agricultural productivity in the Subcontinent, but also make it cost-effective. Collaborative research between these two organisations has already yielded fruits in germplasm and seed breeding. The space programme of India and Pakistan—the INSAT and IRS for the former and Badr-I and Badr-II for the latter—can be coordinated for sharing research results. Joint space programme has already produced rich dividends for Washington and Moscow. Proposal for a direct high-speed satellite data link has been also recently finalised between the Indian Meteorological Administration (New Delhi) and the Chinese Meteorological Administration (Beijing) for Indo-Chinese cooperation in meteorological science and technology. Such cooperative ventures between India and Pakistan should be forthcoming too. Telecommunication networks to promote closer interface between public policy makers, businessmen and academics should be encouraged to buttress the proposed technological links.

Besides, there exist possibilities of Indo-Pak joint enterprises. India has demonstrated its expertise in this sphere outside the region. This competence can be utilised in planning export-oriented joint industrial Ventures, Coordination between multinational units operating in India and Pakistan—probably on the basis of division of labour—can also hasten indigenisation of manufactures and economies of scale. Such all experiment can be readily attempted for the existing Suzuki automobile and Yamaha motorcycle plants. Based on policy papers prepared by industrial lobbies in both countries, the two governments and task forces constituted by the SAARC Secretariat, the following areas can be demarcated for Indo-Pak technological collaboration: (i) automobile parts, bicycles; (ii) glass manufacturing; (iii) machine tools and engineering goods; (iv) telecommunication and scientific instruments; (v) plastic and agricultural technology; (vi) cement; (vii) port and ship repair facilities; (viii) iron and steel; (ix) food-processing and agro-based industries; fertilisers; (x) jute, textile and leather; (xi) rubber and plastic products; (xii) mineral-based industries; (xiii) pharmaceuticals and chemicals; (xiv) telecommunications; scientific instruments; and (xv) sports goods.

A SAARC study group has even recommended a regional industrial restructuring scheme, a programme similar to the one which fostered intra-regional integration in production processes in south-east Asia. This would imply "relatively more advanced economies of the region... (vacating) some stages of production in favour of the others who are laggards in terms of technology and product diversification". It entails new locational patterns of industries and inter-country linkages of supplies and demands. The viability of such an industrial restructuring scheme surely depends on collaboration between India and Pakistan, the region's two leading industrial powers.

Another domain for Indo-Pak technological collaboration is productive utilisation of a common eco-system, rich in biodiversity and genetic resources. The Indo-Pak Indus Water Treaty of 1960 has enabled the irrigation of about 24 million acres of land. An extension of this Indus spirit in harnessing water, energy and other natural resources for developmental purposes will be propitious for one-fifth of the humanity. Studies have already cited how an effective utilisation of water resources can meet the projected shortfall in electricity in the region. The hydro-electric potential is now estimated to be 50,000 MW for India and 21,000 MW for

Pakistan, although only 8.6 per cent and 11.1 per cent of this respective capacity is being realised in practice. But by 2018, Pakistan's energy-generating capacity alone would require increase from the present 12,850 MW to 54,000 MW. A possible means of improving electricity supply in India and Pakistan lies in joint utilisation of the region's hydropower resources and transmission of the generated electricity through an interconnecting Indo-Pak Power Grid System. Discussions have already been initiated on the sharing of waters of the Jhelum river, which flows through the Indian province of Punjab before entering Pakistan. India is successfully cooperating with Bhutan and Nepal in the hydropower sector, and a part of the electricity generated here could be channeled into Indian's northern power grid for transfer to Pakistan. Similarly, electricity imported by Pakistan from Tajikistan and Kyrgyzstan might be connected to the Pakistan grid in North-West Frontier Provinces for supply to the Subcontinent, if necessary. Common electricity grid system involving extensive transmission and distribution networks are already operating in north America, Europe, Africa and West Asia, and the method should logically work in South Asia. A 'synchronous Indo-Pakistani grid system' is not an utopian idea but is functional and economical. At the January 1988 India-Bangladesh-Pakistan trilateral business summit, the then Indian Prime Minister Gujral formally proposed the development of a South Asian electric grid system. Incidentally, from a long-term perspective, hydropower is cheaper and more eco-friendly than thermal power which India and Pakistan have traditionally banked upon. Besides, India accredited with having one of the world's largest solar energy programmes, can transfer this technology to Pakistan for use in provinces like Sindh whose terrain and climate are almost quite similar to the Indian state of Rajasthan, acknowledged as a solar energy enterprise zone. Bilateral collaboration has also been proposed for the use of renewable sources of energy like fuelwood, charcoal and animal residues. A bilateral sharing of energy information, especially in biogas, wind, solar energy and mini-hydroelectric power would be of mutual benefit for the two neighbours.

An essential ingredient for industrial development is natural gas, in which both the South Asian states are unfortunately deficient. While Pakistan will have an estimated shortfall of 1.6 billion cubic feet per day by the end of 1999, India's consumption of natural gas is projected to increase from the present daily level of 65 million cubic metres to 280 million cubic metre in 2010. This shortage, however, can be met if India and Pakistan collectively tap the world's two major natural gas deposits—the Persian Gulf and Central Asia—which are geographically not far off from either of them. Experts have thus proposed a gas pipeline from Iran, Turkmenistan and Qatar through Pakistan to India. The suggested receiving points of this natural gas are Karachi and Sui in Pakistan and Gujarat in India, which have similar topographical features, and hence would not pose any major technical challenge for laying the pipeline. Sections in India are sceptical about this plan since they apprehend that Pakistan may cut off the supply-line in the event of a conflict. But such fears are far-stretched. After all, even during the Cold War Siberia was connected to the West by a gas transmission line. Egypt and Israel are today discussing gas transmission. Besides, as a deterrent against possible Pakistani disruptive actions, India could propose the extension of the pipeline to Bangladesh, Myamnar and ASEAN states with whom Islamabad has favorable relations. Commenting on the possibility of Indo-Pak cooperation in the realm of natural gas, the Indian Petroleum Secretary, Vijay Kelkar, had remarked: "Unlike oil, which can be a cause of conflict, natural gas trade can promote cooperation. The simple reason for this is that in natural gas trade, the relationship between the buyer and the seller tends to be more symmetric and, moreover, contracts are long-term".

India and Pakistan can also fruitfully cooperate in maintaining surveillance on seismic, climatic and other environmental changes for sending advance warnings against drought, flood, and other natural calamities. Collaborative efforts have also been proposed for preserving the region's bio-diversity. Mention may be made of a regional conference on Sustainable Development of the Mountain Areas of Asia (SUDEMAA) in Kathmandu in December 1994, which brought together policy makers, non-government organisations and donor agencies to prepare a plan for cooperative management of mountain areas and improve the living standards of hill people. Obviously, enthusiastic participation by India and Pakistan is required to implement such potentially fruitful environmental management schemes.

Fructification of trading and technological cooperation between India and Pakistan outlined above, requires to be sustained by bilateral investments. Integration of financial capital markets, setting up of offshore financial centres, regional Exim banking service and an Indo-Pak clearing and payments arrangement are essential for creating growth conclaves in the region. Both countries could even think in terms of regional planning. A South Asian regional convention on intra-regional investment has already been proposed. This is scheduled to be followed by the compilation of a common code of conduct for exporters, importers, investors and government officials to work in the new situation. Some commentators even suggest that immediate interim bilateral fiscal arrangements between India and Pakistan could ultimately lead to a regional customs union. The role played by the Australia-New Zealand closer economic relations trade agreement is cited as a case in point.

This discussion has hopefully demonstrated potential realms of Indo-Pak bilateral economic and technological relations where mutually beneficial commonalties, complementarities and substitutabilities exist'. 'Vertical and horizontal complementarities' in bilateral trade, industrial and technological collaboration, and cost-effective utilisation of natural resources are some of the core areas of cooperation. Certain compulsions of international political economy as well as increasing contact between the citizens of its member states within the institutional structure of the SAARC have, as indicated above, strengthened such possibilities of Indo-Pak bilateralism. A growing consciousness for peace and cooperation between the two countries at the popular level was revealed to an Indian journalist and two UNDP officials in Islamabad in April 1997 when they were candidly told by a young

Pakistani from North-West Frontier Provinces: "Who wants submarines and guns, we want schools and hospitals"." In this connection one may also recall the scenes of solidarity and ecstasy demonstrated in Kolkata during the meeting of the Pakistan-India People's Forum For Peace and Democracy in December 1996. Women and legal activists across the borders are also coming together to generate a popular consensus on cooperative actions concerning developmental issues. The leading Pakistani commentator, Samiullah M Koreshi, surely ventilates the growing popular feeling in his country when he writes:

> Even without waiting for the solution of problems, India and Pakistan can work out confidence-buildinty measures that can be implemented to prepare the climate for negotiations. We can move step by step, starting first with confidence-building measures and a controlled level of bilateral trade and the rest can be tackled later (The Nation, March 8, 1997).

Reflecting on the new spirit another Pakistani journalist remarks:

> The mood in both countries is for an improvement of relations between India and Pakistan. Divided families are all for it. Traders would like to see goods moving freely to and from across the border. Budgetary planners are looking for ways to effect economy wherever possible ... It is now up to the political leaders on both sides to take bold decisions and not remain tied down to rigid postures (The News, March 31, 1997).

Interestingly enough, Kashmir was reportedly not seriously raised during the last parliamentary poll in Pakistan. Assuming his office, the recently deposed Prime Minister Nawaz Sharif proceeded to attach no pre-condition to the resumption of official level talks with India, remarking "we are 47 years late, we cannot afford any further delay" '11 Pakistani observers contend that Sharif is the first Prime Minister of the country to have "gone to the Public, speaking of his intention to remove the roadblocks from our relations with India". The former Indian Prime Minister I K Gujral had also reciprocated: "We don't want to be prisoners of the past and (are) trying to get rid of the mind set" (The Tribune, December 21, 1996). The Gujral doctrine sought to improve India's relations with her neighbours without insisting on reciprocity, thereby transforming the Subcontinent into a 'cooperative neighbourhood'. It is also not without significance that Gujral and Sharif perhaps broke with earlier tradition to agree on some concrete proposals for bilateral and regional cooperation at the Male summit of the SAARC in May 1997. A group of eminent persons was constituted to review the functioning of the SAARC and suggest measures for making it more effective and relevant. The October 1997 Edinburgh Commonwealth Summit once again indicated 'excellent personal relations' between Gujral and Nawaz Sharif when, under their directions. The respective foreign secretaries met to keep the dialogue going. The January 1998 trilateral Dhaka business summit between the Indian, Pakistani and Bangladeshi Prime Ministers further reconfirmed the Indo-Pak resolve to expand bilateral economic ties. In the words of the then Indian foreign secretary, K Raghunath: "it is our shared perception that we should continue dialogue. Differences on certain issues should not deter us from resuming negotiations" (The Statesman, January 16, 1998).

Role of SAARC

The Indian Prime Minister Gujral also used the Dhaka summit to suggest an increase in the frequency of goods trains between India and Pakistan from 15 to 30 a month. Projects were mooted for fast track investment and joint sector enterprises in the region. Gujral's Pakistani counterpart, too, promised the removal of bureaucratic bottlenecks impeding regional economic linkages, and announced his intention to host a regional economic summit. The joint declaration of the Trilateral Summit even called for the harmonising of regional laws and regulations for attracting foreign investment. Such processes of cooperative engagement can certainly create conditions of cooperation, belying the realist scepticism about the potency of the politics of cooperation in the promotion of regional peace and stability. In the words of an Indian analyst: "South Asia beckons us all to enrich regional cooperation and carry it forward to new heights".

India, being the major regional power, has to bear the prime responsibility to initiate cooperative regional politics, especially in the realm of her relations with Pakistan. Unfortunately, there are certain disturbing trends in Indian politics like religious sectarianism, which if not checked, would undermine the country's respectability in her dealings with Pakistan. The demolition of the Babri masjid in December 1992, disruption of Pakistani ghazal singer Ghulam Ali's concert by Shiv Sainiks in Mumbai on April 26,1998, ransacking of the house of the famous painter Maqbool Fida Hussain by Bajrang Dal's storm-troopers in Mumbai on May 1, 1998, attempts to foil the 1999 Indo-Pak cricket test series, attacks on Christian missionaries and endeavours to saffronise the Indian education system - all these surely transmitted wrong signals across the border.

India's refusal to sell wheat to Pakistan credit last year [1998] because other buyers were ready to purchase the same in hard currency could have been also avoided. Similarly, inside Pakistan such fundamentalist forces as the Jamaat-e-Islam, which oppose the grant of MNF status to India, need to be isolated. Continuing Pakistani involvement in Kashmir and provocative acts of Islamabad such as the deployment of the long range Ghauri missile have tended to strengthen the hands of those in India who oppose normalisation of relations with Pakistan. The Pakistani leadership should not shy away from improving relations with India, fearing that it might alienate certain sections of the country. As the former Sri Lankan President Premadasa once remarked: "There are moments in life where leaders have to lead and not wait for public opinion"." It would be also worthwhile for Pakistani diplomats not to dampen visions of a new era of Indo-Pak relations.

The nuclear arms race, initiated in the subcontinent in May 1998, also undoubtedly undermined the prospect of normalisation of Indo-Pak relations. Yet, neither New Delhi nor Islamabad have been able to ignore the growing awareness amongst a sizeable number of people in both countries—especially the expanding middle class, intellectuals and a younger generation who had not been directly rattled by the trauma of the Partition—that cooperative methods are worth pursuing rather than fighting wars.

Despite the nationalist hysteria deliberately fomented in the aftermath of the Pokhran-II explosions, a large number of Indian scientists, artists and intellectuals questioned the wisdom of conducting the nuclear tests. Protest meetings were held in major metropolitan Indian cities and dissenting voices found expression in newspaper articles, TV and radio discussions and parliamentary deliberations. The left, particularly the Communist Party of India (Marxist) and the Communist Party of India, have been vocal in highlighting the negative implications of the nuclear explosions which were believed—certainly with reason—to have been actually timed to incite jingoism for bolstering New Delhi's dithering coalition regime. In Pakistan, too, peace groups like the Pakistan-India People's Forum for Peace and Democracy organised rallies in Islamabad on May 14, 1998 not to demand Pakistan's retaliation, but to urge her restraint in the cause of friendship and peace between the people of the two countries. On May 24 a Pakistani International Airlines plane was hijacked by three Baluchis to forestall a possible Pakistani nuclear test in Baluchistan. The Indian government also undertook damage control missions to resuscitate its image in south Asia. New Delhi announced a moratorium on further nuclear tests and on May 21, 1998 suggested to Pakistan the signing of a 'no-first strike pact'. At the first SAARC Communication Ministers' Conference in Colombo which concluded on May 24,1998, the Indian Minister for information and broadcasting even lent support to the proposed 'action plan' to have lowest possible telecom tariffs for the region. Again, the then speaker of the Lower House of the Indian parliament, G M C Balayogi, initiated an exchange of Indian and Pakistani parliamentary delegations to discuss contentious issues, including Kashmir. Indian and Pakistani delegates to the November 1998 Peshawar meeting of the Pak-India People's Forum for Peace and Democracy unanimously regretted that the two countries had spent $ 118 billion on defence between 1988 and 1996 and called for an immediate pullback of troops from Siachen, a bilateral commitment for a nuclear-weapon free world and agreements of Tulbul navigation and Willer barrage issues. Citing substantial public support for Indo-Pak amity the distinguished Pak columnist N B

Naqvi writes: "One's emphasis is on an Indo-Pak dialogue as structured as may be feasible for the doughty peace campaigners and heavens be praised for them—these groups of public-spirited non-officials" (The Dawn, November 20, 1998).

In the same vein another leading commentator of the country, Anees Jilani. notes: "The peace talks should be spread out horizontally rather than vertically with everything lumped together" (The News, November 17, 1998).

The nuclear tension between the two neighbours did not deter the prospect of economic relations in the subcontinent. This was evident from a SAARC-sponsored meeting between Indian and Pakistani industrialists on December 11, 1998 which reiterated specific areas of bilateral technological links. While the Indian spokesmen, Narendra Jamandas Seth and Vinode Kumar of Tata Economic Consultancy Services, referred to information technology, telecommunications, automobile ancillary parts. light engineering products, drugs and pharmaceuticals, textiles, leather and fishery, the President of Pakistan Chambers of Commerce and Industries, Fazlur Rahman Dittu, identified solar energy, fruit processing, mining, marble extraction and PLG cylinders as areas of joint sector ventures. The same meeting expressed confidence that such joint projects would be 'a catalyst' for normalisation of relations between the two countries. It is not without significance that even amidst the sulking over Siachen. And the tensions following detonation of nuclear bombs, the Indian prime minister Atal Behari Vajpayee undertook in February 1999 the historic Delhi-Lahore bus trip. The Vajpayee-Sharif Lahore Declaration and the groundswell of popular goodwill it generated, kindled hopes of a renewal of 'congenital ties'.

The 'Lahore bonhomie' was unfortunately blasted by the open Indo-Pak military encounter in May-June 1999 following the detection of Pak-sponsored infiltrators in the Kargil sector of Jammu and Kashmir. The Kargil crisis incited jingoism in the two countries and the ruling regimes in New Delhi and Islamabad sought to derive political mileage out of it. If Nawaz Sharif wanted to use the crisis to divert public opinion from the pressing domestic issues, the credit for flushing out the infiltrators was appropriated by the ruling formation in New Delhi. It is not without significance that computer games are being developed in India to vent anger on Pak intruders in Kargil. The interactive games—nicknamed 'I Love India' and 'Operation Vijay'—allows passive onlookers, to do something about the Pakistani intrusion into Kargil".

> The beauty of the game is that India is going to win no matter how badly you play it, . . The five minute game starts with a message by Prime Minister Vajpayee urging brave soldiers to fight the intruders and bring glory to the nation. The villains in green fatigues include Nawaz Sharif and Pakistan's fast bowler Sohaib Akhtar with mujahideen and ISI agents advancing into the Indian territory ... The brave (Indian) jawan captures peaks ... to cross the LOC (Line of Control) and march forward to Karachi. As an added bonus, the users can blow up the Ghauri missiles on their way ... At the end of the game the Indian Prime Minister awards the users with bravery medals for courage (The Asian Age, July 28, 1999).

It is equally unfortunate that the Kargil episode is being used to ventilate wrath on the minority community and question its loyalty to the Indian state. The Hindu fundamentalist Organisation—the Visva Hindu Parishad—also undertook a month-long Rashtriya Surakshya Mahayagya from July 28 to August 26, 1999, to raise money for the Kargil martyrs, pray for the safety of the state and energize the people through a religious message. Even Bollywood—the film industry in the country—is cashing in on Kargil to produce a number of overtly chauvinistic films.

There is, however, the other side of the picture. In the aftermath of the crisis both Indians and Pakistanis felt the economic pinch. The conflict cost India anything between Rs 2,000 crore and Rs 2.500 crore, which roughly amounts to Rs 20 crore to Rs 25 crore per day. A July 1999 report of India's Associated Chambers of Commerce and Industry identified the following adverse impacts on the national economy:

(1) The Kargil crisis is likely to register a rise in defence spending from the projected 16.1 per cent to about 20

per cent of the budget in 1999-2000 which will increase the fiscal deficit by 4.5 per cent and accordingly exert a pressure on interest rates.

(2) The fighting will affect capital inflows in the country, causing erosion of confidence amongst the foreign investors.

(3) Prolonged hostilities will severely deplete the oil reserve of the country and result in oil shortage.

The Kargil episode has hit the Pak economy too. The country's defence outlay for 1999-2000 has been increased by 10.9 per cent, although the rate of economic growth declined from 6 to 3 per cent. In Pakistan the banking and financial institutions are in disarray; unemployment is on the rise; poverty has increased: and the health system has been jeopardised.

Voices of popular dissent against Indo-Pak military engagement could be heard on both sides of the border. For instance. In The Frontier Post of June 19, 1999, Afrasiyar Khatak regretted how an Indo-Pak war would be economically, socially and politically disastrous for the two countries in their fight against hunger, poverty, disease and illiteracy. The same daily carried a number of submissions by Farahtulla Babar, warning the Pakistanis that their government was using the Kargil episode to have a temporary respite from the pressing domestic issues. The following quote from an article by F S Aijazuddin also indicates that not all sections of Pakistan's civil society approved of Islamabad's designs in formenting the Kargil crisis:

> It needs to be remembered that Vajpayee's intrusion into Pakistani territory was at our specific invitation. His original plan had been to stand like any inquisitive Indian tourist at the Waggah border. When he was told that it was against our customs to greet visitors at the doorstep without inviting them into the house, he crossed the border, ignoring the apparent snub of being received at the border by his counterpart Prime Minister but not by the Pakistani defence chiefs. He fought back tears moved less by the recital by our Prime Minister of

> his own poem-'We will never let there be another war'—than by the tear gas released by the police against demonstrators objecting to his visit... The Indians came to Lahore with an olive branch. We responded with Kargil. Today, the Indian nation is on a war footing, demanding vengeance, and we are advocating ahimsa. Never in 50 years of independence have we seemed less like a state and more like a 'stringless Pinocchio' capering to a dance choreographed at Blair house (Reproduced from The Dawn in The Asian Age, July 18, 1999).

At a June, 1999 conference in Lahore, the Pakistani Human Rights activist Asma Jahangir, too, asserted in no uncertain terms that the Pakistani women were against war since it was the women who suffer most in wars — religious or political. The conference resolution reflected the apprehension shared by a considerable section of public opinion across the border:

> Both countries are using the electronic media to confuse people and to fan war hysteria. There is no transparency in the events that led to the current hostilities. Both governments have not taken the people into confidence and are pursuing, their agendas by encouraging hawkish elements on both sides of the border.

During the height of the Kargil crisis, public rallies were held in Pakistan demanding end of nuclearisation of South Asia and normalisation of relations between the two countries. Ones such historic gathering was held in Baluchistan on May 28, 1999. The Kargil tensions could not also disrupt the Lahore-Delhi bus service. Almost all passengers coming from Pakistan regretted the escalating border tension. Shortly after the outbreak of hostilities across the Kargil sector an elderly woman ventilated the collective feeling of her co-passengers: "Why cannot they remain in peace and let the people on both sides meet. We do not want war again" (The Times of India, May 30, 1999).

On the Indian side also one could notice a desire for Indo-Pak goodwill. While the armed forces clashed in Kargil, residents living close to either side of the border prayed for peace. "We do not want any more wars", exclaimed Sukhjinder Singh, a farmer. When another agriculturist, Balwinder, regretted that they could never build pucca houses for fear of another war and urged the governments of both countries to strive for peace, he was voicing the feeling of a significant section of subcontinental society. Significantly enough, in the post-Kargil days the Engineering Export Promotion Council of India organised a buyer-seller meet in Kolkata which attracted 44 participants from all the SAARC countries, generating business worth S 50 million." Disregard ing the current Indo-Pak tensions, the business captains at the meet advocated freer movement and removal of non- tariff barriers to spur inter-regional trade growth'. Referring to the fact that Bangladesh and India were the largest producers of jute, India and Pakistan were the biggest cotton producers, and Sri Lanka and Bangladesh constituted the largest tea grouping in the world, the Federation of Indian Chambers of Commerce and Industry president Sudhir Jalan emphasised in a seminar held on the occasion: "We can be a force to reckon with. The only thing required is initiative and the right mechanisms to achieve this objective" (The Asian Age, May 22, 1999). For instance, he reminded his Pakistani counterpart that if the components of the Maruti car or the Vespa scooter were 'sourced' from India, Pakistan would benefit from low prices of these items. Jalan also regretted that although Pakistan directly imported from India only 0.8 million kg of tea, she secured another 45 million kg of the same tea via a third country.

The convergence of an yearning for peace across the subcontinent's national frontiers in the aftermath of the Kargil crisis was aptly demonstrated when eminent citizens of the two countries under the aegis of two organisations—the Association of People of Asia and Pakistan and the Pakistan-India People's Forum for Peace and Democracy—appealed to New Delhi and Islamabad to respect the Line of Control, renew the dialogue process, adopt confidence-building measures, abandon the nuclear race and promote people-to-people interaction. From the Indian side, the signatories included the former governor B K Nehru, the filmmaker and parliament member Mrinal Sen, the journalist and Parliament member Kuldip Nayyar, film actress and parliamentarian Shabana Azmi, the Gandhian activist Nirmala Deshpande and dancer Sonal Man Singh. Pakistani signatories included such leading figures as the National Assembly member Shakil Ahmed Baluch, the educationist Zaki Hasan, the historian Mubarak Ali, women activists lqbal Sultana and Anis Hasan and the journalist Mujhid Barelvi. Mention may also be made of personalities like Suhasini Mule of India making collaborative films on the cause of Indo-Pak peace.

The sudden military coup in Pakistan on October 12,1999 resulting in a suspension of the civilian rule, however, sent new shock waves to India. But what needs to be noted is that the new military ruler of Islamabad, General Pervez Musharraf, did not opt for a belligerent posture towards New Delhi. Instead, he announced on October 17, a 'unilateral military de-escalation' along the border and expressed a willingness to work with India "to take south Asia out of economic deprivation". In fact, neither New Delhi nor Islamabad would be able in the long run to deny the reality that the people of India and Pakistan, despite their 'flawed inheritance', do reason together'. Howsoever the ruling regimes in India and Pakistan remain caught in the whirlwind of the Kashmir question, an increasing social segment in both countries is realising the indispensability of coming closer to each other. This submission has hopefully indicated that escalation of military-political tensions would not be in the economic interest of either India or Pakistan. The path towards Indo-Pak cooperative bilateralism could be strenuous and long. But peace activists and social scientists interested in Indo-Pak cooperative engagement can draw sustenance from the fact:

> There are lots of things that you do now which would have seemed insane to you ten years ago. Those things themselves did not change, but your idea of yourself changed. What was impossible before is perfectly possible now and perhaps your total success in changing yourself is only a matter of time.

The Bone of Contention

In the new millennium, as India prepares to embrace a new age containing unforeseen opportunities, its optimism is dampened by a range of serious problems—both actual and potential. Among them, the conflict in Kashmir occupies a position of paramount importance in terms of its potentials to pose threats not only to India's national stability and security but also to the maintenance of peace and amity in South Asia—an essential requirement for revitalising the framework for South Asian regional cooperation. Next to the unforgettable problem of India's partition, the problem in Kashmir is perhaps the most notable one that still haunts India in its daily affairs. The existing literature on the Kashmir problem is vast and rich. The basic issues involved have been adequately dealt within many outstanding academic works and possible solutions have been debated by politicians, journalists, academicians, etc. Here an attempt has been made to analyse the conflict and the resulting problems from a different angle by evaluating the various conditions that promote sustainable peace in an already conflict-ridden society. After a brief analysis of the nature of the conflict in Kashmir—in terms of the varying levels of violence, an attempt has been made to explore the problems of promoting sustainable peace in Kashmir. In the light of the emerging trends regarding the Kashmir problem, it has been argued that the resolution of this conflict cannot be sought only at the broad level of Indo-Pak consultations and negotiations. A micro 'piece by piece' approach has become more relevant in the post-Kargil era, especially in the light of the recent fresh move in the State in support of greater autonomy.

The history of the problem in Kashmir clearly denotes an evolving trend of increasing complexity and maturity. Whereas the core issue—the question of Kashmir's political future, has remained intact, the dynamics developed by the problem and their long-term impact have resulted in its diversification—both in terms of actors and issues and levels of manifestation. Consequently, a complex web of dynamic linkages of fluctuating intensities has emerged in the arena that signifies an institutionalisation of the entire problem. The actors and issues have not only multiplied and complicated the problem over the years but also they have evolved an organised and set pattern of actions and interactions through which the problem has gained momentum.

As a result, what began as an incipient conflict' in the early years of India's independence, has turned latent over the years and ended in a condition of low-intensity war with distinct and recurrent points of direct and extreme violence (the Indo-Pak wars and hostilities of 1947, 1965, 1971 and 1999, separated by periods of small to medium-scale hostilities, violence and animosity). This has involved not only Pakistan and India but also the people of Jammu and Kashmir, both unorganised as well as organised as various political and religious groups (of which some are banned by the Indian government for terrorist activities), foreign mercenaries who are supported and sponsored by external sources, both state and non-state actors, to fight for the cause of the Kashmiris. This growing change in the nature and intensity of conflict cannot be fully explained by the logic of Indo-Pak relations. The declining situation in Kashmir has been a direct outcome of a gradual weakening of the region's structural stability,' a condition which has aggravated the problem further by nourishing the deep frustrations and rising intolerance of the Kashmiris especially the younger ones.

The nature of violence has changed as well. Today, Kashmir not only depicts a dangerous situation of physical violence but also a place for structural, psychological as well as cultural violence. As a result, the costs of violence have become enormous for all the actors involved in this conflict, but perhaps not enough to deter and discourage them so as to stop the violence in this otherwise peaceful valley. Cases of increasing violence leading to further escalation of the conflict show that the Kashmiri society is in serious need of social reconstruction "energising negotiation and more flexible accommodation of diverse interests as all parties seek to stabilise relations in the face of the appalling consequences of failing to perform such functions".' The conflict has already undermined the democratic structures, processes and practices in

Kashmir and its continuance can further limit the prospects of reinstalling democracy there.

No single approach to settle the conflict can be useful due to a diversification of the problem as the latter has assumed a form similar to that of a chronic disease—a trend which reinforces the need for multiple efforts at multiple levels, to reach a condition of sustainable peace. The following analyses, based on a sustainable peace model of conflict resolution, attempts to explore whether the preconditions for establising sustainable peace exist in the state of Jammu and Kashmir.

Despite several attempts made at official and unofficial levels, consultation and negotiations have never progressed very far because each actor has exhibited considerable rigidity with regard to its fundamental position. This rigidity has strengthened over the years instead of assuming a flexible posture especially in the light of a virtual stalemate over the issue. As the stakeholders in the conflict have multiplied in number and some have been officially banned by the Indian government as terrorist organisations, the task of conducting consultations for meaningful negotiation has become quite difficult. The internal divisions among the Kashmiris over the issue of their political future and the difficulty in locating the main representative bodies that truly reflect the present aspirations and interests of the Kashmiris have aggravated the problem. The environment for the initiation of dialogues and negotiations has worsened especially because of the Kargil war—an event that shook the foundations of all confidence-building as well as peace-building measures taken so far and proved their eventual futility - and the emergence of a military regime in Pakistan headed by General Pervez Musharraf that has adopted a hard-line posture vis-a-vis Kashmir. The worsening of Indo-Pak relations has had a very adverse spill over effect on the status of consultations between India and the various politico-religious groups fighting for the cause of the Kashmiris. The reluctance of India to accept a third country as a mediator and its inability to isolate the local politico-religious groups by severing their external linkages and persuading them to come to consulting terms has brought about a stalemate in the essential tasks of consultation and negotiation.

It has been already mentioned that the conflict in Kashsmir, in its present form, can be attributed to the factor of structural stability. Generally, socio-political and economic structures in a given society and the same in the immediate adjoining region encircling it, play a decisive role in promoting and sustaining stability in the society as well as in the region. A stable, dynamic and progressive society indicates the normal functioning of its social structures. Structural imbalances and malfunctioning generate various forms of disintegrative, conflicting and disturbing forces that may nourish an already existing actual or potential conflict in a society. Therefore, in the context of the conflict in Kashmir, it is necessary to consider the existing condition of each aspect of the societal structure to locate the problems of sustainable peace in the state. The following analysis not only considers the oft-focused social, political and economic issues but also the local education system and associated conditions and the communication/information order. In addition, the question of a possible refugee problem in Kashmir has also been taken up.

Before the accession of the state of Jammu and Kashmir to the Indian Union, there was no democratic system or culture in the state. It was through the accession, albeit under unnatural conditions, that a democratic set up was introduced in the state according to the Indian Constitution. However, attempts to consolidate such structures, inappropriately built on and adjusted to the traditional structures, have been repeatedly undermined by some factors. First, the myopic policies pursued by successive governments in New Delhi and Srinagar have considerably limited the prospects of functioning democratic structures. Whereas New Delhi has indulged in questionable electoral and other political (dismissing state governments on unjustified grounds, frequent interventions, etc.) practices to make its presence felt in the state, Srinagar has repeatedly attempted to extract maximum political mileage from New Delhi on grounds of discontent and apparent apathy towards the political set-up installed in the state by New Delhi. The question of incompatible identities in Kashmir "should be regarded as an outcome of an earlier and distinctly political conflict in Jammu and Kashmir—a struggle for power between the elites in the state and the Central government. Viewing events from this perspective necessitates looking beyond ethnicity as an explanatory factor and focusing more closely on the development of political institutions and the decisions made by the political elite in Jammu and Kashmir and New Delhi".

Secondly, the rise of militancy and terrorism in the state together with Pakistan's continuous unlawful interventions have largely contributed towards creating an undemocratic system and similar environment in the state. Terrorism and militancy have strengthened the base of the secessionist movement to such a significant extent that the Kashmiris are reluctant to accept the existing political structures. Even the conduct of free and fair elections has become a serious problem due to sustained popular apathy and psychological violence incurred by terrorists, militants as well as by the Indian armed forces in their desperate attempts to establish democracy in the state by using force to put an end to the conflict. The active functioning of various politico-religious fundamentalist groups like the banned organisations—the Jammu and Kashmir Liberation Front, the Hizbul-Mujahidden, the Harkat-ul-Ansar, the At Faran, the Hizbullah, the Ikhwan Muslimeen (organised and institutionalised under the All Party Hurriyat Conference), have seriously paralysed the functioning of political institutions in the state. The strong external linkages of these groups and their many international sponsors (states, Islamic fundamentalist groups like the Afghanistan based Taliban, many foreign sympathizers, etc.), have posed serious, repeated challenges to India, creating serious problems for the government to manage the increasingly deteriorating situation. In addition, the increasing number of human rights abuses committed by terrorist groups and allegedly by the Indian armed and paramilitary forces, have elevated the situation of political mismanagement and paralysis to a new height of concern.

The external environment is only partially conducive to the free functioning of democracy in Kashmir. In the Pakistan Occupied

Kashmir (POK or Azad Kashmir as termed by Pakistan), the Orwellian control exercised by Islamabad over the Kashmiris there, has hardly helped them to realise their aspirations—a situation which has disillusioned the residents of Kashmir valley and made them suspicious of Pakistan's ulterior motive in 'liberating' Kashmir from India. The repeated takeover of the state's political machinery by the military in Pakistan (like the present military regime of General Musharraf), the strong base of fundamentalist Islamic forces there (like the Jaamat-i-Islami) and above all Pakistan's very keen interest in freeing Kashmir from Indian control by any means, pose considerable threats to the future of Kashmir's democracy. This, together with the rule of the Islamic fundamentalist regime in Afghanistan led by the Taliban and its support to Pakistan's patronage of cross-border terrorism is also of particular concern. On the other hand, the case of suppression of identity and domination practised by China in Tibet has made the Kashmiris sympathetic towards the issue and has made them more aware of their own conditions. This Tibet factor together with the violent secessionist movement led by the Tamils in northern Sri Lanka provide encouraging instances to the Kashmiri secessionists and have certainly deepened their frustrations and opposition to Indian rule in the state. In addition, it must be noted that the various differences in the social, religious, economic, regional, and cultural arena that India has with Kashmir, have certainly contributed to the contextual background of the problem in Kashmir. The ongoing secessionist movements in India's north-eastern part, the rise of regional forces in the wake of a gradual weakening of India's framework of national integration, the politicisation of the forces of social division and unrest—caste, religion, backwardness, etc.—have had an adverse impact on Kashmir, undermining the role of the democratic political processes and institutions in the state.

Role of Judiciary

A free and efficient judicial system is an essential requirement for any democratic system. Through its traditional role of rendering justice, the judiciary plays a decisive role in strengthening the base of democracy by correcting the deviations from established social practices upheld by law and thereby maintaining social cohesion. In an environment of acute socio-political tensions supplemented by large-scale physical violence, militancy and terrorist activities, the state judiciary can hardly function normally. Such cases of deviant activities leave a considerable burden on the judiciary, so much so that the latter, with its present infrastructure and resources is unable to bear the burden. With the preponderence of the Indian armed forces in the management of state affairs to deter militancy and terrorism, the role of the judiciary has largely shrunk as it is unable to face the challenge of differentiating the just from the unjust—the 'retributive' from the 'restorative'.

The increasing maturity and perpetuation of the conflict denote a situation of social tension, division and unrest created particularly by militancy and terrorism. In addition, three other factors have played decisive roles in augmenting social tensions and unrest. The root of social disorder lies in the problem of the identity of the Kashmiris. Over the centuries, Kashmir has developed its own identity which is popularly termed as 'Kashmiriyat'. In its formative phase, it received contributions from the cultural identities of the Hindus, Muslims, Sikhs, Buddhists and even Christians. And by derogating from the path of Islamic jurisprudence, 'Kashmiriyat' has appeared as a separate form of identity distinct from others." With the accession of Jammu and Kashmir to India leading to an extension of the latter's system to Kashmir, this identity came under the pressure of suppression and dilution. New Delhi's Kashmir policy has done little to preserve and respect this distinctness. In addition to the already formed identity problem, the gradual erosion of 'Kashmiriyat' and its replacement by a hard-core brand of Sunni identity that is bred in the religious seminaries of Afghanistan and Pakistan and spread by local politico-religious groups and foreign mercenaries have added a new dimension to the problem of identity of the Kashmiris. The situation has declined further as a result of the activities of foreign, mostly Afghan, mercenaries in the valley who tried to superimpose their rigid religious system over the all-embracing

Kashmiri brand of Islam despite the distaste of the Kashmiris for the Afghans due to the long history of oppressive Afghan rule over the valley. This has evoked strong but muted reactions.

Next to the issue of identity, comes the significant issue of human rights. Cases of massive abuses of human rights of the Kashmiris have been the result of the continuation of the conflict. Human rights abuses have assumed the form of killings, massacres, looting, rape, torture, and brutality, death in police custody, undue detention, etc., for which not only the terrorist and militant groups of Kashmir and foreign mercenaries are responsible but also the Indian police and armed forces. They are equally responsible for human rights violations through the massive anti-insurgency operations undertaken by them. As a result of such cases of human rights abuses—being the outcome of the activities of each actor involved in the conflict in its respective capacity for the realisation of its objectives—a vicious cycle has come into existence whereby violence and human rights abuses committed by one actor breed the same on the part of another actor by way of reaction. This has given a new dimension to the already deep rooted and complicated Kashmir problem that has evoked harsh criticisms at several international fora like the United Nations, the European Union, the Organisation of the Islamic Conference, etc., regarding India's role in Kashmir. The strong foreign linkages of the terrorist and militant groups operating in Kashmir have been freely and effectively used by the latter to tarnish the image of an allegedly 'hegemonic' India at the world level, drawing international sympathy and attention that are used to pressurise India. Such anti-Indian propaganda is being repeatedly used to force India to come to a political settlement by giving up its control over Kashmir through a blatant dismissal of the Instrument of Accession Act of 1947 that made Kashmir an "integral part of India". The role of the international community has been far from a neutral one. Individual countries and human rights organisations like Amnesty International, etc., have held India fully responsible for the death and torture of innumerable Kashmiris.

Apart from the internationalisation of the Kashmir problem, the human rights issue has had other effects as well. On the Indian side, it has imposed several restrictions on the actions of the police, armed and paramilitary forces in the region, in the name of security. This strategy of the terrorists and militants has succeeded in weakening India's capacity to deal with violent actions, which are reactions to its own actions, by using the Kashmiris as human shields for their objectives. On the side of the Kashmiris, human rights abuses have bred greater resentment, hatred and vengeance among them (especially the younger generation) towards New Delhi, apart from demoralising an already conflict-ridden, divided society through psychological and cultural violence. The vicious cycle of violence which has diversified as well as intensified the Kashmir problem cannot be broken unless every actor guarantees true restraint in its activities vis-a-vis its opponent(s) and abandons a zero-sum approach towards solving the problem. This offshoot of what is essentially a political problem calls for greater alertness and care on the part of India in dealing with Kashmir and re-states the fact that the Kashmir problem cannot be solved by the use of blatant and naked force, apart from highlighting the results of the historic folly of not settling the Kashmir problem at an early stage. It also signifies that instead of solving the problem, the respective policies are creating more problems than they are trying to address and solve a situation leading to a deviation from the accepted and expected path of conflict resolution.

Apart from such factors, the gradual economic decline of the state, for instance, the drying up of the main sources of the state's revenue like tourism, handicrafts, agro-based industries, etc., lack of investment as well as the serious problem of increasing unemployment and popular frustration, has intensified social tensions and unrest in this once peaceful region. Thus, the political and socio-economic conditions clearly denote a lack of structural stability in this region.

Like the disturbing political sphere encircling Kashmir, socio-economic conditions in the adjoining regions are far from being conducive for the settlement of the Kashmir issue, and, in some cases, are worse than the political conditions. Social tensions, conflict and unrest, at varying levels of intensity, are recurrent in the entire region surrounding Kashmir. The economic scenario is better due to the greater economic clout and improved economic conditions of India compared to the gross economic calamities rampant in Pakistan and Afghanistan. However, the crisis in Kashmir and the reluctance of the Kashmir : to accept any form of external intervention—be it in the economic or other spheres—prevents the extension of any positive socio-economic framework to the state.

Educational Development

Over the years the rate of literacy has considerably increased in the state through the spread of education although the psyche and attitude of the local Kashmiris are neither wholly positive nor fully enlightened and conscious. Whereas in 1961, 11.03 per cent of the state's population was literate, in 1981, the figure rose to 26.67 per cent with the percentages of mate and female literates being 36.29 and 15.88 respectively. Educational enrolment multiplied from 78,000 in 195051 to 940,000 in 1992-93, the number of secondary schools from 5,600 in 1950-51 to 262,000 in 1992-93 and that of general colleges from 2,779 in 1950-51 to 34,000 in 1993. However, it is doubtful whether the education imparted to the people is objective or not. In the light of the bleak employment possibilities in the region, the education system has appeared to be less trustworthy in the eyes of the younger generation and the ongoing march of violence and disorder have not only hit the educational institutions adversely (in the form of closures, physical destruction, etc.), but have created a sense of hopelessness vis-a-vis the objectives of promoting education and the role of such institutions.

The political conflict in Kashmir is clearly reflected by the information-communication set-up in the state which, being divided into two broad parts, plays an important role in expressing the concerns, accusations and propaganda of each side against the other. Apart from the Indian government's own information/communication network, the terrorist and militant groups have their own resources for mass communications and mobilisation—newspapers, journals, radio stations, etc. However, Kashmir's proximity to Pakistan and the present revolution in the world of information and communications, have made the task of controlling the entry of foreign information from across the borders (that aim to encourage the Kashmiris in their anti-Indian movement and mobilise support for the activities of the various politico-religious groups and their internal dissemination) extremely difficult if not impossible. As a result, the task of alienating Kashmir from its external supporters by cutting off the means of regular, reliable and efficient communications has become impossible.

There is little information on the issue of refugees created by the conflict in Kashmir. However, as a result of the conflict, a huge pool of internally-displaced persons (around 50,000) has been created. The traditional Hindu inhabitants (known as Pandits) constitute a considerable proportion of this huge pool. The plight of these Pandits who were forced to flee Kashmir in the wake of alarming atrocities committed against them and now live under poor conditions in Jammu, Delhi and in other places, is quite miserable. No progress has been made in resettling the Kashmiri Pandits in their original homeland under state protection. As a result, organisations of the Pandits like Panun Kashmir have repeatedly demanded a separate and safe homeland for themselves in Kashmir. This has certainly contributed towards the ongoing socio-political disorder in Kashmir.

The foregoing analysis clearly indicates the demoralising effect that the conflict has had on the life of the common man. It is doubtful whether the initial enthusiasm and vigour with which the Kashmiris had started their movement still motivate and lead the common Kashmiris. Although New Delhi has failed to resolve the conflict in Kashmir and terminate the alienation of the Kashmiris, at the same time, the Kashmiris have been unable to achieve their basic goals. In this battle of nerves between New Delhi and Srinagar, it cannot be concluded that the morale of the Kashmiris is still strong enough to lead them in the near future in their continued fight. After all, the common man, as in many other similar cases, has been the worst victim of the conflict as he has to lead a life devoid of a dependable and regular source of livelihood, peace of mind and a sense of both objective and subjective security, and above all, a general sense of optimism about the future that possibly is not as uncertain as it is now.

It is hard to determine whether the patience of the Kashmiris over the realisation of their demands is increasing or decreasing. Occasional outbursts of violence do not necessarily signify intolerance because such events are the result of terrorist and militant activities rather than the work of the common man. In this context, mention must be made of the various "senti-mental' walls that the offenders, victims, third parties and analysts have created. These 'walls' have erected greater obstacles before those who are keen on resolving this increasingly alarming dispute. Any future plan for conflict resolution must take note of these 'walls' and attempt to deconstruct them in order to make progress.

The prevailing socio-political and economic conditions clearly reveal the problem of structural stability or rather, instability, in Kashmir, a problem which has attacked the base of objective security in the state and has created severe problems concerning subjective security. No comprehensive attempt has been made to improve both objective and subjective security conditions in the state as security thinking in India remains largely confined to the sphere of macro-external threats rather than micro internal conditions having the potential of destabilising the system as a whole. In the light of continuous Pakistan-Afghanistan patronage provided to the several terrorist and militant groups in Kashmir, strengthening the need and practice of more rigid anti-terrorist, anti-militant and anti-insurgent actions on the part of the Indian government, the prospects of restoring objective and subjective security in the region seem to be dismal.

The external conditions appear to be relatively more stable than the internal conditions although problems regarding structural stability are present in almost all of the surrounding region. Multiple cases of acute terrorism, violent secessionist movements, insurgencies, Islamic fundamentalist outbursts, etc. can be easily located. These, together with a lack of security cooperation among the members of the South Asian Association for Regional Cooperation (SAARC) has made the external objective and subjective security conditions quite weak. This lacuna demonstrates the absence of a security community (similar to that of the European Union) in South Asia. Despite being in a position of relative stability, the objective and subjective security conditions in the region external to Kashmir are not favourable for stability and peace and hence the entire region is conflict-prone.

The preceding analysis clearly shows the absence of the necessary pre-conditions of sustainable peace in the state at the required level so as to end the conflict. This absence has largely been the result of an inappropriate Kashmir policy followed by New Delhi overall these years, a policy which has neither yielded any result in the area of political settlement nor has made any real progress in the area of socio-economic development of the state. Today, the Kashmir problem has assumed other dimensions that must be taken into consideration. Attempts should no longer focus on and deal with the main political issue. The resolution of the Jammu and Kashmir state assembly demanding greater autonomy for the state is a glaring example of this folly of dealing with the matter from one side, with the help of force rather than using other means to address the problem. The Indian government has to bear the burden of its folly in the near future. Erecting the pillars of sustainable peace is a time-consuming matter which should have complemented the previous actions taken at the level of high politics. However, a fresh attempt may not be totally irrelevant even now. Otherwise, this recent move cannot only heighten the problems of high-level hostilities at multiple levels but will certainly alienate Kashmir from India to an unbridgeable distance. It is now in the interests of the common people of Kashmir that confidence-building and peace-building measures with a view to sustainable peace are required at the lowest level of the social structure, i.e., a micro-peace approach is more necessary in the post-Kargil period to deal with the institutional and organised political forces in the state rather than a macro-peace approach. It should be noted that with time, the flexibility regarding the selection of options is disappearing at a very fast rate. At the present level of complexities, no singular approach would yield any result. Without a constructive and re-oriented approach based on the elimination of misperceptions, lack of political will and incorrect assessment of the total situation on the part of the decision-makers and political elites, no solution can be envisaged for the future, a situation which would not be in the interests of any party involved in the conflict.

12

Joining Nuclear Club

Ensuring national security is one of the primary tasks of a state. The national government is responsible for protecting its citizens from external aggression. One way to deter the enemy from launching a full-scale attack lies in the acquisition of nuclear weapons. Though a good many people continue to debate the futility of armed peacc or specifically, of nuclear deterrence in ensuring durable peace and stability, nevertheless, deterrence is still accepted as a means of protecting national security by a sisable community of strategic thinkers. More importantly, the major powers that matter most in the world subscribe to this philosophy. Underlying the strategy of deterrence is the assumption that if deterrence fails a nuclear war would be imminent. In a counter-city strategy-where cities are targeted and held as permanent hostages —a nuclear exchange may result in a horrifying catastrophe. War no longer remains a competition between two belligerents primarily through their armed forces. People are very much involved in a total nuclear war.

When security is viewed in its many prismatic elements, the distinction between internal and external security tends to get blurred. Some argue that in perception at east, boundaries are being obliterated and sub-national security issues are taking precedence. This involves not only the active participation and articulation of interest of social and political groups having a compelling effect upon the decision-making process, but also challenging the authority of the state as the groups resort to using arms to redress their grievances. In other words, groups and individuals in a state should not be alienated or threatened to such an extent that they themselves become a source of threat to the security of the state (Banerji, 1998: 26). One call fully agree on this point but at the same time, one feels that these issues have more to do with the problems of good governance in a plural society ensuring egalitarian economic development, accommodating group interests, effecting a judicious balance between persuasion and coercion and the like. At any rate, these internal security dynamics have very little bearing upon nuclear decision-making though their contribution in creating a conducive or unfavourable decision-matrix is not entirely ruled out.

The government takes decisions regarding national security. People in general can exercise very little control over such decision-making. However, in the ultimate analysis, individuals who occupy different positions in government actually take the decisions and they are susceptible to pressure, persuasion and influence from fellow individuals and institutions. In India, where a vibrant democratic system thrives along with all increasingly sharp media scrutiny, an exploration into the situation at the dawn of a new century may perhaps be rewarding. In a representative democracy, people throw up leaders and messiahs from among themselves who decide their fate in turn. How far these leaders can effectively be controlled is a question that has not been very convincingly answered. This chapter seeks to explore the extent of public control on nuclear decision-making in India—the perspective being a flourishing democracy that enters a new millennium—with a special focus on the role of the leadership.

As individuals, when we confront a situation, we define it first, choose our priorities and act accordingly. The leader of a state also does the same but his choice of priorities and subsequent actions acquire a larger meaning as he takes decisions on behalf of a large community and thereby profoundly affects the developments that shape history. Events that shape history include war and peace—events involving decisions on which people have very little control. War and peace decisions are primarily the prerogative of the men at the top who happen to be at the helm of affairs when these decisions are taken. The impact of a single personality on war policy decisions gains serious proportions when one considers that some leaders in the world enjoy such wide power as to determine the future of humanity. For example, the American President—and now even the Indian Prime Minister has the authority to press a button to start a nuclear war. It is true that the people elect their representatives and they also retain the right to replace these representatives with others. In other words, the ultimate power lies with the people. Nevertheless, the view persists that national security is best guaranteed by the top-ranking leaders with the help of the specialists, professionals and the experts in the field. In effect, the responsibility primarily lies with the political leaders.

People have developed some ways to exercise influence over the decision-makers especially when matters tend to go out of hand. Marching in demonstrations, signing petitions, writing letters, poster and leaflet campaigns and meeting with the decision-makers are generally accepted as useful democratic means of influencing policy decisions. However, spontaneous public emotion is aroused under adverse circumstances when the actual or potential threat to survival or a sense of loss and deprivation assumes a serious credibility. For example, the anti-nuclear freeze movements in Western as well as in eastern Europe in the early and mid-1980s gathered momentum when the Europeans thought that a nuclear confrontation was imminent between the US and the then Soviet Union. Their apprehension was that in such a confrontation, the superpowers would avoid hitting each other and use Europe as a theatre of war instead.

How do the leaders feel about it? In the early 1980s, the view of the Reagan administration regarding these anti-nuclear movements was unsympathetic. The Secretary of State at this point of time was Alexander M. Haig. His perceptions, which appeared later in his autobiography, are quite revealing. He felt that :

> It is the duty of any administration to listen to messages contained in great popular movements and to try to

> understand their deeper meanings. But if the demands of a popular movement are likely, if adopted, to bring about the results opposite to the aim desired by the movement itself, then leaders must not yield to popular pressure.

He further added,

> If democratic governments have an obligation to listen, they have no mandate to yield and must remember that even if there are a million demonstrators in the streets, they remain demonstrators (Haig, 1984: 236-37).

However, the leaders have often changed their position under public pressure. In a way, the freeze movement was instrumental in compelling the Reagan administration to initiate a dialogue with the Soviet Union and paving the way for the Reagan-Gorbachev summit meetings.

In the Central Asian state of Kazakhstan, President Nazarbayev initially claimed nuclear status for his country. He claimed that nuclear tests were carried out within its territory before the nuclear Non-Proliferation Treaty was even drafted. It is generally believed that external pressure and financial incentives changed his plans as Kazakhstan eventually acceded to the Non-Proliferation Treaty. But there was opposition to nuclear weapons from local people in the state as well. In 1991, Nazarbayev had to close down the testing site at Serniplatinsk because of a mass movement against nuclear testing led by a poet.

It has been mentioned earlier that spontaneous public emotion is aroused when a situation becomes directly adverse to the conditions of physical or emotional existence. People generally relish accumulation of strength by the state or its commanding abilities in its relations with other states. In the United States (US), during the Vietnam War, people demonstrated only when the bodies of American soldiers in plastic bags started pouring into America, compelling the state to withdraw from a conflict in a distant land.

The messiahs are leaders with charisma. Millions of people tend to explain the political or economic problems of the state in terms of the "failure of leadership". Only the appearance of a Messiah on the political scene, they believe, will set things right again. This is known as the 'Messiah Complex' and "This craving for a masterful, macho leader is voiced today by even the most well-meaning of people as their familiar world crumbles, as their environment goes more unpredictable and their hunger for order, structure and predictability increases" (Toffler, 1980: 416). Over the years, the people have been a little bit disillusioned but the longing for the ultimate leader continues.

If not already a committed party member in opposition, a voter is always willing to give a new incumbent in office adequate chance to prove his mettle. It is quite possible that the voter is soon disappointed with the level of his so-called representative's inefficiency—he is frustrated and dejected but the search for a new Messiah continues. He tries to make a Messiah out of ordinary men and in the process, loses his own significance as submission to a Messiah, in most cases, submerges individual identity. There are many instances when leaders have been regarded as Messiahs albeit temporarily. Prime Minister Rajiv Gandhi, Mr. Clean in the initial years of office, was heralded as the 21 st century technology Messiah. It was expected that he would make a break with the past and lead the country towards a techno-modern society. Mikhail Gorbachev was regarded as the disarmament Messiah with his unilateral arms cuts and the idea of political solutions for military problems.

Charisma is the ability to inspire devotion and enthusiasm. The tool in the hands of charismatic leaders to derive obedience, is direct emotional appeal. Under the present day democratic set up of governments, where there is a fixed hierarchy of officials and where legal rules govern the organisation of leaders and the subordinates charisma perhaps cannot supersede the Constitutional norms, But within the Constitutional framework, a political leader can skilfully use his charisma to influence policy decisions and garner public support.

Fall from grace, however, takes place pretty often—as it happened with Prime Minister Rajiv Gandhi, with the Soviet

Premier Mikhail Gorbachev, even with Lenin in Russia. Still, the search for new heroes, new Messiahs, continues. This is a potentially dangerous situation. When the public mood reflects such a cry for an effective leadership, it becomes easier for a charismatic leader to go his own way and nourish his personal interests. If the leader can offer to the people at least an illusion of being successful in his conduct of domestic and foreign policies—policies that may or may not benefit the country in the long run—his current standing in public ensures popular support.

A leader may have a Constitutional role but relative influence of the leaders as individuals becomes more important than their role behaviour. Beliefs about the most important issues of foreign policy—those involving war and peace—are usually unrelated to roles (Jervice, 1976: 26). If one considers—the views and acts of various Prime Ministers of India (from Jawaharlal Nehru to Atal Bihari Vajpayee) on issues of military security, acquision of nuclear weapons and various other related matters, one may notice how their beliefs, motives and interests have guided India's security policy, leaving marks of inconsistencies.

Nuclear Policy

When it comes to simple generalisations, it would appear that the Indian nuclear policy has progressed spasmodically, by fits and starts. This is not surprising especially when in ultimate analysis, the Prime Minister and his Cabinet—or more specifically, the Cabinet Committee on Political Affairs—are responsible for analysing and evaluating the internal and external situations and providing direction and policy to the government. Much depends on the Prime Minister as he can and very frequently does make the Committee irrelevant in decision-making. It is not without reason that many watchers of India's foreign and security policy have talked about how the committees have been hijacked by leaders who could not tolerate disagreement or opposition, or how the Prime Minister's Office (PMO) generally superseded the Cabinet Secretariat or the Ministry of External Affairs.

Leaders, when they are gravely concerned about their political survival, tend to act cautiously. However, policies undergo fluctuations depending upon the personality factor of the decision-maker. The assumption is that a maverick would certainly have a different attitude and style than an ultra-cautious calculating mind. Nevertheless, in India, one can detect two very basic objectives of security policy: (i) the obvious duty of the state: to protect its political independence, territorial independence and sovereignty, and (ii) the 'extra-ordinary' and unique effort: to spread the cult of non-domination. Within this perspective, the role of the leaders in making India's nuclear policy needs to be ascertained.

Nehru's Legacy

Nehru shaped the policies in the initial years after independence. He was against the use or threat of use of nuclear weapons and called for nuclear disarmament instead. Just after independence a militarily as well as economically weak India was not in a position to compete with the major powers for ensuring military balance. Rather, the sad experience of the colonial rule, the deep sense of an unjust international system and the fresh and pure aspiration of a young nation came together to take an idealistic blend. But the civilian nuclear programme that developed with Nehru's support was instrumental in providing India with a basic infrastructural facility and skilled nuclear personnel when the need arose. It is generally accepted that the 1962 defeat imposed by China followed by the nuclear tests provided the impetus for India to go nuclear and Prime Minister Shastri gave the go ahead signal. Despite her initial reservations, Mrs. Indira Gandhi found the nuclear issue politically useful as well and authorised the 1974 Pokhran test. What followed next was an era of confusion as nobody was quite sure of Indian plans. Successive governments followed an inactive policy for the next twenty-four years and thereby helped to build up a general consensus that India might not go nuclear unless directly threatened by a nuclear attack, but she would keep her nuclear option open nonetheless. This position was quite acceptable to the public in general.

The policy had its own charm. On the one hand, the issue of national security was not being neglected and on the other, it was in consonance with the moral objective of spreading the cult of non-domination. Whenever India was affronted with pressure from the recognised nuclear weapons states to renounce the option, she could come up with a more moral, more profound stand of total nuclear disarmament, thereby putting the big five on the defensive. This worked quite effectively during the Cold War days but towards the end of it, the disarmament politics became an irritating game. Through the Comprehensive Test Ban Treaty, the recalcitrant states were sought to be roped in, and to a large extent this renewed effort instigated the Pokhran-II tests as India tried to wriggle out from the dragnet.

Interestingly, the leaders played their bit in the process. Prime Minister Rajiv Gandhi was keen on having a breakthrough in disarmament negotiations to achieve a nuclear free non-violent world. He put forward an action plan in the General Assembly of the United Nations to eliminate all nuclear weapons by the year 2010. The Delhi Declaration with the Russian Premier, Mikhail Gorbachev, for a nuclear free world, the Six Nations' Peace Initiative, ail agreement with Pakistan on not attacking each other's nuclear installations. Rajiv Gandhi was a disarmament Messiah in the making. Still when his plans failed to muster enough support and reports on Pakistan's efforts to acquire nuclear weapons continued to pour in, he gave the go ahead for the weaponisation programme.

Weak governments succeeded Rajiv Gandhi during which the leaders were more embroiled with internal political squabbles and economic chaos. However, they kept the money flowing into the nuclear programme. Prime Minister Narasimha Rao reportedly planned for a nuclear test but the American reconnaissance satellites discovered the test preparations and consequently the test was called off.

Public reaction till the Pokhran-II explosions indicated that they were more or less contented with 'keeping the option open' policy and they were against renouncing the option under external pressure. There was a hue and cry over media reports in India in early 1994 when it came to light that an Indian team of officials was secretly holding talks with an American delegation in London on the nuclear future. This embarrassed the government of Prime Minister Rao. Consequently, the government had to downplay the talks and categorically stated that the government will not succumb to any pressure tactics of the United States or any other power. Likewise, Prime Minister Gujral had to cancel the appointment of a noted academician as one of his advisors, because the opposition thought that the concerned person was so on the Western non-proliferation measures that aimed at capping India's nuclear programme. Indeed, despite all the signs of vacillation, the Indian nuclear policy has followed a path over the years where Pokhran-II comes as a climax and not as a departure from the past (Majumdar, 2000: 200-14).

Prime Minister Vajpayee authorised the Pokhran-II tests soon after assuming power. Going overtly nuclear was a clearly known stand of the Bharatiya Janata Party (BJP). How could BJP come to power? One representative analysis goes like this:

> ... After Rao, the absence of a governing ideology left Indian politics in a state of near permanent chaos. Coalition government after coalition government collapsed, necessitating fresh elections, which produced more fragile, aimless coalitions, which collapsed again....
>
> As frustration grew, the Bharatiya Janata Party ... saw its star rise. The party had long been a political pariah. But as the decade progressed, instability bred a burger for order and a tolerance of authoritarianism .... (Beinart, 1998: 25-26).

The same analysis describes the nuclear tests partly as a political play of the BJP to retain power by generating nationalist sentiment and partly as an expression of a movement for worshipping military power and restorating Hindu pride.

Critics have cited many reasons, especially for India, as motivations forgoing nuclear which are not really related to the question of national security. One can summarise some of the main points. To begin with, the aim was to gain international prestige and status and to project her in global politics. Or, it was an attempt to gate-crash into the Security Council of the United Nations (U.N.)

and secure a permanent seat. Or, perhaps, it was a signal to the United States that India would not like to be neglected by the West while China enjoyed cooperative engagement. Again, it was probably a symbolic protest against the current attempts by the West to enforce discriminatory treaties upon India. The motivations have also been linked to the domestic socio-political scene: for example, it was viewed as a deliberate ploy of the Bharatiya Janata Party to derive maximum political mileage and enliven its chances of retaining power (as mentioned earlier). And probably the new generation scientists wanted to make their mark and secure more budgetary allocations in the process. One single act can have many ramifications and the motives for nuclear explosions, too, are subject to explanations based on informed guesses. However, any one of the explanations listed above is not strong enough to hold on its own, though a combination of all these can act as a very potent motivation.

Under the circumstances, does the public have a role to play?

A noticeable increase in the numbers of anti-nuclear activists has been matched by perhaps an equal increase in the number of people who now hold more pronounced hawkish views after the Pokhran-II tests. The general consensus that has been developed over the years—we will not make the bomb but keep our option open—has now given way to a fractured composition of diverse opinion. Today, there is no dearth of writings on issues nuclear in India. The pro and anti-nuclear groups are quite vociferous since nuclearism has its political, economic, social and moral ramifications as well. As some may view it "[nuclearism] is the most depraved, shameless, and costly pornography of our times" (Nandy, 1998: 1).

Nuclear opponents, at the end of the century, are beginning to be assertive as they find a sizeable growth in the numbers of a receptive audience and a few established periodicals or magazines are starting to be sympathetic to their cause as they carry anti-nuclear essays and give those pieces due prominence (Mattoo, 1999: 15). This trend is not absent even at the regional level. An established Bengali fortnightly, Desh, called for the active involvement of artists and writers to prevent nuclear weaponisation in its 30 May 1998 issue and carried anti-nuclear articles and editorials in its subsequent issues, thus generating a debate between the pro- and anti-nuclear groups.

Stategic Matters

On the other hand, the pro-nuclear strategists and academicians are also publishing books, articles or monographs favouring weaponisation and professing their views in seminars and at discussion fora. Interestingly, they have serious differences among themselves regarding the structure of command and control, the number of weapons needed, the viability of no-first-use as an effective principle and the nature of 'credible minimum deterrence'. This has perhaps also to do with the division in the public perception regarding the benefits of having the nuclear weapons or the viability of its use vis-a-vis the pressing issues of economic development—the Guns vs. Butter debate. A government has various structural and non-structural channels to gather information regarding the public mood and perceptions. This information may seem incomplete or inadequate but a rough idea can always be formed. A democratic government cannot remain ignorant or immune to general public opinion. Nevertheless, it is doubtful that the debate thus generated might induce the policy-makers to go either way; rather, the debate may result in a collage of co-existing ideas—sometimes mutually exclusive—making the nuclear policy (and consequently, the security policy) a vague and intriguing affair.

Of course, things change when the people elect a leader who has a pronounced stand on an issue. The opinion of the leader then appears to be backed by the people. Way back in the 1970s, a campaign for armaments in the United States was led by a coalition of neo-conservatives and the dedicated opponents of detente and arms control under the aegis of the Committee on the Present Danger (CPD) of which Ronald Reagan was a member. Forty-six CPD members were serving Reagan during his election campaign and transition process. No wonder, the CPD line of argument, once discredited as alarmist, became respectable, received greater attention, and with the election of Reagan as the President, the ideology of the CPD was given an official stamp, (Sanders, 1983: 283), (Zuberi, 1985: 164-65). In the same way, India's nuclear tests can also be explained to a good extent. When Prime Minister Vaipayee's party—the Bhartiya Janata Party became the majority party in the Lok Sabha, theoretically, the BJP manifesto (which calls for nuclear weaponisation) was expected to be officially implemented. Here, the personality factor plays an important role. Even if the objective conditions are more or less the same, X may succeed and Y may fail, as perceptions of objective conditions and consequent actions of different leaders vary.

There has not been in existence an effective peace-lobby in India, and sporadic anti-nuclear demonstrations often take the colour of opposing political parties trying to score a few points against each other. It is relatively easy to break the consensus on nuclear disarmament (generally taken for granted) in the absence of a strong and broad-based peace movement within the country, as has happened with Pokhran-II (Jayaprakash, 2000: 53 1). Moreover, absence of perceptible protest can also be widely interpreted as tacit consent (Chatterjee, 2000: 149). Re-building national consensus is never free from obstacles, and interestingly, here again the leadership plays the pre-eminent role.

Obviously, states today are not like the Greek city states of yesteryears, and people's participation in policy making is constrained by the complicated administrative structure of the state. However, establishing effective links and networks and maintaining these among the concerned and relevant institutions and organisations, may bring in fresh air into otherwise closed-door deliberations. For example, the Ministry of Defence (MOD) can establish linkages with university departments in various parts of the country on a regular basis to gauge the pulse of the people. Along with keeping track of new research outputs materially helpful in advancing security, it is equally important to understand people's needs and aspirations. In the universities, one comes across people of different generations, different perceptions, with people coming from different sections, economic and social strata, and where there is an established tradition of free and frank exchange of views, to a large extent free from emotion and sentiment or narrow political interests.

The unique process of seeking public reaction through the publication of the Draft Nuclear Doctrine is commendable. However, the debate remains confined to certain provisions of the doctrine and largely among groups who constitute a very miniscule part of the society. The military has war-fighting contingency plans—perhaps even plans that include the use of nuclear weapons. But these do come into conflict with decidedly idealist political pronouncements and when we voice different opinions, we make it easy for the external operators to exploit the situation. If the people, in a united fashion back the policy of the state on national secuıty-the government will not have to fight on two fronts—external and internal. This does not mean that people should not have divergent views. A democracy is marked by the co-existence of opposing viewpoints. Rather, the submission is: people need not wait for the Messiahs, they need not solely depend on the leaders, but on matters of security, they have to assert themselves and build up a consensus of opinion and make the government more perceptive on the security matters as well. This requires an active involvement in the political life of the state. A self-imposed alienation from the political life virtually takes away the right to criticize policies. All and sundry and half-hearted, whimsical, haphazard attempts against state policies, are bound to have the least credible effects upon the decision-makers.

After all, India is not only the land of the Buddha—it is the land of the great strategist Chanakya as well. Effecting a judicious balance between the ideas of these two stalwarts remains a perennial problem for the government and the public as well. The leaders and the people of India inherit the dichotomy as generations fail to come up with a compromise formula. When people remain divided, interest groups peddle their respective agendas in the name of public interest, giving a leeway to the leaders to formulate their policies. In the absence of greater public interest and assertion in peacetime security policies, the leaders choose their ways. As a result, essentially private matters influence issues quite often, which are primarily public. Human ingenuity compels the man to think of devices helpful in exercising increasingly greater control over his fate—survival in a nuclear world is just one important issue. In the meanwhile, however, the cravings and the waiting for a new Messiah, who will set everything right some day, continue.

13

Leader of the Region

Compared to other areas of the world, the emergence of the idea of regional cooperation in south Asia is a somewhat belated development. Regional groupings such as the European Community EU, the Association of South-East Asian Nations (ASEAN), as well as similar entities in Africa and Latin America had assumed concrete institutional shape by the time Zia-ur-Rehman, the then President of Bangladesh, mooted the idea for a similar venture in south Asia in 1980. However, two decades later, cooperation among the states of the region—India, Pakistan, Bangladesh, Sri Lanka, Nepal, Bhutan and the Maldives in an institutional shape, has been in operation for a decade and a half though its progress is not rated by many to be as noteworthy as expected at the time of its inception in 1985. India's size and regional preponderance has often been considered a major factor that has contributed to the somewhat lackluster progress in South Asian Regional Co-operation (SARC) in recent years.

Keeping this perspective in view, this chapter seeks to examine India's role in SARC with the poser: Whether its role has been that of a facilitator or a road block. The chapter is divided into four parts. Part II provides a historical backdrop with an account of India's approach to regional cooperation in Asia in the immediate post- independence years. Part III deals with India's response to the proposal for SARC in 1980. Part IV offers an analysis of the Indian role in the South Asian Association for Regional

Cooperation (SAARC) as it evolved since its inception in December 1985. The final part sums up the arguments advanced in the previous three sections.

Regional Cooperation

India's quest for forging cooperation with other parts of Asia dates back to the pre-independence period. It was in the early 1920s that the Asian National Congress—then spearheading the country's Struggle for freedom—began to display a distinctive independent world outlook. It was reflected in its concern for the other Asian countries, many of which had been subjected to the kind of colonial bondage that India itself was undergoing at the time. While voicing sympathy for particular Asian countries, as a leading historian on the subject notes, "the Congress leaders also thought in terms of sonic kind of Federation among them. Behind this urge for Asian unity lay not only a feeling of a strong cultural and political bond with Asian countries, but also the realisation that their coming together would improve their chances of securing equality with Europe and a voice in world affairs". Both Mahatma Gandhi and Jawaharlal Nehru clearly identified themselves with the need for India's support to fellow Asians in their struggle for emancipation from colonial rule as well as their support for India's movement for freedom from British control. The responsibility to expostulate the Congress positions in this regard fell on Nehru who had become the organisation's spokesman on foreign affairs.

As independence approached, an important landmark in the evolution of India's Asia policy was achieved with the initiative taken to convene the Asian Relations Conference in New Delhi in March 1947. The conference which carried the imprimatur of Nehru's personal interest in Asian unity was the first such gathering of its kind in the post-war era which brought together representatives front all corners of Asia and the Middle East. Extending a warm welcome to the delegates at the conference, Jawaharlal Nehru called for a reassertion of Asia's role in world politics and economy, In Nehru words, the time had come for the peoples of Asia "to meet together, to hold together and to advance together". The special position of India in this regard was Stressed by Nehru, especially its important geographical location as "the meeting point of Western and northern and eastern and Southeast Asia" and also the as "the natural centre and focal point of the many forces at work in Asia".

The spirit of pan-Asianism which had so enthused Nehru was also reflected in subsequent years when India took the initiative to organise a conference in January 1949 to discuss the issue of decolonisation in Indonesia which was agitating Asian minds at the time. The Asian-African Conference, held at Bandung in Indonesia in 1955, was another forum in which Nehru played a notable role and where his quest for a regional identity went beyond Asia in an effort to create a wider Asian-African forum. The venture, which turned out to be abortive, was designed to bring the Asian and African countries together not only to fight imperialism but also to forge greater links to foster internal economic development among themselves.

As mentioned earlier, India's keenness to promote regional cooperation in Asia was also considerably guided by geo-strategic compulsions. India has enjoyed extensive links with West and Southeast Asia by geography, history and culture. Growing Indian trade lies in the 1950s with South and Southeast Asia were also necessitating some kind of institutionalisation of regional cooperation. However, even before any initiative in these directions could be taken, the Cold War entered Asia in the form of the Central Treaty Organisation (CENTO) and the Southeast Asian Treaty Organisation (SEATO). The emergence of an United States (US)-Pakistan military relationship in 1954 and a military strategic relationship between China and Pakistan in 1962 were the other adverse developments which came in the way of regional cooperation in south Asia.

SAARC in Action

Till the end of the 1970s, bilateral and multilateral economic arrangements had existed among the south Asian states, but there had been no proposal for a regional framework. India itself was wary of advancing any suggestions in this regard as it was conscious of the fact that its own size and economic and industrial development could prove to be obstacles for the development of regional cooperation in South Asia. In view of the perceived notion of Indian hegemony prevalent among the smaller neighbouring states, any Indian proposal on the need to cooperate in a regional institutionalised framework had the potential of being seen by the regional states and especially Pakistan as New Delhi's desire to dominate them.

At the bilateral level, New Delhi has experienced difficulties with almost all its South Asian neighbours excepting Bhutan and Maldives. It has been at loggerheads with Pakistan over Kashmir for over half a century, the relationship with Bangladesh has occasionally been marred by the issue of the sharing of river waters; the Tamil issue has been a source of irritation between New Delhi and Colombo; as far as Nepal is concerned, India's relationship with the Himalayan Kingdom has on the whole been good, though from time to time, issues such as those of the Nepalese exiles in India and Nepal's courtship of China in the 1960s. The proposal of Nepal being accepted as a zone of peace in the 1970s and the question of trade and transit in the 1980s, soured ties between Kathmandu and New Delhi.

Apart from these bilateral irritants there were two other reasons for Indian inhibitions in this respect. The first of these related to the more global outlook of Indian foreign policy which was reflected in New Delhi's leadership role in the Non-Aligned Movement (NAM) and the North-South dialogue. The second concerned serious differences in security perceptions between New Delhi and its South Asian counterparts. While India was keen to forestall external intervention in south Asian affairs to ensure regional security, its south Asian neighbours, especially Pakistan, desired such intervention to counterbalance what they perceived as overwhelming Indian superiority in military terms.

It was, therefore, in the fitness of things that the task of initiating regional cooperation fell to one of the smaller and relatively weaker states in South-Asia—Bangladesh—whose

President Zia-ur-Rehman suggested in 1980 that it was possible to organise cooperation within an institutional framework for the common good of the people of the region. It was suggested that the possible areas of cooperation could be economic, technical , scientific, educational, social and cultural. It was further suggested that in order to make regional cooperation meaningful, the venture had to be mutually beneficial to all countries concerned, irrespective of their existing economic disparities.

India's response to the initiative taken by Bangladesh was a cautious one. New Delhi seemed to be caught in a dilemma; in view of the troubled history of the region since independence—especially the turbulent Indo-Pakistani relationship—there was enough ground for reservations. On the other hand, India was not willing to stand in the way and frustrate the venture which, in any case, would have been damaging for New Delhi's image in the region. As a bearer of the legacy of Jawaharlal Nehru, India felt duty-bound to support such an initiative.

Therefore, in spite of its wariness of its neighbours, especially Pakistan, which could rake up bilateral issues in such a forum, India actively participated in and extended its support to the efforts between 1981 and 1985 at the ministerial level, to give a formal institutional shape to SARC. A candid articulation of the Indian approach in this respect was given by Prime Minister Indira Gandhi in August 1983 when she extended New Delhi's strong support for the move which, she argued, had the potential to bring economic and social progress. Inaugurating the Seven Nations Meeting of Foreign Ministers, Mrs. Gandhi regretted that the countries of South Asia had been rather slow in realising this. She noted that in spite of past or present political differences, economic cooperation could give a strong impetus to close friendship and bring about greater stability in south Asia. Complimentarities existed between the economies of the countries concerned and with better planning and greater exchange of information, she felt that it was possible to make optimum use of respective available capacities.

While the Prime Minister assured India's neighbours of New Delhi's commitment to a policy of non-interference in the affairs of others, she was candid enough to add that "ours is a troubled region. Most of our countries are multi-religious and multi-racial. It would be idle to pretend that we are not affected by what happens elsewhere. Even as we are meeting there are disturbing and tragic developments in our neighbourhood—which was a pointed reference to the ethnic violence then sweeping across Sri Lanka. Mrs. Gandhi further asserted that the new regional grouping was not aimed at nations outside the region. Nor was it moved by any ideological or military considerations. According to her, "Our cooperation in no way limits each other's freedom of judgement". Differences among the nations of south Asia existed and these had to be resolved by peaceful means.

This comprehensive statement indicated the broad parameters of the Indian approach to regional cooperation in South Asian optimism tempered by caution in regard to the ground realities. India played an active role in drawing up the charter of the South Asian Association for Regional Cooperation (SAARC) which became a reality at the Dhaka summit of the Heads of State and Government in South Asia held in December 1985. Special care was taken to ensure prohibition in the raising of bilateral issues of a politico-security nature at meetings of the SAARC, as Such a practice was likely to vitiate the environment for enhancing economic cooperation and trade relations, which was meant to be the basic objective of the organisation.

Considering the geo-political realities in the region noted earlier, the success of the states concerned in establishing an association for regional cooperation was indeed a remarkable achievement. Ten summits of South Asian leaders have been held, beginning with Dhaka summit which was a historic event providing a unique opportunity for the first direct contact among the leaders of the region. The institutionalisation of the movement has progressed considerably during this period with a steady increase in the range of activities by the SAARC. A Secretariat has been playing an important role in coordinating activities launched under the Association. Regional institutions like the Agriculture Centre (Dhaka 1995), the Tuberculosis Centre (Kathmandu 1992), the SAARC Documentation Centre (New Delhi 1994) and the Meteorological Centre (Dhaka 1995), were been set-up and are functioning now.

Keeping the sensitivities of the participating states in mind, the first few summits of the Association dealt with relatively uncontentious issues. Some of the notable achievements of SAARC during the first decade of its operation were: establishment of the South Asia Food Security Reserves, a Convention on Suppression of Terrorism, the Prevention of Trafficking in Narcotic Drugs and Psychotropic Substances, the setting up of the Meteorological Centre for weather forecasting, as well as cultural and academic exchanges, etc. The core issues of economic and trade cooperation were taken up for active consideration only from the seventh Summit (held in Dhaka in April 1993) onwards.

The exhortation for initiating cooperation in the core areas of economics and trade cattle from the Indian Prime Minister, P.V. Narasimha Rao. Drawing attention to the changing international economic and political scene in the post-Cold War era of globalisation/ liberalisation, the Prime Minister laid special stress, in a speech, on the South Asian region's "collective economic strength and weight as a mega-market of billion consumers". "Contemporary history tells us", Mr. Rao continued. "that economic development in all its aspects is among the best cures for socio-political ills ... introspection leads us to the conclusion that the content and range of cooperation within SAARC region has been slower than what we wished for. The reasons are the geo-demographic disparity amongst member countries and inhibitions born out of problems inherited from the past".

A ground-breaking agreement seeking to liberalise intra-regional trade within a stipulated period was reached at the seventh summit of SAARC leaders at Dhaka in April 16, 1993. The South Asia Preferential Trade Arrangement (SAPTA) called for a reduction of trade barriers among the SAARC member states." SAPTA, however, came into force only in December 1995 after it was ratified by all the member states of SAARC. Under the agreement, each member state is to offer preferential trading to the other member states by reducing tariffs on specific commodities. Tariff concessions covering 226 commodities, to be offered by all the member states, was the prime feature of the agreement. A hundred of these concessions were offered to the least developed countries of the region such as Bangladesh, Nepal, Maldives and Bhutan. As the region's most industrialised country, India sought to play a leading role in the project by submitting a schedule of 106 commodities which offered concessions ranging from 10-100 per cent of which 62 items were offered to the less-developed countries (LDC's) alone.

The step-by-step liberalisation of trade in the region outlined by SAPTA envisages periodic rounds of trade negotiations for exchange of trade concessions on tariff, para-tariff and non-tariff measures. Provisions to protect the member states during critical economic circumstances have been kept. "At the initial stage a product-by-product approach is to be followed, designed to give each country the benefit of identifying products of interest to it. The possibility of concessions on a sectoral basis or even across the world could be looked into with increased intra-SAARC trade".

The step by step approach led to further negotiations among the member states on strengthening and expanding preferential trade which culminated in SAPTA II in May 1997. Under this dispensation, a total of 1,871 commodities were offered by all the member states for tariff concessions. The Indian schedule was expanded from 226 items to 994 with reduction in duty rates from 10 to 50 per cent. As one writer put it, "SAPTA I and SAPTA II are steps towards the objective of achieving duty-free trade under the ultimate goal of converting South Asia into a free trade area".

The eighth summit of the Association was held in New Delhi in May 1995. Here, India drummed up support for setting up the South Asian Development Fund (SADF). This was to be brought about with the merger of the two funds set up earlier-the SAARC fund for regional projects and the SAARC regional fund (SRF) The SADF is devoted to projects among one or more states of the region which would be of economic interest to more than one country.

The historic ninth summit of SAARC was held at Male, the capital of the Maldives in May 1997. A new milestone was reached here in further promoting regional trade with the decision to form a South Asian Free Trade Agreement (SAFTA) in the SAARC region by 2001; the original target date for achieving this goal had been set for 2005. The Male summit also underlined the need for strengthening economic cooperation with the promotion of investment and joint ventures among the member states.

The tenth summit of the SAARC was held at Colombo in July 1998 against the backdrop of rising regional tensions following the nuclear tests carried out by India and Pakistan in May this year. The substantive deliberations of the summit were therefore overshadowed, quite naturally, by the bilateral talks held between the Indian and Pakistani Prime Ministers on the sidelines of the conference which attracted wide attention from outside the region. On the substantive SAARC agenda, the realisation seemed to dawn that given the regional climate, SAFTA was unlikely to become a reality by 2001 as anticipated. The final declaration of the summit, however, recorded the satisfaction of the leaders gathered there with the articulation of a common position of the SAARC member states at a meeting of the World Trade Organisation (WTO). The need for SAARC forging links with the European Union and other trading blocs emerging in the era of globalisation was also stressed in the declaration.

Notwithstanding his pre-occupation at Colombo with the need to counter the Pakistani propaganda exercise in regard to the Indo-Pakistani bilateral security issues, especially Kashmir and the tensions generated by the unclear tests, the Indian Prime Minister, Atal Behari Vajpayee, made it a point to urge the member states to maintain the momentum towards trade liberalisation. Mr. Vajpayee signalled India's strong commitment in this respect by announcing a decision to remove restrictions on over 2000 products "to help other South Asian states gain access to Indian markets and increase their exports". In order to allay apprehensions—

especially of the smaller neighbours regarding India's much-touted regional ambitions, the Prime Minister reiterated New Delhi's commitment to nuclear disarmament and good relations with neighbours.

The climate for regional cooperation, already surcharged following the Indo-Pakistani nuclear tests of May 1998, darkened further in the wake of the Kargil conflict between India and Pakistan during May to July 1999, and the military takeover in Pakistan on 12 October 1999. The eleventh summit of the SAARC which was scheduled to be held at Kathmandu from 26 to 28 November 1999 was postponed indefinitely by the SAARC chairperson Mrs. Chandrika Kumaratunga, the President of Sri Lanka, in deference to a strong plea by the Government of India. New Delhi argued that the conditions prevailing in the South Asian region following the military takeover in Pakistan were such that it would be appropriate to defer the summit in the interests of a productive meeting at a later date. The official line taken by Colombo was that the summit had to be postponed since there was no unanimity on the issue of holding it (the SAARC charter provides that no decision within the Association can be taken without unanimity).

The postponement of the summit which was scheduled to deliberate on important issues of concern for the regional grouping may convey the impression that India was acting as a spoilsport in preventing further intensification of cooperation in the region. The fact of the matter was that India was not alone in seeking a postponement of the Kathmandu SAARC summit. Bangladesh and Bhutan also urged Sri Lanka to defer the meet because of the regional and international concern and disquiet generated by the military takeover in Pakistan. The Commonwealth had already acted in suspending Pakistan's membership of that organisation. The Indian contention was that it would have been most incongruous and inappropriate to hold a SAARC summit with a military ruler, who had overthrown a civilian duly elected government enjoying a huge majority in Parliament, representing Pakistan.

Though not unprecedented (the Fifth, sixth and the seventh summits had also been postponed due to various reasons), the postponement of the eleventh summit was a setback for regional cooperation in South Asia. The meet was expected to offer specific guidelines for the creation of a South Asian Free Trade Agreement, the blue print of which had been ready for sometime. The conference was also scheduled to discuss the prospects of the south Asian nations—all developing countries—co-ordinating their actions at the World Trade Organisation to safeguard their interests vis-a-vis those of the industrialised nations. The issue of investment, both intra-regional and Foreign Direct Investment (FDI) which is of vital interest to all south Asian states, was also on the agenda for discussion.

However, it has to be borne in mind that the future prospects of SAARC and indeed regional cooperation in south Asia cannot be held hostage to the vagaries of Pakistani domestic politics or, for that matter, the domestic politics of any other South Asian state. While restoration of democracy in Pakistan will be in the interests of all concerned, the postponed SAARC summit would have to be held with, if necessary, the Paskistani military ruler, General Pervez Musharraf, representing Islamabad. After all, with the exception of India and Sri Lanka, the democratic credentials of the other South Asian states are not very sound, to say the least.

The foregoing pages offer a brief review of the role India has played since the idea of regional cooperation in south Asia was mooted two decades ago. It is pertinent to ask now whether the role India played was that of a facilitator or a road block in furthering the cause of cooperation in South Asia.

As noted earlier, India's original vision of regional cooperation had a pan-Asian dimension and was not confined to the south Asian region alone. Jawaharlal Nehru had been keen that a distinctive Asian identity be promoted vis-a-vis the developed industrialised countries of the West, so that an Asian voice could be heard and Asian influence would be felt in determining the course of international affairs. However, the entry of the Cold War in Asia in the 1950s put paid to such hopes and radically altered the strategic scenario for the whole continent.

Naturally, south Asia, too, was unable to escape from the baneful influence of the Cold War rivalries notwithstanding Nehru's brave efforts to build a regional solidarity to counter such pressures. However, the geopolitics of the region and the post-independence, post partition legacies stood in the way. While India strove to counter the entry of extra-regional forces and influences on the plea that these will undermine the independence and security of the regional actors, India's smaller neighbours, especially Pakistan, were wary of India's power and sought external intervention to neutralise it. As noted earlier, in view of this physical and psychological asymmetry, the initiative for regional cooperation had to come from a smaller neigbbour.

Once the moves in this direction were made, New Delhi found itself in a delicate situation. On the one hand, it was not willing to be perceived in the region as a road block to a venture which had become a prime imperative of the time; on the other hand, New Delhi was wary of the potential of such a forum turning into an India-bashing enterprise in view of the bilateral irritants that have plagued India's relations with several of its smaller neighbours.

However, as the foregoing review shows, in spite of its initial reservations, India has extended its unstinted cooperation to various common enterprises (noted above) of the SAARC New Delhi cannot be held responsible for the relative lack of success of the Association which can be ascribed to the interplay of a complex set of factors.

The peculiarities of the geopolitics of the region, already commented on earlier in this paper, continue to be a hindrance. The overwhelming regional presence of India (which accounts for some 77 per cent of the population and 79 per cent of the Gross Domestic Product (GDP) of South Asia), issues of national identity and the diplomatic sensitivities of its smaller neighbours, the continued fragility of politics in the region, water resource management, trade and transit, economic pressures and ethnic sensitivities, are among some of the factors which have deterred rational approaches to the question of regional cooperation. Since foreign policy and security issues were not meant to be brought within the purview of the venture, a common regional perspective on these crucial matters did not emerge, leaving the regional actors to pursue their respective foreign policy objectives in the light of perceived national interests.

It has to be noted that policy makers in New Delhi have always felt that India had a role to play which goes beyond the boundaries of the south Asian region. The pace had been set much earlier in the leadership that India provided in the establishment and guidance of the Non-Aligned Movement. As the Indian economy grew more sophisticated, the need to forge economic and political linkages with other key regional organisations such as the Association of South-East Asian Nations (ASEAN), the European Union (EU) and the Asia Pacific Economic Cooperation (APEC) came to the fore. The drastic fall in India's trade with the former Soviet Union and Eastern Europe in the wake of the radical transformation in this region during 1989-91, necessitated a substantial re-orientation of Indian commerce in favour of the South-East Asian markets. The 1990s witnessed India making serious bids for association with forums such as the Asia Europe Meeting (ASEM) and the Asia-Pacific Economic Cooperation, in an effort to increase its economic and trade linkages with the fast growing east and south-east Asian region. However, these efforts did not yield the desired results as India was unable to gain entry in either of the two forums, though it became a member of the ASEAN Regional Forum (ARF) and an ASEAN dialogue partner.

New linkages also emerged involving India and the states in the Indian Ocean/Bay of Bengal region in the late 1990s. The Indian Ocean Rim Association for Regional Cooperation (IOR-ARC) was set up in March 1997 with a membership of 14 drawn from the three continents -Africa, Asia and Australia—around the Indian Ocean. India was one of the countries which took the initiative in this respect. In June of the same year was born the BIST-EC (Bangladesh, India, Sri Lanka, Thailand Economic Cooperation), the initiative for which was taken by Thailand in January 1996.

The forum aims at specific cooperation projects in the sectors of trade, investment and industry, technology, agriculture, energy, infrastructure and transportation. In December 1998, India followed up these initiatives with a bilateral agreement with Sri Lanka to establish a free trade area between the two countries. The agreement which came into effect recently following ratification by both countries, sets a timeframe for phasing out tariffs on a large number of items.

It is obvious that the extra-south Asian linkages developed by India in the 1990s evolved, apart from its greater international compulsions noted earlier, partly due to New Delhi's frustrations with the slow progress of economic cooperation in SAARC. The implementation of SAPTA was delayed due to Pakistani dilatory tactics. As already noted, the prospects for SAFTA being realised by the revised target date of 2001 received a setback due to the serious deterioration in the regional security environment during 1998-99. As mentioned earlier, the climate of mistrust between India and Pakistan following the military takeover in Islamabad in October 1999, led to the indefinite postponement of the eleventh SAARC summit scheduled to be held between 26 and 28 November 1999, at Kathmandu.

Yet another source of Indian irritation with SAARC summits was the increasing focus bilateral issues were receiving at official and ministerial discussicns. In spite of its steadfast opposition in this regard, New Delhi was forced to concede some degree of informal consultations on bilateral issues at the Male summit in July 1997. The matter came to a head at the meeting of the Council of Foreign Ministers at Nuwara Eliya in Sri Lanka in March 1999. A report of the standing committee was to commend both India and Pakistan for the Lahore Declaration (issued after the visit to Pakistan by Prime Minister Atal Behari Vajpayee in February 1999, committing the two countries to an intensification of their dialogue on all issues including Kashmir). India, however, resolutely opposed any reference to the Lahore Declaration in the standing committee report on the ground that the matter was a bilateral issue between India and Pakistan and should not, therefore, find a place in a report of SAARC, a multilateral forum.

The final consensus at Nuwara Eliya, however, reflected some sort of a climb down on the part of India as the report of the standing committee "noted with appreciation the reaffirmation of SAARC goals and objectives in the Lahore Declaration adopted by Prime Ministers of India and Pakistan with a view to promoting welfare of peoples of South Asia".

In this the twenty-first century, India increasingly finds that its extra-South Asian linkages are becoming more important. The Indian security paradigm (in a more conventional military sense which seems to have assumed greater importance in the determination of New Delhi's foreign policy of late), according to Brajesh Mishra, India's National Security Adviser and Principal Secretary to the Prime Minister, dictates that South Asia had always been an inadequate framework for this nation. India has rediscovered its extended neighbourhood—Central Asia, the Persian Gulf, the Indian Ocean region and South-East Asia—through greater economic, commercial and defence engagements. Next to the US and the European Union, the countries of the ASEAN region have become major economic partners and the Persian Gulf has emerged as an important source of energy, foreign exchange earnings and job opportunities for skilled Indians.

India is, therefore, placed in a delicate if not a complex situation. On the one hand, its location in the south Asian geographical setting is a reality it can hardly disown; the closest possible cooperation with its immediate south Asian neighbours is, therefore, in India's obvious national interest. On the other hand, the extra-South Asian linkages, especially in the context of the broader Asian Continent, are a reflection of the multi-faceted character of the contemporary Indian state and these need to be sustained and nurtured. It is in this context that India's role in South Asian regional cooperation has to be evaluated. Given the geopolitical peculiarities and compulsions under which it has acted, India has in recent years, tried to facilitate greater economic cooperation in the region though not with the kind of success anticipated. On the other hand, its extra-regional linkages and interests have often sent contradictory signals to its south Asian partners and have, to that extent, dampened the spirit of regional cooperation. The SAARC has truly been a test case for India in a difficult balancing act to reconcile its regional and international concerns. It remains a challenge for Indian diplomacy and statesmanship in the years ahead.

Non-Aligned Movement

The current dilemma of non-alignment stems from the crisis of choice confronting Third World states during the nineties. The emergence of a virtually unipolar world following the dissolution of the Soviet Union appears to have made non-alignment largely irrelevant. Yet the rationale of non-alignment clearly laid down by Jawaharlal Nehru in his Discovery of India still retains its appeal despite the parametric changes in world politics which have pushed the members of the Non-Aligned Movement (NAM) into a new situation. "The hundreds of millions of Asia and Africa", Nehru wrote, "...have become conscious of themselves and their destiny and at the same time become world conscious. Large numbers of them follow world events with interest. For them inevitably, the test of each move or happening is this: Does it help towards our liberation? Does it end the domination of one country over another? Will it enable us to live freely the life of our choice in cooperation with others?"

Indeed the driving inspiration behind non-alignment during the Cold War era was the perception that the sovereignty of the new nations that had enlarged from colonial domination and their independence of action in the field of foreign policy could best be preserved by their remaining aloof from the military alliances fashioned by the superpowers. This point was emphasised in the meeting between President Tito of Yugoslavia and President Nasser of Egypt at Briom in July 1956. The two sides commended the recommendations made at the Conference of twenty-nine Afro-Asian states held in Bandung (Indonesia) in April 1955, particularly the Declaration on the Promotion of World Peace and Cooperation. The Briom meeting was important in suggesting the first step towards the institutionalisation of non-alignment. Later Tito recalled, "To be able to uphold successfully the basic legitimate rights and to influence international processes, it was necessary to work towards the pooling of those efforts of ours. Despite all the differences, Nehru, Nasser and I, subsequently joined by Sukamo, Nkrumah and others, had similar ideas and strove after one and the same thing, and we made immediate steps to form the non-aligned movement.

Form the 'philosophy' of non-alignment, there was a gradual transition to the Non-aligned Movement (NAM) during the late fifties. The first NAM summit was held in 1961 at Belgrade. The 25 states assembled there proved to be the nucleus of the vastly expanded movement of the future.

With expansion and institutionalisation, there were inevitable problems determined both by in-group dynamics and the external environment. In the course of the nine summits held before the end of the Cold War, the NAM faced issues and challenges which may be analysed in terms of Samuel Huntington's criteria, viz., adaptability rigidity complexity-simplicity, autonomy-subordination, coherenced is unity. The ability of the NAM during the seventies and eighties to shift its emphasis in changing circumstances can be shown as an index of functional adaptability.

During 1961-1989, the growing institutional complexity of the NAM was self-evident. Ad hoc summit meetings preceded by preparatory conferences had given way to regular procedure and rules of rotation. The Standing Committee became the Coordinating Bureau, steadily growing in numbers and influence, with specialised functional bodies like the Economic Working Group and the Non-Aligned News Pool, the Centre for Public Enterprises, the Documentation Centre and the Computer Bank.

In the context of the developments within the NAM since the ninth summit (which met, ironically, at Belgrade) in 1989, it is significant to note that the increasingly symbiotic relationship of the Group of 77 and the NAM helped in refining the economic objectives of the movement and also in developing strategy and tactics within the United Nations (UN) and multilateral lending agencies. From the beginning, the memberships of the NAM and the Group of 77 were overlapping.

Despite strident Western charges of bias towards the Soviet bloc. the NAM did retain its autonomy vis-b-vis the two superpowers. The Cuban thesis in the Havana summit, 1979, regarding the socialist countries as "natural allies" of the NAM was not accepted; as Julius Nyerere, the President of Tanzania, observed, "the non-aligned countries have no permanent friends or enemies, let alone natural ones". The principle of judging international issues on merit rather than in accordance with superpower interests often did result in the NAM agreeing with the Soviet position on several question. What was involved in this was not so Much ideological affinity as a temporary coincidence of interests; it was an approach based on pragamatism rather than principle. In fact, in the period between 1961-1989, despite major differences within the NAM on such questions as anti-colonialism vs peaceful co-existence (the issue of priority), the movement revealed that it had occasionally clear perceptions of its self-interests in the changing context of the international environment.

Despite this, the NAM failed to develop any degree of coherence on a long-term basis. The expanding membership led to disunity and internal conflicts, not always mitigated by the strategy of consensus building.

The characteristics associated with political institutionalisation which developed in part within the NAM during the nine summits held between 1961 and 1989, were profoundly affected by the post-Cold War developments. A review of the deliberations of the NAM summits held after 1989 would reveal the extent of the transformation that the movement has undergone during the last decade of the twentieth century.

Already at the ninth (9th) NAM summit held in Belgrade in 1989. There were hints of the approaching change in the international environment. Parametric changes were manifesting themselves in international politics. The world of sovereign states was being challenged by 'sovereignty-free' actors at various levels. The issue of international justice was not confined to the demands and counter demands advanced by sovereign states; transnational actors of various types were also deeply involved in the debate on a 'just' new international order.

The tenth NAM summit held in Jakarta (Indonesia) from September I to 6, 1992, highlighted post-Cold War issues. One hundred members attended along with eight observers and twenty-one 'guest' countries. In an ironical twist to the pattern of history, the question of the membership of Yugoslavia, which was one of the founders of the NAM, generated an intense conflict at the summit. Earlier in May 1992, a dispute at the preparatory meeting of the NAM Co-ordinating Bureau held in Bali over whether to allow the Federal Republic of Yugoslavia (Serbia and Montenegro) to continue to hold the seat of former Yugoslavia, turned out to be so disruptive that work on the preparation for the summit could not continue properly. There was a reflection of this in the summit itself: African members were generally sympathetic to the new Yugoslavia, while Malaysia and Iran led the attack of the Muslim members against Serbia. They were upset by the Seth atrocities against Muslims in Bosnia-Herzegovina. Evidently, ethnic and religious differences within the movement were henceforth going to affect its character.

The Jakarta summit sought to strike a balance between the traditional concern for state sovereignty and independence on the one hand, and the new imperatives of interdependence, integration and globalisation on the other. That is did not prevent the NAM leaders from recognising that US President Bush's call for a 'New World Order' was really little more than a demand fora new international alignment. It was argued that the new order should cover economic and social justice as well as security; it should be based on a strengthened United Nations, rather than the unilateral use of force, and claims to use extra-territorial rights.

Reform of the United Nations was high on the summit's agenda. Member states sought to reduce the dominance of the five permanent members of the Security Council, to review their veto power and to expand the elected membership of the Council. They sought also to strengthen the General Assembly, arguing that it should become the central co-ordinating organ for the United Nations. They advocated greater independence and administrative support to the UN Secretary General as well as a more balanced secretariat in geographical and gender terms.

Economic issues were inevitably high on the agenda of the movement. There was qualified optimism over the potential benefits of the General Agreement on Trade and Tariffs (GATT) Uruguay round, including liberalisation of agriculture and an end to Western protectionism against developing country exports. The commitment to international commodity agreements was strongly reaffirmed.

If all this marked an emphasis on older trends for the NAM, there was also demonstration of a new concern for global environmental issues; the impact of the Rio Earth Summit was manifested in an important section of the final document which stressed the need to save Planet Earth from self-destruction and vigorously espoused the concept of sustainable development. It was imperative that environmental and developmental concerns be fully integrated".

These new concerns of the NAM were re-emphasised at the NAM Foreign Ministers' Conference in Cairo held in (May 31 - June 3) 1994. In his keynote address to the ministerial conference, Egyptian President Hosni Mubarak observed that the NAM has to face "new realities" in a changing world. "If we do not act with open minds and great adaptability we will be justifying the argument that the movement has become empty of content, an image without reality".

The last decade of the twentieth century thus witnessed a general transformation of the NAM toward new priorities. The eleventh NAM summit held at Cartagena (Colombia) from October 18-20, 1995, highlighted the attempt at a realistic re-ordering of the priorities of the movement. 109 members attended the summit. The only significant absentee was Federal Yugoslavia, torn by civil strife. There was a noticeable tendency on the part of the members to move away from the earlier radical rhetoric. There was strong support for democracy, human rights, economic globalisation and free trade. At the same time, international terrorism was unequivocally denounced. The older tradition of the movement was reflected in the specific criticism of the dominance of the major industrialised countries, in particular that of the United States.

Concern was expressed about the "damaging unipolarity" and also about powerful members of the international community insisting on their models as standards for universal behaviour. Even as members of the NAM cautiously accepted the liberal free market system, they expressed their support to the role of the government in technology transfer and in handling situations of market breakdown and in controlling the volatility of private finance. In recognition of the importance of economic issues in the UN, the NAM sharply criticised the developed states for their failure to pay their assessed contributions to the UN budget. While sharing the concern of the G-7 countries (expressed at their Halifax summit held in June 1995) that the economic institutions of the UN system should be reformed, the Cartagena summit was of the view that the World Bank and the International Monetary Fund (IMF) should be brought into closer relationship with the UN, clearly implying that they ought to be more influenced by the General Assembly, in which the developing countries had a voting majority.

The Puzzled Situation

The dilemma of the NAM at the end of the century found expression in the rejection by the Cartagena summit of the "unilateral coercive measures" adopted by the dominant Western countries:– these measures included trade restrictions, blockades and embargoes against states like Libya and Cuba. There was also muted criticism against the continuing UN sanctions against Iraq. Also, deep concern was expressed about proposals before the United States' (US) Congress that would confer extra-territorial privileges on US trans-national companies.

By the time of the twelfth NAM summit held in Durban towards the end of 1998, the movement faced several contradictions and contrary pulls. In the first place, the vaunted anti-colonialism of leading NAM countries was revealed to be somewhat hollow in several areas, most notably in the Indonesian stand over East Timor till recently. The role of the Indonesian militia in East Timor, like the Serbian atrocities against Muslims in Bosnia and elsewhere in the former Yugoslavia, brought home the stark reality that non-aligned countries were not necessarily paragons of virtue. Indeed, the sharpened ethnic and religious conflicts within many NAM countries diminished their importance as standard-bearers of democratic development in a peaceful World.

The Cartagena and Durban summits both highlighted the current NAM dilemma of choice between zero-sum and non-zero-sum game policy alternatives vis-a-vis the Western developed states. This point had been acutely stressed by Professor A.P. Rana as early as in 1976: "We have now ventured for several decades to believe that non-alignment is some sort of catch-all, a strategy which we can employ with equal facility within the context of the Cold War... and vis-a-vis our quarrel with the North. Even from a terminological point of view, what, one may ask has non-alignment to do with the NorthSouth divide. What are we non-aligned about? ... Even terminologically ... it makes little sense to be 'non-aligned' in the North-South conflict".

Even if it is contended that non-alignment was never meant to signify 'neutrality' between rival camps, Rana's point has relevance in the area of NAM strategy in developmental issues. Both in Cartagena and Durban, zero-sum confrontation tended to give way to the cautious search for a negotiated settlement of differences on questions concerning environmental balance and a just economic order. As Rana points out, "The Cold War [did] provide us the opportunity to satisfy the paradigm demands—effective competitive generation of national capabilities through the suitable conception and operationalisation of the foreign policy of non-alignment. When, however, the same strategy is attempted to be used in relation to the North-South Conflict, the picture alters considerably, for here the conflict is of a nature which does not provide an opportunity to satisfy the paradigm's demands; however Much we may combine together and expand. Our rhetoric in the councils of the world ... non-alignment cannot successfully engage in such a competitive task against the North".

Nevertheless, it would perhaps be unrealistic from this to contend, as Rana has done, that the policy framework of non-alignment with its undergriding paradigm of the sovereign state system, is not "appertaining" in dealing with the North." The urge for independent' decision making, free from pressures of the superpowers, that had been an important motivating force for the Non-aligned Movement in its formative years, can provide for a variety of alternative policies based upon calculations of self-interest.

The current dilemma of non-alignment at the turn of the century arises precisely out of this situation of multiplicity of policy alternatives of NAM members vis-a-vis the developed world. The plurality creates divisions within NAM ranks, despite proclamations of formal unity on questions of international peace and justice. The problem is compounded by deep internal divisions within NAM countries on ethnic and religious issues. Indonesia, Sri Lanka and former Yugoslavia offer glaring examples of such divisions. Sharp differences have appeared among leading NAM members on adherence to the Nuclear Non-proliferation Treaty (NPT) and the Comprehensive Test Ban Treaty (CTBT). India's explosion of a nuclear device on May 11, 1998 which was followed soon by Pakistan's "retaliatory" nuclear explosion, put the NAM members into disarray. While South Africa openly regretted India's action, many others also expressed their disapproval in a more muted way. Independence of action and exclusive pursuit of security goals on the part of NAM members could, it was apparent, lead to results contrary to the earlier NAM goals. Will this dilemma lead to the marginalisation of non-alignment in future ? The answer to this question lies in the ability of the NAM leaders to continue to strive for social justice and radical, meaningful reform both within the NAM countries and in their negotiations with the North, even as they support and sustain plurality of policy-making, as well as vital internal changes both in the North and the South, with determination to eliminate absolute poverty and to preserve the world with most of its diversity and life support systems intact. This has to be the new NAM agenda for the twenty-first century.

14

People's Power

One major achievement of the 20th century is to bring to focus human development issues in the general development analysis. The concept of human development has come to the surface of socio-economic analysis only in the last decade of the 20th century. However, the initial phase of research is over. The concept is clarified and various dimensions of human development are being incorporated. Also human development levels of different countries are being estimated by the United Nations Development Programme (UNDP), the proponent of the concept, and other researchers as well. Further, many countries are on the way to introducing human development as an agenda for national priority and adopting human development strategies.

The basic objective of development as an extension of human capabilities has never been overlooked in development literature. But excessive emphasis on income growth has overshadowed human development concerns and led to developmental imbalance. The fact that economic growth and human development are complementary and have somehow been kept in abeyance. Economic growth through effective policy management enhances human development and human development, in turn, contributes towards economic growth. Quite late in the 20th century, it has come to be realised that income growth by itself does not automatically percolate towards promoting human development. Countries having similar levels of national income are seen to have different human development levels and similar human development levels are also seen to have been generated from diverse incomes. Per capita income cannot be taken to serve as a surrogate for performances in the quality of life. It is claimed that the ultimate well-being of a society depends on the uses to which income is put rather than on the level of income itself. Correspondingly, human development research has gained momentum.

The concept emphasises that the process of development should, at least, create a conducive environment to enable people to have full access to resources needed for a decent standard of living. It thus concerns more than the formation of human capabilities or human resource development (human capital) and the use of it in the economic development process. So, here the focus is on how the benefits of economic progress are shared among human beings of different strata in an economic society. Human development conceptualised as a process of enlarging people choices encompasses a wide range of factors working upon the overall human well-being. Various attempts have been made to capture these factors in the form of indices such as Physical Quality of Life Index (Morris and McAlpin, 1982), Social Development Index (Mukherjee, M et al, 1981), Level of Living Index (Rajagopalan, 1982) and finally the Human Development Index (LNDP). Of these, the Human Development Index (HDI) has received universal policy level acceptability. This is because it is not burdened with too many indicators and secondly, it is a composite index as it considers income also.

This chapter intends to discuss human development in the Indian context. In section 2 of the chapter, the conceptual development and measurement of human development are dealt with. It studies the main strands of the theoretical advancement of the human development approach and also how the different dimensions of human development other than the major ones are incorporated in this area of research. Section 3 considers the estimations of the Human Development Index (HDI) and other related indices for India and different countries of the world and reviews India's overall human development level as also the individual components of human development in the backdrop of the world scenario. In section 4, a study of the various dimensions of disparity in human development within India is made by making inter-state comparisons of the human development index and the related indices and also of the individual components of human development. Section 5 deals with the human development strategies and public action necessary for the uplift of human development.

The evolution of the concept of human development may be considered in two stages. First, the initial attempts to understand the importance of aspects other than income in human life. This realisation originated in the 1970s and correspondingly attempts have also been made to represent the aspects relating to human well-being in the form of an index. The second phase of research relates to attempts by the UNDP to formulate the Human Development Index, revise the index subsequently in order to make it more representative and consider various dimensions of human development. In this chapter, the major focus is on the UNDP's human development criteria although there is some discussion also on the earlier approaches emphasising the necessity of looking into the quality of life factors. But the UNDP's Human Development Index is different from the earlier ones. The Physical Quality of Life Index (PQLI) or the Social Development Index (SDI) or the Level of Living Index (LLI) and similar others—all consider only the various aspects of quality of life, whereas the HDI includes, along with the quality of life factors, income also, though in a different form. In this sense, the HDI is a composite index. The problem in measuring quality of life is that unlike goods and services in GNP calculations, quality of life indicators have no common numeraire that values them all. The pioneering attempt in this direction was made by Mcgrahanan et al (1972) who took several development indicators such as mortality, morbidity, urbanisation and other economic indicators and examined the correlation among them and used these to describe socio-economic development. The problem of combining these into a single index remained. Morris and McAlpin (1982) were the first to formulate the Physical Quality of Life Index (PQLI). This includes infant mortality rate, adult literacy rate and life expectancy at age one as the component indicators. Countries are scaled between worst and best performances and simple averages are derived to get the index. The Social Development Index (SDI) formulated by Mukherjee et al (198 1) has a much wider coverage. A large number of variables are selected from each area of social concern which includes, in addition to the usual ones, per capita domestic great singer of modern India electric supply, newspaper circulation rate, etc. Rajagopalan (1982) defines level of living as a measure of actual satisfaction of needs or flow of welfare and takes into account a large number of variables including health. education. nutrition, transport and services, etc. These are transformed into indices by measuring their mean and distribution over critical points designated as the satisfaction point or the survival point. All these studies endeavour to measure how people actually live or the quality of their living. The other approach is to redefine poverty by Supplementing income considerations with the quality of life concerns. Desai and Shah (1988) maintained that there were also "other observable variables that explain poverty" and income poverty is only one of the aspects of deprivation that make up the expression of poverty (Kincaid, 1973, p. 172). The multi-dimensional aspects of poverty with the consideration of quality of life have found expression in the UNDP's Human Development Index.

The human development approach itself has a character of its own. Economic growth models focus on expanding the Gross National Product (GNP) rather than enhancing the quality of human lives, perhaps implicitly presuming that expansion of GNP would percolate towards improving human lives. In human resource development analysis, human beings are primarily considered as inputs in the production process. In this perception, human beings are looked upon as a means rather than an end. Welfare approaches consider human beings as beneficiaries and not as agents of change in the development process. The basic needs approach focuses on the provision of material goods and services to the deprived population. Human development conceptually blends all the above perceptions by considering production, distribution of commodities and the expansion and use of human capabilities together. It connotes even more: it analyses all issues in a society from the perspective of people. The concept has basically two aspects: first, the formation of human capabilities improvement in health, knowledge and skills and second, the use people make of their acquired capabilities for productive purposes, for leisure, or for being active in cultural, social and political affairs. Considered from this perspective, the purpose of development that emerges is to enlarge all human choices, not just income. Thus, human development as a concept has a much wider and broader connotation than the index. The process of enlarging people's choices, as the term perceives, can, in principle, be infinite. Of these, the major ones selected are related to acquisition of a healthy life, knowledge, and skill.

In the process of incorporating different dimensions of human life in the human development concept, it was gradually felt that estimation of disaggregated human development indices was necessary since the aggregative HDI conceals the local, regional, social, ethnic and gender distribution of human development indices. In response to this, computation of the human development indices for the urban and rural regions of different economies, as also for different social, ethnic and income groups was felt to be necessary. Of all these, disaggregation of the HDI by gender was considered to be of utmost importance. It came to be realised gradually that "if human development is not engendered, it is endangered," (HDR, 1995, p. 23). In no society was it found that women enjoy the same opportunities as men. In most cases, women's contribution is either undervalued or not valued at all, whose estimate according to the UNDP is somewhere around $14 trillion a year (HDR, 1995, p.6). In order to capture the gender dimension of human development, the Gender Related Development Index (GDI) was formulated by the UNDP. The idea was to bring into focus the disparity between males and females in the availability of opportunities for human development. Alongside the evolution of the GDI, the concept of gender empowerment has also emerged which basically focuses on female participation direct and indirect, and their access to the decision-making power of the society. It also covers participation in the legal, administrative, managerial and professional activities of the society. The Gender Empowerment Measure (GEM) seeks to estimate the extent of female participation in the above-mentioned areas as these are the essential elements of human development.

Over time, considerations about bringing additional choices within the ambit of human development analysis has led to the emergence of new concepts like human freedom, human security, human poverty, etc. In the human poverty concept, impoverishment is taken as multi-dimensional. The concept emphasises that income is not the sum total of human lives; therefore, lack of it cannot be the sum total of human deprivation. Human security is concerned basically with security regarding food, job, and income. The concept of human freedom covers a wide range of factors ranging from the rights to movement and free speech to the right to gender and ethnic equality, the rule of law and other democratic freedoms. The Human Freedom Index (HFl) as developed by Charles Humana examines whether each of these rights is protected or violated.

The Human Development Index as formulated by the UNDP, is only a snapshot of the status of human development in selected areas and not a comprehensive measure. The HDI for each region indicates how far a country has to go to attain certain defined goals. It measures the relative distance on the basis of three crucial dimensions : health, knowledge and skill. The HDI adjusts per capita real income (in $ Purchasing Power Parity) for the diminishing utility of higher levels of income to human development. The idea is that people do not need an infinite income for a decent standard of living. The maximum and minimum values for each variable are reduced to a scale between 0 and 1, with each country placed at some point on this scale. For the knowledge component, the original HDI considered the adult literacy rate. Subsequently, mean years of schooling was added to the adult literacy rate with 1/3 and 2/3 weights respectively. Still later, mean years of schooling was replaced by a combined enrolment ratio at the primary, secondary and tertiary levels with 1/3 weightage as before. The health component has throughout been represented by life expectancy at birth. HDII for the country is computed by taking the simple average of the life expectancy index, educational attainment index and the income index.

In the human poverty index (HPI)[2], the components of HPI-1, which is for the developing Countries, are: percentage of people expected to die before 40 years, percentage of adults who are illiterate and deprivation in overall economic provision in public and private indicated by percentage of people without access to health services, safe drinking water, percentage of underweight children under five. HPI-2 is for the developed countries and is composed of percentage of persons likely to die before 60 years of age, percentage of people whose ability to read and write are far from adequate (i.e., functional literacy) proportion of people with disposable incomes of less than 50 per cent of the median and the proportion of long-term unemployed (12 months or more).

Freedom of the Individual

In the Human Freedom Index (HDR, 1991), for each freedom protected—'one' and for each freedom violated—'zero'—is assigned to each country and the countries are ranked accordingly. The components of the Gender Related Development Index (GDI)[3] are (a) female and male life expectancy at birth, (b) female and male adult literacy rate and female and male combined enrollment ratio, (c) female and male earned income share. The GDI measures inequality in the achievements of men and women. The greater the gender disparity in basic capabilities, the lower the GDI compared with its HDI. GDI is HDI discounted or adjusted downwards for gender inequality. For gender sensitive adjustment, a weighting formula is used, which expresses a moderate aversion to inequality.

The Gender Empowerment Measure (GEM)' expresses inequality in opportunity in selected areas and focuses on female participation in economic and political life. It takes account of the percentages of women in parliament, among administrators and managers, professional and technical workers and women's earned income share as a percentage of men's. The GEM, however, is not meant to be an index.

India is grouped among the low human development countries in the world standard. It ranks 138th in the world out of 174 countries. HDI in India as compared to that of other countries has improved from 0.439 in 1987 (HDR, 1990) to 0.451 in 1995 (HDR, 1998) with its rank going up from 37th to 36th in the ascending order of the index. Pakistan's human development level has also gone up from 0.423 in 1995 to 0.453 in 1998. It is to be noted here that Pakistan superseded India's human development level during the period under consideration. This is because the percentage increase in life expectancy was 4.40 in India and 6.89 in Pakistan, in adult literacy it was 20.93 in India and 26 in Pakistan, and real GDP per capita increased by 35 per cent in India and 39.36 per cent in Pakistan (HDR, 1998, Table 1).

During the last few decades, remarkable improvements in living conditions have taken place in the developing world. However, some glaring diversities have emerged within the developing world itself. Basic deprivation is now heavily concentrated in two particular regions of the world—South Asia and Sub-Saharan Africa. India alone accounts for more than half of the combined population of these deprived countries. It is, however, not the worst performer by any means. Life expectancy in India is close to 60 years. But this is to be interpreted in the backdrop of large regional diversities within India. India and Sub-Saharan Africa do not appear to be very different in terms of either adult literacy or infant mortality. But economic and social inequalities are more acute in India because countries of Sub Saharan Africa do suffer from famines, armed conflicts, etc. The social and economic inequalities, apart from portraying social failures, also imply much lower levels of well-being for the deprived sections of the population than the country or regional aggregates reflect. Gender inequality in India is also greater than Sub-Saharan Africa.

A very common feature of India and Sub-Saharan Africa is the persistence of endemic illiteracy. Compared to some selected Asian countries such as South Korea, Hong Kong, Thailand and China, India's literacy is not only simply far lower than in these countries today, nor is it that India was much more backward than these countries in basic education at the time when these countries jumped forward economically, but the problem is that India today is far behind the level that these countries were at, when they initiated their rapid economic expansion (Dreze & Sen, 1995, p. 32, WDR, 1983, Table 1 & HDR, 1992, Table 2). In spite of having a large body of people with higher education, abysmal inequalities in India's education system represent a real barrier against widely sharing the fruits of economic progress. India's progress is characterised by a local boom concentrated in high-skill industries, but the overall growth for the industrial sector is rather low. This low coverage and poor quality of literacy stand as all obstacle to broad-based economic development which the eastern countries have succeeded in attaining (Dreze and Sen, 1995, pp. 39-40). Regarding the health component, while India's life expectancy at birth is very close to 60 years compared to Sub Saharan Africa with a life expectancy of 52 years on an average, star inequalities are unleashed at the disaggregated levels. A comparison between the three worst performing countries of Sub-Saharan Africa and the three worst performing states in India reveals that while India's infant mortality rate (80 per thousand according to the 1991 census is much lower than that of Sub-Saharan Africa (124) in the aggregate there is no country in Sub-Saharan Africa or perhaps in the world where the infant mortality rate is as high as in the Ganjam district of Orissa (164) (Dreze and Sen, 1995, p. 31). The HDR of 1998 reveal that life expectancy in developing countries has increased from 46 to 62 during the past thirty years with life expectancy of women go in tip by ten years in the past 25 years (20 per cent more than for men). India and Bangladesh, male and female life expectancies are almost the same (in India 61.8 for female and 61.4 for male). The success story of the East Asian countries in having a much better health standard lies in their provisioning of medical facilities through public support for general health care and basic education. China's expansion of rural health care was one of the most remarkable achievements in the pre-reform period. This proved to an "asset of great value" and contributed much to productive work (Dreze and Sell, 1995, p. 41 Coming to the gender question, it is observed that higher performing Asian states have reduced the gender gap in basic education fast with the impact of reducing the relative disadvantage of women in social and economic opportunities. But in contrast, South Asia behind Latin America and Africa in addition to East Asia. In expanding employment options and other opportunities for women. South Asia (including India) lags behind other developing countries (Dreze an Sen 1995, p. 46-47, World Bank. 1993). Gender disparity in India even larger than Sub-Saharan Africa. Among the three worst performing states in India and Sub-Saharan Africa, it was found that there is no region in India or Sub-Saharan Africa like the Barmer district of Rajasthan, where the female male ratio in adult literacy rate is low as 8/37 (Dreze and Sen, 1995, p. 31).

India has a GDI value of 0.401 against 0.919 for Sweden and 0. 16 for Afghanistan. India ranks 99 out of 130 Countries (HDR, 1995). A.K. Shiva Kumar's paper (1996), the GDI for India is estimated to be 0.388, slightly different from the HDR of 1995, although the rank is the same in both the estimations. Only 31 countries have a GDI lower than that of India. The sharp inequality in the male and female adult literacy rate between India and China is worth mentioning in this context. China's male and female literacy rate are 87 per cent and 68 per cent respectively at the 15+ age group whereas in India the corresponding figures are 64 per cent and 39 per cent respectively. The figures for India are for the 7+ age group and if the 15+ age group is considered, the disparity is even more intense.

India is characterised by enormous variations in regional experiences and achievements both in terms of standard economic indicators as well as in terms of social indicators. The relative intensity of deprivation in different parts of the country depends on which aspect or indicator of deprivation we are concerned with.

India does not have any single-problem region. Broad pattern south Indian states perform better in mortality, fertility, literacy and gender equity. It needs also to be remembered that the remarkable performance of Kerala does not imply that other states have homogeneous human development levels. In fact, there exists a heterogeneous pattern of human development and a varying performance of individual components. Rural poverty (Head Count ratio) is high in Bihar, Orissa but less in West Bengal. Child death rates are high in central and north-Western states compared to West Bengal and Bihar. Orissa combines a high incidence of both poverty and child mortality. Tamil Nadu has a fertility rate of 2.2 which is lower than that of all other low income countries except China (2.1) and this is comparable to the fertility rates of the United States or Sweden (2.19). At the same time and in the same country Uttar Pradesh (U.P.) in India has a fertility rate of 5.1 which is significantly higher than that of the average of low income Countries (3.4) (World Bank, 1994).

Shiva Kumar's (1996) study reveals inter-state differentials in GDI in India which are startling. Kerala has the highest GDI (0.565) rank and U.P. (0.293) the lowest. Comparing the GDI of the Indian states with that of other countries in the world, Kerala's 73rd rank is somewhere between China (0.578) and Nicaragua (0.560). Only 13 countries have lower a GDI than that of U.P. and Bihar. Further, the combined population of these 13 countries (112.6 million in 1992) is half of that of the combined population of U.P. and Bihar (225A million). This indicates the intensity of gender deprivation in India compared to the world standard. A comparison of the HDI and GDI values of the Indian states (Shiva Kumar, 1996) reveals that percentage reduction in GDI from the HDI is low in Himachal Pradesh (4.7), Maharastra (6), Kerala (6.2), Gujarat (6.3), Karnataka (6.9). Gender inequality in these states is not pronounced as the levels of human development (measured by the HDI) are not significantly far from the GDI values. Five states with maximum difference between their GDI and HDI values are Haryana (24.35 per cent), Punjab (19.8 per cent), U.P. (15.9 per cent), Bihar (13.6 per cent), and West Bengal (13.1 per cent), in which sharp gender inequalities are indicated . It appears interesting to observe that although Haryana and Punjab are high income states, they have a sharp gender differential. It is not quite recognised that equality in the provision of basic capabilities among men and women can contribute more towards raising income. West Bengal has a very low female-male ratio of average wage especially in the agricultural sector. The low GDI states of Rajasthan (0.309), M.P. (0.312), U.P. (0.293) and Bihar (0.306) comprise 336 million of population which is approximately 40 per cent of the country's population (Shiva Komar, 1996). This serious gender inequality along with the sharp disparity somewhat explains India's low overall achievement.

Human Development

Comparing the Human Development Index for the 16 major states of India for 1981 and 1991 (Bhattacharya B., 1998)5, it is found that significant inter-state disparities in human development existed in India in 1981 ranging from 0.7728 for Kerala to 0.0876 for Bihar. Following Kerala came Punjab, Maharastra and Himachal Pradesh, and the states with low human development levels preceding Bihar were M.P. (0.0948), U.P. (0. 1343), and Orissa (0. 1 597). The pattern remained almost the same in 1991 with Kerala (0.7495), Punjab (0.6866), Maharastra (0.6753) and Haryana (0.5738) occupying the first four positions. Over the 1980s Haryana's human development level improved from rank 5 to rank 4 which that of Himachal Pradesh went down from rank 4 to rank 7 in the descending order of the index. In 1991, Orissa became the worst performer with an HDI of 0.1340 and Bihar went tip to rank 14 (0.1743 in 1991) from rank 16 (0.0876 in 1981). The coefficient of variation for 1981 was 0.54 whereas in 1991 it was 0.47 indicating a reduction in the degree of disparity.

Mention may also be made of the sharper disparities in human development prevailing in West Bengal (Bhattacharya B., 1998) compared to that of India in general. In 1981, the human development levels varied from Calcutta to for Maldah. The worst performing districts preceding Maldah were Coochbehar (0. 1766), West Dinajpur (0.1107), and Murshidabad (0.1707) and the districts following Calcutta were Howrah (0.7374), Hooghly (0.6767), and Burdwan (0.5990). In 1991, the pattern remained almost the same with West Dinajpur's HDI dropping down to 0.0524 with rank 17, the worst performing district and Maldah's rank going up from 17 with an HDI of 0 to rank 14 with an HDI of 0. 1980. The coefficient of variation in 1981 was 0.67 and in 1991 it was 0.58 indicating also a reduction in deprivation as in the state level but in both the years the degree of deprivation was higher in West Bengal than in India.

Migration to Cities

Internal diversities in the form of urban rural disparity in human development facilities have some grave repercussions. The growing concentration of people in cities have almost become a developing country phenomenon. Major population movement to cities actually leads to urbanisation of poverty. "If financial and economic opportunities do not travel toward people, one major result is that people travel towards opportunities" (HDR, 1991, p.80). Urban economies cannot absorb all the rural poor. This has become a very persistent, and therefore, alarming problem. Attempts to tackle urban poverty directly by creating jobs, and providing public services not available in the rural areas, simply attract more of the rural poor. Their migration wipes out the gain and leads to deterioration of urban human development levels. Malnutrition, environmental degradation and other associated problems in the cities follow suit. In several countries, more severely malnourished children are found in low income urban areas than in rural areas. The urban poor may have higher nominal incomes, but real incomes are seldom better. In Kolkata more than three million people live in shanty slums and these refugee settlements do not have even the supply of potable water. Their living is also characterised by serious annual flooding with no way to dispose of refuse or human waste.

According to world standards, India belongs to the low human development country level with glaring internal diversities in local, regional and gender specific human development levels.

It is also revealed that the continued existence of a high degree of regional diversities leads to serious consequences. If India is to sort out these problems, it would have to try to translate its expanding command over material resources, i.e., growth in GNP, into improvement of living conditions for the population at large so that the growing income is put to use for human welfare.

This necessitates national priorities to be attached towards human development which includes formulation of human development policies as also the allocation of public expenditure on health, education and other aspects of human priorities. Instead of adopting ad hoc and abrupt measures, India should prepare human development plans based on the assessment of an inventory of existing human development resources and skills, people's health, education and nutrition, absolute and relative poverty, employment and underemployment and their progress in the demographic transition, etc. It should also address the prevailing disparities between males and females and the distribution of social services in the urban and rural regions and different income groups. Along with all these, cultural ethos, ideological aspirations and real motivations of the people need to be captured. In effect, a complete human development balance sheet is to be prepared.

The next step is to identify priorities and make a feasibility study of the human development programmes. The priorities are to be ranked ascertaining people's preferences which would be in the line of participatory development. Finally, these priorities are to be translated into specific goals for primary indicators, e.g., life expectancy, literacy, nutrition, etc. Among a full range of alternatives, complementarities among the policy instruments and their costs are also to be studied. There is some progress in this direction. Madhya Pradesh in India has published a 'Human Development Report' with a focused perspective on local circumstances. The report unleashes the inequalities and shortfalls in basic consumption and reflects the unequal distribution of income and assets and also of human development facilities.

Apart form the national priorities, the attitude of the state level authorities are also, if not more, important. Educational expenditure is borne primarily by the state rather than by the Central government. There often exist large inter-state variations in per capita expenditure on education and the states with lower educational achievements, where the need for public investment is most acute, tend to be those having meager financial resources.

The second important factor in this regard is the functioning of the public health and educational systems in providing basic facilities. It is important that public resources should reach the poor or improve the basic dimensions of human development. In many developing countries substantial public subsidies are provided for 'private goods', usually consumed by the better off sections of the society, while 'public' goods and services which are likely to have the widest impact on human development, are neglected, indicating inefficient targeting of human development resources. Thus, authorities have a very important role to play. In addition to the expenditure aspect, political activism is also important. In Kerala, the high literacy rate and wide spread of elementary education owes much to the contribution of political organisations. India also has a poor health achievement record despite spending a comparatively large part of its GNP on health (adding up public and private spending). This mismatch between resources and achievements is due to the poor functioning of the public health care system. In general, public policy in India needs to be geared towards reducing the standard of economic inequality in income and land ownership, gender, caste, health and educational facilities. In India, some initiatives taken in recent years may be noted here. The Nutrition Programme in Tamil Nadu, the Employment Scheme in Maharastra and Gujarat, Primary Education in Himachal Pradesh, land reforms in West Bengal, etc., are some examples. Kerala's success story can be traced to the role of public action in providing a wide range of social opportunities like education, health care services and improving the role of women in society. However, in general, a sharp discrimination in the provision of health, educational and other basic facilities exists mostly between rural and urban regions of different states and between genders.

Finally, it is to be noted that much depends on the social value attached by the population at large to the provision of basic facilities. Its importance lies in the fact that it creates pressures from below which could in some cases be quite powerful so as to even alter the authoritative decisions on total expenditure, its allocation as well as the functioning of the system itself. In India, there is little political challenge against the apathy towards primary education. A study by Dreze and Gazdar (1996) reveals how a village school in U.P. can remain non-functional for as long as ten years simply because of teacher absenteeism with no action taken or collective pressure organised through the period. A comparable state of affairs is not even imaginable in Kerala.

Thus, the allocation of expenditure at the centre and the state levels on human development, suitable infrastructure for the distribution of human development facilities, and general human development awareness and people's initiative—all contribute towards an even spread of public facilities as well as the raising of the level of human development standards. In India, it is of utmost importance that all these measures should go towards bridging, at least reducing, the inter-regional disparities, in addition to an overall uplift to catch up with world standards. It is, of course, true that public action cannot penetrate into all facets of human development, e.g., intra-household gender disparities. But deliberate action should be taken in the penetrable areas of human development.

Some state level initiatives are being taken to prepare state human development reports, for example, the Himachal Pradesh Human Development Report is under preparation. This is expected to unleash the most intricate and multiple aspects of human developmental disparities at the disaggregated level. It would enable the state authorities to formulate and implement more planned and effective measures. If other states also come forward, a much better human development performance may be expected by the early years of the 21st century.

It appears important to bear in mind that the concept of human development is more crucial in the development analysis than the index. The index only gives an approximate impression of the overall human development level of a region. The index considers only the major aspects of human lives leaving aside a number of other aspects working upon human lives. Some of these other aspects are reflected in the components of the index while still others are not reflected at all. Many of the aspects are not even quantifiable.

Along with the empirical estimations for diagnozing human deprivation India, it is also necessary to concentrate on formulating human development strategies and undertaking action plans towards the provision of basic facilities. Such human development programmes will be successful only if there is a general human development awareness and a recognition of the human development philosophy.

The debased, disconcerting, disastrous devaluation of values has come full circle.

The national scene is deeply distressing, grotesque, gloomy, grim.

What is the outcome?

The record is bleak and frightening. It makes a depressing catalogue: run-away prices, a steeply rising unemployment spiral, the breakdown of law and order over wide areas of the country, indescribable indiscipline and, above all, corroding moral decay at all levels.

Naked forces, coupled with cunning and fraud, unscrupulous, unholy hotchpotch alliances with unprincipled factions and groups, and false promises and unabashed alibis to hoodwink the masses have become the methods of capturing and clinging to power.

The creed of the majority of politicians, with hardly any exception has become impure: disturbance is the best way to peace, hatred to love, and fraud to sincerity; that vilification and vindictiveness are shortcuts to power grab and power-retention.

The ideal of "Government of the people, by the people and for the people" has degenerated into "Government off the people, buy the people, and far the people". Indeed we have now "Government of the politicians, by the politicians and for the politicians."

With the gradual disappearance of the leadership pledged to team work, and owing allegiance to the majesty of Moral Law, the commanding heights of our national life—political, economic, industrial, educational and social—has come to be dominated by opportunists, devoid of moral scruples and largely motivated by self-interest. This brought in a schizophrenic dualism, double-think and double-talk. This paved the way for the era of politics without principles, commerce without morality, education without character, wealth without work, and social service without service motive. The sources and springs of corporate life have thus become polluted at the very roots. The body politic of India has become vitiated, sapping the very vitality of national life.

Casting aside even elementary decencies and ignoring many urgent, vital and basic tasks, our politicians have become totally engrossed with silly and savage infighting, crafty and crude manipulations, arrant and obnoxious horse trading, unscrupulous and despicable engineering of defections, pulling down and putting up of governments as naughty children do with sand castles.

Self-glorification and self-aggrandisement seem to have become the goal of public life. Trickery and treachery are the sanctified instruments deployed for advancement in life, be it political or economic, social or educational. The result is a political disaster. The collapse of the whole fabric of moral, traditional and legal values is leading the nation to total nihilism.

Today one retires to bed every night, looking forward not to a "brighter morning but praying for a less dark morning."

Dr. Johnson's classical definition that "Politics is the last refuge of the scoundrel", is getting affirmation in our sacred *Bharat bhoomi*.

The dangerous situation raises the momentous question. Can the vital task of regulating the "life, liberty and pursuit of happiness" of our proverbially patient people be left to the sole, exclusive ministrations of the magnates of monopoly power-professional politicians.

"Put not your trust in princes and rulers... in whom there is no help," said the Psalmist. This advice, so correct in regard to the rulers of Biblical times, appears particularly timely in its application to today's politicians and political parties.

But let us bear in mind that we and the rest of the world witnessed Mahatma Gandhi's unique War without Violence in 1920, 1930, 1932, 1940 and 1942.

Tens of thousands of young and old men and women cheerfully courted arrests, smilingly braved lathi blows and willingly sacrificed their all for wresting the freedom of the Motherland from the then mighty British Empire. And in 1947, we witnessed the triumphant culmination of this saga of self-invited suffering and sacrifice in the advent of Indian Independence.

Shall we betray the ideals for which so many sacrificed so much ? Shall we fail to discharge the duty which they enjoined upon us?

Why should so many people suffer for so long the miseries flowing from crass selfishness, self-aggrandisement, incompetence and corruption.

How long shall we keep looking askance at the grinding poverty and miseries of millions of our hapless brethren? How long will they take things lying down?

Emancipation of Common Man

Eternal vigilance is the price of liberty. People get the government they deserve.

Basically it is the people that create their own graves by turning a blind eye to misgovernment and by giving unquestioned obedience to unjust laws, motivated not infrequently by hopes and personal gain.

How long are we to be blind, deaf, mute, and dumb to the appalling conditions in which we are getting engulfed deeper and deeper, day after day?

Let us come to brass tacks. Is it so very difficult to stem the rot ? No certainly not, for us, heirs of the matchless inheritance of satyagraha handed down to us by Mahatma Gandhi, the invincible weaponless warrior.

The dire need of the hour is that people should politely but resolutely refuse to yield. When the root receives no nourishment the branch withers and dies.

And this can be done by adopting the path laid down by the Father of the Nation.

In our 5,000 years of history, we have survived repeated shocks and vicissitudes. However, desperate the situation had been, however hopeless it had looked on the surface, the best elements amongst our people, in times of calamitous developments, always managed to forge unity and mobilise the nation's mental, moral, social, educational, ethical and spiritual forces and usher in a new era.

In the present encircling gloom, we must, like our illustrious forbears, with unflinching determination, set about an all-out mobilisation of our constructive forces from all segments of national life.

For this, all patriots wedded to democratic and moral values must weld themselves together and give a positive lead to the people.

Let us steel our resolve. If we will we can still build up India of Gandhiji's dream.

Utthishthata Jagrata, Praypa Varan Nibodhata:

"Arise, Awake and stop not till the goal is reached."

Religious or God-minded; such a thing there never was even during the Vedic times. In the Vedas do we not come across the lamentation of a gambler ?

The world has always been peopled by atheists, including agnostics, and theists, including the fervent followers of religion, to the lukewarm or near-indifferent type of believers.

Jesus of Nazareth, the Son of God, who came to redeem mankind was crucified, and the kinsfolk of Sri Krishna, the God who came to re-establish *Dharma*, killed themselves in a drunken brawl, all of which only go to prove that religion and irreligion have always existed side by side. Hence it would be foolish on the part of anyone to assert that the world has gone to dogs or that it has suddenly turned divine. But then we cannot ignore the general trends just as we speak of a specific direction of the fight of a swarm of bees though there will be stray bees flying in the opposite direction.

What then is responsible for the present "Swing Back to Religion" trend which is evident the world over? There is a deep-seated reason which is briefly dealt with below.

The nineteenth century perhaps marked the culmination of the Renaissance revolt against decadent religion. That century was certainly the most anti-religious period the West has ever known. And what were the reasons for it ?

Industrial Front

In the wake of the Industrial Revolution, the greatest event of that century, man came to possess powers of which he had never dreamt, and almost concluded that he had discovered the key to ceaseless "progress". With Darwin's (1809-1882) theory of evolution synchronising with the dawn of the industrial era, it almost seemed that God could be safely dispensed with at least as far as the sphere of living and development was concerned.

Newton's (1642-1727) discovery of the laws of gravitation had already come as a rude shock to many believers who thought that now God had no place in the physical universe.

And it was left to Sigmund Freud (1856-1939) to dislodge God from the human consciousness with his startling discoveries in the field of psychoanalysis.

But in the twentieth century Darwin, Newton and Freud, are also the theory of the inevitability of "Progress" have all been found wanting.

Does not evolution also imply involution ? Does not the enlightened man help the survival of the weak, in a sense defying the Darwinian theory of the survival of the fittest ?

When it comes to the realm of science, discoveries in the realm of nuclear physics have destroyed man's belief in matter. "In the 19th century a table was a table; now it is a cluster of whirling electrons which can just as well be called energy as matter," said a scientist.

Sir Jame's Hopwood Jeans, the distinguished British physicist and astronomer (1877-1946) says: "The universe begins to look more like a great thought than a great machine. Mind no longer appears as an accidental intruder in the realm of matter. We are beginning to suspect that we ought rather to hail it as the creator and governor of the realm of matter. Not, of course, our individual minds, but the Mind in which the atoms, out of which our individual minds have grown, exist as thoughts."

And did not Albert Einstein himself proclaim that "Science without religion is lame and religion without science is blind"?

Many of the findings of modern science come very close to, if not corroborate, some of the fundamental concepts of Indian philosophy such as that the entire universe is the manifestation of one Supreme *Shakti* or Primordial Energy.

And Freud's findings in the sphere of human consciousness have been largely improved upon, if not superseded, by later men like Carl Jung, the eminent Swiss psychologist (1875-1961), who was awed by the spiritual experience of a sage like Ramana Maharshi.

In his introduction to Dr. Zimmer's book Der Weg Zum Selbst (The Way to the Self or The Life and Teachings of Bhagavan Sri Ramana Maharshi) Jung says : "The identification of Self with God will strike the European as shocking. It is a specifically oriental realisation, as expressed in Sri Ramana's utterances. Psychology cannot contribute anything further to it, except the remark that it lies far beyond its scope to propose such a thing."

What do all these show ? Only one thing. Those who were looking to the scientists for the repudiation of God have come in for the biggest shock. The "progress" promised by the technological age has also proved to be a mirage, a will-o'-the wisp. Today man knows that culture is something quite different from civilization and that industrial advancement can only ensure the latter and not the former. In fact, material affluence has only taken man farther away from the "Peace that passeth understanding" the goal of religion.

Is it then any wonder that we see today a swinging back of the pendulum from materialism to religion ?

How to accelerate the pace of this swing back and how to slake this spiritual thirst, how to transform and direct this earnest yearning into constructive channels so as to avoid a slide back, is the challenging task before our religious heads and leaders; educationists and constructive and social workers who stand and strive for the re-enthronement of the Majesty of the Moral Law.

Female Power

It is no coincidence that the last general elections of the twentieth century in India should have been prefaced by the drama of one woman and her citizenship. It is no coincidence because over the last two decades of the dying century, the veil of universalism implied in the doctrine of Indian citizenship had been lifted to reveal the substantive non-citizenship of certain groups, like 'backward' castes, and acknowledged by the Mandal Commission report. From Aristotle's idea of citizenship as a status belonging to those who engaged in the activities of political and civic self-government and hence extendable only to free mates, to the French Revolution when women succeeded in claiming address as citizen, the term has connoted respect, status equality, dignity, and the rights that were associated with these values. In the liberal tradition, individual citizens are presumed to have equal status, equal rights and duties—so that principles of inequality deriving from gender, caste, class or other contexts are not supposed to be of relevance to the status of citizenship. In other words, citizens are conceptualised as strangers to each other, they are not related by fields of history, culture, power to each other. The autonomous citizen of thought found herself (and often in the case of Dalits, himself) considerably short of the substantive rights of citizenship.

Citizenship meant free status and the rights attached to that status, such as the right to vote, own property, make valid contracts, the liberty of one's person, the rights to freedom of speech, thought and religious faith—many of which are enshrined in the Indian Constitution as Fundamental Rights of Citizens of India. These rights attached to citizens who were implicitly autonomous, self-governing, self supporting, rational and are not dependent in any way—the problematic idea of 'free and equal persons' which women and the poor in any society are substantively not. The growing awareness within the Indian women is the movement in the past fifty years of the discrepancy between the formal political equality conferred by the vote and the substantive dependence of women led to the emphasis on the political participation of women-as-women, articulated in the Women's Reservation Bill. As one of the leaders said recently, "when a peasant woman asks for her inheritance rights to be part of any agenda of land reform initiated by the state, she is told that women's issues are only part of a bigger problem: do these very people count a woman's vote as half-a-vote?".

However, in the final instance of the contested issue of Sonia Gandhi's citizenship, the debates shifted ground, centring not around the false universalism of citizenship itself, but around the 'foreign' origins of a politically powerful woman. One group of sophists insisted that one who had 'acquired' citizenship by virtue of her marriage to an Indian citizen, and twenty years' domicile in the land of her affines, could not be given identical rights (of heading a government, in this instance) as, in theory at least, belonged to others who had imbibed their citizenship through the blood.' This implied that there were two, or three, hierarchically organised tiers of citizenship: the highest tier made up of 'natural' and 'primary' citizens of birth and blood endowed with the fullest rights and prerogatives, with a corresponding incompleteness of prerogatives according to the level of the intervention of the state in the allocation of citizenship. In other words, this position openly condones discrimination and the racialisation of citizenship on grounds of what is always a historical accident—where or to whom one is born—without attention to social divisions and positions like gender, caste, class.

While the natalism and implicit indigenism of this argument show up the exclusionary discourse of citizenship, there is one aspect of this position that deserves to be singled out for discussion. That is the untheorised distinction between the 'home' and the 'nation-state', entities which have been equated in slogans thrown up in street demonstrations, and indeed, in a statement made by the woman in question herself.' While Sonia Gandhi's use of kinship-activity diametrically opposed the work of 'culture' to the natalism propounded by her detractors, the issues that are raised in turn are equally fraught with political and theoretical implications. In raising the standard of certain normative (self-sacrificing) behaviours expected of a woman, she was presumably resting her claim to Indian citizenship by virtue of cultural assimilation. Apart from the fact that these are roles marked out in relation to a male, there is the more delicate question of whose and which culture. Is there only one cultural way of enacting kinship—whether of bahu (wife) or as ma (mother) or as widhwa (widow)? In the context of diverse and constantly changing cultural landscapes within the sub-continent, the answer is certainly in the negative. Must each 'outsider' then assimilate to one particular group/community/ religion's script of kinship-activity for women? This, in effect will mean assimilating to the script laid down by the most powerful within each community or religion, as Kumkum Sangari so forcefully argued in the context of a gender-just Uniform Civil Code, being debated in the early nineties.

The most important contribution of international feminist movements to social theory has been the recognition that the construction of the boundaries between 'home' and 'nation', as between private and public, is an act of power in itself, and hence political. Hence, it is important to ask ourselves whether the implicit overlap between the home and the state, between the status of a bahu (daughter-in-law) and that of citizen articulated by one side in the latest debate is theoretically significant for feminist purposes. Does the rhetoric of caring-for-kin need to be engaged with as a theory of women's citizenship-activity?

Feminist theorists have evolved a critique of those theories of citizenship which take citizenship to be made up of two emblems the vote and work-employment (the American ideal). If these were marks of civic standing, many of those who worked without wages, for instance, most women's domestic work, and immigrant labourers who worked for wages but did not vote, were excluded from the ambit of this citizenship. Despite feminist concerns for equal pay for equal work, access to paid work and the prevention of harassment at workplaces shared by an international women's movement, what has been attacked by the movement has been the 'second-class' nature of the citizenship of women, based upon the primacy of waged work as criteria of citizenship. Unwaged, domestic work—the nurture of dependents that is principally done in spheres not recognised as workplace, the massaging and maintenance of social and political relationships by the investment of time, energy and emotion—has been the thrust of the new theorising by Carole Pateman. In urging that a sexual contract prefaced the social contract of the seventeenth century, Pateman urged that the continual forgetting of domestic life in the definition of the private/public distinction introduces a negation at the very centre of social contract theory; domestic life becomes by virtue of its disavowal, a problematic boundary of civil society. Hence, she implied that the concept of citizenship, too, be gender differentiated, even if it was according to varying performances of work. That is, if caring of the decrepit and the future citizens is work which women do, then citizenship is different for men and for women. The problems of this position are many: chief among which is the imminent slide from 'is' to 'ought'. If women do the work that they do, then is it what they 'ought' as part of the 'obligations' and 'duties' also carried by the status of citizenship? Is it enough to dignify this work as citizenship activity? What happens to those women who for temporary or permanent terms, do not/cannot undertake this activity?

Rather than resurrect the old dichotomies of public/private, Yuval Davis has suggested three distinct spheres: of state, civil society (made up of informal and formal associations) 'and kinship, for evolving a theory of citizenship in post-colonial states where one's extended kinship and family relationships have continued to be used as the foci of loyalty and organisation.' The value of this is, of course, that it assumes right from the start that citizenship is much wider than just a juristic relationship between an individual and a state. For one, especially in the context of incoming residents and potential citizens, the right to formal citizenship depends upon the rules and regulations both of the country of origin and of the country of residence, and upon the relationships and treaties between these two countries. In other words, citizenship is dependent upon relationships between states, on the one hand, and on the other, is collectively acted upon within social, political and economic relations of conflict and cooperation.' Where dual citizenship does not exist (India), the situation of a bride from Italy is not identical to that of a bride from Nepal or Pakistan or Bangladesh. The reality of an uneven hierarchy among states in the geopolitical system is central to the consideration of the citizenship claims of both brides. In the latter case, the skewed structure between states being what it is, the retention of citizenship does not correspond with any capacity or willingness of their home states to act on their behalf. In the case of a bride from one of the European Union states, the relinquishing of an old citizenship is probably not only an emotional but also a real political dilemma. To insist that every person originating from a dual-citizenship country to a single-citizenship one like India must relinquish forthwith his/her older nationality is analogous to wishing a bit of (north, west and east) Indian patriarchy on the international arena. For only in completely unilineal (and patrilineal) virilocal societies such as these, are women as brides expected to completely erase their previous allegiances and identities in the natal households and regions of origin. In addition to this, such a demand also reverberates with echoes of a slave holder's laws and society in a not-so-old history. It is a history that both sides of the current citizenship debate need to be reminded of. Hence, particularly for a feminist reading of international politics, it is imperative that we resist all attempts to wipe out geopolitical considerations from the history of Indian 'family-constitution'.

It has appeared to me from the moment that I could read, somewhere in the early seventies of this century, that the word 'homely' defined the limit of expectations that the world of adults had of potential daughters- in-law—if one were to go by the number of times it cropped up in the matrimonial advertisements in the English-language newspapers. The word clearly meant many things in one: being skilled in the arts and sciences of home-making like cooking, tailoring, embroidery, nursing the aged, the young and other animals. Homely was a job-definition, across caste, class, region, religion, and household-type, but not across gender—the job of actually establishing, maintaining and reinforcing the structures of the 'home' was something only one set of people did and do. They did this because kinship as a structure of politics situated them in this way, but it was defended as a 'natural' phenomenon. Homely thus appeared as a common characteristic for defining the properties of 'women'. Yet, if anyone living in Indian kinship formations thinks about it at all, women have been historically those who have always had to travel between homes' and cannot ever belong in only one - as a daughter in one and as a wife in another. Women's experiences in the sub-continent have patently shown that they do not belong, and never permanently. Women have found this to be true every time that the issues of dowry surfaced between their natal homes and their marital ones (all through the eighties and nineties, in north, central and east India) and each time they have tried to claim inheritance along with their brothers from their dead fathers (Mary Roy, 1983, Travancore) or maintenance from their husbands (Shahbano, 1985) or even from their non-husbands (Maka tribal women of Orissa, Ratan Devi vs. Paddam Singh, Himachal Pradesh) or custody of their own children (Geeta Hariharan, 1996-7). And that is in mundane peaceful times.

The history of the sub-continent, however, has hardly been of an enduring peace. From the moment of independence in 1947, the discrete states of the sub-continent have been ravaged by different forms of violence—and the consequent trans-border flows of rejected, fugitive and displaced people. In the history of our region, we have had widespread transfers of girls for money and goods across different kinds of households, female-headed and patriarchal, sometimes for marriage and re-marriage and sometimes not. Home has therefore been the horizon towards which all women, both the sold and the unsold, have travelled, and have never fully or comfortably inhabited, never been at home in. Both this travelling, this to-ing and fro-ing, and the pain of never being at home, in the homes women have found themselves in, is what I have chosen to call the politics of the unhomely. Unhomely is not homeless, as Homi Bhabha reminds us, but a state in which the borders between 'home' and the 'world', between private and public, between exchange economy and moral economy do not exist; those who live in this state espouse a politics which reveal the intermeshed ways in which social, economic, intellectual or political life reinforce the discomfort of the unhomely.

From this vantage point, the efforts of the nineteenth century—in the prohibition of sati, the legislation on the remarriages of widows, the restitution of conjugal rights, the age of consent controversies which have seemed so significant to an entire generation of nationalists appear to have been based on an entire miscognition of the state of the unhomely. We are not talking here of the consequences of these efforts for were we to do so, so spectacularly unsuccessful would these efforts appear, that we could tell the story of the last fifty years in the nation's life as another nineteenth century. If the Deorala burning resurrected the spectre of dead wives walking, the Commission of Sati (Prevention) Bill of 1987 drew upon the old colonial legislation of 1829 in treating the widow as a free person making a choice. We are talking here of the premise of blindness that is common to that nineteenth century law and to the twentieth century one—did the state ask itself either then, or later, how such wives came to be wives? How such daughters were allowed to remain daughters? By what routes had they travelled to these particular 'homes'? Elsewhere I have touched upon the historical particularity of language in a colonial setting which distinguished the meaning of a word from the meaning in its cosmopolitan setting (like 'child' which till at least the 1830s in Britain, represented a labourer of a specific sort, and in the plantations of the Atlantic economies denoted male and female slaves, many of whom were in fact adult men and women). Here, I am only touching upon the implications of thinking through the identity-terms that became the touchstone of legal rights and exemptions by taking the history of displacement as the vantage point for the interrogation of identity politics in the country. Familial terms were one aspect of this. Autobiographical accounts of reformist males also touch upon this institution (bharar meye) current in the mid-nineteenth century. One of them specified that since bride-wealth (pana) payments among the Srotriya and Bangshaja Brahmans in Bikrampur district of Dacca ranged from Rs 600 to Rs 1200, the poorer males among these Brahman groups bought 8-13 year-old girls off the boats coming from Sylhet. Since the buying prices of such girls ranged between 100 to 250 rupees, these purchases were economically rational for poorer males, even though they infringed social and moral injunctions. Another nineteenth-century account chose precisely the criterion of disregard of the girls' jati to condemn the institution. Speaking of the ways in which 'brides' could be had without the payment of a heavy pana (bride-wealth) to the bride's father, he said,

> People take a boatload of Bangshaja girls. They may not be Brahmins at all but they are passed off as such and Bangshaja bridegrooms buy these girls from out of the boatload ... poor people buy these girls. Instances have been known when Mahomedan girls sold out of the boatload have been passed off as Bangshaja girls. One such girl after her marriage ... was discovered to be a Mahomedan but she was not driven away by her husband and she remained in the family, as such a procedure would have entailed a loss of caste, and the matter was hushed up.

But whose loss of caste was it that was feared? Not the individual woman's but of the others. Women themselves after all do not appear to have been of any fixed jati or gotra status. In the Presidency of Bengal in the late nineteenth century itself, two girls were reported from Sylhet to have been disposed off [sic] under feigned names to a Brahmin in the Tipperah District as Brahmini Girls" while a woman identified as an 'Ahirun' was sold "for Rupees 60 as a Rajpootin girl" in Goruckpore in 1871.1() Such evidence throws the immutability of 'jati-identity' into question. If women's home in the jati, as well as the qaum could always be volatile changing, then why is it that men and their laws have not recognised this as the starting point for all legislation?

This has some significance for the Indian feminists who wish to distinguish their agenda for a Uniform Code from that of the Right wing forces who also demand uniformity' of laws. Because it reveals that neither religious nor caste identities are permanently sealed off, nor birth-inscribed, for women even historically. In fact, even in the late twentieth century, when women's other democratic groups had fought for a more equitable jati-order, (specifically for 'lower caste' groups against higher-caste oppressions) they have rarely allowed for the possibility that the lower-caste woman too does not belong in the jati or got in a permanent way. She can be sold again and again between different households for different sums of money, as indeed the reports in the newspapers and journals make amply clear-repeating once again the truth of the unhomely state.

Territorial identities were another aspect of displacement of the unhomely. So while British officials, discussing the sales and purchases of children in the Muzzaffarpur district of Bihar, confidently wrote of such children as 'not slaves' but 'kin and family' ("After purchase the condition of these children is often far better than it was before, and though they are considered the property of the master, are not looked upon in the light of a slave, ...often acquire property, and in some cases, even attain to great opulence. The child when purchased is fed and clothed by its master, and when it gets to sufficient age to be of any help, is given a small monthly allowance as well ... To call either one custom or the other slavery would be giving a very wrong impression". 12), on the other hand, when such people tried to claim some rights in their current homes, they were defaulted on grounds of 'not originating' in the region in which they claimed these rights. The most acute example of this was that of an eunuch in the mid-nineteenth century who had originated in some distant shore of the African continent, but had spent fifty years in the region we today call Bengal: this eunuch protested that the lands and houses entrusted to his care by his dead master were being taken away by a particular English officer. In court, the case against the English officer failed because the plaintiff was proven to be 'not Indian'.

Even if in the twentieth century, certain naturalisation laws would come into operation, to give people like the eunuch the status of citizenship, I would submit that when it came to women, the pitfalls of a locational bias remained in the laws. For instance, for an entire generation of women moving between India, Pakistan, Bangladesh, Nepal, Sri Lanka, claims to property through inheritance became either a non-issue in their newly reached homelands, where ' there was precious little to inherit anyway, or a trap with which to lure them back to old homelands (as Urvashi Butalia's account so vividly portrays). Furthermore, for many young girls who were then subsequently relocated through marriage, labour-contracts, or other devices into yet other homes and homelands, varying prohibitions of Land Alienation legislation ensured that the distance between such wives, widows and workers and both ancestral and self-acquired property remained intact. In many states of the Indian federation, for instance, domiciliary status was not tantamount to the right to buy land there, a fact that holds irrespective of gender, but for women workers of the domestic, their deference to the elder males and females of the household, made it difficult to substantiate any greater powers anyway.

There are at least two different accounts of how one's specific interests or group identity (as women) might relate to one's political activity as citizen. One feminist position asserts that democratic political activity has the power to transform the individual, who will transcend her particular identity when in the arena of political dialogue: to which the obvious retort is normally which particularism will she transcend; that of caste, or class, or of gender. And if the latter, then why women's reservation at all? Nor can political activity be equated to a dialogue among equals alone in a country infarcted by vicious inequalities of livelihood, social dignity and ritual rank. Rather than a dialogue among equals, Indian political activity tends always to the visual—of the grand, and sometimes in the case of the debates in the Lok Sabha, a terrifying spectacle. Is that what is in store for both the representative and the participatory politics of women?

The question that is more important to the other group of feminist theorists is the problem of group closure (people coming to define themselves politically through what is only one frozen single aspect of their lives) and the insuperable obstacle of establishing what any group wants. Any group is internally heterogenous with respect to identities, interests and political perspectives; taking the policy proposals put forward by the leadership of these groups as definitive of the interests of all members of the group, presumes that the democratic and egalitarian processes have permeated the group itself thoroughly. It is to be said for the maturity of the Indian women's movement that all of them have treated the Women's Reservation as the beginning of further democratisation, rather than as an end, and are therefore fairly sensitive to this issue of heterogeneity.

The really substantive issue in this debate is the definition of women as a group. Having rejected the biologism of the past, which roots the identity of any woman in her body (sex), the Indian feminist movement cannot now resort to that archaism. Hence the 'community' of gender has been increasingly constructed as the one based on the experiences of a majority of woman. This majority, along with experiences of power and powerlessness in natal and marital households and harassment in a variety of workplaces, implicitly rests on a notion of birth-induced Indianness. It is this that needs to be interrogated: it is here that the Indian women's movement has to extend its ideas of citizenship. Mainstream political theory has tended to focus almost exclusively on relationships of birth and putative common culture for the grant of citizenship. Feminist thinking on this score risks replicating the limitations of this if it only thinks of those who are already citizens of the particular nation-state. It must attend to the fact that even within liberal democratic states, lack of citizenship-as-nationality is a source of particular vulnerability." A political theory of citizenship within the ambit of the Indian Constitution is presumably necessary before one can begin to claim the rights of the citizen.

I am proposing that in the next century, the women's movement in India will recognise this fundamental difference in the identity of the Indian citizen: and will learn that the instability of the identity of the refugee, the exile, the fugitive and the migrant is the point from which all identity-politics must begin. Because women do not just comprise large numbers of such groups, but because all refugees and fugitives share the politics of the unhomely with women. Because like such migrants and refugees spell danger to hawks watching the boundaries of nations in the same way that women have been seen as 'aliens' right from birth in which ever kind of household they have been. This unhomely politics will relate the traumatic ambivalences of forever departing and never arriving home to the wider disjunctions of political existence (globalisation economics, international politics, and sectarian domestic politics), and will finally rework the social contract theory. If this means subjecting the Citizenship Act of 1955 or the citizenship clauses of the Indian Constitution to some cold feminist scrutiny, all the better. The adoption of the unhomely politics of women-as-diasporic will reveal further incivilities of the society that we are supposed to be acquiring citizenship of, by nature, nurture, or negotiations. But more important, it will enable a distinctly South Asian and post-colonial theorisation of 'women's experience' as grounds for knowledge claims as well as for a politics struggling to find common ground, not in the home, but somewhere on the street.

15

Revolution in the Offing

Devoted to life, literature and culture, inspired by the imperishable values of India's ageless culture and sustained by the faith in the fundamental unity of India, the Bhavan has, through the columns of its journal, ceaselessly striven to mobilise the thought of the nation on the cardinal principles of sraddha (faith), samyama (self-restraint) and samarpana (dedication).

The whole world has, from time immemorial, looked upon India as the *akshayapaatra* for spiritual food. India has in the past, to a great extent, continuously provided it for all mankind. It behoves us of the present generation to keep up this age-old, unbroken tradition.

The nation, as the individual, is a complex organic whole. Together, and functioning in unison, it is a living, throbbing and creative entity; uncoordinated, isolated and cut off from one another, it is as good as a dead jumble.

We won freedom in unity. We can retain it only in unity. Therefore, no effort should be spared to retain it.

A great misfortune of post-independent India has been the relegation, if not total neglect, and quarantining of spiritual and ethical values. We should not forget that whatever respect India commands internationally is only because it is the most ancient and inexhaustible repository of higher values.

If only we had continued the tradition of active participation, in the country's administration, of the creators, builders and upholders of moral and spiritual values, it could have greatly contributed to the nation's creativity, enriched those in authority by intuitional wisdom, purified public life by the elimination of sordid selfishness and by the eternal values of *Satyam* (Truth), *Shivam* (Love) and *Sundaram* (Beauty).

Another disquieting factor is that but with rare .exceptions, the qualifications for leadership of most of the ruling politicians today consist in their capacity or adroitness for machinations, manipulations and manoeuvres; skill in fanning lower human emotions and subordinate loyalties for the promotion of their personal ambitions; cleverness in the art of making or collecting money and patronage by all possible means in utter disregard of ethical or moral norms, often exploiting position and power in the process; and a talent for diplomatic hypocrisy and 'sincere lying'-double-think and double-talk. This needs to be corrected.

In sum, it means a successful leader must have an elastic, quiescent conscience which readily acquiesces and easily excuses the misdeeds and misconduct of one's supporters and partymen.

It is a pity that, noble as most of the present-day politicians may be as individuals, when they function a representatives of powerful political cliques, they succumb to perfidious and nihilistic tendencies and, by and large, become conscious or unconscious tools of fraud and foul play in the unholy game of naked power politics, designed to retain or wrest power for themselves or, at best, for their party.

A still more baneful element, corroding our nation life, is aggressive linguisin or 'regional patriotism'.

The talk of regional cultures in India is misleading and mischievous. Are not the so-called regional cultures mere variants of one basic Indian culture ? Can these so-called cultures stand or sustain themselves alone or in isolation from the mainstream ? If the great and inspiring fountainheads of our common heritage—the Vedas, Upanishads, Gita, Ramayana, Mahabharata, Smritis and

Puranas are taken away from the life of any region, what would remain of its culture?

It is a truism that things refuse to be mismanaged long—Resnolunt diu male administrari. It is only a question of time. Every crime, whether detected or not, is punished; every virtue, whether recognised or not, is rewarded; every wrong, whether owned or otherwise, is redressed in silence and certainty. Cause and effect, means and ends, seeds and fruits cannot be severed. This is an unalterable law of nature and this is what gives a hint of optimism.

Human character and noble endeavour spring evermore and make themselves felt. Never is a sincere work utterly lost. Never does an unselfish and ennobling endeavour fall to the ground. Goodness and Truth will prevail.

We must, however, confess to a sense of anguish at the growth of the amoral and divisive forces presently defiling Mother India.

There is, however, a silver lining. People have begun to sense the danger to national harmony. The ranks of men and women pledged to national unity are swelling. But the forces which represent spiritual and ethical values—the essential, ingredients of social and national integration—must be more vigilant and active.

To save the Motherland, a massive, sustained and concerted effort is called for by all patriotic sons of the soil. Saving the Motherland is ipso facto saving ourselves.

Change on Cards

With the ever-widening frontiers of knowledge and rapid strides in science and technology, the leading intellectuals of the 20th century, like the French Surgeon and Biologist, Dr. Alexis Carrel, the American Physicist, Julius Robert Oppenheimer, and the British Physicist and Astronomer, Sir James chose to see beyond materialism. The pioneer of atomic science, Dr. Albert Einstein, declared:

> *Science without religion is lame;*
> *Religion without science is blind.*

One may well pose the question: What type of religion ?

Certainly, not the religion of mere dogmas, rituals and exhibitionism. Not the religion which degenerates into spiritual snobbery. Not the religion which discriminates between man and man. Not the religion which breeds fanaticism and hatred amongst men and nations. Not the religion which is totally other worldly and utterly oblivious of the world we live in. Not the religion which sets its face against all material progress and makes a virtue of self-suffering, self-torture and suppression of legitimate aspirations.

In reality the religion which inculcates the art of understanding and goodwill towards all, unspoilt by the vice of patronage; the religion which erases the ego; the religion which instils humility; the religion which forges the fellowship of man; the religion which stands for sarvabhootahita, the welfare of all in ali its pure forms.

"A flippant attitude towards material welfare is not spiritual, anymore than which pins its faith on mere material welfare," Kulapati Munshiji often used to say.

For a people to be cultured and religious, their basic needs food, clothing, shelter and education should be adequately provided for.

At the same time, we have to be careful that in the process of raising the standard of living, we do not neglect the standard of life. They should go hand in hand. There must be simultaneous fostering of ethical and spiritual values, which go to build up character. And it is character alone that can provide the solid foundation for stable reconstruction—economic, social and political.

As Samuel Smiles, whose works have stood the test of time, has affirmed :

> The strength, the industry and the civilization of nations all depend upon individual character; and the very foundations of civil security rest upon it. Laws and institutions are but its outgrowth. In the just balance of nature, individuals and nations and races will obtain just so much as they deserve, and no more.

And as effect finds its cause, so surely does quality of character amongst a people produce its befitting results.

How to build up national character?

Not by merely opening more and more schools and colleges. Not by organising a spate of symposia and seminars. Not by any amount of preaching and sermons by those who seldom practise what they preach. It can only be done by hammering out an integrated, life-giving, man-making education.

Of course, *Vidya*, knowledge, is necessary-knowledge of the methods and techniques of work, knowledge of the theoretical and practical aspects of a subject. *Vidya* without *shraddha*, faith, is useless tinsel. Without *shraddha*, we cannot achieve the true purposes of education. *Vidya* does not shine without *shraddha*. *Vidya* and *shraddha* are like man and wife, Shiva and Shakti.

Shraddhamayoyam purusho yo yacchraddha sa eva sah. "Man consists of *shraddha*. Whatever be the measure of his *shraddha*, that will be the measure of his life", avers the Gita. What makes one man great and another weak and low is *shraddha* or the lack of it.

Spiritual Values

Ancient India blossomed into the home the *akshayapatra*, inexhaustible reservoir of spirituality because our rishis and munis had unsurpassed *shraddha*. India of the Ages had reached the pinnacle of cultural achievement and also material prosperity, because our ancestors had unswerving *shraddha*. We lost our freedom because we lost *shraddha*. We regained our freedom on August 15, 1947, on account of the *shraddha* instilled in us by Mahatma Gandhi and other leaders.

When *vidya* and *shraddha* unite, creative spiritual energy issues forth.

As Swami Vivekananda asserted:

Learning is not a condition of spiritual growth; scholarship is not a condition .... We attend lectures and read books, argue and reason about God, soul, religion and salvation. These are not spirituality, because spirituality does not exist in books, or in theories or in philosophies. It is not in learning or reasoning, but in actual inner growth.

How then shall we foster inner growth?

How can we release the creative power of spiritual energy which is the goal of real education?

In the Yoga Sutra, Sage Patanjali gives a simple formula:

Happy relations are the end-products only of sincere unselfish love. Enduring achievement is the end-product only of absolute sincerity. Richness of life is the end-product only of absolute honesty. Peace and harmony are the end-products of austerity.

These aphorisms may sound like copy book maxims but their efficacy is indisputable. The lives and achievements of the unbroken line of sages and saints, architects and builders of nations, champions of liberty, equality and fraternity, pioneers in science, technology and social service in all ages are a standing affirmation of their efficacy. It is demonstrated even today in the work and accomplishments of some of our living great.

After 40 years of painstaking labour in distilling what 4,000 years and 20 civilizations can tell us of man's journey through 'war, conquest, creation and self-exploration Will and Ariel Durant, in their monumental 10-volume work. The Story of 'Civilization, have come out with certain significant conclusions:

There is no significant example in history before our time, of a society successfully maintaining moral life without the aid of religion.

Even the sceptical historian develops a humble respect for religion since he sees it functioning in every land and age.

The only real revolution is in the enlightenment of the mind and the improvement of character. The only real revolutionaries are philosophers and saints.

The obligation rests upon us all to do our work in an attitude of Iswara Pranidhana, learning to live in the presence of God, to surrender to His Will in such a measure as we can. And in doing so, let us ever remember that His Will alone determines both the adventure and the outcome; we are only His instruments. But the important thing is that we must deserve to be His instruments.

When Harold Laski enunciated in his Grammar of Politics the political doctrine, "I ought to have what I enjoy only as the result of the services I perform," he was also, perhaps unconsciously, giving form to a moral maxim.

Gandhiji who believed that the "highest religion is also the highest politics" has expressed the same idea in another way. "If we all discharge our duties, rights will not be far to seek. If leaving duties unperformed we run after rights, they will escape us like the will-o'-the-wisp".

In the context of Gandhiji's approval of democracy as the best form of government for free India, he never failed to stress that a democracy, for its successful functioning presupposed that all sections of people would claim their rights only after discharging their duties. That is how it should be but the easiest way to derail a working democracy would be to make all sections of people lax in their attitude towards discharging their duties and make them vigilant about clamouring for their rights.

Laxity in the discharge of duties should invite punishment whatever be the rank of the guilty. Is this happening in our India today ? If crimes, civil, criminal or economic go unpunished people will lose faith in the system and the foundations of democracy will be weakened.

Says Kautilya, the ancient law giver, "Whoever imposes punishment as deserved becomes respectable. For punishment, when awarded with due consideration, makes the people devoted to righteousness (dharma) and work for the production of wealth."

In our epic Ramayana there are any number of sayings to the effect that the ruler who fails to punish the guilty is himself guilty. Therefore, punishment of the guilty is one of the most important duties of the ruler.

In the Book of Life, as the Mahabharata is known, greater emphasis is laid on dharma, the discharge of one's duties. In the celebrated "Yaksha Prsana" which occurs in the 'Vana Parva', the

Yaksha asks Dharmaputra, "What is Tapas?" The answer is "Observance of one's Duty is Tapas'.

Soon follows another question: "What does he gain who is devoted to his duty (dharma)? "The answer is "He who is devoted to his duty (dharma) attains liberation." And liberation is the highest goal of man! Today in the name of liberty, many who commit culpable acts go unpunished. We often tend to forget the phrase 'civil liberty'. The word civil means the opposite of criminal or violent. None is entitled to criminal liberties—the ruled or the ruler.

The UN General Assembly adopted on December 10, 1948, the Universal Declaration of Human Rights. It is equally important that the UN should adopt a Universal Declaration of Human Duties because there cannot be any rights without duties. In India we have enshrined in our Constitution, Fundamental Duties of a citizen.

The term 'duty' may sound gruesome to many because of its association with the drudgery or unpleasantness of imposed work or responsibility. But if we see 'duty' as 'what is due', it can be seen in a new light as is advocated by Christmas Humphreys, a noted thinker.

Two concrete examples will make this point clear before we go into the realm of the abstract.

Think of 'black' money. Money becomes 'black' only because the 'duty' on it by way of tax has not been paid. So much as it cannot bear the light of scrutiny and has to ever remain concealed in darkness. Or take another interesting example. Imagine the delight of owning a 'duty-paid' TV or VCR or any other gadget as against the anxiety and sense of guilt of owning a 'smuggled' piece, meaning one on which 'duty' has been evaded.

Coming to the abstract level, any duty left undone weighs heavily on our conscience. No amount of popping in tranquillisers can ease our conscience.

All duties left undone go to the 'debit' side and our inner self is burdened and this drag affects our efficiency at all levels.

As Ernest Hocking, the author of The Lasting Elements of Individualism has cryptically stated: "costless rights" constitute "moral toxin". Any right claimed by us, for which we have not paid in cash or kind, poisons our system and certainly robs us of our peace physical, mental and spiritual.

Thus, it can be seen that in the single word 'duty' the whole secret of gaining freedom' from bondage is adumbrated. Hence the Gita counsels Karmanyevaadhikaaraste phaleshu kadaachana. Freely rendered it would mean, "Let your concern be the discharge of duties alone and never the fruits thereof because by the discharge of your duties your act is complete, and debt is redeemed and you become a free man.

Gandhiji's words: "Think of one's duties first and foremost and the rights to take care of themselves, for rights follow upon the fulfilment of one's duties and NOT 'vice versa' constitute the best commentary of the above Gita verse.

It is only such people, high or low, concerned about the honest discharge of their duties who are good people, the others are hypocrites, whatever be their field of action-politics, commerce or industry, law or teaching.

Our democracy's survival depends on increase in the number of such 'good' men and the elimination of hypocrites.

Elections are the integral part of the democratic way of life. They are essential for the health of the nation. They are like periodical medical check-ups. They are intended to rid the body-politic of poisonous infections, to chop off diseased limbs, to shed deadwood, to infuse vigour and vitality into health-giving organs, and to give purpose and direction to governance. But aren't they losing their sheen and purpose?

Civilizational Heritage

Indian tradition has always conceived of the kings of the rulers as *rajarishis* or philosopher-statesmen. They wield the reins of power for *jana kalyan*—welfare of the people—the preservation and promotion of which is their *kshatra*-dharma. While assuming power, they take a solemn oath, in the name of God, not to swerve from the path of righteousness. The great ideal of the greatest rulers of all time, Sri Rama, was *lokaradhana* or the service of the people.

In the *Shantiparva* of the Mahabharata, the intricate problems of statecraft are discussed by the venerable Bhishma Pitamaha, as he lay on his bed of arrows. It is a dialogue in the nature of a last testament of India's immortal patriarch. Therein is delineated how King Vena was replaced by a worthier one by the concerted actions of the people when he strayed from the path of *lokaseva* and took to swarthaseva.

Plato dwells on the nature of governments as being determined by the character of the men and women that compose the state. He avers that a government is not composed of trees and stones. Hence the character of the government depends on its citizens. People get the kind of government they deserve.

We are prone to complain of the sorry state of affairs in our land; of the political leaders who exploit caste and communal differences, regional and linguistic rivalries; of trade union bosses who paralyse Production by organising unjustified strikes and bandhs; of the bureaucratic class who are callous and corrupt; of the captains of industry and commerce who are adept in engineering artificial scarcity for price hike and fatter profits; and when elections come, of the legislators who let us down and do not deliver the goods they promise us when they periodically but treacherously seek our votes.

Unfortunately, not a few candidates approach the elections with an outlook that smells of profanity. Profanity tends to bring to the forefront minds that are corrupt. It also inveigles into the body-politic elements that are inimical to the successful functioning of a democracy.

But have we ever turned the searchlight inwards?

Sense of Responsibility

If electoral candidates and the high priests of the different political parties who field them do not make the grade, aren't we, the people, responsible for it in equal measure? Why are we indifferent to public affairs? Why do we let ourselves be deluded? Why do we support men who indulge in double-think and double-act? Why do we cast our precious votes to those who make elections a sort of ribald jugglery and in the process jettison a golden opportunity? Why do we not discard candidates who take to what works for the moment and not to what is correct in the long run?

It is the bounden duty of every patriotic Indian to pose the question to himself: "Am I acting as a responsible citizen of democracy?" Is the precious vote not being wasted?

When talent becomes shy and sycophancy thrives, when promises, hoodwinking and whipping up of jealousy and hatred are deployed to garner votes, when opportunistic and blind support are extended to all kinds of fantastic electoral support, when performance ceases to be the criterion for vote-seeking, when public service, commonwealth and moral standards are given the go-by, democracy faces peril.

When such a situation emerges in any country, the dangers to democracy begin to outweigh its advantages. Political, social and commercial leaderships then begin to prosper at the expense of national interests. The ambition for pelf and power in almost all segments of national life begins to corrode ethical principles and values. Long-term national interests are then gravely undermined.

The root of the matter takes us from politics to religion, to the eternal foundation of all-life dharma.

The continued stability and the even tenor of life on earth is a result of dharma. There is an Eternal Law that keeps the stars in their paths, the sun and the moon in their orbits and makes the cycle of seasons manifest regularly year in and year out.

This Higher Law also relates to human life, its place and function, its relationship with itself, with other fellow beings and what is beyond, which we may designate as God.

This Law of laws, the *Rita* of the Vedic Age, the dharma that binds all life, is inexorable. It has its sway, no matter what we do and how we do. The consequences of actions, good and bad, are inevitable. If we act well, it sustains us, it lends us succour. If we act ill, it blows us off like withered and dry leaves and ditches us into oblivion.

The righteous and wise will lend their shoulders to turn the wheel of dharma. The unrighteous and the deluded will only act to get ultimately crushed underneath its weight.

Lessons from Past

Mythology and history are replete with accounts of rulers who, blind with pride of power, neglected the foundations of their position, the spiritual springs of it and ignominiously fell in the end.

Hiranyakashyapu of yore denied there was any God higher than himself. He wanted all worship and obeisance to be done to him. What was the result? He fell, was torn to shreds despite his foolish confidence that he was invincible by virtue of the boon that the great God had given him. He did not know that even the boon of God would not eternally work against the inexorable Divine Law of cause and effect, action and reaction.

Ravana in Lanka, Kamsa in Mathura, Duryodhana in Hastinapur, Zohak in Persia, Nero in Rome, Charles I in England, Louis XVI in France, Czar Nicholas in Russia are some of the specimens of their own undoing, of steep descent from the sublime to the ridiculous.

In our own times, the rise and fall of Hitler in Germany, Mussolini in Italy, Sukarno in Indonesia, Nkrumah in Ghana, Ayub Khan in Pakistan testify to the disastrous consequences of taking recourse to the pernicious policy of hatred and deceit, vilification and violence, corrupt practices and horse-trading for gaining temporary political ascendancy and domination.

India is the ancient home of dharma. This land of ours is the *akshyapatra*, the inexhaustible reservoir of ethical and spiritual values. The code of right conduct in personal, institutional, and public life was first formulated here. *Tyaga*, sacrifice and *nishkama karma*, unselfish toil, were the badge of our ancestors.

In this punyabhoomi we witness today in the endemic, shameless spectacle of loyalties swinging from one end to the other. The Aya-Rams and Gaya-Rams are poisonous pests. They should be given the short shrift. It is a sin against man and God to lend them any support.

Those to whom we give our votes should be men and women of integrity. Legislators make the laws of the land. They are the guardians of the people. Who shall guard the guardians? If the salt loseth its savour, wherewith shall it be salted?

We must ensure that honesty and integrity flow from top downwards. Politics without principles will ultimately destroy the leaders and their lieutenants and the political parties under whose flag they sail. It will also take the nation to rack and ruin.

Let us heed the warnings of mythology and history to hammer the point of difference between then and now. No individual, leadership, party or nation will be able to survive long, divorcing ethical and spiritual values from personal, institutional and national life. This is the unchanging and unchangeable Divine Law.

Mahayogi Sri Aurobindo cautioned that "if good people keep away from public life, goondas will dominate it." It is, therefore, incumbent on the educated and cultured sections of our society not to keep away from public affairs. They owe an inescapable duty to themselves and to the Janmabhoomi to help provide intelligent and constructive leadership at all levels, in all fields of national life.

Lokaseva is part of one's *swadharma*. But we should be eternally vigilant lest it is misused as a stepping stone to *swarthaseva*.

People are dazed, desperate and despondent. The present situation in the country, reminds us of the horrors of the pre-partition days, especially the atrocious devil-dance, by human beasts on the so-called Direct Action Day observed in Calcutta at the call of the Muslim League on August 15, 1946, following the announcement by the Viceroy Lord Wavell, of the installation of the Interim Government in New Delhi headed by Pandit Jawaharlal Nehru, on September 2, 1946. It eventually led to the vivisection of India and the creation of theocratic Pakistan.

At the time of Independence, it was clear in the minds of leaders as well as the masses that there would be a delinking of politics from religion because the country had paid a very high price by way of partition for mixing religion with politics.

The Constituent Assembly (Legislative), in a resolution adopted on April 3, 1948, unambiguously stated:

"Whereas it is essential for the proper functioning of democracy and the growth of national unity and solidarity that communalism should be eliminated from Indian life, this assembly is of opinion that no communal organisation which by its constitution or by exercise of discretionary power vested in any of its officers and organs admits to, or excludes from, its membership persons on grounds of religion, race and caste, or any of them, should be permitted to engage in any activities other than those essential for the bona fide religious, cultural, social, and educational needs of the community, and that all steps, legislative and administrative, necessary to prevent such activities should be taken."

In spite of this solemn, unambiguous resolution, our post-Independence era proved beyond doubt that we have not stuck to the spirit of the wholesome Constituent Assembly resolution to eliminate communalism from our body-politic. Our political parties, without any exception, have sacrificed genuine secularism at the alter of power.

The addition of the word "secular" in the Preamble to our Constitution in 1976, at the initiative of Smt. Indira Gandhi, was a reaffirmation of our faith in secularism. It was also an expression of our hope that our politicians would, under all circumstances, rise above narrow religious considerations for transient political gains.

What is happening today? Is there a single party which sticks to secularism in letter and spirit?

The great Indian National Congress itself, without any qualms of conscience, in order to retain power, set a bad example, by forming a coalition government in Kerala with the Muslim League.

Once elders deviate from basic principles and resort to unethical compromises it is difficult to reverse the trend. It becomes a dreadful habit as indeed it was in later years.

The Communist Party which loudly swore and still swears by secularism followed suit and courted Muslim League to grab power in Kerala. It went a step further and created in 1968 the new district of Malappuram which has a predominantly Muslim population when the redoubtable E.M.S. Namboodiripad was the Chief Minister.

Lamentably, no political party in post-Independence India has lived up to the true ideal of secularism and fostered robust nationalism. Of course, all of them always nauseatingly swear by the twin ideals. Self-interest guided all their political decisions.

It is time that we cried halt to hypocrisy, double-think and double-talk. Communalism is dangerous, whether it is minority communalism or majority communalism.

Communalism arises from the consciousness of a separate identity in the matter of religion, caste, language, race, social status or culture. Such consciousness leads to a sense of arrogant, aggressive superiority of which one is proud and which one wants to protect at all costs, or a sense of debasing inferiority complex which weakens one's spirit of self-confidence, self-reliance. Both promote intolerance and strife.

The question is: Whither India today?

Even now we do not have a common civil code. The Constitution of the Republic of India envisages only one kind of citizenship. Is this put into practice ? All Indians cannot own a hearth and home in some parts of India. For example, Kashmir.

Here are the guidelines given by the Consolidator and Integrator of India, Sardar Patel, on this all-important minority-majority question:

> It is up to the majority community by its generosity, to create a sense of confidence in the minorities, and so also it will be the duty of the minority communities to forget the past and

> to reflect on what the country has suffered owing to the 'sense of fairness,' which the foreign rulers thought was necessary to keep the balance between community and community.
>
> If the minorities have honestly come to the conclusion that, in the changed conditions of this country, it is in the interest of all to lay down real and genuine foundations of secular State, then nothing is better for the minorities than to trust the good sense and sense of fairness of the majority and to place confidence in them who happen to be in a majority to think about what the minorities feel and imagine how we would feel if we were treated in the manner in which they are treated. In the long run, it would be in the interest of all to forget that there is anything like majority or minority in this country and that in India there is only one community.

What is robust, comprehensive nationalism?

At the height of our freedom struggle, the far-seeing apostle of Indian nationalism, Mahayogi Sri Aurobindo, defined it thus:

> Nationalism depends for its success on the awakening and organising of the whole strength of the nation; it is, therefore, vitally important for nationalism that the politically backward classes should be awakened and brought into the current of political life—the great mass of orthodox Hinduism which was hardly ever touched by the old Congress movement; the great slumbering mass of Islam which has remained politically inert throughout the last century; the shopkeepers, the artisan class, the immense body of illiterate and ignorant peasantry, the submerged classes, even the wild tribes and races still outside the pale of Hindu civilization. Nationalism can afford to neglect and omit none.

Anything done, consciously or unconsciously, to weaken the secular foundation of India is a heinous crime. The moment of truth has arrived. India is at present passing through a very critical phase. We find all around us an all-pervading sense of power-lust and unscrupulousness, frustration and despair, moral decay and disintegration.

The vacuum, in the sphere of social goals and political objectives, caused by the deliberate quarantining of ethical and spiritual values, is steadily growing at an alarming pace.

No son or daughter of Mother India can afford to ignore the deeper import of the recent political melodrama at the union and some of the state capitals.

The politics of power-chase and negativism of destroying other political parties should be replaced by the politics of high purpose, undiluted patriotism, dedicated service and constructive statesmanship.

The delusion that words can be substitutes for action should be given up. The chimera of rights without corresponding duties should be abandoned.

The hypocrisy of not frankly telling the people that wealth cannot be produced without hard and honest work should be forsaken. The shibboleth of noble declarations and ignoble policies should be given the go-by.

The pursuit of higher standard of living should cease to be divorced from the simultaneous pursuit of higher standard of life.

These alone are the sure guarantees of our Motherland's continued freedom and strength, progress and prosperity, greatness and glory.

We can tarry no more. It is time for self-introspection and soul-searching.

16

Twenty First Century

An analyst once opined that technology for a developing economy is like "food to a child's body". While access to technology is important for the growth and well-being of all nations, it is considered to be especially important for developing nations since it can bring about rapid increases in the productivity of both the capital and labour employed in the developmental process.

The process of planned economic growth that was initiated in India in 1951 laid considerable stress on the use of modern technology for ensuring rapid economic growth. However, India's attempt at harnessing technology for the national development effort was unique in the developing world since it involved an ambitious effort to become technologically self-reliant. More than fifty-five years after independence, it is clear that the attempt to achieve self-reliance has not been completely successful. Though India has built up impressive capabilities in science and technology (S&T), the country still remains dependent on imports of technology. This chapter analyses both the successes and failures in India's attempts to achieve technological self-reliance and considers the lessons that past experience holds for future government action.

Self-reliance in all aspects of science and technology has been an important long-term objective of Indian government policy since independence in 1947. In the early sixties Pandit Jawaharlal Nehru while defending his government's decision to produce

Soviet weaponry under license in India, rather than buy Western equipment off-the-shelf, said: "I believe as a practical proposition, that it is better to have a second-rate thing made in our country than to rely on the first-rate things which we have to import". This determination to be self-sufficient, even if it meant accepting lower levels of technology, was an important feature of government policy for more than four decades after independence. While it was accepted that at least initially the country would have to import industrial technology from abroad, national leaders envisaged a future where India would be completely self-reliant.

The Science Policy Resolution of 1958, the first official document in independent India which set forth government policy for the development of scientific and technological research and development capabilities, laid considerable stress on creating an infrastructure for promoting pure, applied and industrial research within the country. As part of this effort, existing national scientific and industrial research organisations were expanded, and new ones set tip, to create research and development (R&D) capabilities in all areas of science and technology. Organisations such as the Council for Scientific and Industrial Research (CSIR), the Indian Council for Agricultural Research (ICAR), the Indian Council for Medical Research (ICMR), the Department of Atomic Energy (DAE), the Department of Space (DOS) and the Defence Research and Development Organisation (DRDO) set up a large number of national laboratories to develop their R&D capabilities. Existing university science departments were expanded, and new Indian Institutes of Technology (IITs) were set up in various parts of the country, to train scientists and technologists to work in these national laboratories.

By the early 1990s India had built up one of the largest and most diverse scientific and technological R&D capabilities in the developing world. Government expenditure on S&T increased from Rs. 20 crore in the First Plan (1951-56) to Rs. 9388 crore in the Eighth Five Year Plan (1992-97).[1] While expenditure on R&D as a proportion of GNP was only 0.81 per cent, in comparison to the average of 2.55 per cent for the developed world, it was still greater than the average of about 0.55 per cent for the developing world—Government R&D organisations spent 80 per cent of the resources devoted to scientific R&D, while private-sector industry contributed the rest. In terms of its breadth, Indian R&D capabilities were comparable to many of the advanced industrialised states.

Development of Technology

Though the commitment of successive governments to the development of indigenous scientific R&D capabilities has remained strong, as illustrated by the development of broad capabilities and sustained increases in R&D funding, it became apparent in the early eighties that this had not translated into increased availability of advanced indigenous technology for Indian-industry. Indian industry continued to depend on imports of technology for new products and processes even after a substantial R&D infrastructure had been developed within the country.' Reports submitted to parliament by four committees between 1954 and 1986 stated that the Council for Scientific and Industrial Research (CSIR), for example, had made only minor technological contributions to domestic industries.' In house R&D carried out by public and private sector firms were devoted mainly to adapting imported technologies to local conditions, not developing new technologies needed for new products and processes. A variety of factors have contributed to this inability of Indian R&D organisations to develop new technologies and successfully transfer it to Indian industry.

The Nature of R&D. The first problem was the nature of the research being carried out in many national R&D laboratories. Planners very often tended to confuse 'science' with 'technology'. Though science research was important for new technology development, that by itself does not generate new technologies that are commercially exploitable. Much of the research that was carried out in national R&D labs tended to be pure scientific research, rather than applied industrial research that could be used directly by Indian industry. Many of the laboratories were staffed by scientists and technologists recruited from universities and research institutes, either within the country or abroad, who tended to see national research labs as institutions where they could carry forward the research they had already completed. The fact that many national R&D institutions were recognised by universities as post-graduate research centres further reinforced this nature of national R&D organisations. Though this improved the quality of the science research being undertaken, the research output was very often was not relevant to the needs of Indian industry.

Lack of Exposure to Market Forces. Scientists and technologists working in government laboratories were assured of government funding for their research projects, irrespective of whether their research output was being used by Indian industry. This assurance of funding meant that national labs did not have to sell their research output to Indian industry in order to generate funds for new research projects. This independence also reinforced the trend towards pure rather than applied research. While pure research led to greater peer-recognition, applied research would only have generated more funds, which was in any case available from the government.

Failure to Develop Mature Technologies. Indian firms that tried to source new technologies from government R&D labs very often found that the technologies offered were not mature enough to be exploited quickly." Firms usually acquire new technologies to gain a competitive advantage over rival manufacture. The speed with which companies can bring newer products on to the market very often decides the success or failure of these products. Technologies offered by government R&D labs had often been demonstrated only on a laboratory workbench and were unsuitable for commercial exploitation. Such technologies often needed further developmental effort to scale it up to pilot-plant level or higher for successful commercial exploitation. While this problem could have been overcome through further R&D, differences often arose over the time taken and the costs involved in such R&D. While the labs were often reluctant to undertake the additional R&D work needed to develop these technologies, the firms were unwilling to provide the resources needed for such R&D.

Lack of Mission-Orientation. In the absence of any need to respond to market demand, research carried out in national R&D laboratories very often lacked focus and was not directed towards the achievement of specific objectives. While government ministries and departments dealing with science and technology were tasked with the job of identifying technological needs and allocating resources accordingly, such planning efforts were rarely successful." This meant that research funds were often spread across a large number of research projects, which did not finally yield technologies which were commercially exploitable,

Though indigenous R&D was unable to generate advanced technologies for Indian insdustry, two Indian R&D organisations were extremely successful in developing advanced technologies needed for national programmes. The Indian Space Research Organisation (ISRO) and the Defence Research and Development Organisation (DRDO) succeeded in making the country self-reliant in many critical areas of defence and space technologies. The strategies that these organisations adopted are worth analysing since they provide some indication as to how other Indian R&D organisations could reorient themselves and develop commercially viable technologies for Indian industry.

Studies in Space

The Indian Space Research Organisation was set up in 1972 with the objective of making the country self-reliant in building and launching satellites capable of providing communications, meteorological and remote-sensing services. The development of space technology required mastery over a wide variety of advanced technologies combining different scientific and technological specialities. The technology used in launching satellites was not substantially different from that used to build long-range ballistic missiles and therefore export of these technologies from the industrialised states was strictly controlled and restricted.

Realising its own limitations when it came to developing all the technologies needed for the space programme, ISRO developed a close working relationship with Indian industry for both development of, and production using, advanced technologies. This interaction, which began in the mid-seventies has increased rapidly both in terms of the number of collaborations and the complexity of the technologies involved." India is at present almost completely self-reliant in space technologies and is considered to be a potential commercial threat by the major space powers.

The interface that ISRO developed with Indian industry was unique in the history of Indian scientific R&D. Three main strategies were adopted to develop advanced technologies and manufacture capabilities indigenously.

Developing Partnerships with Indian Industry. From its inception the Indian Space Research Organisation has built up an excellent working relationship with Indian industry. ISRO has an active technology transfer programme called the Technology Transfer and Technological Consultancy Scheme through which advanced technologies that the ISRO has developed are transferred to Indian industry. Rather than waiting for industries to approach it, ISRO actively searches out potential industry partners and approaches them with offers of technology transfer. Information regarding technologies that the ISRO has developed is also disseminated to Indian industry through specialised publications, product demonstrations and ISRO participation in industry seminars and exhibitions. Since production of components for the space programme requires complex processes, high-precision fabrication skills and superior quality control systems, ISRO teams involved in developing these technologies visit production facilities frequently to provide technical assistance.

Through the Technology Transfer and Technological Consultancy Scheme, the ISRO has transferred more than 220 different technologies to Indian industry. A large number of small, medium and large scale industries now work as sub-contractors for different satellite and launch-vehicle projects that the ISRO manages. Almost 50 per cent of the funds allocated to the Indian space programme flow to Indian industry.

The Consortium Approach to Technology Development. The ISRO realised very early that developing the complex technologies involved in building satellites and launching satellites was beyond the capabilities of any single organisation. Therefore, it decided to adopt a 'consortium approach' to technology development. A large number of R&D organisations as well as public and private sector industries were brought together to develop systems and components needed for satellites and launch vehicles." This process involved an analysis of technologies involved in the development of a particular system, identification of research institutions capable of carrying out R&D in those areas, and the transfer of technology to firms that were capable of producing products or components using the technologies that had been developed.

The consortium approach was made possible by the close relationship that ISRO had earlier developed with Indian industry. Though initially the ISRO itself had to develop the technologies involved and manufacture the final product, since such capabilities were not available within Indian industry, it is increasingly playing the role of a facilitator whose main role is to bring a large number of organisations together for completing a specific project. The ISRO is now attempting to become a pure R&D organisation, concentrating on managing various ISRO-industry technology development groups, while leaving the production of systems and sub-systems needed for satellites and launch vehicles to Indian industry. A major programme that the ISRO initiated in the nineties to develop the technology needed to produce cryogenic engines for geostationary launch vehicles envisages the development of a large consortium to acquire the technology for cryogenic engines and produce them. In addition to the ISRO, six private sector firms are involved in the development and production of these engines.

The RESPOND Programme. In addition to Indian industry, the ISRO also utilised the resources available with academic institutions involved in R&D, such as the Indian Institutes of Technology and various science and technology departments in Indian universities. The Sponsored Research (RESPOND) Scheme that the ISRO administers provided academic and research institutions in India with financial support for undertaking research relevant to specific programmes that the ISRO identifies. About 25 institutions have projects under the RESPOND scheme, which provides academic institutions and University science departments with an opportunity to take part in advanced scientific research. The RESPOND programme is important not just because it provides the ISRO with technologies needed for the space programme, but also because it helps to train young scientists and technologists for space research.

The strategies that the ISRO adopted overcame many of the problems that prevented the successful transfer of indigenously developed technology to Indian industry. Funds were allocated to projects only when there was an ISRO requirement for a particular technology. Since R&D efforts were mission oriented, funds could be targeted at specific institutions and for specified projects. Close interaction between the user of the technology, the ISRO, and the agency developing it meant that the partnership was able to develop the technology to maturity, i.e., capable of commercial utilisation. The large number of agencies involved in the development of space technologies ensured that even in cases where the technology involved was complex, sufficient expertise was available to develop it.

The strategies that the ISRO adopted were later adopted by another R&D organisation, the Defence Research and Development Organisation, to develop a whole range of guided missiles for the Indian defence forces under the Integrated Guided-Missile Development Programme (IGMDP). The DRDO's experience with the IGMDP is unique since it involved an organisation that has traditionally suffered from many of the handicaps afflicting Indian R&D organisations, adapting itself successfully to attain self-reliance in a range of advanced technologies.

Within a few years of independence in 1947, government policy had identified self-reliance in the design, development and production of defence equipment as the primary, long-term objective of Indian defence planning. Self-sufficiency in defence production was considered to be an integral part of the policy of non-alignment, which was to be the guiding principle of India's foreign policy.

Long-term plans for indigenous defence production were laid out in the late 1950s with the proclaimed goal of complete 'self-reliance'. This meant the ability to design, develop and produce weapons systems indigenously. This was to be tailored to the industrialisation strategy being adopted for the civilian economy. The first stage of this process was to be a period of import substitution, followed by indigenous technology development. The 1960s saw the construction of new ordnance factories, the upgradation of machinery in existing units, the creation of new state corporations and the take-over by the Ministry of Defence of some organisations producing military equipment. While initially most of these public sector industries undertook licensed production of imported weapons designs, the expectation was that Indian defence R&D would eventually mature to the extent that the design, development and production of military equipment would become an entirely indigenous process.

Defence research and development in India was carried out by the Defence Research and Development Organisation through its 47 laboratories and establishments. As part of its indigenisaton effort, the DRDO assiduously built up a large number of defence research laboratories to design and develop weaponry for India's armed forces. Though by the early eighties Indian defence R&D had some notable successes, such as the indigenisation of low-tech weaponry and support equipment, the country did not move away from the production of imported weapons-systems under license of production, using indigenously designed and developed technologies. In the early eighties the DRDO embarked on two ambitious projects, the Arjun Main Battle Tank (MBT) and the Light Combat Aircraft (LCA) projects. These projects were aimed at developing a self-reliant and innovative defence-industrial capability within the country. However, while progress was made in the design and development of the MBT for the Army and an LCA for the air force, prototypes of these systems contained a substantial proportion of imported equipment. Nearly 50 per cent of the 'indigenous' Arjun tank, including its engine were imported from Germany. Seventy per cent of the LCA's components were imported because indigenous components of domestic design had still not been developed."

India had enough scientific and industrial resources available within the country for it to attempt autarky in defence production. The obstacles that prevented India from achieving this objective were primarily technical in nature and also caused by poor management of research projects. Defence R&D also suffered from one of the main problems afflicting civilian R&D: the poor relationship between labs and industry. The DRDO labs did not work closely with production on its because of an organisational division between the two. The main users of DRDO developed technology were public sector units making defence equipment which were under the control of the Bureau of Public Enterprises. Though both the DRDO and the Bureau of Public Enterprises were under the control of the Defence Ministry they were autonomous institutions and this prevented close interaction between them.

Though, by the early nineties, India had built up one of the largest and most diverse government-control led military industrial complexes in the developing world, its record in terms of self-reliance was regarded as disappointing. Attempts at indigenous development and production succeeded only in areas of low and middle technology items. More complex defence research and development projects did not progress quite as rapidly as previous government plans had predicted. More worrying was the fact that government-controlled R&D organisations and public sector undertakings found themselves unable to keep pace with the rapid growth of military technology and the increasing complexity of modern weapons systems. This meant that the armed forces continued to rely on imported designs and components for their weapons systems. The problem was Compounded by the easy availability of weaponry and spare-parts from the Soviet Union. All assured source of supply reduced the sense of urgency in the indigenisation effort and India continued to import a large number of major weapons systems from the Soviet Union.

The DRDO also proved unable to tap the talent available in civilian R&D institutions and industries for designing and developing crucial sub-systems for important weapons systems. There was too much emphasis on in-house R&D, which could not produce all the components needed for complex weapons systems.

These failures of defence R&D became apparent at a time when rapid shifts in global strategic alignments were forcing India to reassess its foreign and defence policies. The Gulf War of 1991 and the collapse of the Soviet Union severely undermined many of the premises on which these policies had been based. First, it became evident that the Soviet Union was no longer an assured source of weapons systems and spare parts". Second, the defeat of the Iraqi armed forces in Kuwait demonstrated that the technological gaps between Soviet and Western weapons systems were widening to an alarming extent. This was especially worrisome for India because the armed forces of Pakistan, its traditional adversary, were equipped with US weaponry.

The way forward for Indian defence R&D was identified by the success of a DRDO programme that involved civilian industries and universities in its R&D activities, the Integrated Guided Missile Development Programme (IGMDP). In 1992, Dr. A.P.J. Abdul Kalam, who had successfully guided this programme took over as the then Scientific Advisor to the Defence Minister and Secretary of the Department of Defence Research and Development. Drawing lessons from the success of the missile programme that he had directed, set about reorienting policies and invited the active participation of civilian and private sector industries in defence research and development.

Self-reliance in Defence

In 1983, the DRDO launched an ambitious missile development programme under the leadership of Dr. Abdul Kalam, then Director of the Defence Research and Development Laboratory (DRDL), Hyderabad. With a budget of Rs. 400 crore, the programme was expected to develop a series of surface-to-surface, surface-to-air and anti-tank missiles that would meet the country's needs beyond the year 2000." Dr. Kalam, who until 1982 had been the Project Director of the Indian Space Research Organisation's successful

Satellite Launch Vehicle (SI.V- 1) programme, replicated many of ISRO's R&D strategies in the DRDO. He identified two problems that had contributed to the failure of many DRDO projects: technology control regimes that prevented the transfer of critical missile technology to developing countries like India and the undue emphasis within the DRDO on in-house research without harnessing the talent available within the country.

To overcome barriers to the transfer of missile technologies, the DRDL team first identified five critical technologies that they would have to develop indigenously. These were: phase shifters for radars, impact diodes that act as high frequency power sources, carbon composites for heat shields, sensors for guidance systems and computerised fluid dynamic models. Realising the limitations of the DRDO's in-house expertise, Dr. Kalam adopted the 'consortium approach' that had been pioneered by the ISRO to defence research and development. A wide range of both public and private sector industries, universities and academic institutions were involved in the development of critical components for these missiles. As many as 42 industries, both in the public and private sectors, contributed to the development of five missiles under the IGMDP. These were the intermediate range 'Agni' and medium range 'Prithvi' surface-to surface missiles, the Akash' and 'Trishul' surface-to-air missiles and the 'Nag' anti-tank missile. Within six years, the IGMDP developed to a stage where all the five missiles reached testing stage with the import content in these missiles being less than 10 per cent.

This unique exchange of information and inputs from different laboratories, academic institutions and private industry showed that the consortium approach to technology development could overcome barriers to indigenous development of advanced technologies. It also demonstrated that with proper management and leadership, different departments and laboratories could co-ordinate and integrate with each other to produce modern hi-tech weaponry.

The process of economic liberalisation that began in the early nineties has exposed Indian industry to intense global competition.

Indian industry can no longer afford to ignore the major technological revolutions that are unfolding worldwide. The traditional dependence on a protected domestic market for low-technology, low-quality products is slowly giving way to an environment in which Indian industry can survive only by keeping up with rapid advances in technology that are happening worldwide.

The development of effective national R&D capabilities is crucial in this emerging environment. Easy access to advanced technologies provides firms with a competitive edge not just in the domestic, but in global markets as well. The continued dependence on imported technologies available are often not state-of-the-art, and even when they are available, they are offered on unfavourable terms.

The experience of the past fifty years demonstrates that while indigenous R&D suffers from major organisational and managerial weaknesses, there are instances where technology development efforts have succeeded in developing state-of-the-art technologies. Both the Indian Space Research Organisation and the Defence Research and Development Organisation have succeeded in their efforts because they have developed organisational structures that have overcome the obstacles that hindered the successful transfer of technology from Indian R&D institutions to Indian industry. Indian R&D organisations and Indian industry can draw many lessons from the experience of the ISRO and the DRDO.

First, it has to be recognised that technology development and commercialisation cannot happen independent of each other. The experience of the ISRO and the DRDO conclusively proves that Indian R&D institutions will have to make an effort to move closer to Indian industry. They will have to seek out research projects and sell their technologies to Indian industry if their technology development projects are to be successful.

Secondly, there has to be a recognition that most of the advanced products entering the market today involve technologies that are far too complex for any one R&D organisation or firm to develop and commercialise on its own. The 'consortium approach to technology development that the ISRO and the DRDO adopted was successful because this brought together a large number of organisations in research projects where they used their diverse capabilities to jointly develop complex technologies.

Finally, research institutions and Indian industry should involve themselves in collaborative ventures only after they have developed a clearly defined research agenda. Organisations involved in such projects will have to clearly identify the technologies and products that they want to develop and cooperate closely until the development and commercialisation process is complete. Unless all the institutions involved in a research project clearly identify their expectations regarding the final outcome, technology development efforts are bound to fail.

As technologies become ever more complex, even large firms find it difficult to develop all the technologies needed for their products on their own. The techniques adopted by the ISRO and the DRDO provide both R&D organisations and Indian industry with successful strategies that they could follow to develop advanced technologies indigenously.

17

The Last Word

The debased, disconcerting, disastrous devaluation of values has come full circle.

It has become second nature with politicians and political parties to put the expedient before the equitable to prefer *suruchi* (the ephemeral pleasant) to *suniti* (the eternal just).

Let each Indian honestly assess for himself or herself whether he or she has chosen suniti or suruchi.

Enticed by the glittering image of *suruchi*, most people go astray only to realise, too late, that they are chasing a shadow. Those who hearken to the still, small voice of *suniti* within them are sure to find fulfilment. Ultimate victory is theirs. This is the core of our ancient lore.

In the Upanishadic literature, which has come down to us from the dim, distant past when history had not delineated its characters in clear-cut lines, we find the idea of *shreyas* (the good) and *preyas* (the pleasant) clearly enunciated. The path of the good is not always easy to tread, it is like walking on the razor's edge, but it is a path that leads one to abiding joy and fullness. It alone helps us to expand our hearts and hopes as wide as the world. The path of the pleasant, on the contrary, is laden with immediate but fleeting pleasure. It ultimately takes one to the goal of pain and vacuity.

In the modern jet age, when man has no time even to "stand and stare," there may not be many who would be inclined to coolly weigh the merits of the two paths, guided by the esoteric teachings of the Upanishads, and prefer the transcendental to the transient, permanent to the temporary.

It is with a view to bringing the abstract ideas contained in the Upanishads to the very doorsteps of the common man that the *Puranas* were conceived by our ancients. In the form of stories and parables, these *Puranas* bring home to the people the magnificent truths which would have otherwise been inaccessible to them.

We find in the *Bhagavata Purana* the story of Dhruva, an *epitome* of bhakti and the outcome of preferring *suruchi* to *suniti*.

King Uttanapada had two consorts, by name Suniti and Suruchi. Like most mortals, Uttanapada preferred the alluring Suruchi and neglected the angelic Suniti.

The story runs that, infant Dhruva, the son of Suniti once sought to sit on the lap of his father Uttanapada, along with Suruchi's son. At this, an angry Suruchi brushed away the innocent Dhruva, taunting him that he would have no place in his father's lap as he was born to Suniti.

The king, infatuated by Suruchi, acquiesced in this act of heartbreaking insolence to a tender, loving child. In sum, Dhruva went to a forest, forlorn, and did penance, was ultimately blessed with God's vision and also an abiding place in the firmament as the Pole Star or guiding star to all humanity. Thus, the father who chose the pleasant remained mortal and a permanent object of contempt and ridicule, whereas his little son who chose righteousness gained life eternal and became an all-time inspiration.

The general run of our present day "practising politicians" who masquerade as "servants of the people" so live in the sensation of self-seeking that their personality has almost run to seed. As men, most of them care only for themselves and can read only their news in headlines.

Our present-day politicians have almost desecrated our sacred Temple of Freedom built by Godmen like Gandhi and other great torch-bearers nurtured in ethical and spiritual values, with the blood, sweat, toil and tears of millions of unknown patriots.

Oh! These politicians have reduced Free India to 'a gigantic quilt of jumbled crochet work, a monstrous monument of shame'

"There are plenty of people," said an Irishman, "who are dead without knowing it". "Yes," said his, friend, "only they haven't the sense to lie down."

With the modern politicians' posture of half unworldly saintliness and pretentious selfless service, their penchant for deliberate evasion and vagueness, fidgetting and fuming expletives, idiosyncrasies and eccentricities, artful dodging and shameless self-seeking, their crudely cultivated habit of making statements and taking actions which very seldom, if at all, respond to the test of accuracy and truth, the silken fabric of India's public life woven with the warp and woof of *satya* (truth), *ahimsa* (non-violence), *asteya* (non-possession), *aparigraha* (non-covetousness) has been soiled, defiled, nay, torn to-pieces.

Dr. Johnson's classical definition that "Politics is the last refuge of the scoundrel" is getting affirmation in our sacred land too!

After the stewardship of Jawaharlal Nehru and Lal Bahadur Shastri, our political life was heartlessly polluted, poisoned at the very source. The series of endemic, amoral plottings and sinister actions of the decades have resulted in an elongated catalogue of cursed catastrophes.

In the hollows of their unclean palms, politicians seek to hold the sole control of economic power, demagogic machinations and well-oiled vehicles of unceasing propaganda through plutocratically or oligarchically controlled press and other powerful mass media.

Naked force, coupled with cunning and fraud, unscrupulous, unholy hotchpotch alliances with unprincipled factions and groups, and false promises and unabashed alibis to hoodwink the masses have become the main methods of capturing and clinging to power.

The creed of the majority of our politicians has become: disturbance is the best way to peace, hatred to love, and fraud to sincerity; vilification and vindictiveness are shortcuts to power-grab and power-retention. Who then will guard the guardians *Quis custodiet ipsos* custodes ?

The ideal of "Government of the people, by the people and for the people" has degenerated into Government off the people, buy the people and far the people". Indeed, we have now "Government of the politicians, by the politicians and for the politicians".

Primitive passions and jingoism of the most unredeemed type have been let loose. Forces of anarchy and pedlars of poison are allowed to be on the prowl, befouling, besmirching the placid fountain of civilization and culture. They can no longer be easily controlled, or regulated. We are hopelessly thickening the problems of generations unborn.

A blind, passionate impulse of all-round destruction seems to have taken possession of and is propelling our ruling elite. This must be checked. Otherwise, we will soon pass irretrievably into an era of political prostitution, intellectual bankruptcy, moral nihilism and ethical barbarism, in which India's noblest traditions and values, priceless heritage—an eternal beacon to all mankind would be laid to waste.

This dangerous situation raises the momentous question of our time: Can the vital task of regulating the "life, liberty and pursuit of happiness" of our people be left to the sole, exclusive ministrations of the magnates of monopoly, power-professional politicians ?

"Put not your trust in princes (and rulers)...in whom there is no help," said the Psalmist (Psalm 146:3). This advice, so correct in regard to the rulers of the Biblical times, appears particularly timely in its application to today's politicians and political parties.

By far most of them have shown themselves to be bereft of the minimum intellectual, political, moral and social qualifications necessary for a successful and speedy solution of the tremendous problems facing the nation.

As the Father of our Nation and other architects and builders of modern India have stressed, we must "spiritualise" politics.

"Two things fill me with wonder," said the German philosopher Immanuel Kant, "the starry heavens above and the Moral Law within."

We, the people of India, each from his station in life, must take urgent steps to re-enthrone in each one's life the Majesty of the Moral Law—*Suniti*.

The situation in India today is too critical to attempt a cure by superficial and half-hearted measures, gimmicks and sloganeering.

India is now at the stormiest point in her post Independence era.

Let us ever remember that "all people can be fooled for some time, some people for all time but not all people for all time."

Our people are proverbially patient. But let us beware of the anger of patient men.

What then shall we do?

We must urgently:

Replace the largely obsolescent political ideologies and current tattered values by pragmatic new ones, anchored to the fundamental, but suitably adapted to meet the great and continuing challenge of the changing conditions; and

Re-enthrone ethical and spiritual values in public life which will automatically prevent misuse and abuse of power by each and every political party and government.

The nefarious deeds of the growing tribe of wily pedlars of poison must be put down with an iron hand.

In sum, we can only hope to reach the much sought-after heaven—the Ram Rajya of Gandhiji's Dreams only by mobilising all our mental, moral and other creative forces and harnessing for national reconstruction the best minds, purest hearts and highest consciences still abounding in all regions of our motherland, who shun the politics of power and who are committed to the politics of service.

Bibliography

Andrew, S. J., *India on the Path of Progress*, Asian Publications, Singapore, 2003.

Alfred, John, *The Nation on Rise*, Appolo Publication, Chennai, 2002.

Deshpande, V.N. (ed.), *Poverty: Interdisciplinary Approach*, Somiya Publications, Bombay.

Dreze J., and Sen A., 1995, *India: Economic Development and Social Opportunity*, OUP, New Delhi.

Haig, Alexander M., *Caveat: Realism, Reagan and Foreign Policy*, Widenfeld and Nicolson, London, 1984.

Humana, C., *The World Guide to Human Rights*, Facts on File, New York, 1996.

Jervice, Robert, *Perception and Misperception in International Politics*, Princeton University Press, New Jersey, 1976.

Kincaid, J.C., *Poverty and Inequality in Britain*, Penguin, Harmondsworth, 1973.

Lijphart, Arend, *Democracy in Plural Societies: A Comparative Exploration* Yale University Press, New Haven, 1982.

Mattoo, Amitabh, (ed.), *India Nuclear Deterrent: Pokhran II and Beyond*, Har-Anand, New Delhi,1999.

Mcgrahanan D.V., Proust C.P., Somani MX and Subramanian M., *Contents and Measurements of Socio-economic Development*, Praeger Publishers, New York, 1972.

Morris, D.N. and McAlpin M.C., *Measuring the Condition of India Poor: the Physical Quality of Life Index*, Promilla & Co. Publishers, New Delhi, 1982.

Sanders, J., *Peddlers of Crisis*, London, 1983.

Toffler, Alvin, *The Third Wave*, MacMillan, New Delhi, 1980.

Viqar M. H., *India : Destination 2020*, Emm Publications, Hyderabad, 2001.

Wazir, K. L., *Pathway to New India*, Kem Publishers, Mumbai, 2002.

References

Beinart, Peter, "The Return of the Bomb", *The New Republic,* August 31, 1998.

Butler, David, Ashok Lahiri and Prannoy Roy (1997), 'India Decides: Elections 1952-95", in Partha Chatteriee (ed.), *State and Politics in India,* OUP, Delhi.

Desai, M. and Shah, A., "An Econometric Approach to the Measurement of Poverty", *Oxford Economic Papers,* 1988.

Dreze, J. and Gazdar H., 1996, "Uttar Pradesh: The Burden of Inertia", in Dreze J and Sen A. (eds.), *Indian Development: Selected Regional Perspectives,* Oxford and New Delhi.

Jayaprakash, N.D., "Nuclear Disarmament and India", *Economic and Political Weekly,* February 12, 2000.

Lustic, Ian S, "Lijiphart, Lakatos, and Consociationalism", in, *World Politics, 50,* October 1997.

Majumdar, Anindvo J., 2000, "India-China-Pakistan: Crisis Prevention in the Nuclear Triangale", in Arun Kumar Banerji (ed.), *Conflict Resolution in the Post-Cold War Era,* Minerva Associates, Calcutta.

Mukherjee M., Gayen JL., Roy 1., 1981. "A Quantitative Study on Inter State Variation in Socio-economic Development", *Journal of Income and Wealth,* 5 (1).

Nandy, Ashis, "The Epidemic of Nuclearism: Clinical Profile of the Genocidal Mentality", in Zia Mian and Ashis Nandy, *The Nuclear Debate: Ironies and Immoralities,* Regional Centre for Strategic Studies, Colombo.

Nayyar, Deepak (1998), "Economic Development and Political Democracy: Interaction of Economics and Politics in Independent India", *Economic and Political Weekly*, 5 December 1998.

Shiva Kumar, A.K., "UNDP's Human Development Index: A Computation for Indian State", *EPW*, April 6, 1991.

Shiva Kumar, A.K., "UNDP's Gender related Development Index: A Computation for Indian States', *EPW*, Oct. 12, 1996.

Shakhnazarov, G., 1988, "Political Leadership in the Nuclear Era", *Social Sciences*, Moscow.

"The Puzzle of Indian Democracy: A Consociational Interpretation", *American Political Science Review, 90*, No. 2, June 1996.

UNDP, Human Development Report: 1990-1998.

World Bank, 199 1. World Development Report.

World Bank, 1993. The East Asian Miracle, OUP, New York.

World Bank, 1994. World Development Report.

Index

E

F

G

H

I

□□□